Venice: Lion City

A *Los Angeles Times* Book Prize Finalist

"In *Venice: Lion City*, Garry Wills passes over the picturesque decay of the Baroque city in search of 'an older, tougher town.'"

—*The New Yorker*

"The chapters wind through Venetian history at a leisurely pace, pausing here to look at a wall, a painting, or an arch, there to recollect a battle, a popular cult, a book, or a lawsuit. . . . The pages teem with curiously familiar stories, not just of political intrigue or societal crises, but of ordinary life, of family quarrels, business partnerships, bad marriages and ungrateful children."

—*Chicago Tribune*

"This is a book for those who love Venice, particularly its art. . . . In a work this rich in scholarship, the incidental information is often a delight in itself. . . . To bring this much learning to the understanding of art and history is wonderful, and to share it even better."

—*The Independent* (London)

"For understanding Renaissance Venice in all its mystery, no better book exists in any language than Wills's brilliant, beautifully written, and profoundly erudite tour de force. It will sweep you along with swift delight through art, politics, commerce, and religion to the heart and soul of an almost incomparably rich culture."

—John W. O'Malley, S.J., author of *Praise and Blame in Renaissance Rome*

Venice: Lion City

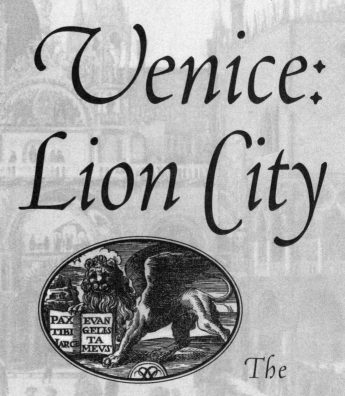

The RELIGION of EMPIRE

Garry Wills

WASHINGTON SQUARE PRESS

New York   London   Toronto   Sydney   Singapore

Copyright © 2001 by Literary Research, Inc.

Originally published in hardcover in 2001 by Simon & Schuster, Inc.

All rights reserved, including the right to reproduce this book or portions thereof in any form whatsoever. For information address Simon & Schuster, Inc., 1230 Avenue of the Americas, New York, NY 10020

ISBN: 0-671-04764-7

First Washington Square Press trade paperback printing September 2002

10 9 8 7 6 5 4 3 2 1

WASHINGTON SQUARE PRESS and colophon are registered trademarks of Simon & Schuster, Inc.

For information regarding special discounts for bulk purchases, please contact Simon & Schuster Special Sales at 1-800-456-6798 or business@simonandschuster.com

Cover design concept by John C. Wills
Picture research by Natalie Goldstein

Printed in the U.S.A.

To my favorite Italian

who took me there

Contents

CONTENTS

KEY TO BRIEF CITATIONS

I. ARTISTS

For attribution, provenance, and date, I append to each artifact a reference to the relevant catalogue raisonné.

BB   Bruce Boucher: *The Sculpture of Jacopo Sansovino*, Volumes I and II (Yale University Press, 1981)

D   Otto Demus: *The Mosaics of San Marco in Venice*, Volumes I and II, each with an accompanying volume of plates (University of Chicago Press, 1984)

P   Terisio Pignatti: *Veronese*, Volumes I and II (Alfieri, 1976)

P-H   John Pope-Hennessy: *Italian Sculpture*, Volumes I through III, fourth edition (Phaidon, 1996)

P-P   Trisio Pignatti and Filippo Pedrocco: *Giorgione*, translated by Marguerite Shore (Rizzoli, 1999)

P-R   Rodolfo Palluchini and Paola Rossi: *Tintoretto*, Volumes I through III (Electa, 1982)

S   Vittorio Sgarbi: *Carpaccio*, translated by Jay Hyams (Abbeville Press, 1994)

SMR   Stefania Mason Rinaldi: *Palma il Giovane* (Electa, 1984)

T   Anchise Tempestini: *Giovanni Bellini*, translated by Alexandra Bonfante-Warren and Jay Hyams (Abbeville Press, 1999)

W   Harold E. Wethey: *The Paintings of Titian*, Volumes I through III (Phaidon, 1969–1975)

II. HISTORIES

C-P   Elizabeth Crouzet-Pavan: *"Sopra le acque salse": Espaces, pouvoir et société a Venise à la fin du Moyen Age* (École française de Rome, 1992)

F   Robert Finlay: *Politics in Renaissance Venice* (Princeton University Press, 1980)

L   Frederick C. Lane: *Venice: A Maritime Republic* (Johns Hopkins University Press, 1975)

M   Edward Muir: *Civic Ritual in Renaissance Venice* (Phaidon, 1981)

McA   John McAndrew: *Venetian Architecture of the Early Renaissance* (MIT Press, 1980)

McN   William McNeil: *Venice: The Hinge of Europe, 1081–1797* (University of Chicago Press, 1974)

R   Dennis Romano: *Patricians and Popolani: The Social Foundations of the Venetians' Renaissance State* (Johns Hopkins University Press, 1987)

S-L   Staale Sinding-Larsen: *Christ in the Council Hall* (L'Erma di Bretschneider, 1974)

Athens of the Renaissance

*If every museum in the New World were emptied, if every
famous building in the Old World were destroyed and only
Venice saved, there would be enough there to fill a full lifetime
with delight. Venice, with all its complexity and variety, is
in itself the greatest surviving work of art in the world.*

— EVELYN WAUGH

THE CITY AS A SINGLE ARTIFACT was what stunned Waugh. Venice is
a thing *made* as no other city is. It created its own site, its chain of islands built
up and hardened in a soup of surrounding marshes. Its buildings were raised on
subaqueous platforms of piles—piles driven, in stripped forests, down out of sight. The
crisscrossing canals that serve as its avenues and lanes were sluiced by guided waters,
with slender boats threading this labyrinth at the touch of a single oar. The very marginality of Venice made it safe, poised between the Byzantine East and the Gothic West,
between papal South and Germanic North. Yet it purchased this marginality by pitting
its skill against rising and falling waters, which perpetually threatened its islands with
spates from the rivers spiraling out into its lagoon, or periodic tides shouldering back
toward it. Venice's level of safety was always measured in inches. Its fragility was the paradoxical source of its stability over time. It had to be very careful about preservation, as
a solid thing on a fluid base. As the city's courtesan-poet, Veronica Franco, put it:

> The sea itself yearns toward this city's realm,
> Holds turbulences off from it,
> While winding through its Eminence

Composed upon a water-woven throne—
A maze of intersecting liquid ways,
An endless plan of serviceable paths.[1]

Other cities, more exposed to the buffetings of war and of land traffic, could be more careless about their past in the confident refashionings of the present. Little has remained from classical Florence or Gothic Rome. Venice not only preserved its Byzantine and Gothic and Renaissance heritages, but ran them together. A Renaissance artist like Giovanni Bellini creates Madonna after Madonna that "updates" Greek icons. Venice combined the extremes of originality and conservatism. It was so aware of its own idiosyncrasy that it was not willing to let any sign of it perish.

A comparative lack of internal rebellion and external invasion made it possible for Venice to keep itself to itself. Its boast was to be *Serenissima*, "Most Undisturbed." This continuity called for a high degree of discipline that goes against the later myths of Venice as the hedonistic world of secret vices. That reputation grew up after Venice had lost the empire that it ruled only by self-rule. By the eighteenth century, Venice had begun its later career as a museum, selling itself to tourists rather than imposing itself on subjects. Francesco Guardi's endless "views" *(vedute)* of Venice reflect the way it had become a place to be *seen*, a quaint religious and social spectacle. Pietro Longhi helped create the impression that everyone went around in domino masks of the Carnevale. Giacomo Casanova made rascality, not responsibility, the mark of Venice. Aristocrats eventually retired to their mainland *(terraferma)* villas—private showplaces, with Tiepolo's frescos on Palladian walls—away from the emptying public places of government.

In the nineteenth century, Byron made Venice a place of delicious decay, of covert loves and political conspiracies. Ruskin mourned the decay and perpetuated Byronism with a moralistic twist to it. Browning's Venetian poetry danced to Galuppi measures ("What of soul was left, I wonder, when the kissing had to stop?"). Henry James's prose moved as slowly as the moldering of a ceiling fresco. Literary visitors threw over the entire city one vast bridge of sighs, with a Turner sunset burning in the waters under it. The allure of this later Venice is measurable in the number of tourists who crowd into shops that sell Longhi masks or trudge through Casanova's *prigione*.

I am interested in an older, tougher town. There will be no Canaletto or Guardi here. My town is a place of admirals and treasurers, not of revelers and rascals. Though my focus is on the Renaissance (the fifteenth and sixteenth centuries), it is a Renaissance that respected and incorporated the best of the city's earlier history. This place was rapacious and ruthless, but in service to a government that valued control of the governors as well as of the governed. It is customary to treat Venice as feminine, as the calm seductress, Serenissima. The older Venice thought of itself as masculine, the Lion City, one that lived under war discipline—not because its walls were scarred with cannon fire or its streets marked with battle monuments (thanks to its physical seclusion, they were not), but because so much of its population had to live out on the commercial ships and war fleets of an extensive empire, storming other people's walls, bringing other cities' treasure back to be absorbed into their own town's distinctive fabric.

When I first started going to Venice, twenty years ago, I saw it through the eyes of Ruskin, my favorite prose master. It took me a while to see how distorted that vision was. Ruskin thought that a primitive Venice, pure in its religion, was corrupted in the Renaissance by the advent of mercantile rationalism. He read Venetian history as an omen of England's doomed empire. Actually, mercantile values were building the Venetian empire all through the "Gothic" centuries Ruskin treated as preimperial. What began to weaken Venice in the sixteenth century was not any loss of religion (it was hardening, then, in adversity) but the lessening of commercial advantage during a time when Atlantic traffic opened up and Turkish expansion ate into Venice's trade with the East. It was not the advent of commerce, but the loss of commerce, that was affecting Venice's power.[2]

Venice's imperialism resembled England's less than it did that of ancient Athens. I realize that Florence is usually called the Athens of Renaissance Italy, the center of learning and art; but Venice has a far better claim to that title. Periclean Athens, a sea empire, used its land enclave as a staging area for ventures into a watery world of restive subordinates or hostile rivals. Athenians, as much as Venetians, felt that they were different from the rest of mankind, separate, autochthonous (sprung out of their own turf). They could preserve that difference from others only by a certain sameness among themselves, a tight internal cohesion. That is why Otto Demus can describe Venice as the "counterpart of a Greek polis."[3] That is why I shall have frequent occasion to mention echoes of Athenian arrangements in the polity of Venice—parallels, as we shall see, with Greek "liturgies," or ostracism, or restriction of politics by bloodlines, or the use of resident aliens (Greek *metoikoi*), or compulsory ritual, or post-term scrutiny of officials (*euthyna*). This was not because Venice was consciously imitating Athens, but because the structure of the two sea empires made them reach for similar solutions to the problems they faced.

The naval skill of the Athenians secured the Delian League, from which they extracted tribute to adorn their polychrome Acropolis—just as Venetian seamen brought back the plunder of Byzantium to be incorporated into the iridescence of their martial shrine, the basilica of St. Mark. Athenian tribute money was brought in formal procession to the theater of Dionysus for the religious contests of that god. In Venice, the rich reliquaries captured in the East were carried about on the feast days of tutelary patron saints. Both cities had an identity marked by idiosyncratic religion. The Athenian commander steering his trireme toward the Athenian port of Piraeus could see, flashing far out over the water, the gold tip of Athena's spear as it towered above her sixty-foot bronze statue on the Acropolis. The Venetian commander saw, from the outer channels of his lagoon, the gilded angel of the Annunciation on the vertiginous campanile in St. Mark's Square, the angel of the Marian feast day on which the city was supposedly born in 421 C.E.

The Venetians were Catholic, but they certainly "wore their rue with a difference." Their religion was specific to their politics, kept at a deliberate distance from the papal and Byzantine forms of faith. As Edward Muir says (M 16), "in Venice patriotism equaled piety." The Athenians would have understood that. Venetians' sense of themselves was endlessly mirrored and remade in the religious pageants that celebrated their patron saints, the guardians of their empire. In a painting (c. 1572) by Battista d'Agnolo del Moro, now at the Arsenal, Saint Mark himself is seated at the recruiting table outside the Doge's Palace, where a man is being paid in advance to serve in the fleet. Mark is so involved in the process that it is hard to tell whether he holds his gospel open in front of him or a list of recruits. He has to guarantee the quality of the men who row and fight and conquer under his flag. His emblem, the Lion of Saint Mark, was emblazoned on the walls of subject cities. Painting after painting represented the way Mark had rescued his naval clients from drowning and various dangers. Other saints important to the city's empire—George, Theodore, Nicholas, Stephen, Jerome—performed tasks different from those Mark made his specialty. There was a division of labor among the saints, as among the Venetians themselves.

The Venetians' very cohesion depended on articulation of the differing and supplemental work each had to perform if the city and the empire were to work. An imperiled society must pull together, even as its members labor on different social strata—just as fighting ships' crews at the oars and on the decks have to coordinate their actions in a fearsome choreography. The Venetian home base was just the headquarters for an intricate network of citizenry scattered over the many ports, dependencies, and targets of military action that maintained trade routes and kept in line both allies and foes. The real sinews of both Athens and Venice were rarely visible in the capital city. Even during the winter, which slowed or stopped shipping, when festivals were held to unite most of the citizens at home, residents of foreign holdings, the imperial or commercial officials and their naval supporters, were kept away from the center. Strong religious and patriotic ties were needed to hold the whole system together. That is why neither Athens nor Venice, in its rise to supremacy, used slaves to row its warships.[4] The skill and loyalty needed for complex maneuverings in battle, with over a hundred oars working in unison on each ship, was not a matter that could be trusted outside the family, as

it were. Besides, warships were coasting vessels, which put into land at night. Oarsmen were not chained in place, like later galley slaves (war captives, criminals, etc.). Desertion would have drained away any slave force in such relatively free circumstances.

The mass of men in both cities were not only seamen; most were oarsmen. Aristotle even called the Athenian democracy "a throng of oarsmen."[5] An Athenian trireme carried, on average, 200 men, and 170 were at the oars. A single operation in a single year could require as many as 2,000 rowers.[6] The Venetians had only 140 to 180 men to a warship, but the proportion of rowers was the same. When we see pictures like Andrea Vicentino's *Battle of Lepanto* in the Doge's Palace, we must remember that those

FIG. I
Battista d'Agnolo del Moro, *Saint Mark at the Recruiting Table*

15

slanting forests of oars on which the ships "walk" were wielded by a vast invisible army, the main structural support of the empire. And the Venetians were full partners in the campaigns, in ways that Athenian rowers could not be. When ships grappled, or invaded a shore, their oarsmen came swarming off the benches with the weapons they kept beside them, weapons supplied by the state (another reason slaves could not be used). Notice the armor on the recruit in Battista d'Agnolo's picture. In Athens, by contrast, men had to supply their own armor and weapons, and propertyless rowers (*thetes*) could not afford their purchase.

The two cities took to the sea, in some measure, because the land was sealed off from them. In the years of Venetian expansion, heavily armed and mounted Frankish knights roamed the land like modern tanks, crushing all opposition (McN 1–3). Their formations were vulnerable only when they took to the sea, where Venice could intercept their movements and interdict their supplies—serving the Byzantine empire, for a period, as a kind of buffer against the Frankish incursions. In the same way, Sparta held undisputed mastery of land war in fifth-century B.C. Greece. Pericles, recognizing that supremacy, persuaded the Athenians not to oppose Spartan invasion of Attic territory—it was a waste of effort. They should wall themselves up in the Acropolis and let the Spartans ravage the city's outskirts. When, in time, Venetians felt coerced to guard their inland trade routes by venturing out of their lagoon onto the mainland (terraferma), they did so with some misgiving. Though they would later organize their land armies with some of the same efficient management techniques they used for their fleets, they thought of this force as secondary to the "true" Venetian métier. Though they put their own fighters on ships at sea, they hired mercenaries to wage terraferma wars.

Once the imperial cities had committed themselves to breathing in life from the sea, they had to keep expanding over it in order to survive. As Pericles said of the Athenian holdings, "It was wrong perhaps to have taken them, but it would be deadly to yield them back."[7] The imperial drive in both cities convinced their opponents that they aspired to world dominion. This was an absurd notion, given the limited population of the two empires' base cities, but it led to frightened coalitions against them. Corinthians warned that Athenians were "incapable of keeping peace themselves or letting any others stay at peace."[8] A French ambassador warned Germans that Venetian plans were for "flinging bridges across the Danube, Rhine, Seine, and Ebro" (F 36). Thus Athenian expansionism led to the Peloponnesian War, and Venetian advances onto terraferma created the League of Cambrai to check them. In both cases, the combined forces won, stripping the imperial cities of much of their power. But they both bounced back, to the amazement of contemporaries. It was only when real world dominators came along—Philip and his Macedonians, Mehmed II and his Turks—that the two finally lost their empires.

The Venetians were more consistently aware of the source of their power and wealth than were the Athenians. Though they both had extensive shipyards that were the technological wonder of their day—Athens at Telegoneia and Venice at the Arsenal—we hear little about the Athenian ship factory. Athens' first military forces were the full-armed (hoplite) formations (phalanxes) of land war—yet even when its real fighting was being done by hoplites ferried in ships, and most combatants were sailors, a literary conservatism made them think of warriors in an anachronistically Homeric mold. Aristophanes could mock mere rowers, as opposed to hoplite troops, even while the city depended on the rowers for its very existence. The Venetians, by contrast, came late to terraferma war. They had no militia or land army of their own. Their first image of the Lion City at war was of sailor-combatants, rowers and archers and siege technicians for shore assaults. They conceived of themselves in fresh terms, taken from contemporary life and not from stylized epic memories.

The Venetian maritime discipline was patterned after early voyages, when commercial ships had their officers appointed by the state, though merchants' representatives were on board to protect their investment, and the masters of the ship consulted them in unforeseen emergencies. Both officers and investors tried to recruit the loyalty of the crew, and when emergencies arose the men were given a vote on specific decisions: "As late as the thirteenth century, the ship's company as a whole had the right to decide whether the vessel should change its destination, whether it should winter overseas, whether an individual seaman should be allowed ashore" (L 50). The crew was also given a share of the booty captured by sea or land (McN 8). The "republic" of Venice was really an oligarchy at home; but it could at times be a democracy at sea.

At home, too, there were democratic aspects of Venetian life that arose outside its formal ruling procedures. These had to do with the unique way Venice was formed and maintained. Athens claimed to be autochthonous because it sprang out of its own earth. Venice first had to make its own earth spring out of the water. Many plots of its land were not wrestled free of the lagoon until the twelfth century, and the perpetual struggle to keep lagoon and land in a proper relationship created a communal discipline closely tied to each person's needs. River inlets to the lagoon had to be guided to flush out deeper channels for maneuvering. Salt pools and marshes inside each patch of recovered living space had to be dried out or filled in. The islets thus linked were, in fact, like a stationary fleet in interdependent formation, one whose safety depended on the performance of many pressing tasks. In a two-volume study called (in English) *Above Saline Waters*, Elizabeth Crouzet-Pavan argues that these spatial realities affected the enduring regimen of Venetian society and politics.

To take just one example, the need for fresh water was an ironic exigency placed on a people "up to their necks in water." The brininess of the lagoon had given Venice its first major industrial operation—the salt pans that made it a major source of that essential preservative. But fresh water was initially available only from the sky, and collection of it had to be systematized. For a while, only the wealthy could construct the system of basins and pipes to convey water from rooftops and courtyards into underground cisterns (*pozzi*) in any stored quantities. Extended families lived around the palace courtyard that had a pozzo, fed by drainpipes inside the walls. In cities like Rome or Florence, a great family and its dependents clustered together to share the safety of fortified palaces with towers. But in Venice, where the palaces were unfortified and open to the air, it was at first the water at the heart of the whole *ca'* (house) that acted as a magnet.

Poorer people had for some time to live from buckets or jars of collected rain, or from barrels of fresh water brought by boats from terrraferma, but this time-consuming and inefficient practice distracted them from other jobs, so public money created pozzi in every square (*campo*), where carved wellheads (*vere da pozzi*) still mark this vital node of communal life (c-p 244–52). The *vere* became centers of social life—there were over a thousand of them in Renaissance Venice—much as inner hearths or courtyard fires were in cold northern climes. The squares (*campi*) were the organizational centers of a city that originated as unconnected islets, each with its parish church or churches. At the beginning of the thirteenth century, the main node of Venice, the Rialtine land cluster, still comprised over sixty small islets, separated by more and wider watercourses than at present. Venice could not grow out from a central forum, like old cities of Roman foundation, or grow inward from containing walls. It was a multicellular accumulation of nuclei tied together by land ligaments or wood bridges or boat landings.

This decentralized beginning led to apparently contradictory things—a sense of separate locale that never disappeared, and yet a need for overall regulation. Since everyone relied on the lagoon and the canals for multiple purposes, resources had to be pooled for their management and orderly use. And the limited nature of the individual units called for common services that none of them was adequate to provide on its own—things as different as a plague hospital and a defensive navy. Certain activities had to be assigned to one area though it served the whole. Dangerous or polluting tasks were sequestered—the fire for forges in the ghetto (foundry) area or the Arsenal, the fire for glass-blowing on the island of Murano. Cloth dyeing, whose offscourings could foul internal canals, was banished to the main body's extremities (c-p 295–96). The painter Tintoretto, who belonged to a dyer's family, came from the parish of Santa Maria dell'Orto (Mary of the Garden), on the northern embankment (*fondaco*) of Venice proper. The same confinement away from the canals applied to butchers and tanners (the latter situated on Giudecca).

Despite these specializations, the integrity of the original units had led to a mingling of people from all classes around the individual campi. Patricians lived where they had parish or commercial ties, diffused throughout the islets. The commercial basis of their wealth kept them near manufacturers, lesser merchants, sailors, and ship builders. Here the aristocrat was not a feudal lord, his castle walled off from the land worked by his serfs. Despite an honorific title, "knight," bestowed for service to the republic, Venetians lacked a feudal hierarchy—no counts, barons, etc. There was a strictly egalitarian code *within* the patriciate, and little to separate the grades of wealth between a poor patrician and a rich notable (*cittadino*) except eligibility to public office. In everyday life, the classes of society jostled along the same alleys and canals; they were members of the same parishes or religious brotherhoods (*scuole*), business firms or military units. The nobles were so active in business affairs that the bottom floor of their palaces was given over to shops, storerooms, or rented apartments—a practice that was maintained even in grand public buildings like Sansovino's Mint (Zecca).

Since patrician women were restricted most of the time to the family palazzo, they formed close ties there with all the different kinds of people frequenting it—tenants and business agents and domestics. As historian Dennis Romano notes, "Nowhere in Venetian society were the contacts between patricians and popolani [commoners] as frequent or as intimate as they were in the households of patrician families."[9] Everyone was engaged in the great commercial enterprise that was Venice. For most of the Renaissance period, even the Doge's Palace was flanked by traders' booths. The merchant on land and the fleet at sea were the key to empire, openly confessed. There was none of the snobbism toward "trade" that land wealth encourages.

Venice was thus not only a water culture—one in which the citizens moved about by boats for their ordinary daily tasks as well as for their imperial ventures abroad—but a hydraulic culture, one that needed a strong social discipline to maintain its "unnatural" physical environment. Historian Karl Wittfogel argued in his famous 1957 book, *Oriental Despotism*, that hydraulic societies were the basis of authoritarianism in ancient civilizations (Assyria, Babylon, Egypt) and some modern ones. He recognized that Venice, like the Mormon settlements in the desert, had a complex regimen of water control, but he refused to call these hydraulic societies, since they were not despotic.[10] The more sensible thing is to recognize that there are two possible kinds of hydraulic civilizations, one founded on coercion and one on cooperation. This does not mean that the Venetians or the Mormons lacked the ordinary governmental powers of coercion, but that those powers supplemented a binding social code rather than caused or replaced it. A strong sense of religion and mission held the Mormons together. It is not enough recognized that Venice had a similarly strong sense of religion and mission, one as idiosyncratic as the Mormons'—and one that, like it, looked heretical to more conventional Christians.

This was expressed in the so-called "myth of Venice," that historical romance the city told about itself to prove that it was set apart from ordinary states. Creating this myth is called by Muir "an act of communal genius" (M 13). It was not just a pleasant tale added to reality like an ornament. It was a constitutive part of the Venetians' identity as they had forged it, making themselves up as they had made up their physical site. That is why I look, in this book, for evidence of the myth in the works of art that were so important in articulating and renewing the myth. Venetian ideals, attitudes, goals, and disciplines are given to us in the visual languages that Venetians perfected for communicating their worldview to themselves and others. We cannot actually attend a Venetian church ceremony of the Renaissance—but artifacts from or about the feasts and processions and cult objects are still vivid and available, easing our reentry into that world. This is generally recognized, but the connection is often slighted—either by concentrating on the history and using art as supplementary "illustration," or by concentrating on the art and using history as perfunctory "background." I mean to look at the history *through* the art, the art *through* the history.

It is possible, for instance, to study the issue of the doge's status in the artifacts created around the entry gate to the Doge's Palace (p. 100), or to watch the fight over credit for a Venetian victory in the funeral arrangements on competing sides of the nave in the Frari church (p. 120), or to judge the merits of the sea empire over the land empire in a Veronese painting in the Doge's Palace (p. 68). Since these artifacts take us so vividly into a different world, I use them constantly—which sometimes means that a work is chosen not for its intrinsic merit but for its usefulness in understanding some historical point. Nonetheless, there is so rich a variety of treasures to draw from that most of the works are stunning in themselves.

Art was at the service of the state in Venice, with an intensity not paralleled elsewhere in Italy. In other cities, art was largely a matter of dynastic celebration. The courts of powerful princes, those of church or state, were centers of artistic commission and display. Even work done for churches and monasteries was generated from these centers. But in Venice there was no ruler's court, no feudal hierarchy, no hereditary office. There were noble families, but they were legally equal, a fact that was impressed on them and others by their required uniformity of dress—nothing but long black robes ("togas") except for officials during their (short) terms of elected office. Sumptuary laws discouraged personal aggrandizement. Even the doge could not be represented in his own private church, St. Mark's, except in his official role as custodian of the body of Mark.[11]

In order to celebrate themselves, influential men had to glorify the state by showing themselves in service to it. A typical example of this is Tintoretto's 1567 *Madonna of the Treasurers* (P-R 1.100), in which the three treasurers (*camerlenghi*, "chamberlains") have commissioned a work to hang, not in their separate family palaces, but in the building

FIG. 2
Jacopo Tintoretto,
*Madonna of the
Treasurers*

of the camerlenghi. It shows them in their (identical) robes of office, making their year's account of the city's treasure to the Virgin, who is accompanied by three patron saints of the state (Stephen, Mark, and Theodore). This is like the Athenians' annual accounting for the tribute money to Athena on her Acropolis. The men's discipline of service is brought out by the rhythms of their choreographed motion, echoed by the similarly graceful but orderly posture of the three attendants who bring the money forward. Venetians, as we shall see, liked to show different ranks of society in responsive coordination with each other, where everyone is simultaneously serving religion and the state.

The family crests of the Venetian treasurers are hung on the marble ledge that half supports Stephen. The men's equal status is expressed by the motto "A Sign of Single-Hearted Agreement" (UNANIMUS CONCORDIAE SIMBOLUS). Here Saint Mark, important as he is to the city, is represented as subordinate to the Virgin, on whose feast the city was born. Mark reaches an approving hand toward the treasurers, and turns to assure Mary that they have discharged their duties to her. This is the myth of Venice in action. Here a disciplined piety, a confidence in divine mission, affects policy, down to the details of economic administration.

It is interesting to compare Tintoretto's painting with Battista d'Agnolo's picture of Mark at the recruiting table. There, too, officials of the state in identical uniforms— the defense ministers (*provveditori all'Armar*)—are accountable to Mark. Instead of reporting income to the Virgin, as in the Tintoretto, they are giving out state money to the citizen who will fight under the banner of Saint Mark, but—just as in Tintoretto's painting—there are three containers of money and an alignment of the family crests of the officials at their task. The recruit, though presumably a commoner, is classically armed to show the dignity of his calling. The same kind of transaction is conducted in these two pictures, though at different levels of society, and Mark is central to such actions of the state. Otto Demus once wrote, "It would be tempting to write a history of Venice in the early Middle Ages from the point of view of the relics of St. Mark alone."[12] There is no better way to start this book than to ask why Mark played such a powerful role in the city's self-image.

Venice: Lion City

PART ONE

Imperial Disciplines

CHAPTER ONE

Contract with Mark

WHEREVER YOU TURN, in Venice, lions strut or lurk, colossal or miniature, placid or menacing. Entering the city from the Basin (Bacino) as diplomats did in the Renaissance, you pass between two high columns on the Piazzetta by the Doge's Palace. One is topped, mysteriously, by a man standing on a crocodile that has a dog's head. The other has the city's famous emblem, a bronze lion with its wings spread for takeoff, its paws already dancing on the ground. It may not look so large, up there on its pillar, but it measures fifteen feet from the tip of its muzzle to the end of its tail and five feet from its perch to the small of its back. Viewed from the balcony of the Doge's Palace, or from the ground with opera glasses, it reveals its natty mustache over a leering grin, its opaque white eyes, its intricately curled mane—not a lion one wants to be on the wrong side of. It has an exotic history. Restorers decided in the 1980s that the bulk of its body is roughly 2,300 years old.[1] The city it guards is a newcomer to this veteran, who has seen empires rise and fall, but has spent his last 850 years at this sentinel post (with only a brief time of Napoleonic captivity in France).

Proceeding deeper into the Piazzetta, one sees more accommodating lions, carved in relief on the façade of the Doge's Palace—two of them, facing in opposite directions, align their backs as a throne for a personified Venice as Justice, who holds in her hands a sword and the scales of judgment. The same configuration can be seen high up on the campanile at the left end of the Piazzetta. And across from it, on the right side of the Piazzetta, a winged lion stands in majestic profile over the formal entry to the Doge's Palace. This is a religious lion—it props up an open book with its right front paw, displaying the words, "Rest here, Mark, my evangelist."[2] So this lion evangelizes. It is a preaching lion. All around this great portal (the Gate of Documents) are little ornamental lion heads projecting from the carved surface. There are also lion heads between the arches all down the long colonnade of the Doge's Palace, as well as over the arches of the Library facing the palace.

Leaving the Piazzetta, one does not leave the lions behind. Go to the Arsenal, where Venice built its famous ships, and you find exotic lions on its front lawn—captured animals brought from Greece, kenneled here. Other lions project from the Arsenal's gates or decorate its flag-pole base. Go to St. Mark's Distinguished Brotherhood (Scuola Grande di San Marco), now a hospital, where lions carved in low relief by the Lombardo family guard the door. Cross to the nearby island of Murano, you will find a casually sprawling lion carved in relief on a little bridge. In the Church of St. Francis at the Vineyard, a very philosophical lion, painted by Tiepolo, peers down at you from the roof of a chapel. Out on the walkway near the Danieli Hotel there are monstrous lions, ten times life size, cast in bronze. One is gnawing at chains that have bound it for a time. (A cat sunning itself on the lion's glistening back does not notice the discomfort of its oversize relative). Above almost every altar in the city there is a lion in one of the quadrants of the vault.

THE LION AS EVANGELIST

The churchy lion is the father of all the other felines in Venice. Its pedigree is even longer than that of the lion on the Piazzetta's pillar. That creature dates from Cilicia in the third or fourth century before the common era (B.C.E.).[3] The lion of the altar vaults dates back to Babylonia of the sixth century B.C.E., where Ezekiel saw a vision of God's chariot-throne, guarded by four creatures. Each of the creatures had four faces, directed toward the symbolic four directions—faces of a man, a lion, an ox, and an eagle (Ezekiel 1.10). This vision was adapted and simplified in the book of Revelation, where the four creatures are, respectively, a man, an ox, a lion, and an eagle (Rev 4.7). They became symbols of the apocalyptic end of the world (like the Four Horsemen of the Apocalypse in Rev 6.1–17) and then of the entire body of revelation leading up to that ultimate fulfillment.

Since the four Gospels—of Matthew, Mark, Luke, and John—were considered the greatest revelation of God's purpose in the world, their authors, the four evangelists, became associated with the four creatures of Revelation. Theologians found ways to show that the four symbols were appropriate for the beginnings of each gospel. Matthew was linked with the man for his supposed interest in human history, Mark with the lion for his opening desert scene, Luke with the ox for his implied reference to Isaiah's ox at the manger, and John with the eagle for his soaring hymn to the Logos of

God. These are the symbols painted in the quadrants over each altar, as witnesses to the mystery they wrote about. They stand, as well, at key places like the mosaic in the dome of St. Mark's basilica that is nearest the altar—where Mark-as-lion is saturnine and vaguely anthropomorphic (D 1.43).

So the lion is in Venice because of Mark. But why is Mark there? Venice did not exist during the time of Jesus, when Mark wrote his gospel. Several cities that did exist then had a better claim to connection with Mark, who was supposed to have spread the faith in them—Rome first, where legend had him writing his gospel; then Aquileia, on the Venetian lagoon's terraferma, where Mark was supposed to have ordained the first patriarch (Saint Hermagoras); then Alexandria, where he founded a church and was martyred. Even Grado, near Aquileia, had a claim prior to Venice's, since that is where the patriarchate of Aquileia was transferred in the sixth century. All Venice could boast was that, as part of the ecclesiastical jurisdiction of Aquiliea/Grado, it had a proximity to a Marcan realm.

The only way Venice could move up to closer association with Mark was to take advantage of a long squabble between the terraferma cities. When the patriarch fled from Aquileia to escape Langobard raiders in 568, he went to Grado, which was safer—it stood nearer the lagoon. When the danger had passed, Grado would not give back to Aquileia the patriarchy's religious relics and other symbols of authority. The two cities maintained their dispute for centuries; but the feud came to a head in the ninth century, when Frankish rulers, now in charge of Aquileia, appealed to the Pope for a ruling. This was delivered at the Council of Mantua in 827, restoring Aquileia to full authority. Venice, which preferred Grado in the dispute, was unhappy with the council's result—so it managed what Otto Demus calls a "coup d'état," wrenching from Aquileia the original basis of its authority, the connection with Mark.[4]

THE CONTRACT

This was accomplished by Venetian merchants, who stole the body of Mark from its Alexandrian shrine in 828 and delivered it to the doge in Venice for safekeeping (it was alleged that Muslims were about to desecrate the relic). Venice's right to the body was confirmed by a new myth—it was said that while Mark was setting out into the Adriatic after consecrating Hermagoras in Aquileia, a storm held his boat overnight in the lagoon, at just the spot where the doge's basilica would later be built, and an angel appeared to him in a dream, saying, "Be at rest here." Literally, the words were "Peace to you, Mark, my evangelist" (*Pax tibi Marce evangelista meus*), which had a first meaning,

"Be not afraid of the storm," but also a deeper meaning (in Venetian eyes), "Rest here"—at Venice—as his final resting place. This is the motto the heraldic lion of Venice props up under its paw. Venice, not Alexandria, was Mark's destined place of final rest. Once he reached it, he would protect the place forever.

This was what Anthony Hecht calls "the major heist of Christendom."[5] Patrick Geary, in his book on the politics of relics, writes: "Every aspect of the translation of Saint Mark has been studied with greater attention than has any other relic theft because of its acknowledged pivotal importance in the history of Venice."[6] The move was so brilliant that it became the basis, over time, for omnidirectional declarations of independence on the part of Venice. It undercut, for a start, both Aquileia and Grado as the true seat of Mark's religious authority. In doing so, it pushed away as well the state sponsors of the competing towns—the Franks ruling Aquileia and the Byzantine rulers who challenged them by backing Grado. All ecclesiastical authority, whether from Rome or Byzantium, was also set at a distance, since the merchants had not delivered Mark's body to an ecclesiastical authority in Venice—it went to the secular head of state, the doge, who kept it in San Marco, his own private chapel-basilica.

Most cities had as their main church the cathedral, the seat of the local bishop, who had authority over local clergy by virtue of his place in the ecclesiastical chain of command. But the center of religious life in Venice was a *political* cult site, where the doge had power to appoint his own chaplains for his own church. The bishop of Venice was shoved to the periphery of its social life, both symbolically and physically—on the island of Castello, where the old cathedral of Saint Peter was located. This expressed an attitude toward Peter's successor in Rome that would be a continuing feature of Venetian life. The living religious leadership was exercised from Mark's shrine. As Muir puts it:

> He [the doge] alone selected the chaplains and nominated the vicar (*primacerio*) for Senate approval, and there remained a closed circle of administrative ties between the doge in his palace and the clerics in their basilica that no outside ecclesiastical or lay power could break . . . Claims that Venice had a special mandate from God, that it was protected by the saints, that it was independent of the Papacy and the Empire, and that all of this was amply proved by history, depended on the ability of the republic to assume the attributes of the doge. (M 261–62)

The doge's very office now depended on his relation to the relic of Mark. He assumed his responsibility by signing a Pledge (*Promissione*) that was, in effect, a contract with Mark. Speaking for the whole Venetian people, he bound himself to defend Mark's relic in return for Mark's protection of the city. This contract brought Venice many advantages. By welcoming a Western saint, Venice not only edged itself away from Byzantium but from the parts of its own past that had been formed in the Byzantine ethos—a cultural dependence expressed by its prior choice of an official patron, the Eastern martyr Saint Theodore, whose relics had been kept in the doge's chapel before it became Mark's resting place. Theodore was "elbowed out," as Demus puts it, to make room for Mark.[7] The demotion of Theodore (who was retained as a subsidiary figure—he is the saint standing on a crocodile in the Piazzetta) went with a reordering of the pecking order among Venetian protectors. Other patrons—Saint George, whose monastery on his own island was an important spiritual center, or Saint Sebastian, whose cult was also Byzantine (based in Ravenna), or Saint Nicholas, who guarded the Lido—had to step down a notch when Mark moved in at the top. Such shifts in importance were reflected in the processions that articulated so much of Venice's understanding of itself. These protocols of saintly status resemble the reshufflings of position in the Kremlin reviewing stand at May Day parades in the old Soviet Union. Western scholars used to study the platform order to see who was up, who down, who was in, who out. That is the kind of adjustment that had to occur when Mark assumed his commanding role in Venice.

SAN MARCO'S MOSAICS

The doge's chapel was rebuilt, expanded, sheathed in the precious spoils from imperial campaigns fought in Mark's name, under Mark's flag. The doge was assisted in his guardianship of the basilica and its surroundings by Venice's "Caretakers" (*Procuratori*), who thus became very high officials. In and around and throughout the doge's basilica, Mark's story is told and retold and referred to in painted and jeweled and sculpted artifacts. San Marco is, in effect, one large reliquary, a huge casket to hold the treasure of Mark's body. It has already been mentioned that the doge himself could not be represented in his own church except in his role as keeper of Mark's body.

That is expressed in the thirteenth-century mosaic over the north door of the entrance (the last surviving one from a set of four) telling the story of Mark's transfer to Venice. In this mosaic (D 2.201–04), two bishops are carrying the saint's body into the church on which this mosaic is placed. The doge, in his ceremonial ermine collar, stands to the right of the entry, deferred to by his son with a yielding gesture. The doge's wife (*dogaressa*) is on the other side of the entry with her retinue of noblewomen.

PLATE I
*Saint Mark's Body
Carried into the Basilica,*
Byzantine mosaic

There are fifty figures in the mosaic, and all but the two bishops carrying the body are laymen, the doge's secular companions. The doge holds a scroll in his hand, the Pledge to defend the body now arriving.

Demus's realization that the scroll was the doge's Pledge made it possible for him to solve the principal mystery of the mosaic—the fact that the saint is going *into* the church's central portal, but the others are coming *out* of its four side doors. The doge who had this mosaic created, Lorenzo Tiepolo (1268–1275), is commemorating the Pledge he ceremonially accepted inside the church, which reenacts, as it were, the placing of Mark under his custody. This thirteenth-century figure is symbolically reenacting the ninth-century event that placed the body in his care. He has come out to testify to the people that his oath is now sworn. The relic is in safe hands.

This mosaic on the façade of the church, which replicates that façade in its narrative, has two companion mosaics inside the church which represent the inside of the church—they tell how Venetians came into San Marco to pray for the rediscovery of Mark's body (lost in a remodeling of the church) and how his body miraculously appeared from inside a pillar. These thirteenth-century mosaics also show, anachronistically, the doge who commissioned the mosaic. He too is reenacting a remembered miracle, in this case one from the eleventh century. Doge Ranieri Zen (1253–1268) leads the people in prayer for the body's recovery (D 2.27–37). He stands just behind the priest at the altar—the church's actual altar, visible across the transept, with its canopy (*baldacchino*). We also see (in this scene) the tiered pulpit to the left of the choir screen, and (in the next scene, of rediscovery) the flat-box pulpit on the right side. We would have seen more of the church presented in the mosaic, but the ends of the two scenes, which originally curled around the corners of the wall that holds them, were destroyed when other scenes were put on those surfaces. We would have seen the church's apse, not only its domes and balcony network (*matroneum*), as at present.

In the scene of prayer for the body to appear, we are shown the whole of Venetian society. Behind the doge stand other officers of the state. Below them are priests, choirboys, and monks bending low in supplication. To the left are male citizens—females would have been included if the part around this left corner had not been lopped off. In the scene where the pillar reveals its contents (D 2.37–44), the doge again stands with male members of his family (one of whom wears the ermine lining to his cloak permitted to immediate relatives of the doge). A group of officials is on the other side of the flat pulpit. After them the dogaressa leads a contingent of patrician ladies. The little girl who holds the dogaressa's girdle is her daughter; but the boy holding another woman's finger cannot be her son—not merely because Ranieri Zen had no son, but because the boy wears a crown, and only two people could do that in Venice, the doge and his wife. Demus makes a convincing case that the boy is Philip of Courtenay, only son and heir of the Latin emperor of Constantinople, sent as a child to Venice as security for a great loan given to the East in Zen's time by Venetian merchants. The lady he attends church with is presumably a matron from the Ferro family's palace (Ca' Ferro), where Philip was lodged during his stay in Venice.

FIG. 2A
Detail of *Apparition of the Relics of Saint Mark*

These scenes, like the one on the exterior of the church, show how Mark's body ordered the whole of society around itself. Elsewhere in the basilica, the story of Mark's life, martyrdom, and transport to Venice is repeated in every medium. He is present even where he did not ordinarily belong. Statues of the apostles, sculpted by the Dalle Masegne family in the fourteenth century, line the top of the choir screen before the altar—but there are thirteen of them, not the scriptural Twelve. Mark, an evangelist but not an apostle, is an honorary apostle in his own church. He also shows up with apostles in the central dome mosaic of Christ's ascension to heaven (D 1.149). In the east dome, the first one a visitor passes under, he is seated with the apostles as the fires of Pentecost descend on them (D 1.193).

FIG. 3
San Marco mosaic, *Noah Leading His Family and the Animals Out of the Ark*

Of course Mark is also present wherever the evangelists are shown, either accompanied by his lion or represented by the lion alone. In fact, the primacy of the lion symbol means that Mark is implicitly present even where modern viewers do not normally recognize the fact. In the atrium mosaics of the creation of the world, for instance, the lions come first in the pairs of animals made on the fifth day (D 2.111). And when Adam is naming the animals, he begins with the lions, placing his hand on the male one, Mark's emblem (D 2.113)—we know it is the male of the pair because it stands on the right, the place of honor. In the Noah mosaics, when the pairs of animals are taken aboard the ark, the lions come first again, and are helped aboard by Noah's two hands (D. 2.120). When the animals come out after the flood, the male lion bounds free at once, while Noah is still guiding the female down the plank (D 1.121–22). The dignity of Mark's lion is emphasized from the beginning of the cosmos—and Mark is there at the end of time as well, in the apocalyptic scheme of the basilica's façade.

SAN MARCO'S HORSES

On that façade, the four classical bronze horses captured from Constantinople pace forward over the triumphal arch of the central portal. The horses were originally part of a quadriga, a four-horse chariot with its driver. There were many such quadrigae in the classical world, above ceremonial arches, at hippodromes, or as votary offerings for victory in the games. All the other horses were melted down for their bronze, and this set alone survives, protected by its religious use. But what is that use? Why are they on Mark's basilica front? To understand that, we must look at the context of the west end of medieval churches. They usually contained a Last Judgment, on the outer wall, or the inner one, or (as at San Marco) on both. This was a penitential barrier before the inner mysteries, forcing one to confess the sins that will be judged at the return of Christ.[8] (The east end, by contrast—with the choir and apse spaces—usually had a message of comfort, delivered by the Savior or his Mother or a protecting saint above the altar.)

The façade of San Marco has a Last Judgment in the recess under the central arch (the present one is a second replacement for the original mosaic shown in Gentile Bellini's fifteenth-century painting of the cathedral front). To go with this End Time scene *below* the horses' pacing, there was originally a relief carving *above* the horses' heads, of Christ the Cosmic Ruler (Pantocrator), who will come again in judgment.[9] The relief was moved to the north (landward) side of the basilica when a window was opened above the horses to let more light into the interior.

Like the Four Horses of the Apocalypse, then, these horses signal the end of the world, the time of judgment, the arrival of Christ's reign. But they are not individual carriers of doom. Rather, as a processional chariot team they draw back the Lord in his apocalyptic Quadriga Domini, with the Pantocrator as charioteer. That quadriga was often thought of in terms of the four apocalyptic animals, the symbols of the evangelists taken from Ezekiel. In fact, Titian did a famous woodcut of the procession of the Lord, called *The Triumph of Faith*, in which the evangelical symbols are hitched to Christ's chariot as a team.[10] Titian lines them up, for visibility, in terms of their rising height, so the eagle is closest to us viewers, the lion behind it, the ox after that, and the standing man is last.

The connection of these symbols with the Quadriga Domini was made clear, in the façade, before the present window replaced the Pantocrator—for that figure was flanked by carved reliefs of the four evangelists, seen writing their Gospels but without the animals that normally accompanied them. They would have been associated, instead, with the horses just below them. According to Jacoff's reconstruction, Mark's symbol would have been the second horse from the left. Everything in Mark's church bears his mark.

FIG. 4
Titian,
The Triumph of Faith

And so did everything in Venice. He was the guarantor of the city's separate religious calling. The republic would be true to him even when it puzzled other nations by its defiance of popes, Christian crusaders, Protestant reformers, and many different forms of religiosity. So identified was the city with its patron and his symbol that people spoke of fearing the lion, or surrendering to the lion, when they were in conflict with Venice. They spoke of giving allegiance to Saint Mark if they formed a treaty with his city. The image of his lion was carved on the gates and in the courtyards of subject cities, and razed at times when Venice lost control of them. But the lion's realm was not itself violated until the nineteenth century, when Napoleon became the first to enter it as a conqueror. He took the Piazzetta lion down from its pillar and shipped it, along with the four horses of the Lord, back to Paris. Then newspaper cartoons showed the lion trammeled in a net, or rolled over on its back, or being toyed with by children. Enemies rejoiced in this downfall of a republic that had been so proud of its lion ways. To defeat Venice was to beard with impunity Mark's lion, to dethrone Mark himself. Do *not* rest here, my evangelist.

CHAPTER TWO

Declarations of Independence

VENETIANS FOUND MANY WAYS to make their possession of Mark's body a sign of their independence from other people, from ordinary cities, almost from common humanity. But they did not rely solely on this symbol of their independence. They deployed other aspects of their own myth to support or reflect the legend of Mark. The sheer number of these reinforcements of the idea of their separateness shows what an obsession it was with them. This chapter considers just three of the ways that Venice declared its distinctive character. It will come as no surprise that, like the use of Mark's body itself, these were political manipulations of religious themes.

THE ANNUNCIATION

Wafted by gondola or shunted by vaporetto, one goes under the Rialto Bridge between two figures that stand out in high relief on opposite aprons of the bridge. On the left is an angel, still in flight but checking his flight, his right arm out in greeting. On the right, a kneeling woman throws her left hand back in surprise—it is the Virgin Mary receiving the news that she will bear the Son of God. This "annunciation" by an angel is often treated in this way, with the figures separated by a wide space. On altar panels, they may be on opposed wings of a triptych. On the arch over a church altar, they signal to each other across the sacred space. On St. Mark's basilica, they inhabit little structures (*aedicula*) on the outermost corners of the façade's frothy upper level. In all these cases, the distance between the angel and the woman is charged with a theological meaning. The incarnation of God, the mystery being enacted, fills the intervening space. In a triptych, the central picture shows some action of Jesus, the fruit of this moment. Over an altar, the transaction points to the Eucharist on the altar below, where God is again mysteriously embodied—this time under the appearance of bread. On the basilica's façade, the whole church becomes a meeting place between God and man, made possible by the God-Man that entered Mary's womb when she said, "Let it happen to me as you say" (Lk 1.38).

But all this just makes the Rialto bridge more puzzling. What passes between Mary and the angel here is a motley crowd of tourists, garbage scows, and gondoliers singing Neapolitan songs in a Venetian setting. The more one knows about the figures in relief, the more their use here seems to border on the blasphemous. But this neglects the serene assurance Venetians had that the Virgin of the Annunciation blesses everything they do. Her announcing angel stands atop the huge brick campanile in St. Mark's Square. She is, in one of her guises, Venice itself, accompanied by the announcing angel in Jacobello del Fiore's triptych of the Virgin City (ante 1439) in the Accademia (SN 442–43). All these artistic summonings of her bear witness to the fact that Venice was founded on the Feast of the Annunciation, March 25, in the year 421. Only the Venetians could be confident that their city, born miraculously from the sea, is an earthly echo of the conception of the Savior himself. So important to them was the story of the Annunciation as told in Luke's gospel (1.26–38) that it entered into other Marian celebrations—as when two priests reenacted the scene at the culmination of a huge procession for the Feast of Mary's Purification (see below).

Though it is claimed that Venice came into being in 421, this date is too early for any sizable settlement to have existed on the scattered islands of the lagoon. Yet even this exaggeration left Venice a latecomer in the antiquity stakes. The other major cities of Italy could point to skeletal remains, often half buried, of Roman forum or temple, amphitheater or aqueduct, testifying that they were civilized places when most of Venice's islets had not been wrestled up above the saline waters. There had been some Roman settlement of the oldest islands, as an inscription found on Torcello proves. But the exiguous signs of this had perished; there was no major ancient structure to keep alive its memory. At times, especially after Padua had become part of Venice's land empire, the city would share in the prestige derived from the claim that ancient Trojans settled in the Veneto region even before they arrived in Virgil's Rome. And the Renaissance prestige of the classics guaranteed that Venetians, like humanists anywhere in Europe, would be very interested in antiquity, as Patricia Fortini Brown and Irene Favaretto have confirmed.[1] But the Venetians continued to make an advantage of their temporal recentness and rootlessness, turning it into a virgin birth, a watery parturition like Mary's delivery of Jesus at the angel's word.

Let others talk of Caesar. The tie with Mary's feast gave Venetians a higher lineage. It declared their independence from pagan Rome. They would use its heritage, like any other country, but without obsequiousness. Their own claims were superior even to those of the revered classical past.

In the fifteenth and sixteenth centuries, official state historians openly disdained ancient Rome. They claimed that Venice was a greater Empire than Rome had ever been because she had never been conquered and she was a Christian Empire . . . Probably the most outspoken Venetian historian is Paolo Paruta, whose *Discorsi politici*, posthumously published in 1599, is essentially a diatribe against ancient Rome.[2]

Belief in the magic date they share with Mary gave a special quality to Venetians' attitude toward the Virgin. All Italian cities were devout in their worship of her. Many (but not Venice) dedicated their most important church (the *duomo*, or cathedral) to her—Florence, Siena, Milan, San Gimignano. They made her a queen or empress, and favored the depiction of her enthroned in majesty (the Maestà pattern) with angels in rapt attendance. When Mary is given a throne in Venice, it is sometimes because her image is merged with that of the personified city on a lion throne.

Other cities prostrated themselves to Mary in a feudal spirit, consigning themselves entirely to her. In Siena, for instance, the mayor made this legal surrender before a Maestà image in 1260: "I most miserable and unfaithful of sinners give, donate and concede to you this city of Siena and all its region, its armies and its holdings, and as a sign of this I place the keys of the city of Siena on this altar."[3]

The Mary of Venice, that nonfeudal state, was less imposing, more human— almost a sister of the city with which she shared a virgin birth. Venetians had special emphases when representing the Annunciation in art (see Chapters 17 and 18). They also had special ways of celebrating her feast. They did not concentrate so much on the Annunciation feast shared with the rest of the Catholic Church, on March 25, though that was the supposed date of their own foundation. They celebrated the Annunciation, reenacting it in drama, on another Marian feast, that of the Purification—known in England as Candlemas—when Mary went to the Temple for the ritual cleansing all Jewish women were obliged to undergo after childbirth.

THE MARK AND MARY PARTNERSHIP

The Purification was a feast in which women had a special role to play, since it emphasized their bond with Mary in the trials of childbirth, and women in Venice never had a larger arena for their action than in its celebration. But that is not what made the Purification feast, during its time of maximum celebration, one of the two major processional occasions in the city. Elizabeth Crouset-Pavan argues that this feast was seized on for special attention because it followed so closely (with only one intervening day) on the feast of the transfer of Mark's body—his Translatio—in Venice (C-P 533). The two events, with the ceremonies on the eve of each, gave Venice four days of ritual activity (January 30–February 2), the longest celebration in the calendar, representing the close tie between Mark and Mary as the city's protectors. We have already seen the interplay of Mark and Mary in Tintoretto's painting of the city treasurers. Many of the large votive paintings in the Doge's Palace repeat the pattern of Mark presenting the people of Venice (or their representatives) to the Virgin.

Titian painted a famous picture of Doge Andrea Gritti being presented in this way for the palace's cabinet room (the Collegio). Though the painting was destroyed by a fire, we know the main features of its composition from an engraving. Mary is seated on a platform with four steps. Mark is standing below so that his head is on a level with hers. On the side of him toward the Virgin, his giant lion crouches, while Gritti kneels on the other side of him. When Tintoretto was asked to replace the picture after its destruction, he raised the platform on which Mary sits, subordinating Mark to her, and he introduced between the two patrons another figure, that of the martyr Saint Marina, on whose feast day Gritti won a famous battle, recapturing Padua in 1509. The joint protection of Mark and Mary was sealed, as it were, by their collaboration with the saint of a particular day. All these votive pictures link the two great patrons with particulars of Venetian history, which is supposed to revolve around them, just as the city, in long processions of perfectly articulated parts, moved through its sacred routes on the paired feast days of Mark and Mary.

This celebration was one of those in which, as Muir says, the constitution of Venice was not so much written as choreographed: "In effect, the ducal procession was the constitution . . . In the procession, position was everything" (M 190). The festivities were meant to tie the original parishes (*contrade*) of the city together. The watery pageant's long route circled through and around them. The contrade took turns in arranging the centerpiece of the ceremony—a ritual boat with twelve wooden statues (six from each of the two contrade presiding for that year) of a "Mary," wearing beautiful vestments and jewelry. These formed a retinue for the Virgin, like the retinue the dogaressa enjoyed—they probably represented the twelve stars forming a halo around the woman clothed with the sun in Revelation 12.1, a passage often taken as referring to Mary. The festival was called, after the statues, "the Feast of the Marys," and its base of operations was the Church of the Shapely Mary (Santa Maria Formosa), the oldest church devoted to the Virgin in Venice, whose contrada was therefore sacred to her and would be the site of the doge's own pilgrimage on Candlemas. Since the Marys went on display on the Feast of Saint Paul, January 25, the festival could be conceived as lasting eight days (C-P 537), outdoing Christmas or Easter in the complexity of its proceedings.

On January 30, the eve of Saint Mark's Translatio, men from the two presiding contrade of the year rowed from their own parishes to the Piazza of San Marco, where they paraded with music before the basilica, before moving on to the campo of Santa Maria Formosa, where they gave out money to poor women for their marriage dowries. On January 31, the parishes again rowed to San Marco, where one parish's priest appeared dressed ceremonially as the Virgin, and the other's priest was robed as the angel Gabriel. The man impersonating the Virgin was rowed ahead to Santa Maria Formosa, to await the arrival of the second contrada's boat carrying Gabriel, who, on his arrival, reenacted the Annunciation, and then weddings of couples from the various contrade were solemnized.

On February 1, the eve of the Purification, the Virgin and the angel returned to San Marco to accompany the doge as he went in procession to chant the vespers of the Marian liturgy at Santa Maria Formosa. On February 2, the climax of the long festival, the priests of Santa Maria Formosa were taken in boats to the westernmost part of the city (Castello), where Mass was celebrated in the Cathedral of St. Peter. Then the Marys were put in boats, three to a boat, attended by women and girls, and rowed to St. Peter's to receive the bishop's blessing. From there they rowed to San Marco for another Mass, and the doge joined the procession of many boats along the Grand Canal. They passed the Rialto Bridge before circling back through smaller canals to Santa Maria Formosa, for a third Mass and festivities prolonged into the night. The procession, by its long route, knit together the contrade, affirming the individual ethos of each, yet weaving them into the whole fabric of Marcan and Marian patronage under the doge. The multiple landings and embarkings, says Crouset-Pavan, "linked land and water together in an expansive spatial dramatization" (C-P 533). The constitution was danced out, article by article.

But after more than two centuries of observance, the festival was suspended in 1379, during the crisis of the Chioggia War with Genoa, and only vestigially restored later—the doge going to Santa Maria Formosa for vespers on the eve of the Purification, but celebrating the feast itself at San Marco. There were several reasons for the feast's not being restored. It had become cumbrously expensive, and the patricians of each contrada, who financed it by their local contributions, were now concentrating their activities around the Doge's Palace. The providing of dowries to the poor, one of the principal aspects of the feast, was being supported by religious brotherhoods (*scuole*). Besides, the festival had begun to blend with the Carnival, subjecting the Marys' dignity to casual treatment by rowdy crowds. The centralizing of the imperial government made it no longer necessary to reintegrate the contrade in ceremonial terms. Yet the long discipline of this communal rite had fused the Venetians under the high aegis of Mark and Mary, giving the city the confidence that its origin from the Feast of the Annunciation set it apart from cities of less exalted birth.

THE PACT OF 1176

Another part of the Venetian myth set it above other powers by celebrating its role in mediating their differences. This function of the republic was traced back to the year 1176, when Emperor Frederick Barbarossa was taking over parts of Italy. Pope Alexander III tried to put a stop to these incursions by forming the Lombard League, which checked Frederick at the battle of Legnano. A treaty was signed between the two forces in Venice, with doge Sebastiano Ziani presiding. The Venetians expanded this tale into one in which they succored the pope, who had fled to Venice incognito and was hiding there. The doge, promising the pope that Venice would protect him, sent a fleet that defeated the emperor's sea force, commanded by his son Otto, on the Feast of the Ascension (thenceforth a day of special Venetian celebration). Since the Venetians had captured Otto, Frederick was forced to bargain for peace. He came to Venice and kissed the foot of Pope Alexander, who placed his other foot on the kneeling Frederick's neck. In gratitude for all this assistance, the pope gave a series of symbolic gifts (*trionfi*) to the doge, gifts which would be paraded in solemn fashion down through the years—a ceremonial candle, lead seals, a sword, a gold ring, a processional umbrella, eight banners, and a set of eight long silver trumpets.

These gifts were given separately, rewarding specific stages of the Venetian intervention, and each had a narrative attached to it, painted by the great Venetian masters. Even when the full narrative was not represented, the trionfi "were common iconographical attributes of Venice in paintings and sculpture" (M 109). The candle represented the pure faith that burns in Venice as the guarantor of religion.[4] The lead seals resembled those of the Vatican, and gave documents of Venice the same authority. The ring signified the doge's union with the sea after the victory on Ascension Day. The umbrella was a portable *baldacchino*, marking the doge off from other men, the way the pope's polygon umbrella did. As Muir says, "The [Pope] Alexander legend so permeated Venetian culture that it was accepted as the single most important source for civil feasts, ceremonies and symbols" (M 118).

The measure of that importance was the huge amount of space given to the legend in the seat of all republican authority in Venice, the Hall of the Larger Council (Maggior Consiglio). After the large new hall was completed in the fourteenth century, the Pope Alexander legend was painted in fresco around its walls, at the leisurely narrative rate of twenty-seven episodes divided roughly into two halves, the first devoted to the growth of the conflict between pope and emperor, the second relating Venice's intervention and accomplishment of the peace. This project was executed largely by painters from elsewhere, including Gentile da Fabriano and Pisanello.[5] Unfortunately, fresco does not survive well in the salt air of Venice, and the pictures deteriorated over time. Thus a new project for large paintings on canvas was launched in the fifteenth century. By this time, Venice had its own great artists, who could celebrate their city with native talent. The new cycle, begun by Gentile Bellini in 1474, told the story of the Pact in twenty-one episodes. It is a great tragedy that this second Pact cycle, too, was destroyed by fire in 1577, since it employed Venice's greatest Renaissance masters—Carpaccio, Giovanni Bellini, Tintoretto, and Titian, among others.[6]

After the disastrous fire, the cycle was painted a third time, this time by lesser artists, and in a reduced version, ignoring the conflict of pope and emperor before Venice intervened. Thus there are only twelve pictures devoted to the Pact on the north wall, and they interest scholars mainly for hints that survive in them of the earlier compositions. The paintings are often obscure in their meaning, and the foregrounds of many are cluttered with homely scenes of everyday life—boys playing with a dog, men rescuing a friend who has fallen into the basin, etc. But several give impressive painted representations of San Marco or the Piazzetta, and there are interesting ideological points emphasized in the myth. In the next to last, for instance (counting back from the front of the hall), which represents the gift of the umbrella, the pope, with his back to the sea, is followed by a crowd in which bishops' mitres stand out emphatically. The doge, who has an entirely secular retinue, stands under strong columns that symbolize a settled authority, the kind of strength that rescued a pope when he was adrift and helpless. That is a point that Venice would recur to when it met with papal opposition, war, or interdict—that the pope should be true to the legacy of Alexander, who gave Venice a separate sphere of authority.[7]

THE DOGE'S CROWN (855)

Venetians liked to tell another story of a pope in distress who fled to them for rescue. In the ninth century, Benedict III was dragged from the papal throne shortly after his election because the Roman emperor of the time, Louis II, was displeased with him. Louis installed a rival pope in the Lateran Palace at Rome, and Benedict had to flee in terror of his life. The Venetians claim that Benedict came to hide, appropriately, in the Benedictine monastery of Saint Zachary (San Zaccaria), where the abbess, Augustina Morosini, sheltered him until his allies in Rome convinced the emperor that his choice was unacceptable. After his safe return to Rome, the pope sent the abbess a jeweled crown, which she gave to the doge. This crown was then substituted for the one that early doges had derived from Byzantium, an uncomfortable reminder that the doge had begun existence as a subordinate military officer (dux) of the eastern Roman empire.

This is an etiological myth invented to explain an annual procession made by the doge to the monastery church of San Zaccaria, making it an expression of gratitude for the instrument of his coronation, derived from the gift of the abbess (and only secondarily from the pope). The pope is present in the myth to help disentangle Venice from Constantinople (M 222). And the abbess is there to keep the doge at some distance from the pope. A fretting over any suggestion of dependence lies behind all these myths and ceremonies and invented history.

Of course, the bishops in Venetian territories had to maintain some relations with the pope, who approved their consecration. But bishops, like all priests, could not (if they were patricians) hold office in the republic, or even vote—and could not (if they were, as usual, patricians) serve on the governing boards of religious brotherhoods (scuole). There was even an attempt, at one time, to disqualify for office patricians with sons or brothers who were clerics. Since those who held ecclesiastical appointments by the pope, or belonged to families with a tradition of such ties, were known as "papal creatures" (papalini), some have assumed that there was always an active papal faction in Venice, but that misrepresents the fluidity of the republic's condition. Pressures for alliance either with the pope or with the pope's foes, as the case might be, shifted constantly, and internal coalitions reflected such continual adjustments, people changing sides to meet each crisis. Besides, as David Wootton points out, the number of papalini in the class that could vote was comparatively small: "Only a tiny minority of the Venetian nobility were papalini, that is, men with brothers or sons holding clerical office. The proportion would surely have been greater for any other ruling nobility in Europe."[8]

The doge, not the bishops, was the protector of religion in Venice, and when conflicts arose with Rome, the clergy were expected to be loyal to the *Venetian* faith. That is what happened during interdicts of 1515 and 1606, when the clergy were forbidden by the pope to exercise their ministry. Most of them disobeyed the pope—those who did not were exiled and their property confiscated. For many of them, the decision was simple. Parishes elected their own pastors, subject only to approval by the local patriarch, and the scuole elected their own chaplains (F 47). They could dismiss priests who refused to follow the government's direction.

At times, naturally, it served Venetian interests to act in alliance with the pope. Venice remained free to move in any direction that would maintain commercial ties with other powers, whether pope or emperor or sultan. This readiness to sit loose to any connection with others gave Venice a reputation as perfidious. On the other hand, it helped foster domestic tranquillity, since factions that had business ties with other regions could be placated by readjusting those ties to reflect opportunity or peril. To keep all these balls in the air, Venice had to develop an international intelligence-gathering operation, and a diplomacy, that were famous for their penetration of other nations' secrets. And if religious ties to the outside were restricted, secular ones were bound to be even more energetically banned. That is why Venice had no division along transpolity lines like the Guelph-Ghibelline quarrels that divided other Italian cities. It was necessary to maintain loyalty among those at home, as well as those who served abroad.

On their home ground Venetians held other nations' ambassadors at arm's length, isolating them from any private contact with the doge or the Senate. They also maintained a police control of their own secrets that impressed outsiders as paranoid. Given the small size of the republic's base, given the fact that its adversaries usually had greater numbers in terms of total population, Venice had to survive by superior knowledge, cleverness, and maneuverability. The price of independence ran high, but its rewards were correspondingly exalted. It was hard to be a city apart yet a trader with the world. The precondition of undertaking the operation at all was a discipline of independence, one fed from deep religious conviction about the service of Saint Mark.

CHAPTER THREE

The Lion's Wings

A S FEDERAL BUILDINGS in the United States have pictures of the current president in courts and bureaus, the administrative offices of the Venetian republic had large heraldic paintings of the lion of Venice as certifications of their authority. Later, when most of these offices were closed, some of the lion emblems were moved to the Doge's Palace, where they are now displayed together. Though the pictures conform to official type, they were done with individual touches by leading artists. One of them is now attributed to Cima da Conegliano. Another—the most famous one—was done by Carpaccio for the Treasurers' Office near the Rialto. This lion shows its teeth in an odd grin that is supposed to suggest the grimace on the bronze lion atop the pillar in the Piazzetta.[1] It is an amphibian creature—though one paw holds the saying of the angel to Mark, the other is planted on terraferma, suggesting the lion's tread onto Venice's land empire. But the lion's hind paws are in the lagoon, which is mistily evoked in the background. The lifted wings of the lion are the spread sails of the empire's sea holdings, launched from the lagoon.

Like their lion, the people of Venice were amphibian. They were at home on water from birth, learning the ways of boats the way other children learn to walk. It has been estimated that as many as ten thousand gondola-type craft at a time were threading the lagoon's watery maze during the Renaissance.[2] The skill of the men who stood up to maneuver such craft is visible in their poised leaning and poling on the edge of the gondola in Carpaccio's painting *Healing of the Possessed*, for the Scuola Grande di San Giovanni Evangelista. That skill remains a marvel in the dwindling number of gondoliers today, as it was in the nineteenth century when Mark Twain—who knew something about maneuvering in straits as a pilot on the Mississippi River—was dazzled by it:

The stern of the boat is decked over and the gondolier stands there. He uses a single oar—a long blade, of course, for he stands nearly erect. A wooden peg, a foot and a half high, with two slight crooks or curves in one side of it and one in the other, projects above the starboard gunwale. Against that peg the gondolier takes a purchase with his oar, changing it at intervals to the other side of the peg or dropping it into another of the crooks, as the steering of the craft may demand—and how in the world he can back and fill, shoot straight ahead, or flirt suddenly around a corner, and make the oar stay in those insignificant notches is a problem to me and a never diminishing matter of interest. I am afraid I study the gondolier's marvelous skill more than I do the sculptured palaces we glide among. He cuts a corner so closely, now and then, or misses another gondola by such an imperceptible hair-breadth that I feel myself "scrooching," as the children say, just as one does when a buggy wheel grazes his elbow. But he makes all his calculations with the nicest precision, and goes darting in and out among a Broadway confusion of busy craft with the easy confidence of the educated hackman.[3]

FIG. 5 (BELOW)
Vittore Carpaccio,
The Lion of Saint Mark

PLATE IV
San Marco mosaic,
Vision of Saint Mark

Ease on the water and familiarity with the lagoon gave the Venetians many advantages—for fishing, for drying salt, for dredging sand of many grades to make glass. The sense of the lagoon's blessings comes through in the mosaic of Saint Mark's legendary stop within it during the so-called "foreshadowing" (*praedestinatio*) of his body's final return to the lagoon city. This mosaic, on the ceiling of the Zen Chapel of San Marco (D 2.185–91), shows the haloed Mark asleep in a small skiff while an angel is swooping down on him with a message from God. This is Venice before there was a Venice. Mark's saintly companion has tied up the skiff in a stand of sedgy reeds. The ripples of the lagoon gently rock Mark. The boat has a gondola-style oarlock near the prow and an anchor on the cable at Mark's end of the boat. In the middle is a man without a halo (the figure is heavily restored)—presumably the pilot, since Venice required all boats coming into the lagoon to have a pilot familiar with its labyrinthine channels and bars. The sand of such a bar shows through the water near the sedges, a masterly use of mosaic tesserae to suggest translucence. The tesserae, of course, were made from sand of the sort portrayed here.

Despite this idyllic picture of the lagoon, Venetians knew that its principal benefit to them was military. It was a large watery wall shutting out invaders. If an enemy tried to penetrate it in heavy warships, the markers for the channels could be removed, leaving the hostile ships to be mired on shoals. If the city was in truly desperate peril, the channels themselves could be clogged with sunken material, so only the lightly skimming boats of the Venetians could maneuver there. William McNeill points out a special military use of the lagoon, for testing under controlled conditions the new ship designs invented in the city's technologically sophisticated boatyard (Arsenal)—much as modern airplane designs were tested in the manipulable conditions of wind tunnels (McN 11).

Yet the empire had to be forged out beyond the lagoon, in the large fighting ships that Venetian oarsmen made so mobile in the confused scramble of combat. These ships ensured the fame of the Arsenal that created and maintained them (Venetians formed the term *arsenale* from the Arabic word for "factory"). This installation, toward the east end of the city, was in its time the largest industrial complex in the world. At the beginning of the twelfth century it was still a modest eight-acre naval depot. But as the Venetian empire spread, and a high-efficiency fleet became an urgent necessity, all of the city's ship-related production activities were concentrated here behind protective walls. By the sixteenth century the Arsenal had grown to its present extent—sixty acres (a circumference of three miles), and it could, in a crisis, produce fifty galleys in a month, besides servicing, periodically inspecting, and repairing the ships that were Venice's muscle and bone as a world power.

> The Venetian Arsenal was a genuine industrial concentration, comprising all the various processes of manufacture . . . With its stock of hemp, its timberyards, its gunfoundries, and its sailmakers, the arsenal was completely autonomous. For a very long time this fact made it unique among European arsenals.[4]

Arsenal workers had the early equivalent of security clearance to work in this sensitive precinct. They were given special favors and status. Their families were provided for in case of industrial accident.[5] They had a wine allotment (five or six times a day) like the grog allotment of men at sea.[6] In fact, many of them went out to sea with the ships they made, as experts on repair and maintenance in action. They also did duty as crossbowmen when they were not exercising their craft.[7] They were felt to have a special relationship with the doge himself. They built his ceremonial barge, the Bucintoro, showing off their skills at luxury work as well as military precision. (The Bucintoro was kept in a fine classical building in the Arsenal, one designed by the architect Michele Sanmicheli in 1555.) They bore the newly elected doge in the ceremonial of his first procession, and when he died they guarded the palace while a new doge was being elected. Finally, they carried torches in the doge's funeral procession.

They were called on, as well, for special police duties and for firefighting emergencies. Fifty of their leaders guarded the Larger Council hall when it held meetings.[8] Any successful rebellion in Venice would need to wrench these disciplined workers from their loyalty—which is one reason no rebellion ever succeeded. Theirs was the most important (because essential) set of crafts in the empire: "The managers of the Arsenal did not regard the craftsmen as factory hands but as a valuable arm of the state which it was their duty to strengthen."[9] One government document called the Arsenal "the heart of the state."[10]

So important was the Arsenal routine that the city's time was set by its demands. The workday began at dawn, when the largest bell in the piazza's campanile rang for the Arsenal workers. The bell was called Marangone ("Carpenter") in honor of its craftsmen. It rang for half an hour, establishing the period within which men must reach the Arsenal gate. It rang again for a half hour at noon, telling workmen when they had to be back after lunch.[11] Most of those employed in the Arsenal were masters of their craft, and skills put in play there were reflected in the work done elsewhere when there was a lull in state activity—for instance, in the "ship's keel" roofs of various churches.

Since the Arsenal had from the outset adopted the keel-and-ribs construction of ships, as opposed to the ancient practice of creating the hull first and then putting in its inner braces, an early version of Henry Ford's assembly line took shape, along with specialization of tasks (McN 10). In fact, the entire operation of creating and servicing the fleet was a concentrated image of the Venetians' collaborative form of life. Timber experts felled, seasoned, and sawed choice wood for the ships' carpenters—the wood was resistant oak, which the rib-and-keel method could use for the first time, since this form of production did not depend on cabinetmaker's intricate fitting of the joins but on skilled caulk-ing (McN 11). Caulkers had their own guild. The Arsenal's cable-weaving shed was longer than a football field. Seamstresses worked on the sails. Foundries and smiths cast the fit-tings of the ship, as well as its cannon. The workforce, at the empire's peak, was at least two thousand skilled artisans, running up to three thousand in times of maximum pro-duction. Their precision drill was such that, in a demonstration for a visiting king of France (Henry III) in 1574, a galley was rigged, armed, and launched within an hour.

Dante had toured the Arsenal when he was in Venice, and the caulkers' fires came to his mind when he tried to describe the flames of hell:

> As dark fires in the Arsenal at Venice
> Heat pitch, to caulk the hulls of homing ships,
> Remade in winter when they cannot sail—
>
> (Some hammer at the prow or at the stern.
> A boat's ribs, sprung from heavy voyaging,
> Are straightened back. The boats regain their rigs,
> Their sails can fly as mizzen or as main)—
>
> Just so, in fires not made of man, I saw
> Foul pitch crawl up, erasing boundaries . . .
>
> – INFERNO, 21.7–18

The knowledgeable pride of the Venetians in their naval and merchant fleet shows in the loving depiction of ships by artists of the time. Carpaccio was so accurate in painting different kinds of vessels that he is used to illustrate structures in naval history books. His cycle of paintings for St. Ursula's Brotherhood, now in the Accademia, shows the whole range of ships most in use as he was painting the series (in the 1490s). In his *Ambassadors' Return* (s 88–91), a long sleek greyhound of a boat has docked in the harbor—the kind called a "thin galley" (*galia sottil*). Its sail is being furled around the lateen yardarm (longer than the boat itself). Such ships were known for their arrowy lines, their speed and maneuverability, letting rowers close on enemies with deft target-ing. The huge sail was used in favorable winds, but it was rowers' work to get the ship into difficult harbors as well as into the crunch of battle formations. The oars also made time in lulls at sea or against an opposed wind's buffeting—more than a hundred of them (each weighing about 120 pounds) working rhythmically. Though this kind of

FIG. 40
Vittore Carpaccio,
The Terms Accepted

galley was not designed to carry cargo, its speed and its military prowess made it good for rapid delivery of small but precious items (gold, spices, rare dyes, rich fabrics).

The normal merchant ship was round hulled, with high platforms on either end—called a "fat galley" (*galia grosa*). One of them is winched over for caulking in the English harbor depicted in Carpaccio's *Ursula United with Ereus* (s 78–8). In the background of that painting are four other carracks maneuvering into or out of the harbor (L 383). In *The Marriage Bid* (s 82–87), one man steers a gondola-type boat that has a sail. In *The Arrival at Cologne* (s 72–73), Saint Ursula and the pope are about to disembark from a cog (*cocha*, L 127), whose prow has pointed lines, not the forward "castle" of older merchant ships. (Note the man who has shinnied up the yard to furl the sail at the top of the picture.)

It is impossible to relate here what prodigies the Venetians worked with the magnificent instruments their ship builders gave them. They were in use for half a millennium of imperial achievement. The ceiling of the Larger Council hall in the Doge's Palace is full of painted naval battles, most of them quite confusing to the modern viewer, since grappling an enemy ship for hand-to-hand combat creates mob scenes of inarticulate density. Tintoretto's shop, working to his designs, solved this problem in *The Battle Near Garda's Shore* by isolating a heroic figure as he leads his men across a gangplank onto the enemy's ship. We see him from below, as if we are at water level and the men are pounding across the planks over our heads.

To suggest something of Venice's naval history, I shall mention just four engagements, stretched over six centuries, to illustrate different kinds of battles at sea. The legends of these victories were kept alive throughout the Renaissance in celebration of their dates and in artifacts recalling them.

1. DURAZZO (1081)

Venice began to establish control of the upper Adriatic in the year 1000. By 1081, it was fighting for control of the lower Adriatic, along the Albanian coast. The Norman invaders of the time were led, in this sector, by Robert Guiscard and his son Bohemond, who laid siege to the Albanians' coastal city of Durazzo. The Venetian fleet, coming to the aid of Durazzo, arrived at sundown and could not enter the harbor. It prepared for battle in the morning by creating an "island" blocking the harbor's exit. The fleet's round-hulled ships were grappled together, and lifeboats were strung up between their masts. Men clambered up into the suspended lifeboats, pulled huge weighted logs after them, and propelled them out onto the boats that attacked them in the morning.

FIG. 38
Vittore Carpaccio,
The Marriage Bid

PLATE XVI
Vittore Carpaccio,
Ursula United with Ereus

FIG. 42
Vittore Carpaccio,
*Ursula's Arrival
in Cologne*

FIG. 6
Jacopo Tintoretto,
*The Battle Near
Garda's Shore*

When this battery from above had sunk or repulsed the enemy assault, the Venetians'
rowed galleys, which had been kept in reserve, put the Norman vessels to flight (L 28).

2. CONSTANTINOPLE (1204)

When the Venetians captured Constantinople in 1204, during the Fourth Crusade,
they brought back plunder (including the four bronze horses for San Marco) and
acquired the choicest parts of the city's Byzantine empire (including Cyprus and
Crete). So important was this event that it is commemorated in a cycle of eight paintings on the south wall of the Larger Council hall in the Doge's Palace.[12] The fleet was
led by the fighting doge, Enrico Dandolo, who—though blind and in his eighties—
used the claims of a rival for the Byzantine throne, Alexius IV, to justify Venice's conquest of its own former ruler (L 36–41). Dandolo's ships sailed into the back bay of
Constantinople, named "the Golden Horn" for its crescent shape, and demanded that
Alexius's legitimacy be recognized. When the city refused, the Franks in the crusade
besieged the city by land, and Dandolo sailed his fleet up to the walls that rose from the
sea. The city capitulated and installed Alexius, but he was unable to maintain control

of the city, so a full-scale siege had to be mounted again. Domenico Tintoretto (Jacopo's son), in the sixth painting of the cycle, represents this triumphant operation.

In attempts to take a walled city, the attackers are at a disadvantage if they try to climb the walls, since they are exposed to the missiles of defenders above them. The

FIG. 7
Domenico Tintoretto,
*The Conquest of
Constantinople in* 1204

solution to this problem is to create siege machines as high as the walls and trundle them up—we see such rolling towers in movies like D. W. Griffith's *Intolerance*. The Venetians used their *ships* as moving towers advanced against the sea towns they attacked. The fortifying engineers of Constantinople thought that battlements rising abruptly from the sea would be doubly hard for enemies to climb, since they must clamber up from the tricky water itself. They did not count on Venetian rowers, who could bring ships up snug against their walls. In Domenico's painting, men crawl from the ships' masts over "sky bridges" to the city parapets. The invention and use of this technique was a Venetian specialty, which made the doge more confident of attack from the sea than from the land (which the Franks had advocated). Constantinople was taken, and a Frankish emperor friendly to Venice was crowned there.

3. CHIOGGIA (1379)

No enemy captured Venice until the arrival of Napoleon. But the city almost fell in 1379. Venice spent much of the fourteenth century fighting with that other great port city, Genoa, over control of trade in the Mediterranean. In the great plague year of 1348, Venice had lost half of its population to the "Black Death," and it was weakened for a generation after that. While it was still recovering its former strength, the Genoan fleet struck at the lagoon while the Venetian fleet was absent, and occupied the island of Chioggia, at the southern tip of the lagoon. The Genoans brought in added troops from the city of Padua, which was held by Hungarian allies of the Genoans. The Venetians tried to negotiate a way out of their plight, but the Genoese repulsed the attempt, confident that they could starve the city into submission.

At this, the whole city pulled together for a desperate defense. Women donated their jewels to the effort; patricians set up food distribution services for the poor. The Arsenal worked overtime to create a new fleet, thirty-four galleys for which new oarsmen—artisans called away from their shops—had to be trained, rowing in drills back and forth from the city to the Lido. Another doge already in his eighties, Andrea Contarini, oversaw this operation himself, out on the ships with the recruits. The Senate, which had earlier imprisoned the popular sea fighter Vettor Pisani—acting on a suspicion the elders always had of patricians who attract a following of commoners—now had to turn him loose and put him in charge of military operations. When he came before the crowd on his release, they cheered, "Hurrah, sir Vettor," but he responded: "Enough of that, boys. Cry rather, 'Hurrah the good evangelist, sir Saint Mark!'" (L 193).

Contarini's and Pisani's great coup was the way they made the lagoon itself fight for Venice. Genoa had brought its fleet into the lagoon, finding the Chioggia channels for its ships of deep draft. The Venetians, working by night, towed barges and heavy vessels weighted with stones into that channel and sank them, blocking the Genoese fleet's egress. When troops from Chioggia tried to clear a way out, Venetians, using shallow boats, launched highly mobile strikes from the Lido to foil them. The Lido had been given greater fortification and it was protected with the new fleet trained by the doge. When artisans tired of sentry duty there, and wished to go back to the city, Contarini shamed them by proclaiming that he would stay with the defense effort and not go back to his palace till the city was delivered.

The Genoans had sent another fleet to rescue its first force, now trapped in Chioggia, but before it could arrive the Venetian fleet returned, under the great naval commander Carlo Zeno—he too had been imprisoned earlier in his career for being too popular, but now he was greeted with rapture. Rather than engage the new Genoan fleet at sea, Zeno put his ships between the two enemy forces and prevented their uniting. The relief fleet from Genoa had to stand off the entry to the lagoon, helpless to sail in or to lure Zeno out. Finally, it withdrew in frustration. Meanwhile, the Genoans on Chioggia, who had threatened that they would starve out the Venetians, were themselves starving. A mercenary leader (*condottiere*) fighting on terraferma for the Venetians had recaptured Padua. No supplies could get to the Genoans by sea or land.

At last the stranded Genoans surrendered. The city had passed its greatest moment of danger. The doge's ceremonial ship, the Bucintoro, sailed to the Lido to bring the doge back home at last, after six months of hard duty with his men, and almost every boat in Venice accompanied him as he returned in glory, followed by the captured vessels of those who had occupied Chioggia.[13] The complete mobilization of the city's resources, in its time of ultimate peril, was a culmination of the cooperative ethos developed to face just such crises. There was such gratitude to various families for their service that select nonpatricians were admitted to the ruling class, in the greatest opening of the Serrata ("Lock-Up") that had fixed the number of the nobles. Those in other grades of the populace were rewarded for their services, and even the foreigners in town who had lent their aid (including Jews and Turks) were given new privileges. Yet human beings had not fought unaided in this war. It was a sea fight won by the sea, by the lagoon the Venetians knew how to use against those who violated its sanctuary.

4. LEPANTO (1571)

The last major sea battle of Venice, in 1571, has been called the greatest naval engagement from the age of oared galleys—Lepanto. The Turks had been making inroads into the Mediterranean—they had conquered Venice's province of Cyprus and were threatening Crete. Pope Pius V formed a league, the Holy Alliance, to wage a crusade against the Turks, and he put a twenty-four-year-old Spaniard, Juan, the bastard son of Emperor Charles V, in charge of its fleet, which hunted down the Turkish ships at Lepanto, off the western coast of Greece. Better known as Don John of Austria, this young leader brought the restive allies into accord—sending Spanish troops, for instance, to fill out the crews of undermanned Venetian galleys. Venice was now able to build more ships than it could man, and it was continuing earlier experiments in cannonry for sea combat.

Initial use of cannon on the galleys had been difficult—a gun in the prow could be aimed only by changing the boat's course; guns on the side interfered with the oars of the rowers. One expedient developed by the time of Lepanto was the use of huge galeasses (*galeazze*) as gun platforms that could be moved by their own oars under placid conditions but had to be towed into place when cleared for action. Six of these Venetian vessels served at Lepanto, which has made some call this the first battle of the seaartillery era. That seems an overstatement. The Turkish galleys were intimidated by the floating fortresses, which broke up their assault on the middle of the line; but they struck effectively at the wings of the Alliance's formation. Arquebuses were used more than cannon, as men shot at the foe from platforms and the ship's rigging, where crossbowmen had heretofore been the snipers. But these guns were hard to reload in the grappling stage of battle, and even their importance has been overstated. It is best to think of this as the last great battle of the hand-to-hand era. The sea was turned into a killing ground, soldiers hacking at each other with spears, swords, knives, and clubs. The huge number of ships involved—more than two hundred on each side—practically paved the sea as the battle surged back and forth from ship to ship (Don John's command vessel was invaded twice, its boarders each time repulsed).

Venice provided almost half the ships for the Holy Alliance—110 of them—and only sixteen of these were rowed by slaves (necessary in this case to eke out the manpower), while most other Christian ships—and all those of the Turks—were propelled by men chained at their oars (L 369–70). The Venetian captain general Sebastiano Venier fought in support of Don John at the center of the line. Already in his seventies, Venier fired bolt after bolt from his crossbow (which a soldier standing by had to crank into the cocked position, since Venier was no longer strong enough to do it). The commander of the Venetian fleet on the left wing of the line, Agostino Barbarigo, was killed by an arrow in the eye, and twenty Venetian ships' captains fell at their posts that day— only the Genoans, Venice's old rivals posted on the right wing, performed poorly. Eight thousand Christians died (to the Turks' thirty thousand killed and wounded, and three thousand taken prisoner). All but thirty of the Turks' three-hundred-plus ships were destroyed or captured, while only ten galleys were lost by the Alliance. When fifteen thousand of the Turks' Christian slaves had their chains struck off, there was—to quote Chesterton's poem on the battle—

> Thronging of the thousands up that labor under sea,
> White for bliss and blind for sun and stunned for liberty.

Voltaire famously mocked Lepanto as a battle of no real consequence, but Fernand Braudel says that he ignored the consequences that would have followed on the Alliance's *not* winning:

> The Christian victory had halted progress towards a future which promised to be very bleak indeed. With Don John's fleet destroyed, who knows, Naples and Sicily might have been attacked, the Algerines might have tried to revive the flames of Granada, or carried them into Valencia. Before joining Voltaire in his ironic comments on Lepanto, we would do well to measure the immediate impact of the victory, which was breathtaking . . . The spell of Turkish supremacy had been broken.[14]

As Iain Fenlon says, "The effect of Lepanto on Venetian morale, at every social level, was beyond calculation."[15] The city remade itself in song, procession, and artifacts to celebrate this rebirth of imperial pride. The fleet's home, the Arsenal, had a new winged lion and two Winged Victories added in carved relief to its formal gate, and the pediment was topped with a statue of Saint Justine (Giustina), on whose feast day, October 7, the battle was fought. She became one of Venice's principal patrons from that day. On her feast, the doge led an annual procession to her church. When Goethe was in Venice on October 7 in 1786, he saw the doge's boat arrive at the little square of her church, and watched brightly clothed officials file in through the captured Turkish standards, still brought out as trophies two centuries after the battle.[16] To indicate the importance of her patronage to the fleet, a new statue of her was carved by Giroloma Campagna and placed over the formal entrance to the Arsenal.

October 7 became the Feast of the Rosary, thanks to the victory prayed for on these beads. A new brotherhood was created to honor Mary's connection with Lepanto, the Scuola del Santo Rosario, and Alessandro Vittoria designed a grand new Chapel of the Rosary to be the meeting place of the scuola in the Dominican Church of Saints John and Paul. (Dominicans had been great promoters of the rosary as a form of devotion to Mary.) Tintoretto painted an elaborate allegory of the battle for this chapel—which was destroyed when the chapel caught fire in the nineteenth century.[17]

There are many surviving memorials devoted to Lepanto. The best-known painting is Veronese's, now in the Accademia, which shows Saint Mark and Saint Justine interceding with the Virgin to bring victory to the fleet. A more detailed look at the action is Andrea Vicentino's painting in the Hall of Investigation (Sola dello Scrutinio) of the Doge's Palace. The Christian fleet is on the right of the picture, with Sebastiano

Venier standing under the flag of Saint Mark in the bow of the ship, above the conventional red Venetian oars. Don John's ship is behind it, with the papal flag of the crucified Lord. The Turkish fleet is on the left, with Ali Pasha, its admiral, under the white flag with crescents near the edge of the picture. Turbaned men are shooting their arquebuses from the rigging of the Turkish ships, while Christians return the fire from their platform behind the main ship's gunwales.

Elsewhere in the Doge's Palace (the Collegio's meeting room), Veronese painted the hero of the fleet, Sebastiano Venier, offering thanks for the victory, with Saint Justine by his side (p 1.155–56). He still wears his battle armor, though he has thrown over

FIG. 8
Palma Giovane,
*The Doge Mocenigo
Thanks the Virgin for
the Victory at Lepanto*

it the doge's cloak that came to him on his return in victory. The man who was doge while the battle raged, Alvise Mocenigo, was painted by the Younger Palma offering thanks in San Marco at hearing the news from Lepanto (SMR 380). He pours out his gratitude to the Virgin, who is flanked by Mark and Justine, the patrons of the victory. This painting, in the Church of St. Fantin, shows every social class participating in the joy of the moment—including a portrait of Mocenigo's wife and a self-portrait of Palma looking over the shoulder of the man on the picture's left.[18]

Despite all these rapturous celebrations, the era of galley warfare was ending. The development of cannon would make rowing into close contact with the enemy less effective than maneuvering by sail for vantage points from which to fire broadsides, using the longer-range and more accurate artillery being developed. The future belonged to sail, not oars; to artillery, not hand-to-hand combat; and to the Atlantic, not the Mediterranean. Great ships of the line would go out from the countries facing west, from Spain and England, to conquer the New World. The Crusades were over. But Venice had been been present at this climax of an era, along with Miguel Cervantes, who was wounded in one of the Spanish ships of the Holy Alliance at Lepanto. He would be ironic and mocking about chivalry in his novel *Don Quixote*; but he was dead serious when he boasted that Lepanto was his finest hour—and Venetians thought it was theirs, too.

CHAPTER FOUR

The Lion's Tread

C ARPACCIO'S LION PACES FIRMLY up onto terraferma—which overstates the Venetians' own readiness to move inland. They were more at home on a ship's deck than on horseback. The difference in ethos between Venice and land powers is obvious at a glance, just from the architectures of the various sites. The government buildings on the mainland were fortresses—rugged stone structures with large internal courtyards for the assembly of mounted troops. Even private palaces had this military aspect. In Florence the great family citadels boasted towers that had to be torn down periodically, when they became centers of intestine war between the city's clans. Venetian buildings, by contrast, were fairyland fabrics. The Doge's Palace has a crenellated top derived from saw-toothed battlements, but here it looks like lace on a doily. The precious stone slabs on palace façades are not meant to brave artillery fire. The thin brick walls of the palace's seaward flank could afford to be fragile, since Venice, like ancient Athens, had "wooden walls"—the hulls of its fleet—to keep the enemy off.

Then why go westward at all, risking confrontation with forces drilled for war on terraferma? Well, a certain amount of land control was necessary from the outset. The city had to assert rights over the territory surrounding the outlets of the rivers that flushed its lagoon. It was always damming, diverting, or clearing the streams that maintained the tide levels and salinity of its native element, its estuary. Then, upriver, the trading routes for movement of products to and from the East had to be maintained. The Venetian imperative here was the same as in the Adriatic and Mediterranean—the empire did not want territory, just links for transit of her goods. But, on land and as well as at sea, the trading post often had to be taken from the regime in which it was embedded. And after that it had to be defended from rapacious neighbors. All this entailed land armies. How was Venice, whose manpower was barely sufficient to supply the navy, to create such things? It lacked the natural breeding ground for the cavalry and infantry of the later middle ages and early Renaissance—the feudal land units, with their rural castles, from which an agrarian aristocracy organized its troops.

The Venetians obviously had to do what even some land powers did, hire mercenaries. Cities like Florence were urban and commercial—they too did not want to devote large parts of their manpower to professional military use. They had more money than fighting men. The former must call up the latter. This was the era of the contract commander (*condottiere*), whose conduct (*condotta*) was bargained for. Humanists like Machiavelli, Guicciardini, and Paolo Giovio had warned the Florentines against trusting a city's fate to such adventurers, and Venice had special doubts about surrogate defenders, since it had manned its own galleys with its own populace for so long. But those hiring the troops felt they had little choice.

The risk for Venice was underlined in 1423, near the beginning of the city's major land thrust, by the dying words of a respected doge, Tommaso Mocenigo, who said that Venice would be weakened in its struggle with the growing Turkish menace at sea if it drained energies off into land wars. Yet the very next doge to be elected, Francesco Foscari, led Venice into a long conflict with Milan for control of the Lombard plain. The city was tempted toward this when Milan's great condottiere, Francesco Bussone, called from his birthplace "Carmagnola," offered in 1425 to betray his former employer and lead troops for Venice. For seven years Venice paid well for erratic service from this brilliant but ailing general. But then the government found evidence that Carmagnola was playing a double game with his former masters in Milan. He was summoned to Venice for "consultation," seized, tried, and hanged in the public execution space between the pillars of Saint Mark and Saint Theodore in the Piazzetta. Venice, it turned out, had an advantage no other city did in dealing with its condottieri. No hired general could lead his troops into this city. The lagoon was still Venice's best weapon.

COLLEONI

After further wars with Milan, the Venetians acquired a condottiere, Bartolomeo Colleoni, who managed their land holdings with skill and doggedness for twenty years (1455 to 1475). Colleoni, who came from Bergamo, had served an apprenticeship fighting for other great condottieri—Carmagnola, Francesco Sforza, and Erasmo da Narni (known as Gattamelata, or "Honey Cat"). He shifted sides and loyalties as he rose to eminence. But Venice gave him a feudal holding on terraferma (Malpaga) and a contract that allowed him to acquire immense wealth for that estate. That Colleoni had dynastic ambitions of his own is clear from the ornate funeral chapel he built for himself in Bergamo. This reserved a privileged spot for a life-size equestrian statue of him in gilded wood. But Colleoni (like other condottieri, including Carmagnola and Gattamelata) had no sons, and Venetian emissaries rushed to his estate upon his death to reclaim most of his treasury.

Venice did feel obliged, however, to honor (at least in part) one bequest in his will. He left a large sum for a colossal equestrian statue of himself to be raised in Venice, in the Piazza before Saint Mark's basilica. But that site was sacrosanct. Not even the most respected Venetian had any statue there. (It was felt that Alessandro Leopardi had violated the spirit of the place when he put a small medallion of a doge on the base of his bronze flagpole before the church.) It is commonly said that the Venetians evaded the will's clause by putting the statue in another square of Saint Mark's— since the statue was raised beside St. Mark's Distinguished Brotherhood (now the city hospital), which is partially patterned after San Marco itself. But the fact that there was extensive official debate over other sites proves to Andrew Butterfield that the republic did not feel bound

FIG. 9
Andrea del Verrocchio,
Equestrian monument
of Colleoni

by a provision so outrageous, and the present site won on its merits, not as part of a legal dodge.[1] Colleoni's mounted statue, by the great Florentine sculptor Andrea del Verrocchio (P-H 2.387–89), can be seen advantageously from every angle in the large campo where it was placed. Dramatic as it is, even now, against the skyline, it was more impressive when first put up. It not only stood on a large brick "carpet" raised above the rest of the campo, but it was entirely gilded, both man and horse.

Though Venice discouraged aggressive individualism in its warriors, Verrocchio won this commission in competition with other artists by submitting a design that breathes haughty power and personal energy. Colleoni, envisaged as leading his troops, is about to launch his horse at a gallop toward the enemy—the mount's raised front leg and head are already projected out beyond the high pedestal on which it stands, and its left rear leg is advanced far in front of the right one. The horse is tense for takeoff, its thigh muscles rippling under the skin.[2] Its musculature is so sharply articulated—and based so clearly on vivisection studies—that an early sixteenth-century critic (Gauricus) called the horse "flayed" (*denudatus*). There is even reason to notice the proud mount's realistic testicles, since Colleoni, punning on his own name, included testicles (*coglioni*) in his heraldry. His coat of arms, at the base of the statue, has these coglioni— Rona Goffen says, "They look like double quotations marks, very cute."

Verrocchio's rider has reined the horse's head to the left, where his own fierce gaze is directed. The two of them have the enemy in sight and are poised to charge. Colleoni is as tense as his mount. His legs are straight in the stirrups, lifting him in the saddle as he leans toward the foe—hips forward, back arched—his body communicating urgency to his horse. Colleoni's body turns on its axis, throwing his left shoulder up and out toward the foe. The armor on this side is made subtly larger than that on the recessive right side, making his very body a shield. Verrocchio had also noticed something about Donatello's equestrian statue (in Padua) of the condottiere Gattamelata (1453)—the man's body looks small when seen from below, even though Gattamelata's body is in accurate proportion to the horse's. So Colleoni is made disproportionately large in relation to his mount (P-H 2.207).

Colleoni's face is a mask of contempt, based not on realistic portraiture but on physiognomic studies of aggressive expression. Here are all the qualities he was paid for by Venice. There was no need here for a ruler's benignity, for the classical calm that Donatello imitated by reference back to the ancient equestrian statue of Marcus Aurelius in Rome. Colleoni's energy was not for domestic use, but for foreign intimidation. He is a kind of apotropaic (averting) sign confronting Venice's enemies to the west, the direction he faces, the landward side of the republic. (He is also an assurance to his successors as condottieri that Venice rewards its mercenaries.)

Verrocchio had entered the competition for this commission with a life-size model of the work (probably shaped in wax on an armature). When he won the assignment, he moved to Venice, where he could supervise the casting of the bronze in sections (the joins are clearly visible now, after erosion of the surface by time). But he died before the foundry work was done. The job of completion was given to Alessandro Leopardi. A certain coarseness in the hero's face, the minute ornamentation of the armor, and the stylized horse's tail are Leopardi's finishing touches—as opposed to the individual ringlets of the horse's mane, the whole carriage of man and mount, and the torsion of the human body, which are trademarks of Verrocchio's mastery. It is the composition as a whole that shows the Florentine artist's mind at work. As Andrew Butterfield points out, Verrocchio's statue continually recomposes itself before your eyes as you circle around it, unlike the Gattamelata of Donatello. That work should have been more easily arranged for viewing from all sides, since it is so stable and lacking in complex motion. But it is awkward from more than one angle. Verrocchio, by contrast, puts us in motion by a kind of contagion from his subject's active thrust: horse and man flow into new patterns as we respond to the impulse to move with them. Verrocchio had done a famous study of such flowing curves, which draw one around their never-ending spirals, in his *Putto with a Dolphin* in the Palazzo Vecchio of Florence.

Donatello, for all his psychological intensity, normally composed for a frontal or a favored view. By contrast, the choreography of Verrocchio's work begins with the torque of the warrior's body to the right, counterbalancing the turn of the horse's head to the left. All other details flow from that first balletic interplay. Butterfield describes some of the details:

> He accomplished this by building his composition out of basic shapes that can be viewed as a complex of interrelated forms [seen] from different points. For example, from a three-quarter view to the left and rear, the acute angle made by the left elbow is repeated in the acute angles of the hocks of the legs, while the curve of the right arm is balanced by the curve of the horse's head and tail. Likewise, in three-quarter view from the right front, a harmonious composition emerges: Colleoni's right leg and the right legs of the horse form nearly parallel lines, and the lines of his right arm and the left hind leg of the horse also resemble one another. This aspect of the sculpture's design may have been broadly recognized [at the time]. According to Vasari, when some sculptors debated with Giorgione the relative merits of painting and sculpture, the sculptors used the Colleoni horse as proof of their art's superiority "because the sculpture showed in only one figure different poses and views as the spectator moves around it."[3]

THE LEAGUE OF CAMBRAI

By a combination of severity (as in the case of Carmagnola) and generosity (as with Colleoni) in dealing with condottieri, the Venetians were able to win and keep their land empire in a series of wars during the first half of the fifteenth century. The wars were sporadic and expansive during the first quarter of the century. After a legendary siege of Padua (1404 to 1405), in which many patricians of Venice took part themselves, this system was vindicated in two decades of struggle with Milan. The second half of the century was largely peaceful on the land, during Colleoni's reign and its aftermath. But early in the sixteenth century the whole structure seemed to collapse. When Cesare Borgia died in 1504, the Venetians began to expand south into the papal states he had ruled. This so angered Julius II, the old warrior-pope, that in 1508 he formed a combination (the League of Cambrai) with the Austrians, French, and Spanish.[4] It was their joint determination to dismantle the Venetian land empire and parcel out its components among themselves.

In April 1509, the League forces won a great victory at Agnadello, on the western border of the Venetian holdings. The republic's armies were sent staggering back across terraferma, unraveling their earlier conquests as they neared the lagoon. Even Padua, the city with which their imperial expansion had begun, fell to the enemy. Venice itself

FIG. 10
Palma Giovane, *Allegory of the League of Cambrai*

was in danger for the first time since the Genoans had taken Chioggia over a century before. But the city responded to danger just as it had in that crisis, under the doge Andrea Contarini. Now another doge, Leonardo Loredan, called for sacrifice and total mobilization—an act that was later remembered in the Doge's Palace with the Younger Palma's painting of the clash with this formidable combination of enemies (SMR 143): The enemy is represented as "Europe" (the bull of Europa) carrying a warrior on whose shield are the crests of all the countries in the League of Cambrai. In the background is the city of Padua, where the struggle reached its height. Under Loredan's guidance, the goddess Justice/Venice looses the lion of Saint Mark to attack the bull, protecting the allegorical figures of Peace and Plenty on the left side of the picture.

Palma took the representation of Loredan from Giovanni Bellini's great portrait of the man, now in the National Gallery in London (T 158–59). This was painted just after the doge's election in 1501, eight years before the League made Venice reel; but Bellini captures, already, the ascetical determination that the city rose to in that test of nerve. Bellini is painting the empire, not the man—Loredan was wrathful and rapacious in his private dealings; but here he is made to embody the code enunciated by Horace in his poem *"Aequam Memento"* (Odes 2.3): "Retain, in roughest times / Unruffled steadiness."[5] This icon of such steadiness is best described by Rona Goffen:

PLATE V
Giovanni Bellini,
Leonardo Loredan

> Bellini's Loredan was evidently one of the first frontal portraits of a reigning doge [for which the traditional ceremonial portrait had been in profile]. Such frontality was more often associated with sacred characters, not mortals. The doge's portrait is distinguished from its fifteenth-century predecessors and from other portrayals of Loredan himself not merely by the frontality of the face but also by the self-possession and tranquility of his character, portrayed with such conviction by Bellini . . . The faces of some of Bellini's other portraits have a diffidence or even wistfulness inherently unlike this calm assurance, and the combination of Loredan's expression and his frontality endows his portrait with a quality akin to that of sacred images.[6]

While Loredan marshaled the forces of the city in the lagoon, the great hero in the field was the patrician Andrea Gritti, who retook the city of Padua—its populace cried "Mark to the rescue" (Marco! Marco!) as he entered the walls (L 245). Since Gritti won this battle on the Feast of Saint Marina, she became another patron in the pantheon of Venetian protectors. Every year on her feast, July 17, the doge led a grand procession to her church in the eastern part of Venice.[7] Titian, it was mentioned earlier, painted

PLATE VI
Titian,
Doge Andrea Gritti

Marina as participating in the victory celebration of Andrea Gritti, and Tintoretto retained her in his substitute painting after Titian's was destroyed. Later on, when Gritti had himself become doge, Titian painted him as an aging lion (w 2.108–9). Though he wears the same ceremonial garb as Bellini's doge Loredan, the spirit of this painting is entirely different. Loredan is self-contained, contemplative, immobile as a statuary bust. Gritti is on the prowl, his massive body facing to his left, through he shoots an imperious gaze back to his right. The damask cloak with the spherical buttons is tossed aside, then gathered up in a hand modeled on that of Michelangelo's Moses—an ironic echo, since Michelangelo created his statue of Moses for the tomb of Julius II, the pope Gritti defied as he took on the League of Cambrai.[8] This is a moving storm of a man, his restless energy struck off in the flickering brushwork of Titian's later manner.

VERONESE ON THE LAND EMPIRE

PLATE VII
Paolo Veronese,
Mars and Neptune

In the second half of the sixteenth century, the gradual shrinking of Venice's sea empire before the expanding power of the Turks made the city look to its land holdings as more secure than its ports in the Mediterranean. The consensus on this shift in policy is registered in Veronese's 1578 painting for the Collegio hall in the Doge's Palace (p 1.139). The two aspects of the empire are figured as Mars and Neptune, just as in Sansovino's statues for the "Giants' Staircase." But here Neptune is old and wrinkled, his trident at rest on his lap, the ship's masts and pennons fading in the sky behind him. His putto-genius brings him an unmilitary seashell, and the lion of Saint Mark looks back at him fondly, as if sharing his reverie, while his body is turned toward Mars, who is vigorous, in his prime, holding his commander's baton upright while his putto-genius brings him the helmet he is ready to don. His horse snorts with eagerness for the fight. Though Venice had vindicated its sea skills at Lepanto less than a decade before this painting was completed, the omens were clear. The city of the sea must rely more on its terraferma holdings than on its galleys. In fact, the painting suggests that it will be reborn in this element—a little-noticed figure is the small lion cub lurking in the cloak of Mars, peering cautiously around his war baton. The city will have a new life on the mainland.

TITIAN ON BRAGADIN

Actually, one of the worst blows to the Venetian sea empire was delivered in a land battle, waged over the city of Famagosta on the island of Cyprus. Such imperial posts were held by a patrician as local lord (podestà), with a staff of Venetians who employed condottieri for their land wars. The podestà in Famagosta was Marcantonio Bragadin, who had fortified his city as the Turkish threat came closer. To protect the town, a series of engineering specialists—Zuan Hieronimo, Alvise Brugnolo, Girolamo Maggi—devised imaginative defenses. Maggi planned to poison the fodder of invaders' horses, to swing cannon out on ropes (as invaders had crossed from masts to walls in earlier Venetian exploits), and to create pits that would absorb dirt flung into the castle's moat by those trying to cross it.[9]

The devices were too clever to be workable, and a year's siege brought the Venetian stronghold to its knees in August of 1571. Although the Turks offered honorable terms of surrender, they violated them afterward, butchering the defenders mercilessly and subjecting Bragadin to the most theatrical and detested torture of the century. He was dragged around the city with stones strapped to him, then hoisted to the yardarm of a ship for everyone to ridicule. Brought back down and tied to a stake, he had to watch his skin being peeled from him—he did not expire till his flayers had reached his waist. After the rest of the skin was removed from his corpse, this human leather was stuffed with straw and, tied to the back of a cow, sent in mock procession through the streets. The skin was then taken back as a prize of war and presented to the sultan in Constantinople. This humiliation of Saint Mark was so resented that Venetian raiders on Constantinople later retrieved the skin and brought it back to Bragadin's family, who had it placed in a niche behind an urn just inside the main door of the Church of Saints John and Paul.

Bragadin was reverenced as a martyr of the state, and his ordeal was mingled, in a hazily religious way, with the almost simultaneous news of the great naval victory at Lepanto. Though that battle took place two months after the flaying of Bragadin, details of the two events reached Venice in overlapping messages of great distress and almost hysterical rejoicing. The whole relationship of the unwanted but necessary land empire with the endangered but vindicated sea power made Bragadin's sacrifice the dark underside or sacrificial condition of the bright climax of hope at Lepanto.

The interplay of these conflicting emotions in the fall of 1571 led to one of the most strange and mystical paintings ever produced in Venice, Titian's *Flaying of Marsyas* (w 3.153–54). Though the work is now at the Kromeriz gallery in Czechoslovakia, it still breathes the passions of Venice in the 1570s. Titian, already in his eighties, was engaged in the smoldering last works that create their own victory out of fading strength in hands and eyes. Under the stimulus of Bragadin's sacrifice, Titian turned to

PLATE VIII
Titian,
The Flaying of Marsyas

69

a myth that Venetians had often drawn on, the story of the satyr Marsyas, a story given the moral resonance of Christian self-sacrifice.[10] Before the myth was moralized, by Plato and Dante and others, it was a rather brutal celebration of Apollo's might. Athena invented the musical pipe, but stopped playing it when she saw how her cheeks puffed up unattractively when she blew into it. She taught it, however, to the satyr Marsyas, who challenged Apollo to a musical contest, his lowly pipe against the god's lofty lyre. With King Midas acting as judge, Apollo won the contest by cheating—he either tricked Marsyas into playing the pipe upside down, or he sang while playing on his lyre (which, obviously, Marsyas could not do while his mouth was engaged with the pipe). As punishment for Marsyas' presumption, Apollo flayed him alive.

Plato deepened the meaning of this story when he had Alcibiades compare Socrates, with his satyrlike features, to Marsyas, ugly only on the outside (*Symposium*, 215b). Plato is referring to a Greek toy—a hollow figure of a satyr which, when you opened it up, held the image of a god inside. In later treatments of the myth, the honor of Apollo was rescued by making the story express the power of music to reveal inner truths, often through suffering. This gave a higher meaning to Marsyas' dying cry in Ovid's *Transformations* (6.385): "Why me from me remove?" (*Quid me mihi detrahis?*). In Christian times, flaying became a symbol of self-sacrifice under the influence of the legend of Saint Bartholomew, who was supposedly flayed alive under the orders of an Indian king (Astyages). Dante used the myth as a symbol of purification in *Paradiso* 1.19–20, where he prays to God:

> Enter my heart and fill it with your breath,
> As you extracted satyr Marsyas
> From his own skin's external envelope.

Michelangelo was so taken with the thought of flaying as a shedding of the "earthly" self that he put his own features on the skin Saint Bartholomew holds in his Sistine Chapel *Last Judgment*. This striking personal intrusion into the chapel's iconography seems less odd if we consider the way skinning recurs as a theme in Michelangelo's poetry. He echoes the cry of Ovid in a poem where he asks to shed his past self as a snake sloughs off its skin: "Denude me of myself!" (*Spoglia di me me stesso!*).[11] Elsewhere he speaks of time that "moults" (*muda*) his skin, and in a masochistic poem he envies the animal that was skinned to make the leather glove his beloved is wearing.[12] Bartholomew in the *Last Judgment* twists his body around, giving him the midriff of the ancient marble fragment Michelangelo so admired, the Belvedere torso. This torso, once taken to be of Hercules, is actually part of a seated and bound Marsyas, its pose familiar from vases and statues, and from an ancient medallion familiar to Michelangelo (it was in the Medici collection in Florence).[13] Michelangelo seems to have associated Bartholomew with Marsyas in a way that gives the myth its profoundest treatment before Titian's painting, executed four decades after the *Last Judgment*.

In Titian's painting, Marsyas is suspended upside down, in a pose taken from a fresco by Giulio Romano. The victim looks out at us with a puzzled or pleading expression (the image is emotionally powerful precisely because of its ambiguity). The laurel-wreathed Apollo himself, not an assistant as in other treatments, kneels to perform this sacrificial act. Radiography shows that the assistant was at first playing Apollo's lyre, but now he holds a viola. Marsyas' pan pipes are hung above the standing musician, as if the viola mediates between the plucked lyre notes and the sustained tones of the pipe, uniting the higher and lower music, the divine serenity of Apollo and the human anguish of Marsyas (an unconscious anticipation of Nietzsche's description of Attic theater as a combination of Apollo and Dionysus, of the static eternal and the roiling temporal).

King Midas, the judge of the contest between the god and the satyr, is seated contemplatively on the right of the picture—it is a self-portrait of Titian in the pose of Michelangelo's Jeremiah on the Sistine ceiling (w 3.92). Midas, with the ass's ears of myth almost hidden in his sparse hair, is weighing the meaning of this portentous event. The two dogs on the scene are like those in the Carpaccio painting *Two Women*, signifying alertness (the dog checked by the putto) and fidelity (the dog that licks the blood spilled from Marsyas' body). As we shall see, drinking redemptive blood was a theme very close to Venetian patriotism as well as piety—and dogs were part of the eucharistic iconography.

FIG. 43
Vittore Carpaccio,
Two Women

The blending of these thoughts on human suffering, on harmony, and on transcendence was accomplished under the stimulus of Bragadin's sacrifice at Famagosta. The patrician code called, at its best, for self-sacrifice. Bragadin was a great hero in Venetian annals not because he was a conqueror but because he was conquered yet magnanimous. The strength of a community lies not in what it achieves but in what it is willing to suffer for its goals. That made Bragadin the model patrician, and the perfect subject for Titian's art.

CHAPTER FIVE

Disciplines of Time

THE SIXTEENTH-CENTURY VENETIAN DIARIST Girolamo Priuli wrote that "Time does much for republics, because they never die."[1] The Venetians had a sense of time different from that observable in other Italian cities, where regimes came and went, of longer or shorter duration, marked off from each other by violent wrenches, by sharp changes in personnel, constitutions, and character. The life of the lagoon republic seemed, by contrast, a seamless continuity. There were external shocks, of challenge or loss, and internal strains that bent structures without breaking them. Doges came and went, in glory or dishonor, but the office itself was continuous. Government by overlapping committees, with staggered schedules and frequent rotation of office, made it hard to think in terms of separate administrative eras. Individuals rose or fell, but the corporate entity perdured. Sir Dudley Carleton, the British ambassador to Venice, called the republic "a clock going with many wheels and making small motions, sometimes out of order, but soon mended, all without change or variety."[2]

Commercial ventures entangled people in projects with different time returns, so that a kind of hook-and-eye weave of them all into a common undertaking was the result. The republic governed all this activity with rules ensuring continuity and uniformity of rules. Weights and measures, value of goods, maintenance of quality, gave deals and products a sameness over the years. Frederic Lane notes how the extensive use of double-entry bookkeeping made people think in terms of complex equations, holding together separate investments with overlapping periods of completion.[3] Investment partners of different ages and status made contracts binding them together, and any one merchant normally had a web of such engagements. As Antonio says in Shakespeare's *Merchant of Venice* (1.142–44):

My ventures are not in one bottom trusted,
Nor to one place; nor is my whole estate
Upon the fortune of this present year.

Time had a special significance for the city that traded so widely through different cultures and varying customs. The merchant of Venice had his mind on climates far off, on products being matured in countries widely scattered, on the weather favorable for war on sea or land, on the times for sending precious cargoes upriver or down the Adriatic, on the holy seasons setting calendars elsewhere. Time was fungible. The constant in this wide spectrum of juggled schedules and calendars was the time of Venice itself, marked by recurring festivals, varying day lengths, unvarying liturgies. Precisely because Venetian time formed a continuum, ways had to be found for measuring its different aspects. In the tapestry of Venetian time, bells daily rang the hours for devotion and business, astrological phases marked the months, allegorical figures made vivid the four seasons of the year and the three ages of man, ecclesiastical ceremony haloed special times, and saints' feasts jostled each other in the dense stream of passing days.

Edward Muir notes that time itself was elastic in Venice:

Through its power to arrange ritual life, the government attempted to impose its own political concerns on the cosmos by restructuring time, which was still in the Renaissance a comparatively flexible dimension defined by the saints' feasts and the office hours of the Church rather than by the inexorable mechanisms of the modern age. The length of an hour in Renaissance Venice, for example, varied according to the season; so time was truly relative. (M 231)

THE CLOCK TOWER (TORRE DELL'OROLOGIO)

The great bell of the Campanile (Marangone) rang at dawn and dusk, as those hours shifted with the sun's cycle, and divided the day evenly within these longer or shorter spans. Even when clocks came into use, there was a double-entry time keeping, pitting human work against clock work. After 1499, there was another tower across the piazza from the Campanile—Mauro Codussi's clock tower (Torre dell'Orologio), which itself kept several times. It told not only the hours and minutes but—on its inner face—the phases of the moon, which provided vital information for a city that lived by the tides. Astrological time was indicated by the zodiac signs running around the inner face of the timepiece. Liturgical time was referred to in the statue of the seated Virgin above the clock face. Every year on the principal feast of the city, the Ascension, Magi came out of a door to the left of her, circled before her in reverence, and disappeared through the door on the other side. Seasonal time was indicated by the giants on the top of the tower, who struck the hour with sledgehammers, workers keeping to their schedule. The giants came to be called "Moors" after the bronze, formerly gilded, had blackened with the time being measured. These figures, cast in the foundries of the Arsenal, are like Arsenal workers themselves.

The way times revolved around this tower was far clearer when Codussi completed it than it is now. The long row of offices on the left side of the piazza (as one faces the basilica) was only two stories high at that time, and the clumsy wings attached to the tower itself had not been built. The tower was a slim vertical, a punctuation point for those arriving at St. Mark's basin and looking straight toward the clock through the twin columns of the Piazzetta. And if the tower looked to the sea on its piazza side, its arch opened inward to the main street (Mercerie) binding the piazza to the districts north of it. There was a simpler version of the clock face on that land side, completing the tower's role as a coordinator of times and aspects of the piazza setting.

Codussi made the tower fit its surroundings in multiple ways—with the basilica, by its arches of similar height and its polychrome surface; with the Campanile, on the other side of the piazza, by its profile and bells; with the entry to the basilica, by its ring of zodiac symbols; with the portal into the Doge's Palace, by repeating its relief of the lion of Saint Mark with a kneeling doge. This latter consonance was destroyed by Napoleon's forces when they razed from both structures the image of the doge. A simulacrum of the doge over the gate to the palace was put up later, but the clock tower still lacks its doge, making the lion stand off center, facing a blank space.

SAN MARCO: TIME

The deepest consonance between the clock tower and the adjacent basilica of St. Mark lies in the dense ridges of sculptured figures that line the great central portal of the church. This opening has three arches built out over it, two superimposed upon the first. Each arch is lined, on its underside and on its face, with carved sequences of a programmatic nature. The one that concerns us here is the middle one, whose underside is filled with symbols of the months, each attended with its sign in the zodiac.

Though the iconography of the months is familiar to us from places like the northern "books of hours," Otto Demus has proved that these figures are markedly

Byzantine in their references, thus entirely appropriate to Venice's sea empire: "All the stylistic components of this masterpiece have already been absorbed in the atmosphere of Venice."[4] The months and their signs, on this curve of the arch, rise to or descend from the keystone figure of Christ at the top, with the Sun (Apollo) to the left of him and the Moon (Diana) to the right. They are in the positions given to Saint John the Baptist and the Virgin in Last Judgments, echoing in a minor key, as it were, the large mosaic of the Last Judgment above the door, the commanding feature of the whole façade. The façade's four bronze horses of the Apocalypse fit into this pattern of motion through time toward eternity. In the doorway arch, Christian time is ordered eschatologically, saying that Venice is a lasting republic, but only so long as earth will last, before humankind is swept up within a larger framework by the final Judgment.

The six months rising to the keystone of the arch have, above them, their astrological signs—wavy (watery) lines for Aquarius, two fish for Pisces, a ram for Aries, a bull for Taurus, a roundel with twin faces for Gemini, a crab for Cancer. Descending on the right side of the arch, the carved signs are a lion (Leo), a maiden (Virgo), scales (Libra), a scorpion (Scorpio), a centaur with bow and arrow (Sagittarius), and a goat (Capricorn).

DOGE'S PALACE: TIME

A similarly multilayered approach to time can be seen in three sculptures created a century after the doorway calendar, in the second quarter of the fourteenth century. These are three of the richly carved capitals on the colonnade to the Doge's Palace. Two of the three, as especially fine, were removed in the nineteenth century and can be seen now in the Museum of the Palace. Copies have been substituted out on the colonnade. The most famous of the ones in the museum is known as the zodiac capital, which originally stood under the statues of Adam and Eve at the corner of the palace (P-H 1.274). It has eight sides, seven of them devoted to the then-known planets, depicted in their astrological "houses."[5] The eighth contains a Creation of Adam: God the creator sits on an elaborate throne (signifying the richness of the cosmos) and holds the right arm of a small naked Adam, as if drawing him up out of nothingness. His left hand is placed on Adam's head in a blessing gesture. Adam has a dreamy look as if just coming to consciousness. Ruskin wrote: "In the workmanship and grouping of its foliage, this capital is, on the whole, the finest I know in Europe."[6]

Of the planets, perhaps the finest representation is that of the Moon. Standing in a boat with the balance of a gondolier, she leans into a wind that makes her light dress shimmer like water stirred by a breeze. The crescent in her right hand echoes the larger curve of the boat carrying her. The mutability of the moon is suggested in this wavering image, just as the stable lion throne of the Sun, on the pillar's other side, shows his immunity from waxing or waning.

The second capital in the museum that deals with time is that devoted to the months, distributed one or two to a side around the eight surfaces. Blustery March blows a large horn, and blithe June carries delicately shaped cherries in a basket. January warms his bare feet at a fire, and February roasts the fish of Pisces. The capital is not as well preserved nor as vividly expressive as the zodiac one.

The third capital traces the seven ages of man, each governed by the appropriate planetary influence—Moon for feeble infancy, Mercury for the learning child, Venus for the adolescent, Sun for a burgeoning hunter, Mars for the warrior, Jupiter for a mature magistrate, Saturn for the aged man at prayer—and the eighth side shows an "ungoverned" body stretched dead on earth, heedless of the planets and unheeded by them.

COSMIC SEASONS

Another time scheme that recurs in Venetian art is the depiction of the four seasons, a favorite theme for Tintoretto. He painted the four seasons as putti on the ceiling of the Board Room in St. Roch's Distinguished Brotherhood, and on the ceiling of the Golden Atrium in the Doge's Palace (the room at the top of the Golden Stairway). He also placed allegorical figures of the seasons, done in grisaille, around the clock in the Reception Hall of the palace. But his most ambitious treatment of the theme is now in the anteroom to the Reception Hall (Collegio) of that palace. These four large paintings were given conflicting interpretations in the past, because they no longer hang in the space they were created for—the Square (Golden) Atrium, where (as was just noticed) he had already painted the seasons as putti on the ceiling. Charles de Tolnay realized that, in their former setting, the paintings were explications, as it were, of the seasonal symbols above them, and of the cosmological motifs of the room.[7]

FIG. 11 (ABOVE TOP)
Doge's Palace,
Creation of Adam

FIG. 12 (ABOVE)
Doge's Palace,
The Moon

Each painting is concerned with a (changeable) time of the year and with one of the four (lasting) elements of the cosmos—earth, air, water, and fire. The first painting, devoted to Spring and the element of earth, shows the three Graces with Mercury. Two of the nude goddesses are making way for the third to join them on a flowery mound, to which Mercury has guided them. The sinuously leaning and turning figures are arranged to display woman's body from all three sides, a traditional aim in pictures of the Graces. Usually, however they are standing in a circle that makes us see one figure from the front, one from the side, and one from behind. Tintoretto has cleverly arranged his figures to achieve the same exposure, but without the static or vertical formality of most compositions. The gracefully turning figures that rise onto the mound suggest the appearance of flowers from the earth. They rise in a helix motion. And Mercury, the god of commerce, here equipped for flight, reminds us that Spring opened the sea-lanes for communication and trade.

Summer is presented as the wedding of Ariadne and Bacchus. The grape-crowned Bacchus, arriving at the island where Theseus abandoned Ariadne, is led by a flying

FIG. 13
Jacopo Tintoretto,
*Mercury and the
Three Graces*

Venus, who does a slow barrel roll over the couple, deftly placing a crown of stars over the now-deified bride and, at the same time, holding Ariadne's hand out for Bacchus' wedding ring. De Tolnay thought the element for this picture was water, since Venus is born of it. But Venus is made decidedly airborne here, and air seems the arena appropriate for her feat.

In the Autumn canvas, Peace is taking the milk of kindness from the breast of Concord, holding out a basin as the wet nurse does in Tintoretto's *Nativity* on the upper floor of St. Roch's Club. The goddesses have been interrupted, as the pitcher tipped over on the ground suggests, by Mars in his armor. Minerva, also armed, thrusts her body between the women and the warrior, saying that the time for peace has come. This is appropriate for autumn, when the season for sea battles was coming to an end in the Venetian calendar. The toppled pitcher indicates the liquid element intended by this scene, since water is the dissolver of other elements.

There is no doubt that fire is the right element for the picture of Winter, personified as Vulcan at his forge hammering armor on the anvil. Vulcan is shown against a snowy backdrop, as a white-bearded old master directing the work of three younger apprentices. The painting would instantly call to mind the work of armorers in the Arsenal, who had the winter months to devote to foundries where equipment was readied for the fighting season.

The way the figures in each of these paintings circle about each other, weaving four separate "dances to the music of time," makes the scenes revolve, as well, around each other, completing a larger cycle of advance and return in the recurring years. They express perfectly that temporal differentiation within a temporal continuity that made up "republican time" for the undying Venetian state.

The cosmically ordered seasons that bind earth to heaven are the subject of another Tintoretto picture, now in London's National Gallery, though it was painted c. 1580 for Emperor Rudolph II, who had astrological interests.[8] This is now called *The Origin of the Milky Way*, though it originally linked heaven and earth to describe the simultaneous appearance of the Milky Way in heaven and of lilies on earth (P-R 2.212–13). Copies show that the canvas was cropped slightly at the top and heavily at the bottom, upsetting the composition. Jove flies down toward the sleeping Juno with Hercules, his son by the mortal Alcmene, in his arms. He is putting the demigod to his wife's breast, so that he can suck immortality from her milk. This divine sustenance will give immortality to his son by a mortal woman. Though Hercules sucks enough milk to accomplish his father's purpose, Juno wakes and twists her nipple away from the baby—which makes her milk spurt up into the sky, forming the Milky Way, while the other nipple, sympathetically reacting, spurts drops onto the earth, where they form lilies.

In its reduced present form, the picture seems too crowded. The attributes of the god and goddess—Jove's eagle with his thunderbolts, Juno's peahen—are surrounded by

FIG. 16
Jacopo Tintoretto, *The Origin of the Milky Way*

amoretti deploying Cupid's useless arrows and net, in an effort to fend off the Father of Gods. The diagonal traced by the flight of the putto under the peahen moves up through Juno's twisting body—and this thrust was echoed, before the removal of the picture's lower part, by the slant of a reclining body under Juno's, that of another nude goddess, Tellura (Earth), receiving the shower of lilies from Juno's breast. This strong diagonal running up from the right, one launched by a putto's body, was originally countered by a line running up from the left, one also launched by a putto's body—though only the upper part of that body survives now. This line was carried up through Juno's extended arm and Jove's rolling arrival in flight. The seasonal flowers of earth are here tied directly to the cosmic phenomena of heaven, just as Venice's ships sailed seasonally in response to the astrological sequences of the sky.

THE AGES OF MAN

FIG. 30
Pietro Lombardo,
Tomb of Doge Pietro
Mocenigo

Another time sequence that fascinated Venetians was the three ages of man. The three Magi were always presented as exemplifying youth, maturity, and age. The life span of fallen heroes could be presented with a reference to their own three ages, as in the three caryatids who bear up the sarcophagus of Doge Pietro Mocenigo on Pietro Lombardo's tomb in the Church of Saints John and Paul. De Tolnay argued that the four seasons of the year are blended with the three ages of man in Giorgione's *Three Philosophers* (T 164–67) in the Vienna Kunsthistorisches Museum—he sees, moving right to left, "the blossoming trees of summer, the half-leafless tree of autumn, the bare trees of winter, and the delicate tremulous sapling of spring."[9] Whether this is true or not, a progress in the same direction moves across the three male figures in the painting, going from an old prophet in profile on the right, to a mature man in Asian dress looking out at us, and then on to a young scholar seated and looking intently to the left, as if awaiting the fulfillment of some process unfolding in the three men. They are taken by De Tolnay and others to be (reading right to left again) Jewish, Muslim, and pagan wise men looking to the coming of Christ in the cave of his birth. In that case, this would be a more abstract reading of a pattern common in pictures of the Nativity, where the Magi are presented in terms of the three ages of man, expanding the prophetic text of Joel (2.28)—"Your old men shall dream dreams, your young men shall see visions"—with an intermediate age between the two, covering the whole span of hoping humanity. But the "backward" time scheme of seasons does not fit with the normal sequence of revelations in the three religions.

Others see different patterns in the picture, including a reference to the cave of Plato's *Republic* rather than of Christ's Nativity.[10] But a Christian reading seems indicated by the two sources of light—one natural, one miraculous—in the picture. This was often used to suggest a supernatural light intruding on the natural order (see, for instance, Carpaccio's *Dream of Saint Ursula* or *Vision of Saint Augustine*). In the *Three Philosophers* the natural light is dawning over the horizon—it shines through the sapling on the left and throws the trees to the right of the picture's midpoint into silhouette. But another and a brighter light comes from the left, where the cave is paradoxically darkened. This light floods the face of the seated man and touches into fire the red and gold garments of the standing men, whose faces are not turned directly into the light. They seem to have an achieved and a remembered wisdom, while the young man is first encountering wisdom, his right hand tracing its obscure message. Whatever interpretation one gropes toward in this rich and teasing work—three religions, three schools of philosophy, three stages of initiation, three degrees of truth, and so on—they all, despite varying subtleties, build on the "three ages of man" convention.

A symbolic work with elements resembling those of the *Three Philosophers* is Titian's *Allegory of Prudence* (w 2.145–46). Here too are three faces, the mature one in the middle facing out at us, while the older and younger features are averted. But Titian's three faces are not associated with contrasting landscape backgrounds. Rather, they are linked with animal heads just beneath them, suggesting the ethos of each age—dog for boy, lion for mature man, and wolf for aged man. As Erwin Panofsky was the first to realize in modern times, the painting combines the ages of man with an allegory of Prudence based on an Egyptian treatment of the three-headed god Serapis, with the head of a dog facing to the right, a lion looking straight out at the viewer, and a wolf facing to the left. Titian has superimposed on this Egyptian motif a thoroughly Venetian set of values, one based on his own family. The old man facing to our left is a self-portrait of the artist as an old man; the mature man facing us has the features of Titian's son Orazio, then (c. 1570) in his forties; and the boy facing to our right is Titian's nephew Marco, the artist's only surviving close relative still in his teens.[11]

Light falls on the ensemble from our right, making the young face glow fuzzily with hope and a canine eagerness. The same light molds the middle face with partial shadow, deepening the full intelligence of man in the leonine strength of his prime. This leaves the old man on the left shadowed entirely, only his vulpine cunning left him to deal with the darkness he faces. The animal emblems, when used as a symbol of Prudence, play on the folk etymology of that virtue, *pro-videntia*, "seeing ahead." The central features, those linked with the Venetian lion, combine a foresight of what will be needed in age, based on the experience of youth as chastened by maturity. In Titian's personal reading of the allegory, his own life is circling back to the youth and prime he has left, the ages of man creating a succession that continues through its different stages and strengths. It is a

FIG. 41
Vittore Carpaccio, *The Dream of Saint Ursula*

PLATE XXVIII
Vittore Carpaccio, *Vision of Saint Augustine*

PLATE X
Titian, *An Allegory of Prudence*

tragic vision, yet a hopeful one. Youth is continually coming along to complete the human experience, giving an eternal aspect even to growth and decay. Man contains and is contained by time, which does not cease with any one person. Each person participates in what all share, effecting individual completion and communal fulfillment. A three-dimensionality is achieved by making the central face sharper in feature while the other two recede from us into vaguer lines. This suggests that they are on a rotating stand, as part of a cycle, where age returns to youth and retraces its course—just as time changes and remains the same in the republic of Venice.

CHAPTER SIX

Disciplines of Work

THE PILLARS THAT HOLD the statues of Saint Mark and Saint Theodore in the Piazzetta stand on stone bases with almost totally effaced carvings on them—but when they were still decipherable, they were identified as reliefs showing craftsmen at their work. These twelfth-century figures represented, on the Theodore column, smiths at the forge, fishermen, basket makers, and wine sellers. On Mark's column there were fruit sellers, butchers, and cattle dealers.[1] The city was based on its laborers' effort and skill. We have already seen how true that was of the indispensable workers in the Arsenal. But other workers were just as needed in the economic life of the city, and their work was literally sacred. Each craft had its patron saint. Each had religious ceremonies linked to the performance of its specialty (*mestiere*—the word we know better in its French form, *métier*). The ship builders had as their patron Saint Foca, the bishop and martyr who had worked in a shipyard as a young man—he stands with Saint Mark on the painted emblem of the guild in the Correr Museum.[2]

THE CAPITELLI

If we move across the Piazzetta from the pillars to look at some carvings still legible—those on the series of little capitals (*capitelli*) in the arcade of the Doge's Palace—we find a capital devoted to the Four Crowned Ones (Quattro Coronati). These men were stonecutters, crowned because they were martyrs who refused to carve idols for the emperor Diocletian. As presented on the capitello, they are working with students and onlookers who are not (like the four) crowned and haloed. The Quattro Coronati were patrons of the stonecutting (*tagliapiera*) guild. The most interesting of these sculptor saints is the one called Claudio in an inscription, since he is shown carving one of the sons in the *Drunkenness of Noah* corner sculpture on this very building.[3]

This is the son closest to Noah, who averts his head and holds up his left hand in refusal of the bad son's invitation to gaze on his father's nakedness.

Since architects did not have their own guild, they were included in the stonecutters' guild—which is why three of the figures on this column are performing architectural labors, one at work on a column, another on a pillar, and the third on a row of five arched Gothic windows. Ruskin noticed that there were bits of colored marble in the window scheme.[4] This could mean that the architect is shown at work on the doge's palace itself, just as the sculptor on this capital is creating the statue for the palace's corner relief.

Only one other capitello is devoted to a single mestiere, and it is one of the most prominent, on the first column on the southeast side of the palace, under the *Drunkenness of Noah*. It can surprise the modern viewer that this place of honor is given over to barbers; but they had exalted pretensions, based on a tradition of service as apothecaries and performers of minor surgery. One had to be literate to act as an apothecary, which gave barbers a status they clung to fiercely. We can see that from this capital, where one barber has scissors and comb for cutting hair, another a razor for shaving, but the third has a lancet for bleeding the sick. The barbers called themselves "barber-surgeons" (*barbieri chirurghi*), and took for their patrons the doctor-saints Cosmas and Damian. They commissioned statues of their patrons from the sculptor Antonio Rizzo, for the altar of their guild in the Church of the Servites (Santa Maria dei Servi). When that church was destroyed, the statues were placed on the inside entrance wall of the little church of Santa Sofia (near Ca' d'Oro). Cosmas holds a mortar, and Damian a potion.

A third capitello on the Doge's Palace contains the figures of eight workers. A stonemason's assistant is grinding the mortar to hold his bricks in place, a goldsmith is making a small bowl, a boy cobbler is making a shoe, a carpenter is planing a board, a corn merchant is weighing grains, a farmer is hoeing, a notary is writing, and a smith is hammering on his anvil. The different head-dresses of the figures show that all levels of work are meant to be included. Masters of their profession wear bulky caps with cloth hanging down behind (the notary, the stonemason, the goldsmith). Day laborers wear tight caps (the stonemason's assistant and the smith). And an apprentice has no hat at all (the boy cobbler).

SEASONAL LABORS

The entry arch of the basilica, already considered for its time emblems, links its different times to different tasks for human performance. Even though these illustrations of the seasons were traditional, it may seem odd that Venice, islanded in the lagoon, marks the seasons with agrarian work. But the arch depicts efforts that were a continuing part of Venetian life, like fishing and fowling. Of course, there were originally orchards and vineyards in Venice's core islands themselves, before they were crowded out by people and buildings. We catch reminiscences of that in names like Holy Mary of the Garden

FIG. 18
Capitello of barbers

(Santa Maria dell'Orto) or St. Francis at the Vineyard (San Francesco della Vigna). Elizabeth Crouzet-Pavan notes that some islands in the lagoon—especially Torcello, Burano, and Mazzorbo—continued to supply fruits and vegetables to the Rialtine center. The island known now as San Francesco del Deserto was originally Two-Vineyard Island (Isola delle Due Vigne). Torcello was a busy producer of wines in the fourteenth and early fifteenth centuries, though high tides brought salt to the soil, affecting the grapes. Torcello wine was inferior, and making it had to be abandoned. Though the Arsenal drew timber from northern forests, the constant need for firewood was also satisfied, in part, from growth on the islands.[5] But even aside from the produce of the lagoon itself, Venetians had to be alert to the seasonal work that brought them food. The rhythm of the seasons affected the quality and quantity of their food supply. The freshness, measurement, and prices of food products were regulated for the guilds that distributed them. There were separate organizations for the vendors of vegetables (biavaroli), of oil and cheeses (ternieri and casaroli), of fish (comparavendi pesce), of fowl (gallineri and buttiranti), and of bread (forneri).[6]

The months were carved in the central arch of San Marco in the thirteenth century, when much of the produce of Venice was cultivated on its own islands; but even later, when the bulk of the city's food had to be imported, the connection with the production of it was still vivid in the minds of Venetians as they bought produce at the market. They would respond to the extraordinary vitality of the monthly labors

displayed on the underside of the middle arch. Ascending on the left side are:

January: A man carries firewood.

February: A man, in the slack season for farming, warms his feet at the fire. The roaring flames lick around the acanthus vine that encircles all these scenes.

March: The warrior Mars holds a shield with the lion of Venice emblazoned on it. The winds of March, blown by a kneeling "genius" of the season, whip his hair back. The tongue of his sword belt is tugged down, making this allegorical figure very realistic.

April: A shepherd balances a lamb on his shoulder with one hand while the other uses his shepherd's crook for walking.

May: The young year is crowned with flowers.

June: A reaper cuts grain with his sickle, the curve of his back exactly conforming to the acanthus tendril here.

Descending on the right side of the arch:

July: A man, hoeing, wears a broad hat to keep off the summer sun.

August: A boy, faint with the heat, fans himself. His inability to find rest in the elaborately carved chair is conveyed by the awkward splaying of his body.

September: A wine maker carries grapes in a wicker basket, which has long ropes woven into it for carrying purposes.

October: A boy with a conical hat puts a foot on his spade to break the hard earth.

November: A fowler who has limed a tree takes a fluttering bird out of the lime with his right hand. In his left hand he holds a stick from which hang three birds already captured.

December: A man slaughters a pig. He has pinned it with his legs, so one hand can twist the head back (holding the mouth shut to prevent squealing) while his right hand plunges the knife into the exposed throat.

These figures bend to their labors, echoing or counterpointing the loop of the acanthus vine that encircles them all, binding them into a continuity of human struggle and survival. The polychrome vivacity of the whole is only partially suggested now, after the recovery of some of the original colors in the 1980s.

THE CRAFTS

To contrast with this sequence of seasonal tasks, the year-round work of the guilds is presented on the underside of the basilica's outer arch. Where the months were oval in shape, these are rectangular in composition. They are not united by a single acanthus vine throwing spirals around them, as the months were. Rather, each scene is separated from the next by a lion's head mask in a carved acanthus setting. And the keystone is not the cosmic Christ of the astrological sequence, but the Lamb of God, suggesting humble labor. Between two and four men are shown engaged in every craft, a bearded master and his beardless apprentices. The master here wears a skull cap, sometimes of leather, sometimes of woven cloth—though the master cooper wears a broad-brimmed hat.

Carved slightly later in the thirteenth century than the cycle of months, these reliefs are, according to Otto Demus, "by far the most complete and most lifelike representations of the Trades in mediaeval sculpture."[7] Demus agrees with Ruskin that the trades should be read from the lower right hand up and around the arch to culminate on the lower left side with the greatest of Venetian trades, shipbuilding. The crafts are, rising from the right:

Fishermen: The master sits in the boat and dangles his line, while the apprentice stands and spears his fish.

Blacksmiths: The master and one assistant hammer at the forge.

Sawyers: Master and assistant work the double-handled saw. Here the apprentice wears the woven skull cap and the master is bareheaded. The pose of these workers is taken from the mosaic of Noah building the ark in the Zen Chapel of San Marco (D 2.119). The master braces the log the same way in both scenes, and the boy, who works from a seated position, has a skull cap in them both. Here the basilica's exterior pays tribute to an artifact inside it.

Carpenters: The master is using an adze. The apprentice's arms are broken off, so his task is unclear.

Cooperage: The master is hammering the hoops around the barrel, while two apprentices (one in a cap that ties under his chin) bring him more hoops.

Barbers: The apprentice is shaving a man, twisting his head around violently, which shows his lack of skill. The master is manhandling a person even more severely, but in pursuit of that higher form of barbering, minor surgery. He is pulling a tooth. To pin the squirming man, he has reached under his arm with his left hand, which holds the mouth open so his pliers can get at the tooth.

Cobblers: The seated master has neither beard nor hat. The apprentice is using a model cast of a calf and foot, for fitting shoes and boots.

Descending on the left side, from the keystone:

Masons: The master is using a plumb line to keep the wall vertical. One apprentice brings a load of bricks up the ladder, while the other uses a trowel to lay mortar and a hammer to tap the brick into place.

Milk and cheese merchants: A woman shows up only on this relief and on the one devoted to bread and fish, both times as a customer. Here the master pours milk for her pitcher, while one apprentice hangs up soft cheeses, and the other cuts into a wheel of hard cheese.

Butchers: While the master kills a cow, putting the knife in at just the point matadors choose for a sure kill, one apprentice brings in a sheep, and the other seems to be sharpening his axe to use on a ram behind the cow.

Bakers and fishmongers: The master has sold his customer her fish and is giving her some bread, while the two apprentices bring fresh loaves from the oven.

Vintners: This master has two apprentices and two (male) customers. As the master broaches a keg, the customers are testing their purchase.

Ship builders: Here are the "assembly line" craftsmen of the Arsenal, turning out a galley with their customary speed and specialization.

The sculptors of this series have created a whole race of men with proportions adapted to the exact spaces that they fill. They are an "abbreviated" people, but

they do not look dwarfish or freaky. Details are emphasized—features or hands or tools—to bring out their narrative importance, and one accepts the body's distortions as easily as one does the shrinking of a whole ship or an entire building to fit its role in the story. The scenes are economical; they share a formula that is continually varied; they are busy, but not crowded in ways that would confuse. They reveal a sharp observation of what each task calls for. The men performing them have a certain dignity. Even the barber pulling a tooth from his thrashing patient goes about his work with a contemplative air.

This was appropriate, since every form of work in Venice was a service to the state. That is the significance of the solemn charters (*mariegole*) drawn up by each guild for the approval of the government and the regulation of work under an appropriate patron saint. A model for such relationships was the bond between cobblers and Saint Anianus. He was the cobbler whose hand Mark miraculously cured in Alexandria, leading to Anianus' conversion, priesthood, and martyrdom. Anianus was sculpted on the façade of the cobblers' meeting house by Antonio Rizzo, and the Younger Palma painted the same event for the building's *albergo* (SMR 136, now in the Accademia). In fact, the curing of the cobbler is a regular part of Venetian iconography. It is in the ceiling mosaics of San Marco. It makes up one panel in the Pala d'Oro behind the altar of the basilica. It gets its panel, as well, on the covering for the Pala that Paolo Veneziano painted. Tullio Lombardo created a relief of the cure on the façade of St. Mark's Distinguished Brotherhood. Other crafts' patron saints were not as obviously related to Saint Mark. But all the guilds found some way to make their work an act of both piety and patriotism. All their saints were companions of Mark.

FIG. 23 (ABOVE)
San Marco,
Stories of the Ark of Noah

FIG. 22
(OPPOSITE, TOP)
San Marco,
Sawyers

FIG. 24
(OPPOSITE, BOTTOM)
San Marco,
Barber

PART TWO

Imperial Personnel

CHAPTER SEVEN

Doge

HEN THE BODY OF MARK was given into the doge's custody, that entailed a responsibility for protecting the city—which was a larger reliquary holding the reliquary of San Marco. Only the doge could give the standard of Mark to the highest military authority, the naval commander in chief (*capitano generale dal mar*). A uniting of all forms of authority—religious, political, and military—might have given the doge a hold on power as total as any pope or emperor possessed. But he was supposed to embody the *republic*'s honor, not that of any person or dynasty—a truth that found accidental expression in the fact that the crown given him was too heavy, from accretion of jeweled ornament, to be worn.[1] The crown had to be replaced for everyday use by the biretta with a peak on the rear called a "horn" (*corno*), a far humbler head-dress that accorded with his limited scope of action.

The doge's office in the Middle Ages was a subordinate post of the Byzantine empire, a position from which he worked himself free with the help of local election by an assembly. Then, having shaken off control from above, he was forced by his peers to get free of control from below. This was accomplished when the right to elect him was restricted, in the thirteenth century, to the prominent families that made up the patriciate (roughly 2,500 males during most of the Renaissance). Now he was in the control of his fellow *nobili*, a control he might chafe at but could never entirely escape. Patricians were all equal in legal terms—they all (even the doge) had only one vote in the Larger Council, the basic expression of their caste. There were, of course, different degrees of power among the patricians. Families "in the forefront" (*primi*) had more wealth, connections, prestigious history than the poorer or less active ones. But a corporate ethos of the whole body continually opposed concentration of power in individual men or families. So the history of patrician rule was one of increasing the *symbolic* powers of the doge, as an expression of the republic's religious and civic identity, while subjecting each holder of the office to continual surveillance and control. The higher he was propped up, the slenderer became the stilts that held him on high. He could not charge about on such rickety underpinnings.

Not only was the doge heavily regulated. So were the members of his family, and of his wife's family. Safeguards were erected and continually readjusted to fence him away from merely personal aggrandizement. Of course, such prickly boundaries would not have been patrolled so energetically if there were not real powers being reined in. Doges had resources they could mobilize within the patriciate itself, according to character and circumstance, for getting their way despite opposition—especially in time of war, when executive powers are increased in almost any form of government. But the fact that no doge succeeded in throwing off the patrician system—the only two who overtly tried were executed or deposed—is one reason for the longevity of the institution. There were no dynastic quarrels that overthrew a reigning family, no coups, no breakup of the patriciate that led to expulsion of the losing contingent.

THE GERONTOCRACY

Despite a labyrinth of regulations surrounding the doge, some of the most effective checks were informal—including a tacit consensus on the age requirement. No legal minimum for holding the office had to be enacted, since it was unthinkable that he should be young. The average age of doges at their election was seventy-two (F 130). This reflected a general attitude toward age that made political careers in Venice culminate late in life. The nobili strove to let only tested and trusted men enter higher office. There were long years of seasoning and observation, of service at lower posts, of diplomatic or military assignments, preceding elevation to the government's central positions. Men rarely reached the Senate until they were in their fifties or sixties. This practice was in great contrast to the cult of energetic young leadership in other Italian cities of the Renaissance. Lorenzo the Magnificent ruled Florence from the age of twenty-three to that of forty-three. But his was just the kind of aggressively individual and familial rule that Venice was determined to prevent. The highest offices were kept beyond a man's expectable reach, in Venice, until he was old and had little time to build any power base separate from those who had elected him.

Francesco di Filippo Foscari was a chief of the Ten at 84, and Francesco Bragadin held the same position at 72. In August in 1514 all three of the chiefs were over 80 years of age. Both Alvise Priuli and Sebastiano Giustiniani were members of the College at 74; Marcantonio Barbaro died while serving on the Collegio at 77. Marcantonio Morosini was 89 when he sat on the Collegio in 1506. Marco Bollani was 86 and the oldest patrician in Venice when he was elected to a special commission of the Ten in 1517. Paolo Capello was 82 when he served on the same commission in 1532. (F 130–31)

Here again, Venetian attitudes approximate the ancient Athenian ones. Solon, who wrote the line "I age ever deepening in knowledge," prescribed fifty as the minimum age for addressing the Assembly.[2] When young Athenians had to speak at trials, they apologized for their youth.[3] In the Homeric poems, which shaped Greek attitudes, Nestor is accepted as the wisest leader since he is the oldest.

In Venice, the age criterion was strengthened by supplementary considerations. It was better for a doge not to have sons holding office or showing ambition—the doge who was deposed (Francesco Foscari) suffered because of his son's schemes. In fact it was best to have no sons at all, who might use their father's power to increase their own (F 134). It did not hurt, either, for a doge-elect to have outlived his wife (if any)—which meant there was often no dogaressa whose relatives could gain advantage from her connection. Other things being equal, the ideal candidate for doge would seem to have been an eighty-year-old man who had no surviving relatives, who had never married (to acquire relatives on his wife's side), and had no children who could marry into other families. Celibacy could not actually be required (as it was, supposedly, in the papacy), but the condition was sometimes approximated.

One might think that a doge installed under these circumstances would not need further barriers to self-promotion, but these were added in abundance, throughout his service and even posthumously. The ideal of an intestate old man as doge could not be achieved at every election, since the oldest candidates might be objectionable on grounds other than age. In fact, special needs of the empire or skills in the candidate could at times lead to choice of a person as young as in his fifties. It was clear, therefore, that more codified restrictions were necessary, to go along with the informal barriers.

There were four main stages in the checking of a doge's power—first at his election, followed closely by his renunciatory oath, then during his tenure of office, and finally in the punitive scrutiny after his death.

1. Election. The labyrinthine method of choosing a doge involved staggered exercises in voting and sortition—choosing men by lot was just one of many ways Venice resembled Athens in its choice of officers. The process had ten steps (L III):

From the Larger Council, thirty men were chosen by lot;
then nine were chosen by lot from the thirty;
then the nine voted for forty;
then twelve were chosen by lot from the forty;
then the twelve voted for twenty-five;
then nine were chosen by lot from the twenty-five;
then the nine voted for forty-five:
then eleven were chosen by lot from the forty-five;
then the eleven voted for forty-one;
then the forty-one elected a new doge.

Complex as this already sounds, such a schematic presentation cannot convey all the peripheral controls that were tinkered with, reinforced after periods of laxity, or gone through as rites to purify the process. Minimum numbers of votes were required for each member of the elected panels. The key groups involved had to be sequestered, and when it came time for the final vote, an impartial vote counter was acquired by sending an official out the west door of San Marco to pick the first boy he saw under fifteen to be the *ballotino* (ballot boy). The ballotino would count votes in the Larger Council throughout the new doge's reign, and he would march with him in the city processions (M 191, 288).

2. The Pledge. Once elected, the doge could not be crowned until he swore to the Pledge (*Promissione*) especially drawn up for him. This stated the fundamental duties of the office, but it also incorporated any new limits felt to be necessary for this candidate at this time—including bans based on what was considered dangerous or unacceptable in the previous doge's reign. When, at a later ceremony, the dogaressa (if any) was crowned, she too had to swear to a promissione specially drawn up for her. It was after effective doges' reigns that the promissione tended to be most severe, even if the doge in question had taken necessary steps in war or popular ones in peace. In fact, personal popularity (as opposed to ceremonial majesty) was suspect and could be punished. As Finlay says, "the high tide of antiducal sentiment always crested at the death of a doge, and was channeled into the oath" (F 111). To remind themselves as well as the doge of his obligations, the promissione was read aloud to him every two months of his tenure.[4] As we saw earlier, this document was such a condition of legitimacy for a doge that Lorenzo Tiepolo is shown carrying it, rolled up in his hand, on the mosaic on the basilica's façade.

3. Tenure. The doge served with every important governmental body in Venice's complex system—which both gave symbolic legitimacy to its actions and guaranteed that he never acted alone. If he gained a dominating position in one board or council, his influence could be opposed in others. To keep him from acting outside the joint authority of the republican institutions, he was not allowed to see ambassadors privately, to open mail by himself, to go out of the palace without authorization and an entourage, to confer with relatives unsupervised, to aggrandize his domestic quarters in the palace (which were modest by the standard of Renaissance rulers). How, thus hemmed in, could he exercise any personal leadership at all? He could build coalitions within the various parts of the government, aided by the fact that he had life tenure while the makeup of most government panels was constantly shifting because of their members' brief terms (which kept the Larger Council continually holding elections). He could use his important relatives and wealthy friends to lobby their fellow patricians. He could emphasize commercial or military need for his policy, since he had access to information from all the organs of government. He alone in the administration had long dealings with all of the permanent bureaucracy, made up of non-noble citizens with considerable impact on daily governance. He could collaborate with the only other life-tenured officers—the "Caretakers" (*Procuratori*) of the physical fabric of the city, or the Chancellor, who came from the citizen class and spoke for it.

The doge's power was resented but could never be erased. For one thing, the leading patricians wanted members of their own family to be remembered as a doge. For all its limits, the office itself was deeply revered as well as feared, and never lacked for aspirants. The whole patrician caste needed the prestige and dignity it brought to their most prominent member. Knowing that, a doge could push very energetically against the barriers thrown up around his action.

4. Term-End Scrutiny. In 1501, after the death of an especially unpopular (because powerful) doge, Agostino Barbarigo, the official body drawing up the promissione on the basis of his performance was supplemented with a body authorized to scrutinize the doge's whole reign, with the aim of punishing his relatives for any infractions. This body became permanent, and represented a real threat to the family of any deceased doge. Agostino Barbarigo's relatives were fined because he spent too much of his personal wealth seeking popularity, but the family of the next doge, Leonardo Loredan, had to pay because he had not been sufficiently generous to maintain the dignity of his office (M 277).

PORTA DELLA CARTA

The struggle between doge and patricians could leave its marks on the historical structures of the state. Some of the grander monuments connected with the palace are actually battle scars, the frozen blows and counterpunches of a power struggle. This became clear as Renaissance humanism spread to Venice in the fifteenth century, introducing new concepts of individualism and heroic leadership. The first to put these concepts into visual form for the glorification of the doge's office was Francesco Foscari, whose long reign (1423–1457) ended, as we have seen, by his being unseated for the extravagances of his son, which were taken as evidence that the Foscari were aggrandizing themselves through the office of the doge. Francesco had in fact indulged new ways of enhancing his office through a building program undertaken with the sculptor-architect Bartolomeo Bon.

It has already been mentioned that the doge could cultivate the life-tenured Procuratori, who were in charge of building programs and maintenance. (Procuratori were chosen from the pool of aging high officials from which future doges would be drawn, and they had an interest in aggrandizing the doge's role.) Though construction of public buildings required financial authorization from other bodies of the government, those were mutable bodies with a continual influx of new members. The doge could acquire a powerful influence, during the years of his reign, over the appearance of official buildings. He was not supposed to make his personal quarters more glamorous, but he could arrange for subtler and more important celebrations of his status through the public face worn by the republic. So the Foscari doge schemed to create a triumphal arch at his end of the public palace, one that carried his own life-size portrait, a kneeling statue, as its most prominent feature. This was the Porta della Carta (Document Gate) raised by the artists of the Bon family, probably to Bartolomeo's design (P-H 1.277–78).

The whole gate was originally gilded and painted, as we can see from Gentile Bellini's 1496 painting of the piazza—it was literally a Golden Gate, an entry to paradise (a theme that would be taken up on the inside arch by life-size statues of Adam and Eve). Kenneth Hempel, who conducted the restoration of the gate in the 1970s, found that

FIG. 63
Gentile Bellini,
*Procession in the
Piazza San Marco*

> The surface of the Istrian stone was almost all painted in lapis-lazuli blue on the
> inside of the niches of the [statues of] the Virtues and of St. Mark, as well as inside
> the frieze of the crowning arch. The leaves of the frieze were gilded, as indeed were
> the canopies above the Virtues, the capital supporting Justice and the tracers around

the window. The marble [of all statues but Justice], on the other hand, was not painted, the only exception being traces of red and yellow pigment on the Foscari armorial shields, and gilded decoration on the robes of the Virtues.[5]

Although the statue of Francesco is kneeling, over the gate, before the lion of Saint Mark, whose standard he holds in his hand, his is hardly a humble posture—as Napoleon's troops realized when they tore the statue down in 1797 (a replica is in its place, though the original head is preserved inside the palace). The kneeling doge has his head on the same level as the lion, suggesting what Debra Pincus calls a "parity" between them—he looks more like the lion's keeper than its servant.[6] This should be contrasted with votive paintings in which the doge is on a lower level, with intermediaries between him and the picture's main patron saint. We might contrast this gateway, also, with the mosaic over the northwest entry door to San Marco, where the doge is just one of fifty figures, part of the community he leads. With Foscari's image, Renaissance humanism has arrived in Venice, and with it the lone heroic leader.

JUDGMENT OF SOLOMON

We may sample something of the changing atmosphere if we look to the corner of the palace near the Porta della Carta, where a statuary group was added to the angle as part of the same emphasis on justice that organizes the Porta—*The Judgment of Solomon* (P-H 1.276), where the king discerns which of two women claiming a baby is the true mother (III Kings 3.16–28). This large sculptural group is meant, also, to correspond with those on the other exposed corners of the palace, done in the preceding century; *Noah's Drunkenness* (Genesis 9.18–29) and *Adam and Eve in Eden* (Genesis 3.1–7). These scenes are Gothic in their rich foliage and sinuous tracery of form—Noah's languidly sprawling arabesque contrasted with the energetic arabesque of the vine that flourishes over him, populated by birds and lizards.

Each of the corner groups presents a situation calling for the execution of justice, and each has the statue of an archangel on the level above it, to impose the sentence.[7] In the

PLATE XI
Judgment of Solomon

FIG. 25 (TOP)
Drunkenness of Noah

FIG. 26 (ABOVE)
Adam and Eve in Eden

case of Noah, the angel will execute the curse on the son, Ham, who mocks his father's drunken nakedness. Ham is already severed from his family—his statue stands outside the corner group, across the arch that abuts the corner. Above Adam and Eve, the angel is poised to drive them from Paradise as soon as they eat the forbidden fruit.

At the Solomon corner, however, though an angel also stands over it, the administration of justice has now come down to earth. Gone are the Gothic groups' billowy lines and the neat division of the scenes' two planes at right angles to each other, joined only by the vine or tree at the corner point. Though Solomon's court also has an anomalous tree at its corner (imposed on the artist, perhaps, by his commission, to connect with the other scenes), the artist cleverly suggests the feeling of a single plane creating a cornice above Solomon's throne that seems to run through the right angle at the corner of the palace, then drawing the true mother out beyond the tree, suggesting a cluster of figures against the single cornice. (The mother is so exposed that her head was knocked off at some point and has been replaced with a replica.)

FIG. 25A
Detail of *Judgment of Solomon* (PLATE XI)

This scene is composed as a compact unit, with five figures in it (as opposed to two in *Adam and Eve* and three in *Noah*). Each of the five people in the *Solomon* shows different emotion in reacting to the drama. The false mother lags behind, indifferent to the baby's fate, only wanting to hurt the other woman in the scene. The real parent rushes forward to put a restraining hand on the shoulder of the military executioner, who is about to divide the child with his sword. Her other hand touches her breast, as if to relieve her labored breathing. The soldier is grimly stoic about his task, the baby dangles helpless from his grasp, and Solomon looks off into space as if attentive to some inner prompting.

The soldier's lifted sword is suggested but not seen, and Solomon's hand checks its descent with a touch on the soldier's arm—as if Solomon were communing through this executioner's body with the mother who touches him on the other side. The virtuoso accomplishment of the artist can be measured in the flowing robes set off on either side of the soldier's jointed and robotic armor. The soft line of the baby's flesh runs along the soldier's mailed thigh, which in turn shoves itself against the tree trunk—three different textures juxtaposed in a vertical thrust that gives the scene its central axis. The other corner groups' scenes unfold in a leisurely and expansive way, but here the narrative is locked into the tight interactions of its dramatis personae, and Solomon sits serenely in control of the whole event.[8] Wolters believes that this crowned figure in his court is meant to represent Il Serenissimo himself, the doge inside his palace, and the group is best read in conjunction with the celebration of Doge Foscari on the nearby gate.

ARCO FOSCARI

One might expect that reaction to Foscari's deposition from office would interrupt the process of inflating the doge's importance. But succeeding doges continued and expanded Foscari's plan to make the entrance to the palace a form of self-celebration. Cristoforo Moro (1462–1471) and Pietro Mocenigo (1474–1476) completed an inner triumphal arch (Arco Foscari) matching the outer Porta della Carta, and Agostino Barbarigo (1486–1501) added a ceremonial flight of stairs as the climax of the *via triumphalis* these works had inaugurated. The key artist of these later developments was the sculptor-architect Antonio Rizzo, who fell from favor with his final patron, Barbarigo, who was the victim of his own triumphalism.

Debra Pincus contends that the Arco Foscari's elaborate program of statues presented the doge as the ruler of an orderly realm built on natural learning and martial virtue in the service of Saint Mark.[9] Here, too, on the inner side of the entrance to the palace, there was a kneeling doge on a level with the lion of Venice.[10] But the outstanding figures on the Arco are Rizzo's life-size statues of Adam and Eve (P-H 2.420), quite different from the corner group at the southwest angle of the palace's exterior. The latter group, done perhaps half a century earlier, shows Adam on the verge of eating the forbidden fruit (a fig in this case). Eve has taken the fruit and she gestures for Adam to join her. He raises his right hand in rejection of the offer, but his left hand (the sinful one, in classical and medieval belief) is moving, as if against his will, to pluck the fig. It is an image of weakness and inner division.

Rizzo's Adam is far from weak. He has already eaten part of the fruit (a pomegranate) he holds in his hand, but he takes responsibility for his act in an almost strut-

FIG. 27 (TOP)
Antonio Rizzo, *Adam*

FIG. 28 (ABOVE)
Antonio Rizzo, *Eve*

ting posture of accountability. This figure is alert, his eyes up, his mouth opened, his back arched to address God above him.[11] He will not hide—unlike Eve, who is withdrawing into herself, her eyes down, her body's curves enclosing her as if to hide her nakedness with her nakedness. With one hand she covers her pudenda, while the other (with the fruit still in it) is moving up to cover her breasts (the Venus Pudica pose). The consciousness of sin has disabled her, while it seems to have emboldened her partner. He is still capable of working his way up to the learning signified on the Arco by the statues of liberal arts, and to the virtue symbolized by warrior figures, if—like the doge—he is true to the service of Mark.

The Adam and Eve now on the Arco Foscari are bronze copies of the marble originals, which are kept inside the palace. But even those originals, darkened by time, do not look as they did at first, when they were polychrome. Some think they were painted to suggest gold or bronze. But the example of other figures by Rizzo, and of the polychrome stairs that he built to face the statues, suggests that the figures had tinted skin and colored hair. The green of the vines on Adam and the colors of the fruit would have stood out. Rizzo was a friend of the painter Antonello da Messina, and he aimed at painterly effects in his statues.[12]

So far this entrance through two triumphal arches allowed some ambiguity about its intent. Though the doge was celebrated on both outer and inner façades, the symbols of justice could apply to the republic's protection of that virtue. The entrance, after all, gave access to the entire courtyard—to the complex of offices and seats of government agencies that took up most of the palace, not merely to the (comparatively) restricted area of the doge's apartments. But Doge Agostino Barbarigo crowned the triumphal course through Porta and Arco with an unambiguously literal "elevation" of the doge. In going under the Porta and back out from the Arco, one passed through a windowless vaulted passageway of six bays, emerging into the bright light of the courtyard, where—after Barbarigo's artistic coup—one faced directly onto a polychrome and marble ceremonial staircase (the Scala) sweeping one up to a platform intended as a coronation site for doges.

RIZZO'S STAIRCASE (SCALA)

External stairs were common in Venetian palaces, but they were attached to a wall of the inner courtyard. This free-standing stairway in several stages was something new, and Rizzo executed it with gorgeous craftsmanship (drawing on Lombard sculptors as his workmen). The risers of the Scala were decorated with gilded lead arabesques—

something Tintoretto would imitate in his painting of Solomon's temple for his c. 1552 *Presentation of the Virgin* (P-R 2.164-65).

The doge for whom Rizzo built the stairway had one of the most fiercely contested reigns of the Renaissance. Agostino Barbarigo was not popular with his peers; but when his popular brother, Marco, died after only nine months as doge, the majority faction broke normal procedure and let a member of the same family succeed him. They did this even though Marco himself had told his brother, "Messer Agostino, you do everything in order to succeed to our position, but if the Larger Council knew your character as well as I do, it would quickly elect another" (F 56). The majority faction among the Primi was made up of families of short ("curtailed") lineage, the so-called Curti, who represented recent estates (*case nuove*). They contended for primacy with those of long lineage (the Longhi), from ancient estates (*case vecchie*). The Longhi's original predominance had been eroded as those of newer wealth came to outnumber them. The Longhi had only 24 of the 150 family clusters (*casade*) in the patriciate. The outrage of the Curti's carrying a second Barbarigo to office in succession made the Longhi declare Agostino's election invalid, and Agostino had to make a passionate personal plea to the Larger Council, arguing that to unseat him would advertise a lack of stability in the Serenissima, giving a weapon to her adversaries. That stilled the opposition—for a while.[13]

This initial hurdle did not inhibit Agostino's aspirations to grandeur, aspirations which—among other things—pushed forward the project of a ceremonial coronation stairway leading up to his apartments. A recent fire in those apartments had prompted his brother Marco to begin restoration, which included a stairway, but it was Agostino who turned the project into a blatant proclamation of dogal primacy. Rizzo's chastely carved reliefs on the Scala present the doge as a conqueror. They include trophies (*trionfi*) of classical origin, some of their symbols hermetic with the ingenuity of the Venetian literati's conundrum book, *Poliphilo's Dream-Combat of Love*.[14] There are dozens of references to Agostino in the inscriptions, and his portrait is on the corner pilaster of the complex, in an oval frame borne up by two lions, while the sun of Justice sheds its rays on him.[15]

The audacity of the doge can be seen in the square grilles that stand on either side of the Scala's understructure. John McAndrew, in a brilliant discussion of the stair flight's architecture, says that these grilles have no purpose but an aesthetic variation of the surface, since the cramped room lit by the grilles' light is too small to be usable (McA 99). He misses the astonishing presumption of Agostino. The grilles lit a holding prison, in which the doge's victims were placed under his feet, like a conqueror's captives trailed behind his chariot in the formal celebration of a Roman triumph.[16] The attitude expressed in this artistic masterpiece and propaganda blunder helped disgrace Agostino—his was the reign, remember, which caused the establishment of a posthumous scrutiny of a doge's offenses. Rizzo shared his patron's disfavor. He was prosecuted for embezzlement and had to flee the republic, disappearing into obscurity. Though Rizzo may have stolen some funds, what outraged the patricians was the great time and expense involved in this ambitious project, and Muraro believes that Rizzo was punished as a form of rebuke to Agostino. Rizzo's name was literally erased from memory, as other generations ascribed his works, the Adam and Eve as well as the Scala, to different artists, making him a nonperson.[17]

FIG. 29 (ABOVE)
Jacopo Sansovino,
Neptune

THE GIANTS (GIGANTI)

Resentment of the stairway's pretensions continued, until the government found a way in the 1560s to reduce its importance, literally overshadowing it with the giant statues, by Jacopo Sansovino, of Mars and Neptune, standing for the imperial power of Venice over land and sea. The were put there, as Muraro says, "to blot out the implication of the stairway." The merely personal and hermetic message of the stairway's subtle imagery is brutally swept aside by the assertion of the empire's twofold sway. The patricians curbed dogal arrogance at an aesthetic cost. The statues simply negate, since they cannot compete with, the subtlety of Rizzo's Scala. Sansovino was a better architect than sculptor, and a better sculptor on a small scale than at the colossal level. The statues are undistinguished— though the substitution of carved wavelets across the sea god's genitals in place of a loincloth is clever.[18]

Rizzo's Scala, by contrast, is a fairy structure, grand yet light and airy. The reliefs of personified Victories that flank roundels on the side arches are little miracles. Neither contained in their carved frames nor totally outside them, they seem to brush across the marble as if wafted there by a lagoon breeze. Tinting would have made them even more Giorgionesque, as Muraro claims: "Marble from Greece or Carrara, capable of every subtle shadowing, was given the preference over Istrian or Veronese stone. In the individual figures as in the overall relief, barely emerging images succeed each other, embodied with a mastery that dispels all stiffness of treatment. In many of the more deeply carved figures of the Scala, the example of Verona and Padua lingers like a far-off echo, and appears to confirm the dream of Venetians, who tend to transform every art into color."[19]

PLATE XII
Antonio Rizzo, relief,
Scala dei Giganti

THE LOGGETTA

Though Sansovino served his patrons' purpose more by assertion than artistry with his "Giants," Mars and Neptune, he had remade the surroundings of the palace, twenty years earlier, in a subtler and more powerful way. Working with the Procuratori under an enlightened doge (Andrea Gritti), Sansovino effectually reversed the doge's triumphal route, reading it backwards as an approach to the celebration of a *patrician* domain. Under the Campanile, attached to it, he placed the Loggetta—a meeting place for the Primi, where their importance could be proclaimed in the public space.[20] This is the first thing seen as one comes out of the Doge's Palace, passing through the six-bayed passage from the inner Arco Foscari to the outer Porta della Carta. Deborah Howard describes the impact of this approach to the Loggetta, planned to reveal its significant architectural components stage by stage: "It can hardly be accident that from the top of the Scala dei Giganti, the upper edge of the main door of the palace, seen through the Arco Foscari, blocks out the Loggetta [just] at the level of the main cornice; while from the [Scala] landing half-way down, the door cuts the [Loggetta's] façade at the upper cornice." Then, as one goes through the six-bay darkened passage, "the width of the Loggetta is revealed bay by bay."[21]

The gorgeous structure thus dramatically unfolded is as much one of Sansovino's great masterpieces as the Scala is one of Rizzo's—though some of the Loggetta's original impact is blunted by additions to the structure. The high attic level on the façade lacked the two side panels that match the bays beneath. Sansovino wanted a gradated narrowing at the top, to link the building with the narrower Campanile behind it. More important, the building is now sealed off from the public by a platform with a balustrade (placed in front of it in the seventeenth century) and a bronze gate (added in the eighteenth century). The stairs up to the platform originally went straight from ground level to the sill of the Loggia's door. This brought one close to the building,

PLATE XIII
Jacopo Sansovino,
the Loggetta of the
Campanile of
San Marco

where one could read its iconography's rising levels, and see up close four statues Sansovino put in the ground bays' niches. The three arches of the façade were open in the days when the building was a display case for the patricians gathered there. The main arch was a grand entry, and the other two were spacious windows.

The recent restoration of the building has brought back some of its opulence of color. The framing elements are of red Verona marble, meant to chime with the red brick of the Campanile behind it and the red paving of the Piazza that surrounded it in the sixteenth century. Carrara marble is used for all the pilasters of the design, and Istrian stone for the reliefs. But the eight columns standing free before the main pilasters are of richly colored Asian marbles. Against this glowing backdrop, with only the open arches penetrating it, Sansovino's bronze statues stood out more prominently than they do now. These are gods who express allegorically the nature of Venice's wise patricians, whose monument this is—reading from left to right, Pallas (Minerva) for wisdom, Apollo the lyre bearer for "harmonious" government, messenger Mercury for diplomatic eloquence, and Peace putting war's equipage to the torch.

The statues are part of an iconographic ensemble that was better read when one could go right up to the structure on the piazza level, since the scheme logically began with the scenes carved in relief *under* the bronze statues. These scenes use images of sea power that had been introduced to Venice by Alessandro Leopardi in 1505, when he installed the mythically encrusted bronze bases for the three standards holding giant flags before San Marco.[22] Above Sansovino's reliefs are his bronze statues, sinuous and curvilinear in the Mannerist fashion—far from the lumpiness of his Giants on the Scala. At this scale, he could create small models for casting hollow bronze figures at two-thirds life size. The result is immeasurably superior to the later Giants. According to Pope-Hennessy, "More than any other works these statues determined the form of the bronze statuettes that were turned out in Venice in the later sixteenth century" (P-H 3.2,237).

The outer figures (of the four) are female divinities, with frontal stances that close off the series at either end. The two middle figures, male gods, turn toward the door as if protecting the Primi who enter it. The Mercury is sometimes mistaken for a David, since he wears shepherd's clothes and has a giant head at his feet—but the head is that of Argus, not Goliath, and the tale of his killing him is in the relief above Mercury. These reliefs over the statues, matching the panels below the statues, give narrative glosses on the gods represented. Pallas, for instance, kills the Giant, and Apollo skins Marsyas, who challenged him with inferior music. Over the statue of Peace, that goddess is shown offering a cornucopia to a warrior—the prosperity that comes from a just war's conclusion. This final panel reiterates a theme that runs through the dialectical arrangement of all these images, as a climax to the sequence of statues. On the left is war (Pallas the giant slayer), fully armed. On the right is Peace (the war rewarder) destroying armor. In the middle, Apollo is in contrast to his neighbor Pallas as a peaceful bringer of harmony, and Mercury is in contrast to his neighbor Peace as the conqueror of Argus. There is an intricate weave of bellicose and pacific themes, complementary so long as they are held in the proper skein of relationships—which is the task of the patricians whose prudent tempering of all considerations is given elaborate expression in this, their gathering place. Sansovino's statues are not meant to be looked at singly, but to carry on a continuing dialogue among themselves, one of increasing complexity. They provoke from us a continuing mental rearrangement of their values.

Crowning the whole façade are the three large reliefs on its attic level, the central one by Sansovino, the flanking ones by assistants working to his design. These pick up again the Venus images in the bottom row of reliefs, and the three scenes on the central standard of Leopardi. On Sansovino's attic, the left panel shows Jupiter, the legendary ruler of Crete, protecting the island's shore, and the right panel shows Venus, the legendary patron of Cyprus, at the watery edge of her domain. Jupiter's eagle flies to him with the thunderbolt (war), while Venus' Cupid brings her a woman's jeweled ornament (peace). In the middle panel, Venice-Justitia sits on her lion throne, signifying Venice's rule over both Crete and Cyprus, those old pillars of her sea empire. At the bottom of the panel, statues of river gods pouring out their waters indicate that Venice is the ruler of land holdings as well as the sea.

The interior of the Loggetta is now darkened by the filling in of the two great window arches (finestroni), and it is cluttered with the sales operation for the elevator ride up the campanile. But it was originally decorated with tapestries, with Sansovino's small statue of the Virgin in a niche, and with conference tables for the Primi.

Around the entrance to the Doge's Palace, we find an astonishing number of masterpieces—the *Judgment of Solomon*, the gilded arches of Porta and Arco, the *Adam and Eve* of Rizzo, the Scala, the Loggetta. Each repays study in itself, but it is useful as well to see them as reflecting the great power struggle between the doge and the patriciate. Here we can watch a tug of war. First we have the doge introducing a new theater for his own display, taking us through outer and inner arches, then up Rizzo's stairway to his coronation spot. Then we can watch the patriciate visibly rebuking his effort, first by the installation of the Giants at the top of the stairs, then by reversing course, going back out through the arches to reach a new terminus, the Loggetta, the intricate throne of the patriciate in its public aspect. Here, as elsewhere in Venice, history and art are interpenetrative.

CHAPTER EIGHT

Patricians
(Nobili)

WHERE WAS THE REAL CENTER of power in the Venetian government—with the doge, the Senate, the Ten, the Collegio, the Larger Council? Looking for the inmost node is like looking for a pea under the flying shells of a master con man. The whole trick of government in Venice was to have no center. It was, as Robert Finlay puts it, government "by an endless succession of committees" (F 34). All its agencies, made up of constantly shifting personnel, were designed to intrude on other agencies. It was hard to build on a power *base*, since power came from being on the move from board to commission to council.

> [It was a government of] rapid rotation in office, diverse responsibilities within individual magistracies, dedication to collective decision making, a multitude of temporary commissions, overlapping competencies of councils, complex and lengthy voting procedures, and a consistent weakness of executive authority at almost all levels of government . . . Perhaps the relationship between the councils of government is better compared to the city of Venice itself, to the winding alleys and canals that always seem to bring the wanderer back to a familiar *campo*, although seen from a different perspective and entered by a different approach—a maze whose order only emerges from observing the passage of others through it. (F 38, 40–41)

Outsiders could only wonder at this mystery: the most stable of governments had the most kaleidoscopic system of governing. What held the whole thing together? Not any agency of government, but the single *source* of government—a compact patrician class that had a secure monopoly on all the shifting positions. The unity of the caste was purchased at the cost of cumbrous execution. The Venetian patriciate was unlike other noble classes, which grew up by tradition or landed settlement or competing dynasties. Venice created its caste as another polity might create a constitution—by a deliberate political act, on a specific occasion. It was legislated into existence, in 1297, by the Serrata ("Lock-Up"), which froze the prominent families of the moment into permanent possession of their status. This was "the most crucial event in Venetian political history" (F 41).

Prior to this event, rival families in Venice were going down the spiral of conflict that shattered other Italian cities. The obvious course in such cases is to maintain some body, above the fray, that can adjudicate the disputes—disputes which, nonetheless, are bound to break out again in some new form. Venice, instead of creating a separate body to adjudicate between rivals, just engulfed them all in one body. The patricians would be legally equal to each other, as a way of preserving their inequality with the rest of the community (its majority). There was thus no single center of power, but a single sphere of it—the patriciate.

The "locking" had, necessarily, two aspects. It was, in the first place, a locking *into* privilege of the rivals, to blunt their conflicts (L 114). But that, of course, involved locking *out* all others. Later, the locking out would be the more obvious feature of the move, but its genius lay in the initial purpose of locking in. This was a unique way of achieving unity out of the very conditions of division, and all later theorists of the Venetian system (including the city's own) who tried to approximate it to classical ideas of "divided government" or "mixed government" just confuse the astonishing reality.

The problem with such a frozen and impermeable elite was obvious—how to keep it from ossifying, sealed off from the rest of the community, whose envy of its status would pose problems of majority discontent and rebellion. The patricians were aware of this danger, and took many measures to prevent a centripetal enclosure of the class away from the larger society. Some alleviation came from the circumstances of the city itself. The *nobili* were merchants, and trade is naturally centrifugal. The patricians needed partners and adjuncts at home, and active agents abroad, to maintain their commercial empire with its accompanying military forces. Lower classes had to be recruited, dignified, rewarded, and placated if they were to perform important tasks. A rich variety of privileges other than patrician status were used as bribes, rewards, distinctions, and bids for popularity.

But perhaps the best tactic of all was the elite's agreement that it should bind its own members and impress others as a class based more on duty than on privilege. Service to the state was expected of all patricians. Since the class was a gerontocracy, with high office beyond the grasp of men until they reached middle age, and since unwillingness to serve in the earlier years would disqualify one for consideration later on, there was a discipline of performance imposed by ambitious families as well as by individual aspiration. This code of elite duty imposed one of Venice's many resemblances to ancient Athens—a form of "liturgy tax." In Athens, performances of public service with an individual's money were called liturgies ("people services"). There was, for instance, the trireme liturgy, by which a wealthy citizen built, manned, and managed one of the city's warships (triremes) out of his own pocket.[1] In Venice, too, patrician galley commanders were expected to recruit and pay their own troops, as well as to furnish their own ships. The state would later reimburse them for basic expenditures, but bonuses and special equipment and better provisioning came from the commander's own resources, and these were necessary if a man was to keep his ship at maximum performance level (L 365–66). His reputation rode on it, and any failure in battle could bring heavy punishment—fines or exile or death. Diplomatic assignments also required private expenditure, while on mission at foreign courts, to uphold personal honor as well as the city's reputation. We saw in the last chapter that even a doge could be fined retroactively if he did not show patrician largesse while in authority. Every officeholder had to expect official investigation of his performance after laying down any responsibility.

This is another point of resemblance to Athens, where *euthyna* was the term for an official's postservice audit and account of his actions.[2] In Venice, the official body of scrutinizers that made all patricians, even those not holding office, fair game for continuing investigation was the legendary Council of Ten. This body was established in 1310, after the defeat of an attempted insurrection by a noble out of office, Bajamante Tiepolo (L 114–16). The Ten became a large part of the Byronic legend of Venetian authority as spying and despotic. The legend had some later truth, in the days of decadence, when the Ten could be a threat to *cittadini* or commoners. But the panel's first and principal use was as a way for the patriciate to police itself. The ruling caste felt that any danger to the republic would come from its own ranks, not from the lower classes—a point that sets Venice apart from modern stereotypes of class warfare.

The patriciate's determination to maintain a discipline of service was declared, as we have seen, in its dress code. In public, all nobili had to wear a uniform, a plain black robe (called a toga), and they had to observe other sumptuary laws against conspicuous consumption. This limitation came partly from merchant attitudes toward thrift, but it was also meant to stress the equality of the caste's members (avoiding flagrant signs of inequality) and to impress others with the discipline of service to the state. It was felt that public displays of wealth would create envy in those who had to serve the empire without the privileges given the ruling caste.

Exceptions to the dress code were made only for those holding important office, as emblems of the state's own majesty—we have seen examples in the bright uniforms of Tintoretto's treasurers or Agnolo's ministers of defense. Prescribed colors were donned when a man was elected to office, to be shed at the end of his (usually short) term— scarlet for Caretakers, violet for Cabinet (Collegio) members, purple for senators, and so on. But the normal attire shows up in portrait after portrait by Titian or Tintoretto—stern men in black presented as models of sober responsibility. This was a new clerisy, of political monks sworn to service.

Needless to say, the Venetians did not live up to their code—who does? Donald Queller is shocked—shocked!—to find electioneering, family pressure, fraud, and bribes in the politics of Venice.[3] One proof of that is the need for reiterated legislation to cope with pullulating abuses. But, of course, persistence in addressing such infractions shows that the code lives on, continually adjusting itself to the need for it. The cohesion of caste was never entirely rent, and when decline did set in, it was not—as Ruskin believed—because of an inner loss of faith or piety or discipline, but from outside influences (the growth of the Turkish empire, the opening of the Atlantic, changes in the technology of war at sea). Venice simply had too small a base to maintain its empire for more than its five centuries of success. That is quite a record, and a testimony to the ethos of the ruling elite.

HOMES (CASE)

Patricians did, naturally, try to aggrandize themselves. Since they were so often checked in the political realm, they dramatized their importance in the private realm, in the building of family palaces, in acts of conspicuous piety or charity, in the endowment of chapels with stunning funeral monuments or votive paintings. The building of ambitious homes (case) was not governed by sumptuary laws, though there was some regulation of exotic furnishings. Beautiful dwellings were actually encouraged, as were majestic public buildings like the scuole. For one thing construction with private funds reclaimed and made firm more land at a time when the fixing of the islands against the flux of lagoon and canals was a continuing task. Terraferma was, as we have seen, mainland bordering the lagoon. Venetian territory itself was called, simply, terra—a thing carefully shored up against the water. Terra, in fact, could be used as a synonym for the city itself, or even for its government (F 55–56). Reclaiming terra was a patriotic act. When patricians laid out gardens where there had been marshes, or added a building along a canal front, or sank more pilings for weighty additions to a structure, they were contributing to the terra.

There was a further reason for desiring more secular and domestic structures. Where the terra was portioned out on islands, large monastic and other religious establishments were sometimes felt to be expanding over too much of the available space. This led, at times, to governmental restrictions on their growth. Another motive for permissiveness where palaces were concerned was the Venetians' perception of their city in theatrical terms, as a series of striking backdrops for the religious and civic rituals that trailed along its canals or through its campi. We can see this loving treatment of the Venetian scene in the religious events recorded in the Distinguished Brotherhoods' series of narrative paintings. Private wealth abetted public display. The Grand Canal, as the "Main Street" of the city, was meant to impress foreigners and delight natives. We have only a dim sense of what the canal looked like in the Renaissance, when the *case* that lined it had painted fronts, often frescoed by major artists (Carpaccio, Titian, Tintoretto, Pordenone). There are sixty-seven frescoes of this sort on record, and there must have been more, the notice of whose existence did not survive.

The *ca'* that gives us some idea of the sumptuous façades from that time is the House of Gold (Ca' d'Oro), built between 1421 and 1433. But even this jewel-casque of a building, recently restored, is a pale image of what it looked like originally. Its builders were the Bons, whom we have met as the creators of the Porta della Carta on the Doge's Palace, a project they took up just after finishing the Ca' d'Oro. The Ca' was— as the Porta would be—gilded and polychromed. The various balls and flowers of the façade on the Grand Canal had gold leaf applied to them, as did the crenellations along the top, the braided moldings running vertically alongside the windows, and the little lions perched at the ends of the balconies. Expensive lapis lazuli paint made the gold stand out more effectively—it was used on the heraldic emblems incorporated in the façade and as background foil to the capitals and lions. White lead paint was applied to the tops of arches, to the cornice, to the reliefs of flowers and vines, to the "string course" running across the façade above the ground-floor arches. Black paint further set off these white features.[4] The Venetian love of color enriched Renaissance artifacts in ways we find it hard even to imagine.

PLATE XIV
Ca' d'Oro façade

TOMBS: MOCENIGO FAMILY

Another place where the nobili could indulge themselves was in family tombs, raised in churches heavily endowed by the families that were rewarded with space for family burials. These were private, not state, projects. If there are a number of doges memorialized in the more ambitious tombs, that is because families took pride in members who had reached that office—the size of the monument often reflects family commitment more than any achievement of the particular doge. Families had at one point been allowed to erect chapels for their dead doges in the atrium or baptistery of San Marco—never in the church itself.[5] But that practice was discontinued, and the fate of each doge's memorial was left to his family.

FIG. 30
Pietro Lombardo,
Tomb of Doge Pietro
Mocenigo

Sometimes what is celebrated is not the dead man's performance as doge, but something he did before reaching that office. A good example is the tomb of Pietro Mocenigo, who was doge for less than two years (1474–1476), but had a more glorious career beforehand than did his brother, Giovanni, whose equally large tomb is nearby, and who served as doge for seven years (1478–1485). The inner entrance wall of the Church of Saints John and Paul is reserved for the Mocenigo family, since close family ties with a religious order (in this case the Dominicans) earned prominent display in their churches. Pietro was remembered for exploits with the fleet, which staved off Turkish advances year after year.

Although Mocenigo was not the victor in any major battle, he conducted raids all over the Aegean, collected much booty, and had his fleet at the right places at the right times so as to keep the Turkish armada bottled up at Constantinople and to enable Venice to win control of Cyprus without any fighting. After four and a half years of continual service, Pietro Mocenigo returned to a hero's welcome and in 1474 was rewarded with election as doge. (L 359)

The booty he won at sea was the source of the money that raised his monument, as the monument itself declares in a large inscription: EX HOSTUM MANUBIIS ("from spoils of foes"). Reliefs of trophies at the bottom of the work make the same point graphically.

Pietro's wall tomb is the first and best of the Mocenigo works of funerary art on this wall. Completed by Pietro Lombardo and his sons in 1481, it was recently restored, and it stands resplendent in the light from the high windows at this end of the nave—

though it lacks the pigments and gilding that animated its surface when the Lombardo artists completed it. The ornamentation of the luxuriantly foliaged arch was originally picked out in gold and green. The restorers found many traces of pigment, especially in the eyes of the various statues (P-H 2.422). The doge himself, represented standing on his own casket, was holding a standard with his ensign flying from it—which explains the way his cloak is thrown back on his right arm and then regathered with his left one.

This work of the early Venetian Renaissance is basically a Roman triumphal arch; but touches of older Venetian tradition remain, especially the way a row of statues runs up along either side of the arch. This reflects the construction of great altarpieces with rows of painted or sculpted saints flanking the central scene. A trace of that tradition is seen, as well, in the Porta della Carta, where statues of the virtues stand in side niches. On the Mocenigo tomb, the rows of three soldiers arranged in their separate arches on either side of the arch were initially climaxed with free-standing statues of the patrons of Venice, Saint Mark and the warrior-martyr Saint Theodore—but these were removed to decorate the tomb of a later Mocenigo doge (Alvise), a tomb that surmounts and surrounds the entrance door.

The inclusion of the lesser-noticed patron Theodore strikes the right military note for this iconographically complex assemblage of fifteen (originally seventeen) statues and seven carved reliefs. Even the risen Christ, who stands above the whole ensemble, had a political meaning in the Venetian empire (see Chapters 15 and 16)—and Christ's statue, too, once held a victor's standard (vexillum) in his hand. This should qualify the judgment of Ruskinians that the Jesus on top, standing above a relief of the Marys at his tomb, is just a pious gesture added incongruously to an entirely secular work.

Even the reliefs of Hercules' labors, carved at the basement level of the tomb structure, continued a religious tradition in Venice, where two of Hercules' labors were placed on the façade of San Marco itself—a symbol of Christ's defeat of evil forces, as Erwin Panofsky argued.[6] The Mocenigo tomb is limited to two labors in its basement story—Hercules' conquest of the Nemean lion, to the left of the trophies reliefs, and his conquest of the Hydra to the right of them. Reliefs on the sarcophagus above celebrate two of Pietro's actual victories. On the left, he comes to the relief of Christians besieged by Turks at Scutari in Albania (1471). On the right, he hands over Cyprus to its Venetian queen, Caterina Cornaro (1474).

The sarcophagus with these reliefs is held up by caryatid statues representing the three ages of man, that favorite Venetian theme, to symbolize Mocenigo's service as young diplomat, mature warrior, and sage doge. (Compare Titian's painting of the three ages with their characteristic virtues.) By variation of statue sizes and poses, through-out the chastely relieved architecture that was Pietro Lombardo's trademark, the tomb achieves an astonishing combination of massiveness and delicacy, of Renaissance form and Gothic feeling. It is both monumental and airy. The dead warrior is integrated within a politico-religious system that is both a replication and a renovation of the Venetian myth.

TOMBS: PESARO FAMILY

Though the Dominican church of Saints John and Paul has more doge tombs than any other, the Franciscan church of St. Mary of the Friars (Frari) was the other preferred place for ostentatious burial. This is not surprising, since the mendicant religious orders built huge churches meant to draw people from all parts of the city to hear their star preachers. Since these basilicas existed outside the network of parish churches, they had no geographical boundaries assigned to them—though they stood far apart, on different sides of the Grand Canal, each at some remove from its rival. Families that had branches scattered about through several parishes could unite their resources in a Mendicant church, instead of creating smaller parish monuments.

There were many patrons of the Frari, but something like the Mocenigo dominance of the west end of the nave of John and Paul is to be found in the Pesaro family's promi-nence on the side walls of the Frari's nave. And there was one spacious precinct that the Pesaros commanded entirely—the sacristy to the right of the east end. This large room, originally sealed behind a gate, was the burial chapel of Pietro Pesaro's wife, Franceschina, an heiress of the great Tron family. Though her tomb in the floor is a modest one, the real memorial to her is the 1488 tryptych Giovanni Bellini painted for the family over the sacristy altar (T 136–38). This shows four saints in attendance on the Virgin, and they are chosen because they are the name saints of Franceschina's husband (Peter) and three sons (Nicholas, Mark, and Benedict).

Like many of the works done for the Franciscans' church, the painting pays special homage to the friars' favorite doctrine (over which they fought with its Dominican deniers)—the Virgin's Immaculate Conception (her entire exemption from original sin). The inscription in the mosaiced apse of the painting's fictive architecture is taken from a liturgical office composed for a feast of the Immaculate Conception, and Bene-dict holds his Bible open to the chapter of Ecclesiasticus that has a text supposedly referring to the Immaculate Conception.[7] Bellini collaborated with the frame maker, Jacomo da Faenza, to make the frame's gilded columns match those of the shrine where

Mary sits in the painting. We know this is a shrine, not an enclosed church, since we catch glimpses of landscape on either side. Bellini wants the impossible structure to be open to a flood of soft light from the left, making the scene both naturalistic and transcendent in its radiance.

The most compelling of the four saints is Benedict, not only because (to us modern viewers) he looks exactly like Sean Connery, but because he alone in the picture looks directly out at us, with an imperious challenge. This was appropriate for Benedetto Pesaro. Though he was still a young man when this picture was commissioned (and so could not have been the model), he was the most energetic and successful of the three ambitious brothers. At a time of peril from the Turks (1500), Benedetto was made special commander of the fleet (*generalissimo del mar*), and sailed off to a rapid series of victories in the Ionian islands. With a decisiveness worthy of the Benedict in Bellini's painting, he beheaded those Venetians who had not been firm enough in defense of the islands he had to recapture, even though one of the men executed was a close relative of the reigning doge, Lorenzo Loredan (L 360). Benedetto died at sea in 1503.

Not surprisingly, Benedetto was the brother who received a grand tomb at the entrance to the sacristy dedicated to his mother. The sacristy door is turned into a triumphal arch, with Benedict standing in a pedimented balcony above it. He is flanked by nude statues of Neptune and Mars (anticipating by half a century the use of the same gods on the Scala dei Giganti to signify conquest by land and sea). The architect-sculptor Lorenzo Bregno put two reliefs of the islands recaptured by Pesaro on the base of his statue—Cephalonia and Leucadia. The gilt and painting of the tomb are still dimly visible. The golden armor under Benedetto's cloak must have been particularly striking, along with the reliefs of golden galleys against *verde antico* seas, their two gold islands set in porphyry backgrounds.

VOTIVE PICTURES: THE PESARO FAMILY

Another form of patrician display was the commissioning of votive pictures, those that show the patron at prayer before God, the Virgin, or the saints. One of the earliest votive paintings done by Titian (c. 1512) was for a cousin of Benedetto Pesaro, and it commemorated one of the battles (Leucadia) that was celebrated on Benedetto's tomb. Jacopo Pesaro, though himself a Venetian patrician, was the warrior bishop who, as legate to Rome, had been put in command of the papal fleet that collaborated with Benedetto against the Turks. Each cousin felt the other was less responsible for victory than he, and Jacopo chose to emphasize his separate contribution by showing himself with the pope thanking Saint Peter for the victory won by *papal* ships (W 1.152–53).

Jacopo did this despite the fact that the pope he served was the notorious Alexander VI, the Borgia Pope, who was hated in Venice for the way his son, Cesare, used papal land forces to wrest terraferma cities from Venetian control. The profile of the Borgia Pope is taken from Pinturicchio's fresco of Alexander praying to Christ at the

Resurrection in the Borgia apartments of the Vatican—so Jacopo must have brought back to Venice a print of that painting (the profile is reversed as in a print) to serve as Titian's prototype. Jacopo is defiantly holding the rose-colored flag of the Borgias. Peter sits on a pedestal with classic figures in relief, a sign that Rome, unlike Venice, was founded on a pagan past. This past has become a platform for supporting the keys of the kingdom of God, which lie at the platform's edge. The seascape behind the figures has the fighting galleys of the force Jacopo led, and the bishop-admiral himself has just taken off the helmet that gleams in the foreground.

Not only did Jacopo call on Titian to paint this picture with Alexander VI (which was probably displayed in his home), but his family commissioned the same painter in later years to do a large altarpiece celebrating the bishop's victory at Leucadia, the conquest claimed for Benedetto on his tomb. The picture stands beside Jacopo's wall tomb, which is framed in the same architectural elements as the painted altarpiece. The painting is the famous Pesaro Madonna of the early 1520s (W 1.101–03), still hanging in its original site on the left side of the Frari nave—aimed, as it were, within firing distance of Benedetto's tomb on the other side of the church. Rona Goffen has shown how the family feud is captured in the conflict between Bregno's sculpture and Titian's canvas—a battle of the tombs, resembling the struggle of the monuments that pitched Rizzo's Scala, on one side of the Porta della Carta, against Sansovino's Loggetta on the other side.

In the Frari picture, two architecturally inexplicable columns offer counterpointed verticals to strongly slanting compositions—the Borgia flag on the left aligned with the slant downward, on the right, from the cherubs to the baby Jesus below, whose glance travels on, down the gesturing arm of Saint Francis (who stands in the pose from Bellini's *Ecstasy of Saint Francis*). Another strong diagonal crosses this one, moving up from the kneeling Jacopo through an interceding Peter to the Virgin, who gazes down on Pietro.

The commissioning family of Jacopo is assembled on the right of the picture, under Francis's gesture of blessing relayed from the Child. The family members, all male, are Jacopo's brothers and his favored nephew, Leonardo, the boy who looks out at us as if into a future that belongs to him.[8] His father is Antonio, so the saint behind Francis is Saint Anthony.

In this painting, Jacopo does not himself hold the Borgia standard. One of his soldiers does, and the soldier drags a captive Turk behind him as living spoils. Jacopo, the fighting bishop, is now in service to Mary, not to Peter (who merely serves as intermediary in the hierarchically structured painting). The negotiation of rights between cities, between cousins, between pious offices and patriotic achievements, was continually going forward in the patrician class of Venice. Yet in terms of political symbol and social fact, they all ended, as it were, in the same church. The solidarity of the patriciate was the basis for the serenity of the republic.

CHAPTER NINE

Notables
(Cittadini)

THERE WAS ANOTHER elite group in Venice, of about the same size as the first one, but of lower rank, unable to hold elected office. These were the *cittadini*, a term it is misleading to translate as "citizens." We think of citizens as the body of members in a polity. But the cittadini were a minority (about five percent) of the population of Venice, set apart by certain privileges. There were three classes of notables—one privileged by birth (*cittadini originarii*), and two privileged by long residence. The born notables could carry on trade in the imperial ships, with the city's exemptions from customs in various ports. Notables by residence could, after ten years, share all the privileges of trade within the city (*cittadini de intus*). After twenty-five years, they shared the full rights of originarii in international commerce, making them *cittadini de extra*. As these rules suggest, many notables belonged to the powerful merchant class, and some were very wealthy.

The Venetian caste system was not based on wealth, though it obviously overlapped with some rankings by possession. Since the patrician class was "locked in" permanently, *nobili* whose business affairs went poorly, or who suffered other family misfortunes, could become impoverished without losing their patrician status. Though the patriciate tried to rescue its own from dire straits—e.g., by giving them salaried government jobs—many of its members could not compete in business with the wealthier notables. One solution to this problem was intermarriage. If a noblewoman married a rich merchant, her financial status would improve, but children born of the union would not be patricians. If, on the other hand, a nobile married a rich notable's daughter, he not only had her (often substantial) dowry and her family's business connections, but their own children became patrician at birth.

There were other ways the notables' class could exercise influence on the government. Since some of the notables had superior education, they supplied the staffs of governing agencies and diplomatic missions, making them privy to state secrets. Their expert knowledge and advice could be enlisted in the making of imperial decisions. This bureaucracy of notables did not labor under the patricians' limited terms in office, so it supplied the institutional memory for many governmental operations.

> High-ranking secretaries, such as the four who served the Council of Ten, were the workhorses of government. They were often sent as representatives to foreign powers and as paymasters to the army . . . They knew the ins and outs of official procedure and how to lay hold of necessary files. Legislation by the Ten in 1514 stated that the secretaries were "the heart of our state." According to Bolognetti, secretaries entered affairs of government "hand in hand" with patricians. (F 46)

These claims do not overstate the role of notables. Though patricians supplied most of the high drama of politics and much of the raw courage of warfare, the notables gave Venice the shrewd continuities of risk and caution that explain its success—what William McNeil calls its "niggling effectiveness of official bookkeeping":

> The state was run like a business firm, with skilled clerks to keep the books, directed by magistrates who were themselves accustomed to working within limits set by debits and credits entered in a ledger . . . The result was a relatively high level of rationality in distributing and redistributing state-managed resources . . . (McN 72–73)

But the main activity of notables—as the method of categorizing them by trade privilege shows—was as merchants. They had to be given the trading privileges of patricians so that the latter could tap into their wealth for commercial projects. One of the joint trading forms in Venice was the *colleganza*, in which a partner with smaller capital supplied something else—family connections, commercial information, or labor (like sailing with the ship carrying the partners' merchandise and negotiating its foreign disposition)—to earn an equal share of the profit (L 138–40). Shakespeare picked up a vague awareness of such contracts in his source for *The Merchant of Venice*. In that play, Bassanio is a nobleman down on his luck who undertakes the trip to Belmont to woo an heiress with funds advanced him by Antonio. It is a colleganza, with Antonio as the merchant venturing capital and Bassanio as the impoverished noble undertaking the labor of travel and negotiation.[1]

SOCIAL BROTHERHOODS (SCUOLE)

Besides the means so far mentioned for a notable to gain prominence and influence—the bureaucratic and commercial means—there was another path to fame closely associated with the activity of patricians: benevolence. Pious and/or patriotic bequests earned public recognition and gratitude. Many of these charitable works were individual; but some of the more spectacular acts of charity were performed by groups in which notables were prominent, guilds, parish associations, or "brotherhoods" (scuole)—especially the six scuole singled out as distinguished (scuole grandi), authorized by the government to take part in the official processions that articulated Venice's constitution in choreographic form.

These major clubs had begun in the thirteenth century with three scourging brotherhoods (scuole dei battuti), which performed the public penance of self-flagellation for the city in times of plague or other misfortune. By the sixteenth century, these clubs numbered six, and their civic service had become less that of public penance (though some formal gestures were made in that direction) than of social work for the poor. The clubs were preeminently the sphere of notables. No patricians could hold office in the scuole grandi—nor could priests, despite the religious nature of their activities. These scuole had begun as lay organizations with small quarters granted them in large monastic or pilgrimage establishments—which is why they kept the term "lodging" (albergo) for their boardrooms after they had moved out and built their own ambitious headquarters.[2] The clubs' government mimicked the offices and bureaucracy of the republic itself. The highest official of each distinguished club, the Guardian Grande, was allowed to wear luxurious sleeves patterned on those of the doge.[3] The clubs not only provided charitable activity for their own members and others, but performed such patriotic duties as raising military recruits in an emergency.

Each club became a kind of mini-Venice. As the republic formed itself around the relic of Mark's body, of which the doge was the chief caretaker, so the "guardian" of each scuola tended its precious relics, which were taken out for local or citywide processions.

As the public palace of the city celebrated itself in narrative paintings around the chamber of the Larger Council, so the clubs commissioned narrative cycles for their alberghi. St. Mark's Distinguished Brotherhood, for instance, had Saint Mark's ring, which it paraded every Sunday around the campo of the local monastery-church, Saints John and Paul, before taking it into the church to be enthroned during the Mass.[4] The

PLATE XX
Jacopo Tintoretto,
Paradise

PLATE XXIV
Jacopo Tintoretto,
Crucifixion

Doge's Palace has Tintoretto's vast painting *Paradise* behind the dais at which the doge presided. The clubs had similarly ambitious works proclaiming the dignity of their officers—e.g., Tintoretto's huge *Crucifixion* behind the dais of the albergo in St. Roch's Club (Scuola di San Rocco). The republic's rulers encouraged these arenas for middle-class display, as safe vents for ambition that might otherwise aspire to the patriciate itself. When the clubs vied with one another to put up ever grander headquarters, the city subsidized the effort by exempting a club temporarily from some of its charitable duties or by allowing it to swell its membership in a fund drive.[5] In the processions graced by the doge, the major clubs deployed ambitious floats with tableaux vivants or mini-dramas, both secular and sacred, that became the highlights of the parade.

At times the expenditure on great celebrations and showy headquarters cut into the charitable work of the clubs, and the government had to admonish them. In 1541, Alessandro Caravia caused a major sensation when he published a satirical poem, "Caravia's Dream," attacking the major clubs, and especially St. Roch's, for wasting on showy columns and staircases the money that should have gone to the poor. The scuola seems to have taken the message to heart, and it was soon administering major bequests for the advantage of the needy throughout the city, not just for club members, including these:

1. Income from four scattered estates was set aside for the poor.
2. Poor girls not in the club were given dowries.
3. Five buildings were constructed to house ten families of the poor.
4. Four blocks of housing for the poor were put up on the island of San Giorgio Maggiore.[6]

Civic purpose was measured by benevolence, even in clubs where social prominence was also being sought.

TOMMASO RANGONE

Perhaps the easiest way to suggest what services and honors a citizen could aspire to in Venice is to look at several notables and the mark they left on Venetian art. Of these, the most flamboyant was probably Tommaso Rangone (1493–1577). Rangone was born in Ravenna, educated at Bologna, and did not reach Venice till he was thirty-five years old, yet he was knighted by one doge and declared Champion of Religion and Defender of Virtue by another.[7] The Guardian Grande of a major religious club was supposed to be a cittadino originario, yet Rangone held that highest office in two of the six distinguished brotherhoods (St. Mark's and St. Theodore's) and was reelected twice in one of them. Honorary medals were struck to celebrate him, and three Venetian structures had his statue on their façade. His reputation was international, and the Emperor Maximilian II made him a Palatine count.[8] He exemplifies the three main ways a citizen could be active in and for the city—bureaucratic, commercial, and benevolent.

His *bureaucratic* contribution began as a physician to the Venetian fleet in the Turkish war of 1534. He had experience in such affairs because of his earlier service under a wealthy general (*condottiere*), Guido Rangone, whose name Tommaso took instead of his own (which was Giannotti). He stayed on in Venice after the war in 1534, a consultant to the republic on hygiene (an important subject in the lagoon), the plague, and syphilis (a timely matter in this city with a reputed eleven thousand prostitutes). Since he had taught successfully in Rome, Bologna, and Padua before coming to Venice, he became a lecturer on anatomy in the city, and founded a school for Venetians and Ravennans in Padua. His *commercial* success, in investing the properties won from his many patrons in and outside Venice, can be measured by his immense *benefactions*—gifts to churches, convents, and scuole.[9] A prolific author on scientific subjects, he was famous for his how-to books. The most popular were *How Venetians Can Always Stay Healthy* (1565) and *How a Man Can Live More than 120 Years* (1556)—though the plague killed him when he was eighty-four. His library of learned volumes and rare manuscripts, which was called "miraculous" in its day, he left along with his scientific instruments to the Redentore monastery on Giudecca.[10]

While Rangone was clearly an ingenious, industrious, and ingratiating man, he is famous today mainly for his vanity, since his life was one long campaign of self-promotion, a campaign that succeeded in being memorable because he recruited to it three great artists, the architect Jacopo Sansovino, the sculptor Alessandro Vittoria, and the painter Jacopo Tintoretto. When Rangone donated a new façade to his parish church, San Geminiano, he tried to have the architect, Sansovino, put his (Rangone's) bust on it, but the government forbade this, since San Geminiano faced on the Piazza San Marco, where no individual could be celebrated—so Rangone had the bust (by Vittoria) put on the church's rear façade.[11]

This was a small beginning for Rangone's self-celebration. The next step was to put a new façade on another church he patronized, San Giuliano, which fronted on the busy street (Mercerie) connecting the Piazza San Marco with the Rialto. Sansovino again supplied the façade, but his apprentice Vittoria created the bronze sculpture for the lunette over the door.[12] This lunette reflects all Rangone's achievements (and pretensions). By a skillful linking of low relief with a fully rounded statue, it puts in sculptural terms what was a commonplace in painting—the scholar's study.[13] And it does this in combination with a regular Venetian device, the funeral casket on which the spirit of the figure inside stands (in this case sits) looking as he had in life. The small

FIG. 32
Jacopo Sansovino,
San Giuliano façade

casket in this case is symbolic, an indication that the real tomb is (or will be) inside the church Rangone was providing for his own burial during his lifetime. He often planned for posthumous fame, as when he planned the triumphal funeral procession to this church, in which Sansovino's model of the church would be borne ceremoniously along.[14]

The left side of the San Giuliano lunette reflects Rangone's terrestrial concerns. He is holding on this side a botanically correct healing herb, the sign of his medical practice, though the globe and the books indicate his interest in other earth sciences, which are inscribed in the panel flanking the door column on this side: geography, hydraulics, topography, and cartography. The other side of the lunette is devoted to celestial matters. On this side he holds a tablet with astrological signs—concentric spheres, a lion (the constellation Leo, Rangone's birth sign and one favorable to the Lion City) and a dragon (the sign Draco). A sphere of the heavens balances the globe on the other side, and it also bears astrological signs, Leo (again) and Libra. Here the panel flanking the column names the subjects of books we are to imagine in the chest on this side: cosmology, astrology, astronomy, and theology.[15] Rangone holds all these things in balance, as if weighing the things of earth against those of heaven—and he is turning away from the former and toward the latter.

The third work of sculpture presenting Rangone on the façade of a religious structure was over the porch of a convent he patronized, that of the Holy Sepulchre, where he was given the form of a standing statue of his name saint, the apostle Thomas. As we shall see, it was not unusual for people to be painted as their name saint in votive pictures. Rangone's greater stretch after fame, here, was his memorialization in the form of a statue.[16]

Rangone was as eager to be preserved on canvas as in bronze or marble. Tintoretto had created several portraits of him, and when Rangone became Guardian Grande of

St. Mark's Distinguished Brotherhood in 1562, he commissioned for it three large paintings by his favorite painter, ensuring that he would be included in the sacred scenes. His motive was timely: he had just been made a knight of the republic by Doge Giovanni Priuli, and he wanted to be portrayed in the reddish cloth-of-gold robe this honor permitted him to wear. He would be prominent, swinging out the voluminous sleeves of this garment, in all three of Tintoretto's pictures. He was so proud of this mantle that he later donated it to the scuola on the condition that it be carried in public processions with the repeated cry, "Hail to the famous Knight of Ravenna, defender of the poor!"[17]

The subjects for these paintings posed a problem. The ordinary cycle of Marcan histories had already been covered (by Gentile Bellini and others) in the normal place for such narrative sequences, the scuola's boardroom (albergo). Admittedly, Tintoretto had already created, in 1548, an extra-canonical image of Mark for the large meeting hall of the scuola; but that work, *The Miracle of the Slave* (P-R 2.157–58), had initially been rejected by the club, as too eccentric in its iconography. Now Rangone was proposing to commission three more paintings, outside the normal treatment of Mark, done by a man suspect to the club's other officers. Rangone overruled the resisters of his plan by paying the painter out of his own pocket, not from scuola funds. This, he believed, gave him the authority to make Tintoretto include him, and no other member of the club, in the paintings.

This was unprecedented. It was customary, in these club paintings, to show the scuola as a body present in meditation at the scenes represented in the paintings. Tintoretto, for instance, had put a group of the San Rocco members in the left corner of his great *Crucifixion* for that club's albergo. Titian had done the same for members of the Scuola Grande della Carità, in his *Presentation of the Virgin*. But Rangone did not want to share the spotlight with anyone else, and he said, in effect, "I *paid* for this microphone" to broadcast his own merits. He obviously caused resentments that festered for some time, breaking out years later. In 1573, a decade after Tintoretto's three paintings had been installed in the scuola's meeting hall, the board sent them off to Rangone's home, indicating that they were his property, not the club's. Rangone refused to accept them, saying he had commissioned them only for the club. So now the scuola's officers dispatched them to Tintoretto's workshop, saying they would accept them back only after the artist had painted Rangone out of them.[18]

Tintoretto did not have to deal with this ultimatum, since Rangone soon regained favor in the club, where he was re-elected Guardian Grande. The favor to him, however,

PLATE XXIV
Jacopo Tintoretto,
Crucifixion

PLATE XXX
Titian, *Presentation of the Virgin*

FIG. 33
Jacopo Tintoretto,
*The Rescue of
Saint Mark's Body*

was never extended to Tintoretto, who was not invited to become a member of the club, even though he was a cittadino originario, and Rangone himself was only a notable by residence. (The Bellini family of painters, themselves cittadini originarii, were honored members of St. Mark's Club.) Given this stormy background of the three Tintoretto paintings, it is interesting to see how Rangone's inclusion in them affected their meaning.

Since the standard episodes of Mark's life and his body's transfer to Venice were already covered in the albergo of the club, Tintoretto was forced to stay with unusual iconographical schemes, like that of his controversial *Miracle of the Slave*, in the meeting hall. That is clear in the first picture, *The Rescue of Mark's Body* (P-R 2.183–84), which today's viewers can too easily equate with the capture of the relic for transport to Venice. But the painter goes back to an earlier and obscure part of the saint's legend, in which pagans were about to burn Mark's body immediately after his martyrdom. A miraculous rain doused the pyre's flames, and Christians were able, under cover of the storm, to bury his body secretly.

FIG. 34
Jacopo Tintoretto,
*The Identification
of Saint Mark's Body*

In Tintoretto's work, the pagans scurry for shelter as a mysterious rain sweeps the plaza. Rangone, directing the Christians, seizes the body of Mark—Tommaso's position at the head of the naked corpse resembles that of Tintoretto himself in the *Deposition from the Cross* he later painted for San Giorgio Maggiore. There is a subtler tribute to Rangone, as well, in the structure at the end of the dramatically foreshortened plaza of the picture—its lower part echoes the Sansovino façade of San Geminiano (known to us from prints) that Rangone had wanted to decorate with his own bust. Thwarted in that endeavor, he has his gift to the church celebrated here.

The subject of the next picture presupposes the story of Tintoretto's first one. Since the body of Mark was hidden, finding it becomes a problem. The Venetian merchants who went to steal it from Alexandria are shown in *The Identification of Mark's Body* (P-R 2.184) lowering various corpses from the mausoleum in Alexandria. Their escape route is being held open with a torch at the far end of the vault while they frantically open tombs (the dramatically shadowy scene evokes their tense mood). Mark himself has appeared as a spirit lit miraculously in the foreground, indicating that the outstretched body is his, the contrast between his strong vertical figure and the body's foreshortened horizontal lines marking the difference between eternal life and temporal death. In a test common for verifying true relics, the body is miraculously curing a man with the plague (its mark is on his forehead), who is under the care of the kneeling Rangone, that spe-

FIG. 35
Jacopo Tintoretto,
*Saint Mark
Saving a Turk*

132

cialist in plague treatments. The woman distraught by the plague victim's suffering may be the wife of a club member who was healed by Rangone (with Mark's blessing)—which would then be the occasion for this odd treatment of the legend.

The third picture (P-R 2.185) deals with a late legend of Saint Mark.[19] When a Turkish ship with Venetians aboard is hit by a storm, the Venetians scramble into the boat's skiff while the Turks stay with their ship until it is sunk. One of the Turks bobbing in the waves calls out to Saint Mark, who comes shining over the water, plucks him from the sea and deposits him in the skiff. Rangone is shown dipping his gorgeous sleeve into the water to pull up another Turk, and gesturing to the miracle as a way of converting the endangered Saracen—a reference to Rangone's Christian apologetics. It may well be questioned who is getting more credit in this stunning series of paintings, Saint Mark or Ser Tommaso.

ANTONIO MILLEDONNE

Though Rangone was effective at putting his face and form all over Venice, there were many citizens more powerful than he who were art patrons on a less Madison Avenue scale. One of these was Antonio Milledonne, who held many positions in the higher bureaucracy—secretary to the Senate; aide to ambassadors in Rome, France, and Trent (where he wrote a journal of the council being held there); secretary to the Council of Ten. On two occasions he came close to being elected lifelong Chancellor, the highest post for any notable.

FIG. 36
Jacopo Tintoretto,
*The Temptation of
Saint Anthony*

He wrote political and devotional treatises. Books were dedicated to him, and a biography written of him.[20] He endowed his own funeral chapel in the Church of San Trovaso, for which Tintoretto painted his name saint, Anthony of the desert (P-R 2.208), giving the desert hermit Milledonne's features (according to the latter's biographer).

Four devils tempt Anthony in the painting, three of them taking the form of beautiful women, the fourth a devil with horns, tail, and whip. Stationed two on either side of him, these spirits tear Anthony's clothes from him in a crisscross pattern that represents the tug and pull of wealth (the golden chain on the left side of the picture) and lust (the fire in the bowl on the right side). The saint twists himself up in fierce vertical resistance to these horizontal strugglers, and looks only to the Lord, who flies toward him with comfort and strength. Eternity rises up through temporal efforts to hold it down. In this way Milledonne's spirit is represented, escaping the clinging attractions of fame and political office.

ANDREA ODONI

The paintings that indicated a notable's prominence did not all have to be commissioned for the churches, hospitals, or monasteries. Andrea Odoni was a rich merchant and famous collector of art, books, and scientific specimens, who generously opened his

FIG. 37
Lorenzo Lotto, *Portrait of Andrea Odoni*

house to those who wished to view his collections. They would also see there the painting he commissioned from Lorenzo Lotto, where he puts himself on display in the midst of his treasures. Since he holds a statue of the idol Diana of Ephesus, critics for years tried to work out whether he was praising the classical art around him, as opposed to the fertility goddess in his hand, or vice versa. It was only during a recent cleaning, for the 1997–98 exhibits held in Washington and Bergamo, that restorers uncovered a literally crucial detail that had been covered over in a 1952 restoration—a tiny gold crucifix held between the fingers of his other hand.[21] This shows that Odoni was keeping his multicultural objects at some distance from the thing closest to his heart, the sign of the Savior. Religion and learning are put in the proper balance by this quiet profession of his inmost belief. The counterpoise of the two hands is a chamber-music equivalent of the dramatic-oratorio spread of hands in Rangone's statue on the lunette of San Giuliano. Each man is weighing the value of temporal and eternal things.

Thus notables upheld their values, public and private, in a world where their status could not be eclipsed by that of the patriciate.

FIG. 37
Lorenzo Lotto, *Portrait of Andrea Odoni*

CHAPTER TEN

Golden Youth

I PLACE HERE, between the notables and the commoners, those patrician males who had not reached the age of twenty-five and put on the black toga of severe duty. Those young patricians were privileged, of course. They were destined to be the rulers of their world. But before they were burdened with military and civic offices, their public role somewhat resembled that of notables in their brotherhoods and commoners in their guilds. Like them, they formed voluntary organizations, bodies without direct political authority—though, like them, they were under regulation by the state. The principal voluntary organizations for these young bloods were the stocking clubs, or *compagnie della calza*—groups that peacocked about in semitheatrical costumes, with elaborate identifying badges on their cloaks or sleeves, and a distinctively designed bit of hosiery on one (the right) leg.

The touch of theater in their apparel was appropriate, since the young were given a period when they could be "slumming" with professional actors and musicians, arranging for them to put on elaborate shows at feast days, weddings, and—especially—diplomatic receptions. The young could be allowed to patronize less dignified forms of art than did their patrician elders. They adopted favorite "buffoons," like the popular acrobatic clown Zuan Polo.[1] They mounted the entertainments called theatrical masques, or "mummeries" (*momarie*), and called on famous artists to design the sets or build the pavilions on which they were mounted. Vasari and Palladio built such *tribune* for them.[2] We shall see that they had a special relationship with the painter Carpaccio.

The clubs' processions, plays, banquets, and mock battles, put on for the marriages of their members, evaded some of the sumptuary limits placed on families of the spouses—though the state could step in when the clubs' competitive displays became too extravagant. Authorities took a special interest in the entertainment of foreign dignitaries by the clubs.[3] This was a convenience for the state, which nonetheless had to make sure the ceremonies were not offensive. Since private meetings with foreign representatives were forbidden to the city's rulers, the young men could admit them informally into the social ceremonies of the place. Important young foreigners were even allowed to become honorary members of the clubs during their sojourn. In the process, the young patrician hosts were exposed to international relations and Venice's role in the world.[4]

The clubs came and went according to the economic conditions of the state and of the members. There were at least forty-three clubs recorded—and no doubt more that went unrecorded—between the middle of the fifteenth and the middle of the sixteenth centuries.[5] They tended to take high-minded names (the Ardent, the Modest, the Eternal) or pastoral ones (the Gardeners, the Horticulturalists). Rules of the club had to be drawn up and submitted for approval to the Council of Ten, after which an inaugural Mass launched the club's active life. A slate of officers was elected, and fines were imposed for infraction of the rules. An echo of the republic's governing principles could be found in the existence of a council meant to check any misconduct of the highest officer, the prior.[6] A minimum of upkeep for fine clothes, and for donation to joint ceremonies, was exacted, limiting membership to the wealthy—with the expectable result that some rich notables had to be admitted on occasion, and at least one club for notables only (the Faithful) was authorized.[7]

Since diplomatic embassies and noble weddings were the clubs' special province, it has been convincingly argued that the clubs played a leading role in the ceremonies, stretching over more than two decades (1468–89), that ushered Caterina Cornaro out of Venice and back in again, with initially giddy, then nervous, insistence on her dignity. Caterina is known by the Italian form of her name, not its Venetian-dialect form (Corner), because of her prominence in international relations. Her family had long-standing connections with the island of Cyprus, a Crusader kingdom whose ruler, James of Lusignan, succeeded in driving out of the island's eastern port the Genoese rivals of Venice. He formed an alliance with Venice to keep defying Genoa. In 1468, Caterina's uncle (Andrea) and her father (Marco), friends of the king and agents at his court, persuaded James that he could seal his alliance with Venice by marrying Marco's fourteen-year-old daughter.[8] Caterina, still in Venice, was promoted by the doge to the new title of "Daughter of Saint Mark," to make her marriage one with the highest nobility of the city. She was formally wed in a long-distance ceremony marked by great festivities— Venice had its first queen. Given the unsettled state of James's realm, it was four years before she departed to join her spouse—and the sailing was another occasion for great pageantry. The doge in his ceremonial ship escorted her out of the lagoon, with accompanying boats decorated for the occasion.

Caterina arrived in Cyprus in October 1472, her husband died in June 1473, and the son born shortly after his death did not live long. Without a husband of the ruling line or a legitimate heir to it, Caterina was vulnerable to multiple plots by rival claimants to her throne. She had to turn to Venice for protection, though that made her resented as the puppet of a foreign power. She resisted manipulation herself, but she also needed the protection Venice could provide. By 1489 the Venetian government, finding it too clumsy to rule through her fragile claim on the throne, forced her return to Venice and took over the island outright. Her embarrassment was covered with a show of pomp celebrating her return, and she was given the little "kingdom" of an estate at the foot of the Alps, in Asolo, where she held court for the twenty years left of her life, entertaining artists in the salon that Pietro Bembo memorialized with his *Asolan Dialogues (Gli asolani)*.

The return of Caterina was linked with the action of a brotherhood devoted to the martyr Saint Ursula, as can be seen in the interknitting of these dates:

1. October 1488: The Council of Ten decides to recall Caterina.
2. November 7: Her brother is dispatched to Cyprus on this mission.
3. November 16: The Scuola della Sant'Orsola, which has close ties to Cyprus through its members in the Loredan family, decides to remove the Loredan tombs lining its scuola walls, and to paint on them a narrative cycle devoted to the brotherhood's martyr patron.
4. June 5, 1489: Caterina returns in a riot of pageantry.
5. September 1490: Carpaccio completes the first painting in the Saint Ursula cycle.

What makes these dates significant is the fact that Carpaccio's paintings play up the resemblance between the myth of Ursula and the life of Caterina, whose career had been watched with fascination by Venetians over the years, a career reaching its climax just as the paintings were begun. Ursula, too, was betrothed in her youth to a foreign prince, after negotiations carried on by a kind of "shuttle diplomacy," with ambassadors traveling back and forth between England and Brittany. She too delayed her meeting with her spouse, and when the two were joined they met trials and disaster, in which the husband was killed first, before her own martyrdom. Though Caterina was not killed, her sufferings and the exile from her realm made her a martyr to power in many people's eyes.

Caterina's piety was famous—she was shown holding a rosary and accompanied by her train of women in Gentile Bellini's 1500 painting for the Distinguished Brotherhood of Saint John the Evangelist—*The Miracle at the Bridge of San Lorenzo.*

Modern scholars—given these links among Loredan (Cypriot) politics, Loredan piety in the Brotherhood, and membership of young Loredan men in the stocking clubs—now explain the large role played by these golden youths in the Carpaccio series by supposing, plausibly, that those clubs had been very active in the ceremonies that marked Caterina's marriage, dispatch to Cyprus, and return to Venice. Such embassies and dynastic marriages were precisely the arena where these clubs shone. Michelangelo Muraro and Ludovico Zorzi go so far as to think the paintings are based on actual mystery plays, masques, or momarie performed by the clubs.[9] Other scholars hesitate to make Carpaccio such a literal transcriber of ceremonies; but they honor the way Muraro and Zorzi have alerted all later writers to the thoroughgoing theatricality of the Ursula cycle. Françoise Bardon, Vittorio Sgarbi, and Giovanna Nepi Scire have drawn selectively on the Muraro-Zorzi thesis, to great advantage for their own work, on which I am relying here.[10]

Carpaccio began the actual painting near the end of the story, with a relatively small painting (Number 6 below) and with the altarpiece at the end of the chapel. This was no doubt because he was working (in the altarpiece) above the altar already in place, and with the first space opened up as the Loredan tombs were being dismantled. But I shall treat the pictures in their narrative sequence, not the order of their execution. The story begins on the viewer's right, as one stands at the far end from the altarpiece (the opposite of the modern entry at the Accademia). The pictures on one's right are all diplomatic—the tale of the embassies that led up to Ursula's wedding. This profane half of the story is given ampler treatment than the separate episodes on the religious (or mystical) left wall—which is the privileged *right* side as one looks from the altar, a fact that confirms that the present order is the correct one. Carpaccio dwells on the leisurely diplomatic procedures because this is the part of the story that most resembles the life of Caterina, and it emphasizes the part played in her ceremonies by the stocking clubs. The picture at the far end of the hall—under which one would have entered—is the largest of them all. It forms the connection between the profane and sacred walls as a kind of bridge, and it appropriately shows Ursula and her fiancé spanning the distance between their two countries. The scene is, proleptically at least, a wedding celebration, and the stocking clubs knew how to signalize such an event. Now I follow the paintings around the room beginning near the altar on the right side:

1. *The Marriage Bid* (s 82, c. 1496). The English (Anglian) king has sent emissaries to ask that Ursula, the young daughter of King Maurus of Brittany, be wedded to his son, Ereus. The reception hall in which Maurus is throned resembles no diplomatic chamber in Italy. It is a shallow free-standing structure, open to the weather on three sides and with the bedchamber of Ursula inexplicably stuck on at the right. It has rightly been recognized as the kind of ornate pavilion the clubs had prominent architects raise for their specially grand festivals. The only logic that could "bring on" Ursula's bedchamber for its use in the story is stage logic.

The theatrical ambiance is confirmed by the figure standing at the extreme left of the picture (and almost out of it). He serves, as did the narrator (*festaiuolo*) at momarie as a personified prologue, or "introducer." His pointing finger cannot be interpreted with any confidence because the picture has been cropped on the left side, as happened to many large canvases when they were moved to tighter quarters. The shadow thrown along the left edge of the picture comes from a missing column that matched the

"orphaned" candelabrum column, which stands on the ground (another architectural anomaly that indicates an ornamental, not a functional, structure).[11] The pointing finger must have drawn attention to something in the picture's lower left corner— something like a symbol of the scuola, or the crest of the Loredan family, or a signature by Carpaccio. In line with this latter possibility, Rodolfo Palluchini suggested that the prologue figure is a self-portrait of the artist.[12] Luca Signorelli put himself in just this

FIG. 38
Vittore Carpaccio,
The Marriage Bid

FIG. 39
Vittore Carpaccio,
*Sending the Marriage
Terms*

position at the entry point to his *Last Judgment* sequence in Orvieto (1500–1504—just the years Carpaccio was working on the Ursula cycle). Zorzi objects that the toga is that of a *patrician* in ceremonial red garb, suggesting that the patron is pictured here.

The young man standing just to the left of the candelabrum-column has on his right leg an ornate club-*calza*. And in the very center of the picture, the youth leaning on the far railing has on his sleeve the prominently displayed emblem of the Ortolani stocking club.[13] He is observing the proper procedure of emissaries to a foreign ruler, the kind exacted from ambassadors meeting the doge: They advance from the chamber

FIG. 40
Vittore Carpaccio,
The Terms Accepted

entrance by making three genuflections as they approach.[14] Though King Maurus favors this alliance with Anglia, he either knows or will find out soon that Ursula has objections to it. The small scene at the right may represent what is going on in the king's mind as he conducts the public ceremony.

Ursula is ticking off her conditions, in the gesture that artistic convention gave to those making logical argument—Pinturicchio's Saint Catherine uses it (in the Vatican's Borgia apartments) to count off the arguments against the pagans with whom she is engaged in dispute. In the Ursula scene, there is comedy in the king's resigned air as she tells him what must be, perhaps reflecting the difficulty Venice's rulers had in getting Caterina to take their direction. The woman seated on the step leading up to Ursula's chamber, if she is her nurse, must also be expressing resignation to the ways of her strong-willed mistress.

In the legend, Ursula makes four demands before she will wed Ereus. First, she must fulfill her vow to remain a virgin for three more years. Second, Ereus must spend those three years preparing for his baptism as a Christian. Third, her father and the Anglian king must give her a train of ten virgins, and assign to each of them a thousand other virgins. Fourth, ships must be prepared to carry this large company on pilgrimage.[15] (The usefulness of this story, insecurely anchored anywhere from the third to the fifth century C.E., was that it explained the vast number of virgins' relics made available by the martyrdom of so large a company.)

2. *Sending the Marriage Terms* (s 92, c. 1496). King Maurus is on the left of this picture, though he is on the right in the flanking ones. This follows a left-to-right logic for the direction of the ambassadors' journeys. Maurus is receiving messengers from across the British Channel in the other two pictures. Here he is *sending* one over the Channel. He submits Ursula's conditions to be taken to Anglia. A scribe records the transaction for the archives. The principle of variation makes this picture an interior scene, comparatively private, as opposed to the open-air ceremonies on either side of it—a musical rest between two scenes of pomp.

Yet touches of theater are present even here. The figure in the doorway to the right is directing with a hand gesture the rest of the diplomatic delegation, which is "off stage" on the right (we have before us a train with only two genuflections, not three). And the young boys incongruously present at this private communication of officials have been thought to be performers at a celebration for the visitors, conning their parts (s 92).

3. *The Terms Accepted* (s 88, c. 1496). It is generally accepted that the scene shifts, here, to the Anglian king's court. Though the features of the seated monarch resemble the ones in the first two pictures, he seems to grimace with discomfort. Why would that be the case for the Anglian king, who has sought this alliance in the first place? Ursula's father, on the other hand, is just realizing that his daughter will be taken from him on a long pilgrimage with her Anglian spouse. In the next picture, where the couple is about to depart on that journey, Ursula's mother has tears streaming down her face. It has been objected that Maurus, who has a crown in the first two pictures, is now wearing a *bareta*—as if that would indicate a change of personnel, introducing the Anglian king. But the bareta is what Venetian patricians wear.[16] Maurus himself is wearing this Venetian bareta in the very next picture.

And that picture shows us what Anglia is like—a country rocky in landscape, medieval in architecture, just as rough as this cycle's Brittany is smooth. The present picture clearly takes place in Venice-"Brittany." Zorzi, one of the few who thinks this picture is still in the kingdom of Maurus, points out how Venetian is its style, with the Doge's Palace crenellations and the Codussi window traceries on the large building by the water, with balustraded Paglia Bridge and the Arsenal's towers in the background.[17] Ursula's homeland was an imagined Venice in all the pictures on this wall of the scuola.

Those who think this picture is in Anglia suppose that the ambassadors are returning there with Ursula's conditions. Why should that end the process? Obviously the Anglian king has to accept those conditions, and report his acceptance to Ursula's father, before the story can proceed. *She* is the focus of the story, and the return of the ambassadors puts the seal on what she has accomplished. We are in the world of the stocking clubs. The man seated on the left, with the great baton, is a *scalco* who beats with it to mark divisions in the ceremony (s 88).

FIG. 40A
Detail of *Ursula United with Ereus* by Vittore Carpaccio (PLATE XVI)

The little violin player is the kind hired by the stocking clubs, one of whose members has dressed in a turban for his part in the pageant (we see his *calza* peeping out below his wrap). Another youth with an elaborate *calza* on his right leg is approaching the smartly dressed figure with his back to us, who holds a document that has been called the "script" for this ceremony.[18] The monkey in senator's dress lends a touch of carnival. The pavilion, or *tribuna*, is the kind the stocking clubs raised for their outdoor entertainments. The crowds that have waited at the embankment for the sleek ship that brings the diplomats is celebrating Ursula's accomplishment. This brings to a happy end the profane sequence on the south wall, to be contrasted with the premonition of suffering that begins the sacred sequence of the north wall, leading to her martyrdom and burial.

4. *Ursula United with Ereus* (s 78, 1495). This large canvas gives us four episodes in a single image. The episodes occur in two countries (and in the English Channel between them). The leading male character (Ereus) undergoes four costume changes, the leading female (Ursula) three. The different time zones are marked by the fact that the many flags and pennons (just try counting them) are whipped by winds from different directions. On the left we see Ereus parting from his father in Anglia, leaving a pagan

PLATE XXVIII
Vittore Carpaccio,
Vision of Saint Augustine

FIG. 41 (BELOW)
Vittore Carpaccio, *The
Dream of Saint Ursula*

land with no churches within its massive military walls and towers. In the rowboat that will take him from the pier are two young men ready to conduct him, one wearing on his shoulder the emblem of the Zardinieri stocking club, which shows a sun breaking through clouds. The emblem contains the initials FZ (*Fratres Zardineri*) and AS (*Amicorum Societas*). Though we do not see the legs of the man standing in the boat, he too presumably belongs to the Zardinieri, which had important members from the Loredan family, the historic patrons of the scuola. The standing man holds a scroll with an acronym saying that Nicholas Loredan commissioned this painting to the honor of the virgin saint Ursula.[19]

On the other side of the great standard dividing the two countries, Ereus arrives in a rowboat from his ship, and Ursula is there on the pier to greet him. Then the two are blessed by her parents. This is not an actual wedding scene. There is no clergyman, and Ursula must die a virgin—she is still testing Ereus with the pilgrimage he must make with her. In the background on the right, she and Ereus, now wearing their traveling clothes, are in the boat that will take them out to the convoy carrying the whole company of virgins to Rome.

5. *The Dream of Saint Ursula* (s 74, 1495). An angel comes bringing the palm of martyrdom to Ursula. We see what she is dreaming. There was always debate about the placement of this picture. She departed for Rome with her fiancé in the last scene, yet she seems back at home here, alone in her Venice-Brittany house with its Murano glass windows, not in some pilgrim's hospice. On the other hand, the crown at the foot of her bed seems to indicate she has married the prince Ereus. On the last point, *The Golden Legend* seems to be dispositive: the *martyr's* crown is prominently mentioned three times in the brief entry on

her. Though the angel appearing to her bears one symbol of martyrdom, the palm, that does not preclude the use of another martyr symbol.

The placing of this scene in the narrative sequence is thematically right. As the only painting with a single (human) subject, it introduces the inward meaning of Ursula's life, as opposed to the external pomp of the scenes so far displayed. From this moment, she will be carried along with the pilgrims toward the death now being foretold. The angel enters in a flow of light over the bed. We know it is a supernatural light because natural light is entering from the opposite direction in the small cabinet in the rear of the picture. Early engravings show that the painting has been trimmed on both sides. The word on Ursula's pillow, *Infantia*, has lost its initial letters. It cannot refer to Ursula herself as an infant—she is, after all, four years beyond her betrothal, when she was already a clear-headed young woman. Sgarbi makes the brilliant guess that Ursula-Caterina sleeps with the mournful memory of *Caterina's* child, lost in its infancy (s 74).

FIG. 42
Vittore Carpaccio,
*Ursula's Arrival
in Cologne*

This painting, like Carpaccio's *Vision of Saint Augustine* for the Dalmatian Brotherhood, is a high point in the painter's "magic realism." The very literalness of detail makes the prayerful hush of the scene more powerful. The angel is wearing the fashionably ballooned male garb of the International Gothic style still prevalent in Venice.[20] The slippers are placed as neatly as the crown, keeping ordinary life and mystical symbol on a par. The bedchamber of this virgin is like that which the angel enters in Annunciations to the Virgin Mary—but she is allowed to lie in the bed, which serves as mere backdrop for the Annunciation scenes. The importance of the bed in the composition—its great length spanning the picture, islanding Ursula off from the mundane life around her—must account for the anatomical absurdity that puts her feet so far off from her head. The expanse of bed (greater before the picture was cropped to the left) would dwarf her if her body stretched only so far as nature would allow. The toes obey laws of composition, not of anatomy.

6. *Arrival in Rome* (s 72, 1493). The long train of Ursula's virgins winds in from the horizon while she kneels in a cluster of mitres, with the humanist Ermolao Barbaro (in red toga as an official at the Curia in Rome) playing the role of commentator on the scene. Castel Sant'Angelo in the background establishes the locale. The mythical pope Cyriacus is so overcome by Ursula's piety that he resigns the papacy (to an equally mythical successor) and joins her on her pilgrimage. (*The Golden Legend* neatly explains the absence of these popes from the official list by saying that the Curia was so angry at Cyriacus' action that it expunged their names.)

7. *Ursula's Arrival in Cologne* (s 64, 1490). This, the first picture painted in the sequence, shows the long caravan of ships maneuvering into the harbor. In the lead ship, Ursula and the pope (still wearing his triple crown though he is supposed to have resigned) peer out warily. They have reason to be wary. Treacherous Romans have sent word ahead to the Huns, who are besieging Cologne, telling them to kill the religious troublemakers. The man who delivered the message sits near the pier, with his bow across his knees, this traitor juxtaposed with a dog, the symbol of fidelity. (Why has the pope joined a trip to *Cologne?* Ursula had to end up in Cologne, the traditional site of her martyrdom—in *The Golden Legend*, she was going to meet Ereus there.)

8. *Martyrdom and Burial* (s 68, 1493). While others are being cruelly slain by the Huns, their leader, Julius, hesitates to use his sword on Ursula because he has been smitten by her beauty. A bowman (clearly the same traitor who brought the message) steps in to kill her with an arrow. In the second half of the picture, Ursula is given a formal burial in Venetian style. These first scenes painted are not as well composed or executed as the later ones—they are also less well preserved.

9. *Ursula in Glory* (s 66, 1491). Ursula stands on a weird victory column made up of all the virgins' martyr palms, bound together by a belt made up of burning cherubs' faces—not the happiest of the painter's inventions.

The golden youth of Venice had many spectacular triumphs of an ephemeral sort, pavilions thrown up overnight and disappearing just as fast, great shows put on by Zuan Polo, musical greetings to famous foreigners, chivalrous service to Caterina Cornaro when she left Venice and when she came back. But only Carpaccio took their dutiful exuberance and made it into something permanent, the essence of their festivals frozen in time and fixed on canvas.

CHAPTER ELEVEN

Commoners
(Popolani)

THE THIRD CASTE in Venice made up ninety percent of the populace. Like the other two castes, it was not an exclusively economic category. There were wealthy *popolani*, just as there were poor *nobili* and *cittadini*. That is why the caste was roughly divided between a "weighty" group (*popolo grasso*) and a "slight" one (*popolo minuto*). There was not even a sure distinction between trades, in terms of wealth. Some artisans could be or become as wealthy as some merchants. Guilds were supposed to be brotherhoods of equality, but Dennis Romano has demonstrated that the wealthier masters found ways to keep themselves apart from their workers (R 77–90). Yet, oddly enough, this inner division of single groups helped them cohere with other groups up and down the social ladder. Each was a kind of Venice in miniature, with overlapping structures. The commoners aped the other two castes, in their family discipline, their social-insurance groups, their religious ceremonies, their benevolent activities (R 50–64). The commoners not only had guilds, but minor brotherhoods (*scuole piccole*) with the same functions that the distinguished clubs performed—charitable activities for members in need of dowries or burial funds or other care; religious ceremonies in honor of a patron saint or special feast day; votive offerings for the group's prosperity. The guilds (*arti*), with their trades (*mestieri*), were, for most purposes, identical with their scuole.

Most of the commoners, as a result, had multiple ties with others in the "network of networks" that was Venetian social life. In terms of religion, for instance, one person had many bonds with different groups in the city's fluid life—with the parish of his or her (or the spouse's) birth; with the parish of current residence (where baptism and other sacraments were received); with parishes of family burial; with the church, hospital, or monastery where one's guild met; with the mendicant church where one heard the famous preachers of the day; with the sacred site of the moment where one went for urgent prayer requests; with the celebrations of parish, club, sector (*sestiere*), or whole city. Venetians were recruited for military service largely by sector, parish, or scuola—which bore some responsibility for wounded veterans or for the children of men killed in action. The city itself took over some of these duties when other means failed (R 216–29).

The result was a cohesion in smaller groups, which were porous to reciprocal intrusion. It was noticed, earlier, that patrician families did not have enclaves around fortress palaces, but spread their members through the city. To some degree even popolani escaped confinement in a single space. Though the trades tended each to have a street (*ruga*) where they displayed their wares and did their business, artisans were often moved to other districts, where they had contacts through members of their family, scuole, business associates, or military companions. Many workers had to move about often—e.g., all the many kinds of boatmen, craftsmen engaged in the building trades (who went where construction was occurring), and food distributors. We have seen that the parishes were woven together into a citywide entity in the Feast of the Marys. Though that was trimmed back drastically during the Chioggia War (1379), Edward Muir argues that the patterns of thought instilled by its long tradition perdured (M 154–55). Venetians of all classes threaded their way through each others' lives and living space. Sometimes initiatives arising from the popolani could reshape the civic environment—most spectacularly, perhaps, in the building and adornment of that architectural gem, the Church of the Miraculous Mary (Santa Maria dei Miracoli).

SANTA MARIA DEI MIRACOLI

This church did not begin as a church, and it existed outside the monastic, mendicant, and parish organizations. Nothing caused the project to arise, or to be expanded, but the people's demand for a site to honor a wonder-working painting of the Madonna. That picture had originally been displayed in a niche on the outer wall of a home in the parish of Saint Marina, where it had become a favorite spot for people to stop and pray to the Madonna. There was talk of prayers answered over the years, but the breakthrough occurred after August 23, 1480. On that day a woman coming back from court, where she had testified against her brother-in-law, stopped to pray according to her custom. While she was praying there, the brother-in-law came along and beat her senseless. But when people came to her rescue and revived her, all her wounds had disappeared (C-P 620). Her torn and bloody clothes were left before the image as a thank offering—the first of many such ex-votos that would pile up in front of the painting. There were forty-four miracles attributed to the statue in that first year of 1480, seventy-one in 1481, thirty-eight in 1482 (C-P 628). Since the crowds drawn to the picture clogged the street, its owner, Angelo Amadi, moved it into the courtyard of his palazzo, but allowed the public to have access to it there, where clergy from the nearby parish church sometimes celebrated Mass before it.

As devotion to the picture continued to grow, permission was sought for the patriarch to give it a permanent chapel of its own. It was put in temporary housing while a competition was held for the design of the chapel.

> Neither the State nor the Church had commissioned it; the funds came from the unprecedented donations made by the local gentry and devotees of the miraculous picture. For years past and years to come, no other church in Venice would be able to draw on such generous sources, or be so independent of the economic realities distressing the State. (McA 155)

In 1481, the design competition was won by a simple building of brick, sheathed with rich stone panels. The modesty of the plan made the commissioners content with the meager site on which it was begun. When a small contingent of Franciscan nuns was brought to the site to keep vigil before the picture, a house across the narrow lane from the church had to be demolished, and an enclosed bridge was created to let the cloistered sisters cross over the lane from the second story of their convent to the choir loft of the church.

Pietro Lombardo was chosen to put up the building according to the model—which was apparently not his own design. Lombardo, the head of a carving and gilding clan, was known at this point less for his architecture than for ornamental carving, but it was felt that he could raise the low rectangular building originally envisaged—it was just the first story of the nave of the present church, without a chancel (the raised sanctuary) at the end. But funds and offerings kept rolling in, and in 1485 Lombardo's commission was broadened to include a second story for the nave and the addition of a chancel. The fame of the picture had spread to Rome, whence the Franciscan Pope Sixtus IV gave indulgences to those praying before it. He demanded that the chapel be dedicated to Mary under the title Franciscans were defending at the time, the Immaculate Conception—the doctrine upheld, as we have seen, at the principal Franciscan church in Venice, the Frari.[1] The chapel was growing into something grander.

Since parts of the church were added higgledy-piggledy to the first plan, the parts do not fit together in architectural logic. The classical "orders" of the outside pilasters are not in the proper vertical sequence. The pilasters of the ground floor were given Corinthian capitals, since this was going to be the only floor. When the second floor was added, there was nothing to do but use Ionic capitals, in a "forbidden" upward progression from more ornate to less. The arches of the two orders do not support anything, or even pretend to, since they end short of the level above them. The walls are only two inches thick, so there was no pretense of structural solidity. When the new contract called for a vaulted roof on the nave, Pietro could not construct a real one—the walls would not bear it—so the richly coffered "vault" is in fact a floating wood structure suspended from the real roof.[2] That outer roof, a near-semicircle of wood with lead tiling, would itself push the walls apart if tie bars across the nave were not added to hold them together.

Inside, the patterns of bays, windows, and coffers are not coordinated—each just runs along to its own pattern. "Everything seems as though bought by the yard, piecemeal, and then laid up haphazard, in rhythmically unrelated layers" (McA 164). Yet this very irrationality and insubstantiality lend the building its magic. It is a suspended dream—and was much more so when the original skin of rare stones was still in place. Deterioration of the stones—e.g., from floodwaters absorbed up into the brick core and leaking out through the precious sheathing—led to their replacement over the years, and the recent restoration can only partly recapture the iridescent colors of original materials like *cippolino* ("onionskin" stone), *zebrino* ("zebra-striped" stone) and *paonazetta* ("purplish" stone).

When Pietro had to add the chancel at one end of the nave, the cramped site left him no room for a sacristy, so he had to place it under the altar space, lifting the sanctuary up from the nave floor, and this new area had then to be topped with a high dome to escape the confines of the nave's false vaulting. All these necessities worked serendipitous wonders. The miracle-working picture was given a high place of honor under a serenely floating dome. And all the relief carvings of the column bases, capitals, and moldings were created by the Lombardo masters in a riot of rich imagery. McAndrew points out that the playful mermaids and mermen and other creatures who frolic between the sanctuary columns' feet and their bases are defiant of structural reality, as if the columns floated on a vision of fairy sprites. The creatures' separate world was originally set off by gilded strips above and below it.[3]

The present chaste simplicity of the interior—with no side aisles or altars or supporting columns in the nave—is partly the effect of later changes. An organ originally stood in the balustraded place above the sacristy. The organ shutters, when closed, displayed paintings of the angel and the Virgin of the Annunciation (by Giovanni Bellini's workshop—the panels are now in the Accademia). A supposedly ancient frieze was on display (now in the Archaeological Museum). The organ was moved to the choir loft when the nuns' bridge was destroyed and they no longer chanted the office there. By the seventeenth century the nave was lined on both sides with tombs and votive altars—witness to the ongoing popularity of the magic image, which people wanted to be buried near or pay homage to. This pious lumber was not cleared away until the late nineteenth century.

MINOR BROTHERHOODS (SCUOLE PICCOLE)

Though it was rare for popular clamor to raise a beautiful new center of devotion like the Miracoli, the trade guilds and other *scuole piccole* did have votive altars in parish churches or elsewhere, and some of them were prosperous enough to build their own headquarters. Tourists now circle around one of these on their way from the San Tomà boat landing to the Frari church—it is the small building in the Campo San Tomà where the guild of cobblers (*calegheri*) met. Antonio Rizzo's relief of Mark curing a cobbler's cut hand is on the façade, and the Younger Palma's painting of the same event—now in the Accademia—used to be on the inside. A grander scuola piccola was that of Saint Ursula—we have already looked at Carpaccio's Ursula series for it. By the seventeenth century, many trade scuole had impressive buildings.[4]

But during the Renaissance most of the scuole piccole—there were roughly a hundred of them—met at votive chapels or altars in churches or monasteries or hospitals. Almost every church in Venice had one such guild site, and some had as many as four or five.[5] In the artifacts the various trades commissioned to honor their own altars, the guilds showed the same combination of piety and patriotism that the major brotherhoods did. They expressed devotion to Saint Mark, to the Virgin, to the Eucharist, as well as to the special patrons of their calling. Many scuole were formed that had no guild or trade restriction—for instance, the many clubs of the Blessed Sacrament (Scuole del Sacramento), devoted to keeping the altar where the Eucharist was preserved. Tintoretto painted a whole series of eucharistic pictures for these scuole (see Chapter 16). Marian clubs distinguished themselves from each other by concentrating on different feasts of the Virgin—her Presentation, or Annunciation, or Visitation, or Purification, or Assumption.

Many guilds commissioned depictions of their patron or favored saint. The rich Merchants' Guild (Scuola dei Mercanti) indicated its dependence on sea trade by having Lorenzo Lotto paint Saint Nicholas, the patron of sea voyages. The bargemen (*Scuola dei Peateri*) had Tintoretto concentrate on the running waters of the river Jordan in his Baptism of Christ for their altar in San Silvestro (P-R 2.218). Peter Humfrey and Richard MacKenney assembled a list of fifty-six known altarpieces created for the trade guilds, and there were undoubtedly many more that cannot be traced at this remove in time.[6]

The presence of heraldic arms in some of the paintings shows that nobili could belong to the scuole piccole—just as they could donate to the building of Santa Maria dei Miracoli. But ordinary workmen, too, could belong to them, and hold office—even the highest office (*gastaldus*): "A wool shearer was gastaldus of a scuola at the Frari, a tailor was gastaldus of the scuola of San Giacomo, a cobbler was a gastaldus of the scuola of Sant'Agate, and a schoolmaster [rector scolarum] was gastaldus of the scuola of Sant'Angelo" (R 112). What is more astonishing, given this period in Italian history, was the presence of women in the scuole piccole (in contradistinction from the scuole grandi). They were auxiliary members, but that meant they could elect their own leaders of the women's branches, handle their own money, and make their own decisions. "Costanza, widow of a furrier, was deaconess of the scuola of Santi Pietro e Paolo in the parish of San Polo. Maddalena, a gold-thread spinner, was *gastaldatrix* of the scuola of Sant'Angela. Margarita a Zolonibus was *gastalda* of the scuola of Santa Fosca, and Pasqua was deaconess of the scuola of Santa Clara" (R 112).

Though the scuole, like most aspects of Venetian life, were regulated by the state, which had to approve their charters (*mariegole*), the field they opened for members' ambition, distinction, and participation was very broad. These organizations were flexible to many purposes, social, civic, religious, professional, and military. The very fact that the cittadini and popolani could not elect or be elected in the general government gave them more independent life, in some ways, than Florence's fewer guilds, which were more tightly integrated into ruling structures.[7] This led to subdivision of the pullulant Venetian scuole into many varied activities. Romano's study of the popolani lays great emphasis on the consequent networking function of the scuole piccole:

> For individuals from a variety of social backgrounds, the scuole provided a sense of identity with a group of people with whom they might otherwise have had little in common. The confraternities brought together people from different backgrounds and from different parts of the city and allowed them—in moments of ritual behavior—to dispel differences of wealth, kinship, and power that in their everyday lives

kept them apart. For the popolani the scuole provided opportunities to exercise power and enjoy prestige. Devotion to the saints and concern for the dead allowed early Renaissance Venetians to set aside their differences and come together in a spirit of sacred community. (R 112)

The charitable offices of the scuole are exemplified in the will of the painter Vincenzo Catena (1531—Titian was one of the members of the painters' guild charged with executing the will): one hundred ducats were left to poorer guild brothers, another one hundred ducats to provide dowries for members whose daughters had none, and the rest of the bequest to purchase land for a guild headquarters—which was accomplished by 1532.[8] When a guild neglected its charitable or egalitarian duties, the state could force it back into line. In 1511, the painter Cima da Conegliano tried to change the makeup of the painters' guild board, to favor the "figure painters" over lowlier brothers like painters of masks and shields and miniatures. The government rebuked him and maintained the constitutional balance of the guild.[9]

I do not mean to idealize the social participation of the popolani. It is fashionable now to say that the degree of social concord in Venice has been overstated—which is undoubtedly true. There is never an earthly paradise. But the stability and cohesion of the Venetians are what struck contemporaries, both friendly and hostile observers. Those were the qualities that stood out on further acquaintance with the place, and not only because of the contrast with a more raucous and riven social atmosphere in other Italian cities. What may be wrong is not so much the stress on Venetian "serenity" as the explanation for it. It used to be attributed to the planned or fortuitous machinery of the city's institutions. But institutions, good or bad, work only if you want them to work. And the motive for maintaining the solidarity of the Venetian project did not come from lack of unrest or from perfect devices for controlling it. It came, as much of all social esprit does, from the sense of mutual need in a situation of peril. The Venetians were performing a high-wire act, and they knew it. Usually safe at home, they were never secure there.

The lagoon city was an exotic, in perpetual need of food and supplies—timber for its ships, access for its trade, the respiration of a larger air than the lagoon could provide. It needed precariously balanced and always shifting alliances to prop up its imperial holdings. Though the home base was solid, all its diplomatic and commercial and military outworks had a Tinkertoy fragility and interdependence of the parts. The base *had* to be solid because the far-flung outworks that rested on it were so vulnerable.

People cooperate with vigor, follow leaders, coordinate their efforts, when they act from a sense of shared danger and reciprocal need.

American presidents who are considered great were usually presidents in a period of crisis—war, depression, international pressure. They are great because the urgency of others to cooperate against peril *made* them look great. A man at the tiller of a boat can make it respond in a second when the winds are high. In a calm, he can work the rudder back and forth continually, yet accomplish little. Those of us who remember World War II know that, despite graft and corruption in the war effort, there was an unusually high degree of social mobilization—a willingness to comply, to accept discipline, to respond to calls for sacrifice. This is the mood that is missing from descriptions of Venetians as sybaritically content within their watery enclosure. Our momentary sense of threat in World War II was a continuing condition with them. We are deaf to the muted trumpet calls that trilled their way through all Venetian labors and celebrations. Patricians and popolani needed each other. Theirs was a nervous serenity, a steadiness under danger.

We can perceive this social interdependence in some of the period's paintings, especially those of Tintoretto, who was a favorite of the scuole piccole. The popolani are present and important in many of his works. He was, after all, the son of an artisan—a dyer—as his familiar name indicates (Tintoretto means "little dyer" or "tinterling"). Even in a scuola grande (San Rocco), his Virgin of the Annunciation (P-R 2.225) is more an earthy mother at her sewing table than one of Florence's porcelain-pretty Madonnas. Another picture in the same scuola warmly evokes the communal spirit—the *Adoration of the Shepherds* at Christ's birth (P-R 2.204). Here the shepherds are not a few lads from the hills offering a lamb as if for sacrifice at the Temple. A neighbor group has mobilized, with a sense of crisis, to care for the couple in a rickety hovel—who clearly need their assistance. A man on the ground floor of the barn is lifting a cloth-covered plate of warm food for Mary and Joseph. A woman in the loft with the couple is getting ready to spoon some gruel moistened with her own breast milk into the child's mouth. Three women and four men are coordinating all their activities to give much-needed succor. This is less an adoration of the shepherds than a rescue by them. The sacred family does not take pity on the poor. It needs the assistance of the poor. At their best, Venice's leaders recognized a similar need.

PLATE XXV
Jacopo Tintoretto,
Annunciation

PLATE XVIII
Jacopo Tintoretto,
*Adoration of the
Shepherds*

CHAPTER TWELVE

Women

ENICE WAS, LIKE ATHENS, a state of merchant-warriors. Commerce and rule, diplomacy and combat, were exclusively male occupations. Venetians did not quite say to their women what Thucydides makes Pericles say to his—"Your glory is not to fall below the level of a woman's nature, and not to be talked of among men, for good or ill"—but they came close at times.[1] For them, too, woman's place was in the home, and religious feasts were among the few public activities open to them—at least to the patricians among them. Looser rules applied to citizens and commoners. As we have seen, women of the citizen and popolani class could be officers of the scuole, and of course popolani women worked at many tasks. They were even employed in the high-security precinct of the Arsenal, where they sewed the canvas sails. In what we think of as the "higher arts," Carlo Ridolfi mentions five women painters who became well known.[2] There was also a surprising number of women writers who gained an audience despite male dominance of education—Isotta Nogarola, Cassandra Fedele, Modesta da Pozzo, Gaspara Stampa, Tullia d'Aragona, Veronica Gambara, and Irene di Spilimbergo (who was also a painter in Titian's shop).[3]

Naturally, there were also "working women" of the sort that show up in any port city—the number of prostitutes in Venice, said to be eleven thousand, shocked even those familiar with other entrepôts (F 15). Guido Ruggiero, who has specialized in Venetian sexual history, says that number is exaggerated, but the scale of the business was undoubtedly large.[4] This was a line of work that was open not only to Venetian commoners, but to foreigners, and even slaves. Like all other parts of Venetian life, it was heavily regulated, less as a crime in itself than to curb other crimes associated with it, especially in the foreign communities. But there were also high-class prostitutes, the so-called courtesans of repute (*cortigianne honeste*), of whom Veronica Franco was a famous example. Of *cittadina* status, she became an acclaimed poet with patrician protection. A celebrity herself, she was introduced to visiting celebrities, and even to royalty, as an ornament of the city.[5] Other courtesans were specialists in exotic sexual practice. Titian's friend Aretino the satirist has a courtesan in his dialogue *Six Days* give this menu:

> Some like it boiled, some roast. They have devised a way of getting in from behind— legs on one's neck, à la Jeannette, stork-wise, tortoise-wise, the church on top of the steeple, the browsing sheep, and other positions that are weirder than any acrobat's.[6]

Despite the success of some women writers, painters, or courtesans, political life was so barred to women that when an exception occurred—when, that is, the patrician Caterina Corner was made the queen of Cyprus in an external dynastic marriage—the city did not know what to do with her when she was recalled from her island kingdom. A strange creature like a woman ruler did not fit into the city's scheme of things, so she was given comfortable exile in her villa at Asolo.

The plight of patrician women is summed up in Carpaccio's famous painting *Two Women* (c. 1493–1495). Since sumptuary laws tried (ineffectually) to prohibit extravagance of dress among noblewomen, this painting was for a long time known as *The Courtesans*, but now it is more neutrally called *Due Dame*. There is a patrician crest on the vase with the lily stem, which prostitutes could not display. Moreover, scholars have noticed that all the objects in the picture symbolize married fidelity and chastity—the lily of virtue, the turtledoves of love, the myrtle of constancy, the peahen of simplicity, the orange of united sections, the parrot of outspokenness, the pearl strand of equable continuity.[7] The two canines display, respectively, the affection of the lapdog and the tenacity of the watchdog—the hound is literally guarding a scrap of paper caught under its paw. The assessment of the picture was also affected by the discovery, in the 1960s, that its companion panel, now in the Getty Museum in California, shows men with crossbows moving freely and easily about the lagoon as they hunt from boats. The lily blossom in the lower section of the Getty panel matches up with the lily stem at the top of *Two Women*. The boy in the latter work, once thought to be playing with the birds, could well be reaching for the message the dog has cap-

FIG. 43
Vittore Carpaccio,
Two Women

tured, which the boy just brought from the hunters to the women (s 100). The contrast between the two scenes—the sheltered and idle women waiting at home, the active men out dominating nature—is almost didactically proto-feminist in its sympathy for those left in their gilded cage.

NUNS

Another aspect of the patrician woman's plight is the convent. There were many communities of nuns in Venice, and they were disproportionately inhabited by patricians, many of them forced into the convent. There were more than forty convents in sixteenth-century Venice, and three-quarters of their inhabitants were patricians—an amazing number if we consider that the patricians made up roughly five percent of the population.[8] Women, as half of that five percent, made up less than three percent of the community at large, but seventy-five percent of the religious communities. Why did the upper class seem to have a monopoly on female piety? There were several reasons, of course. Poorer women's labor was often needed at home. They were also less likely to have the literacy needed for singing the liturgical office. Their families could not support the establishments as the patricians could. But the greatest reason, Jutta Sperling has argued, was the "dowry race" that consumed so much patrician energy in the late Renaissance.

Families of assured "nobility" had to marry advantageously to keep their financial rank up to their social one. This meant that poorer patrician women could be less desirable to patrician men than were the daughters of wealthy nonpatricians. These men could marry notables, since their children would be patrician; but patrician women who married outside their class could not beget heirs to the patriciate. They would beget rivals for their own class. For these and other reasons it was often not possible to find "proper" marriages for patrician daughters, even superfluous daughters of wealthy patricians, and the only other respectable life for them was felt to be devotion to the Lord.

Their consignment to a convent was presented to them as a matter of family duty, and even of patriotism. They were keeping up the honor of their class, to which they were supposed to be a pious ornament. Families would be more proud of a daughter in a convent, especially an abbess, than of a daughter marrying "down" out of her class. Even lesser dowries for such marriages would be "wasted" in terms of advantages returned to the patriciate—yet dowries for a "higher" marriage were either lacking or would deplete resources, in patrician families of limited wealth.

In 1580, Nuncio Alberto Bolognetti informed the pope, who was eager to have Venetian convents inspected for their compliance with post-Tridentine clausura [cloister] rules, that a stricter discipline in nunneries would deter many patrician girls from taking the veil, and that this would "cause the ruin of many families because of the excessive dowries noblemen usually give their daughters to marry."[9]

The government thus felt obliged to keep up the convent system, which seemed to relieve economic pressures on the patriciate, even though long-term consequences were bound to be damaging to it. Half of the class's reproductive population was removed from the scene: "Marriage strategies that encouraged women to marry 'up' but limited their choice of partners to a steadily diminishing pool of candidates aggravated the destructive aspects of the patriciate's 'war of conspicuous consumption' against outsiders and lesser members of its own class."[10]

Since deploying the religion of empire was part of the government's mission, it promoted and regulated (more of the former than the latter) the lives of women in religious orders. The sisters were integrated into the celebrations of the peculiarly Venetian saints and relics. Processions to historical convents were part of the annual calendar. We saw earlier how the wealthy convent of San Zaccaria gave the doge his crown. The state's relationship with the nuns of Santa Maria delle Virgini was so close that every newly elected abbess underwent a symbolic marriage to the doge.[11] When the city defied the pope during the period when he placed it under interdict, the convents stayed loyal to the city ruled by their relatives. The nuns were influenced by the religious values of Paolo Sarpi, who justified the morality of defying Rome.[12]

The nuns were not only supported by the government, but were able to exert influence on it, through family connections that were emphasized rather than minimized in fashionable convents, especially those of the Benedictines and Augustinians. A papal nuncio in Venice wrote back to Rome that "convents functioned as a kind of clearing house for political careers."[13] It is not surprising, given this situation, that Rome had trouble trying to impose reforms mandated by the Council of Trent. Despite promulgation of a papal rule that abbesses should be elected to terms no longer than three years, the doge defiantly installed an abbess with life tenure.[14] Enforcement of stricter cloister and austerity measures was taken over by the state itself.

But the state had difficulty regulating its own daughters. In 1619 the Venetian patriarch, Giovanni Tiepolo, argued that the state owed these women certain luxuries, since they were serving its interests under duress:

More than two thousand patrician women . . . live in this city locked up in convents
as if in a public tomb . . . they are noblewomen, raised and nurtured with the highest
delicacy and respect, so that if they were of the other sex, they would command and
govern the world . . . they have confined themselves within those walls, not out of
piety, but in obedience to their family, making of their own liberty . . . a gift not only
to God, but to the fatherland, the world, and their closest relatives.[15]

Under these conditions—where many were not present of their own choice, where
they came from pampered backgrounds, where they were able to exercise political
influence, where access to them was easy because of loose enforcement of cloister—
laxity and abuses were inevitable. Some convents became notorious as love nests.
Sant'Angelo di Contorta, a Benedictine convent of women from wealthy families, was
an egregious case.

The Avogadori prosecuted fifty-two cases of sex crimes involving nuns from the convent between 1401 and 1487. Some were even perpetrated after the convent was offi-
cially closed. Nonetheless, the convent's records suggest that there was a much higher
level of unprosecuted sexuality.[16]

Six of the nine most prosecuted convents in the fifteenth century were Benedictine.[17]
In 1497, a Franciscan preacher thundered in the doge's presence that "when some lord
comes to Venice, he is shown the convents of nuns, not convents as much as whore-
houses and public bordellos."[18] A preacher has license to exaggerate. There were many
women of piety, learning, and discipline behind convent walls. But a system that
imposed a way of life on so many women against their will was bound to function
badly. Sexual intercourse in such a context is a form of political protest. It was only by
depriving them of liberty that the city turned so many of its nuns into libertines.

MARRIAGE ART

If Carpaccio's *Due Dame* shows women literally "all dressed up with nowhere to go,"
other paintings of noble wives show them in a startling state of undress. Matrimonial
pictures present the bride as an erotic nude. Indeed, many Venetian pictures of a reclining nude Venus, once thought to be idealized portraits of courtesans, are now considered wedding pictures representing patrician brides.[19] Perhaps the most surprising
example is now at the Metropolitan Museum in New York. It was painted by that most

FIG. 44 (TOP)
Lorenzo Lotto,
Venus and Cupid

FIG. 45 (ABOVE)
Lorenzo Lotto,
*Marsilio Cassotti and
His Bride Faustina*

pious of artists, Lorenzo Lotto, who here seems to be a naughty artist. I have seen people at the Metropolitan stopped in their tracks with surprise at his *Venus and Cupid* (1542). The lush nude figure of Venus has the portrait head of an individual on it—a combination as surprising as the portrait heads of noble Roman matrons on statues of Venus. These were funerary statues that proclaimed the eternal womanhood of the deceased ancestor. The essence of feminine beauty was contained in the woman's life.[20] Lotto's Venus is a bride, not a deceased wife.[21] Lotto probably painted it for a relative while he was living with him in Venice in 1540 to 1542, and the relative was giving it to a friend as a wedding gift.[22] The symbols of fertile union are all around the nude woman—Cupid urinating through the ring of a bridal wreath to symbolize the wedding penetration, accomplishing the literal "deflowering" registered in the scattered petals below; a shell with its vivid vulva opening. Cupid is the impresario of this wedding, just as he is in Lotto's double portrait of *Marsilio Cassotti and His Bride Faustina* (1523), where he puts a yoke (*jugum*) over the conjugal pair.[23]

In Titian's famous and misnamed *Sacred and Profane Love* (w 3.175–80, 1514), the bride is literally two people, the historical woman in her bridal gown and the eternal Venus who is her double. It was a seventeenth-century catalogue that gave the painting the wrong name, apparently taking the commonsense view that the nude was the profane image of lust and the properly garbed lady was "sacred."[24] But in 1930 Erwin Panofsky wrote an essay claiming that the nude is a Neoplatonic embodiment of pure love and the clothed woman an earthly image of false adornment. This interpretation held the field for decades, though the heraldic emblem on the sarcophagus had been identified as that of Niccolò Aurelio as early as 1939.[25] When, in 1975, Alice Wethey thought she could see the family arms of Laura Bagarotto in the bowl on the sarcophagus, that seemed to prove that this is a painting of the 1514 wedding of Niccolò and Laura. Though the recent restorer of the canvas, Maria Grazia Bernardini, doubts the identification of the stemma in the bowl, collateral evidence collected by Rona Goffen indicates that the painting does celebrate the wedding of Laura, a rich young Paduan widow, to Niccolò, a Venetian *cittadino originario* in his fifties.[26]

PLATE XIX
Titian, *Sacred and Profane Love*

If the clothed woman is the bride, as her dress proves, then she can hardly be "profane love." Does that mean that the nude is profane love after all, to be renounced by the husband in favor of his properly clothed bride? Certain conventions might indicate that. The two sides of the picture follow convention for virtue-vice contrasts, the good on our left (the picture's own favored right side), the bad on our right (the picture's "sinister"). The steep hill of virtue is behind the bride, as is the taming of the horse (symbol of passion) in the sarcophagus relief. On our right, there seems to be a castigation of lust on the sarcophagus, and a copulating pair in the landscape. But the nude not only has the same features as the clothed woman. She looks with affection on her sister self. The intermediation of Cupid between the figures is symbolically erotic—he stirs the water that spurts from the pipe of the sarcophagus, a subtler version (Goffen argues) of the Cupid who "ejaculates" in Lotto's picture. The bride has a Venus within her, just as she had Venus' body in the Lotto. The quiet of the bride's pose, where no wind stirs the petals of her deflowering, is more complemented by than contrasted with the right side, where winds of emotion toss the flaming red cloak of Venus. Here, as Goffen says, chastity is not at war with erotic passion but reconciled with it by marriage. The fact that the figures are two aspects of the same reality is underlined by Titian's treatment of them as literal fact and emotional symbol. The bride is picked out in firm, sharp details. The patterns of her dress are as insistent as her calmly focusing gaze, or her collected and settled posture. Venus, by contrast, is softly molded, and she turns in the fuzzy slow motion of a dream ballet.

Goffen argues that Titian's *Venus of Urbino* (w 3.203–04, 1538), at the Uffizi in Florence, is also a wedding picture. The large chest (*cassone*) in the background is a frequent symbol of marriage, since it was a typical wedding gift, a container for items in the wife's dowry. Goffen also puts in words what Mark Twain said he was afraid to, that the woman is masturbating. Here is Twain:

> You enter [the Uffizi], and proceed to that most-visited little gallery that exists in the world—the Tribune—and there, against the wall, without obstructing rag or leaf, you may look your fill upon the foulest, the vilest, the obscenest picture the world pos-

sesses—Titian's Venus. It isn't that she is naked and stretched out on a bed—no, it is the attitude of one of her arms and hand. If I ventured to describe that attitude, there would be a fine howl—but there the Venus lies, for anybody to gloat over that wants to—and there she has a right to lie, for she is a work of art, and Art has its privileges. I saw young girls stealing furtive glances at her; I saw young men gaze long and

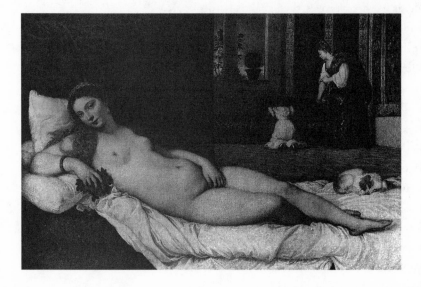

absorbedly at her; I saw aged, infirm men hang upon her charms with a pathetic interest. How I should like to describe her—just to see what a holy indignation I could stir up in the world—just to hear the unreflecting average man deliver himself about my grossness and coarseness, and all that. The world says that no worded description of a moving spectacle is a hundredth part as moving as the same spectacle seen with one's own eyes—yet the world is willing to let its son and its daughter and itself look at Titian's beast, but won't stand a description of it in words. Which shows that the world is not as consistent as it might be. There are pictures of nude women which suggest no impure thought—I am well aware of that. I am not railing at such. What I am trying to emphasize is the fact that Titian's Venus is very far from being one of that sort. Without any question it was painted for a bagnio and it was probably refused because it was a trifle too strong.[27]

FIG. 46
Titian, *Venus of Urbino*

Goffen points out that in the classical "chaste Venus" type, the Venus Pudica, the alert goddess puts her hand in front of her pudenda to bar others' invading gaze. But here there is no one she is sheltering her body from. She does not conceal herself from anyone, she "caresses herself" during her soft revery.[28]

But how can this be a *wedding* picture, if the woman is engaging in a solitary erotic act? The answer is that some medieval Christian theologians had made female masturbation a duty for the purposes of conception. The ancient medical writer Galen taught that a woman's orgasm releases female "seed," needed for successful conception.

So theologians concluded that for a woman deliberately to avoid orgasm was a contraceptive act, a sinful denial of her husband's right to an heir. If a woman did not reach orgasm during intercourse, it was recommended that she masturbate afterward in order to fertilize the male seed just deposited in her—Jean-Louis Flandrin, in a survey of medieval theologians, found that fourteen of the seventeen who discuss this matter approve the practice. Also, six of the theologians say that the ideal circumstance is for the partners to achieve simultaneous orgasm, which means that a woman can masturbate before intercourse if that gives her the "head start" needed to reach climax when her husband does.[29] Goffen argues that this is what the bride is doing here. Giorgione, the curiously learned painter who provided the model for Titian's reclining Venuses, had been the first to show the hand curled to touch the pudenda, and that indicates that his Ur-painting put the whole genre in the category of wedding picture.

This encounter with nudity where we might least have expected it, in painted epithalamia, calls for a reconsideration of Tullio Lombardo's high-relief busts of couples with bared breasts—one (c. 1495?) still in Venice, at the Ca' d'Oro, the other (c. 1505?) in Vienna, at the Kunsthistorisches Museum. Alison Luchs argues that it would be "indecorous" to show a respectable woman with naked breasts; but she was obviously not considering the evidence of the paintings.[30] Sarah Wilk seems on the right path when she finds models for Tullio's busts in northern paintings of married couples.[31] It is true that the Vienna pair identifies the man as Bacchus (since he has grape leaves in his hair), but the presentation of brides as Venus shows that a mythological reference is appropriate in wedding art. There is no mythical story suggested in the busts. It is the concord of the pair that is important. The nudity is not more daring than in Lotto's *Venus and Cupid*, which is unquestionably a wedding picture. Tullio's nudity would have been bolder than it seems now when the busts had their original color—traces of black have been found in the pupils of eyes, of red on the lips, of black

FIG. 47
Tullio Lombardo,
Bust of a young couple

in the background of the reliefs.[32] The white flesh of the bared shoulders and breasts would have stood out dramatically against this dark foil.

ROMAN LUCREZIA

The frank eroticism of this wedding art suggests that the Venetians had a highly charged romantic vision of marriage, especially in the patriciate. The small world of interlocking families no doubt thought, as all Italians did at the time, of marriage as a

familial property arrangement; but such a small world also had the ideal of noble women vying to display their sexual allure in its proper arena. The nude wedding pictures were not only a frank recognition of female sexuality but a model and reward for it. There was clearly a market for the work of Giovanni Marinella, a prominent Venetian physician and philosopher, who published *Women's Ornaments* in 1562, with the right formulas for dyeing hair blond, whitening teeth, and otherwise accentuating the attractions of women.[33] Marinella brought up his own daughter, Lucrezia, to be a learned poet. She proclaimed the dignity of women in her own book of 1600, *The Nobility and Excellence of Women and the Defects and Vices of Men.*

FIG. 48
Lorenzo Lotto,
Lady as Lucretia

Lucrezia based her claims for female excellence precisely on women's beauty. She cites the many male poets who had extolled the beauty of women, then produces Neoplatonist arguments that corporeal reality reflects ideal reality, making the beauty of a woman's body the sign of her exalted soul.

> The greater nobility and worthiness of a woman's body is shown by its delicacy, its complexion, and its temperate nature, as well as by its beauty, which is a grace or splendor proceeding from the soul as well as from the body. Beauty is without doubt a ray of light for the soul that pervades the body in which it finds itself, as the wise Plotinus writes . . . The greatest poets teach us clearly that the soul shines out of the body as the rays of sun shine through transparent glass. The more beautiful the woman, the more they affirm that it is her soul that renders grace and loveliness to her body . . . Divine beauty is, therefore, the first and principal cause of women's beauty, after which come the stars, heavens, nature, love and the elements.[34]

The fact that women did not have to wear the black toga of patrician males was a recognition of superior female status. Women wore colored fabrics, gold and jewels, while "these things are forbidden to men, apart from rulers."[35] Displaying a superb knowledge of literature, ancient and modern, Lucrezia discusses the hundreds of women who showed superior knowledge, courage, piety, and prudence. Among the brave she lists her namesake, the Roman Lucretia, who killed herself rather than suffer dishonor.[36]

That Lucretia was a symbol of female honor can be seen from Lotto's portrait of a Venetian patrician proclaiming her own standard of honor by holding up a picture of Lucretia killing herself. It is likely that the woman's own name was Lucrezia. The quotation below the drawing of Lucretia is from Livy, who describes Lucretia as dying with these words on her lips: "Let no woman live on in shame by appeal to Lucretia as a model." Some argue that the woman is a courtesan, since her dress is extravagant, her veil is pulled back, and her necklace is drawn down to expose her breast—but Peter Humfrey more plausibly suggests that she is showing herself as willing to bare her breast to the knife rather than suffer dishonor.[37] The gorgeous clothes, contrasted with the nakedness of Lucretia in the drawing, are like the collection of refined artifacts in Lotto's portrait of Peter Odoni—possessions he contrasts with the deepest value of his life, the crucifix he holds next to his heart. The woman in this portrait is prepared to sacrifice all the comforts of her undeniable status should her honor ever be at stake.

FIG. 49
Titian,
Tarquin and Lucretia

The popularity of the Lucretia story is seen in works of Titian and Tintoretto. Titian painted his work for Philip II in Madrid (w 3.180–81, c. 1568–1571) and it is not so much a defense of Lucretia's honor as, on the one hand, a study in the psychology of fear and, on the other, a rich play of textural contrasts—of the pillow, the flesh, the bed cover, the drapery, the layers of rich stuff in which Tarquin is wrapped. Lucretia is gazing in anguish directly at her attacker, who thrusts his knee between her naked thighs. The picture evokes all fear and pity for the helpless woman. There is no suggestion of the later episode, in which the intrepid woman kills herself as a public example.

Tintoretto's picture of the rape by Tarquin (P-R 2.229, c. 1585–1590) could not be more different. Here it is the woman's passionate defense of her honor that is dramatized. Lucretia, far from looking passively into the eyes of her rapist, has twisted her body around and braced her legs sturdily against the long vertical tug of Tarquin, whose paral-

lel arm and leg are dragging her body into the diagonal slant that dominates the picture. She has struggled so mightily that two of the female statues that serve as bedposts have been toppled (symbolic of her degradation). In Titian the piled pillows echoed the cushiness of Lucretia's body. Here the one pillow is caught in midfall, not yet having hit the ground—like seven of the pearls broken from her necklace and still raining to the floor. (The contrast is with the unbroken continuity of a pearl strand like that in Carpaccio's *Two Women*.) Lucretia has even knocked the knife out of Tarquin's hand, and its prominent position in the foreground reminds us of the use she will soon make of it.

FIG. 50
Jacopo Tintoretto,
Tarquin and Lucretia

As usual, Tintoretto does not rely on facial expressions to show the terror and anguish of the scene. It is all *danced out*, in the contrast between Tarquin's muscular strain and her softer but flailing effort against it. The calligraphy of zigzagging light on the silken bedclothes is a kind of turbulent musical accompaniment to the struggle. (The abraded right side of the painting is damaged beyond recovery of what counterbalanced the frenzied rustle of the bedclothes.) This Lucretia is a woman of courage as well as chastity, just the kind of woman described by the doctor's daughter who shared her name, Lucrezia Marinella.

CHAPTER THIRTEEN

Artists

T HOUGH WORKS OF THE GREAT Renaissance painters, sculptors, and architects are discussed throughout this book, this is a place for considering the artists' social status and working conditions, beginning with the fact that art in Venice was a *family* business. In Renaissance Italy, the artist was still an artisan, subject to guild regulations. But the craft guilds, like *scuole*, were more flexible in Venice than elsewhere, and the major controlling principle in an artist's workshop (*bottega*) was the family. This was especially true of painters' shops, but it applied also to sculptors and architects like the Dalle Masegne, Bon, and Lombardo families. Skilled assistants who did not begin as family members often married into the master's clan. This could even be a condition of full partnership. Jacopo Tintoretto's German assistant, Sebastian Casser, was tested for the quality of his work and only then allowed to become a full partner in the firm by marrying Jacopo's daughter, Ottavia.[1] Sons and grandsons, brothers and in-laws, cousins and nephews were the favored assistants in each bottega. This was a pattern adhered to by native-born artists like the Vivarini and Bellini and Tintoretto families, but followed as well by those who—like the Bon, Lombardo, Titian, Veronese, and Bassano clans—came to Venice and set up their shops there.

Bassano, a member of the da Ponte family named for the town of his birth, trained all four of his sons to be painters, and he made assistants, as well, of his nephews and grandsons.[2] Tintoretto had as one of his assistants his daughter Marietta.[3] Paolo Caliari—called "Veronian" (Veronese) from the town of his birth in the Venice-controlled terraferma—was apprenticed to his uncle, Antonio Badile, and married Badile's daughter, Elena, with whom he had the sons, Carletto and Gabriele, who (with his brother Benedetto) helped run his shop in Venice. (A nephew, Alvise del Friso, was the continuator of the family business.)[4] Benedetto described in his will the family ties on which the busy shop was based:

> I Benedetto, the son of Gabriele Caliari of Verona, separated from my other brothers, set myself up here in Venice in partnership with my brother Paolo, the famous

painter, whom I loved as a father. He was favored by God with a greater talent than mine, and he treated me in truth as a son and brother, and often conferred benefits on me as we lived together for forty years . . . After his death I was in charge of the effects guaranteed me by law because we were always partners.[5]

These strong ties safeguarded the resources of each shop—the training methods and tools, the formulae for pigments and preparatives, the drawing patterns and brush techniques. The value of such assets was made clear when Gentile Bellini guaranteed that his brother Giovanni would complete a major painting by making that a condition of his getting their father's drawing book.

Drawings of the master were not only valuable items in trade but means for the training of apprentices, who copied them. The students drew also from casts of ancient and modern statues, like those mentioned in the wills of Palma, Tintoretto, and Jacopo Bassano. These essential tools of the shop helped attract students. In the fifteenth century, an extensive collection of casts contributed, in great part, to the success of Squarcione . . . Tintoretto's collection of casts was extraordinarily well-known—we have already mentioned that [his son] Domenico Tintoretto left four casts to [his brother-in-law] Sebastiano Casser, among which he refers to "una testa del Vitelo," a head of Vitellius, from which Tintoretto and his students often made drawings.[6]

Coins, medals, casts, fabrics, jewels, patterns, and other props were also collected by the artists for use in drawing and coloring.[7] The concern to keep the shop's resources intact through family bonds is evident in the Younger Palma's will of 1621:

I leave to my grandson Giacomo, Lucrezia's boy, my entire shop—including paintings, drawings, reliefs, books and every sort of tool needed in a painter's calling—on condition that he is willing to devote himself to that calling. Otherwise, that my shop be divided between my two daughters, Giulia and Lucrezia, so that, if a grandson should wish to become a painter, he may use them—if he takes the name Palma to preserve a living memory of that calling in our line.[8]

To leave a master could entail suspicion or bitterness, since one was taking away skills, if nothing else, that were developed in the shop.

Some of the trade secrets a shop might want to keep for itself are suggested by modern chemical analysis. In paintings, the expensive lapis-lazuli blue was normally toned up or down by mixture with white lead. But Giovanni Bellini also used a different technique:

> Occasionally Bellini also mixed the lapis with a little smalt, a pigment that consists of finely ground potassium glass in which the colorant is cobalt. Given that smalt is a product of the glass industry, and was very rarely used in painting before the sixteenth century, its employment by Bellini—albeit limited—may be indicative of his interest in the technology of Murano glass and its painting with enamel.[9]

There are stories that Titian kept some of his projects even from his own students, locking them up when he was away. Giovanni Bellini kept his secrets by not letting anyone watch him while he worked.[10] Tintoretto observed the same discipline, according to Carlo Ridolfi's 1648 biography, "because the techniques of this demanding art, which aims at applause, are always kept secret by its masters, since the skillful acquire them only by long study and labor."[11] It is easy to see, in such conditions, why family ties led to greater trust and solidarity in working relationships.

1. THE VIVARINI FAMILY

The first important painters' shop in Renaissance Venice was that of the Vivarini. Michele Vivarini was a glassblower (*fiolario*) in the glass factories of Murano. His sons, Antonio (c. 1415–c. 1480) and Bartolomeo (c. 1432–c. 1499), became painters. Their shop was augmented by the marriage of the painter Giovanni d'Alemagna to one of Michele's daughters, and by the training of Antonio's son, Alvise (c. 1446–c. 1503), to be the inheritor of the bottega. Despite differences in their technique, all these painters were characterized by bold juxtapositions of bright colors, reflecting no doubt the Murano glassmakers' interest in the effect of different dyes. It has been suggested that Florentine painters achieved their shot-silk effects (*cangianti*) of shifting hues from interest in the dyes used by their city's fabric industry. We will probably come closer to the Venetians' skill in using color, not by ascribing it to some magic of atmospheric light or of lagoon reflections, but to the guarded technology of the Murano glassworks, where fire writhed out the colors of clouds and flowers. Anthony Hecht describes the kinds of miracle wrought there:

And all the silicate fragility
They sweat for at the furnace now seems
An admirable and shatterable triumph.
They take the first crude bulb of thickened glass,
Glowing and taffy-soft on the blow tube,
And sink it in a mold, a metal cup
Spiked on its inner surface like a pineapple.
Half the glass now is regularly dimpled,
And when these dimples are covered with a glaze
Of molten glass they are prisoned air-bubbles,
Breathless, enameled pearly vacancies.[12]

PLATE XXVII
Santi Giovanni e Paolo,
window

Venetian mosaicists benefited from the improved lucidity (*lucidezza*), achieved on Murano, of the tesserae they used in their work. Paul Hill has registered the Venetian painters' interest in the increasingly complex coloration of Murano vases and cups and bowls. It is not surprising that the most spectacular stained-glass window in Venice—in the south transept of the Church of Giovanni e Paolo—came from the Murano workshop of Gian'Antonio Licinio da Lodi, and had cartoons for its figures from Bartolomeo Vivarini.

FIG. 51
Antonio Vivarini, *Polyptych with Crucifixion and Stories of Christ's Passion*

Antonio, the older son of Michele, collaborated with his brother-in-law "German John" (Giovanni d'Alemagna) on a series of Gothic altarpieces set in elaborately carved and gilded frames. Two good examples of these are in the crypt-chapel of San Zaccaria. The firm became known for this product, for which many orders came in from terraferma churches as well as Venetian sites. But Antonio could, on a smaller scale, be a lively painter of narrative, as in the famous polyptych of the Passion now in the Ca' d'Oro.[13] The twelve small scenes of Christ's sufferings and resurrected life have numerous human touches and psychological details, like the varied reactions of the disciples at the Last Supper. That these are based on deep theological reflection is shown in the Resurrection panel, where Christ stands above a tomb still closed with red sealing wax, to prove that he passed out of the tomb without disturbing it—as he appeared in a room that was locked by the disciples (Jn 20.19). This emphasis on the sealed tomb was used to support the idea that Christ also passed out of Mary's body without disturbing her virginity (the seal of the hymen).

After Giovanni d'Alemagna's death, Antonio collaborated with Bartolomeo until the former's death. Bartolomeo tempered the bright colors of the bottega with volumetric shadings of his figures, bringing the firm unambiguously into the Renaissance. His paintings of the Virgin at half length drew on the great series of such paintings by his contemporary Giovanni Bellini, but Bartolomeo had original touches of his own to add. Where Bellini put the Virgin behind a parapet, on which the child was often propped, Bartolomeo—in his Madonna for the Church of Giovanni e Paolo (now in London's National Gallery)—put Mary before the parapet, and two attendant saints behind it, in a different reality but contemplating hers.[14] The child expresses dependence on the mother, whom he clutches, and all in the group are sadly meditative as they foresee what lies ahead for the frightened baby.

Though the Vivarini have a corporate identity, the generations of the family reflected changing styles in Venice. Alvise, Bartolomeo's son, had already adopted the sinuous poses and elongated proportions of Mannerism, as we can see in his *Risen Christ* for the Church of San Giovanni in Bragora.[15] This classical nude with his flamboyantly curling banner of victory (*vexillum*) crowds out of the picture the two soldiers who witness his resplendent apparition. Only a winding road, the path to his death triumphantly one-upped by the winding and winning banner, is left to situate the picture in time and place. This image was so arresting that Carpaccio copied it for the statue of the risen Christ in his Scuola degli Schiavoni painting, the *Vision of Saint Augustine*. Since Alvise's picture was done for a Club of the Blessed Sacrament, its use by Carpaccio must indicate that there is a preserved Eucharist at the altar in Augustine's study.[16]

FIG. 52
Alvise Vivarini,
Risen Christ

PLATE XXVIII
Vittore Carpaccio,
Vision of Saint Augustine

2. THE SOLARI FAMILY

Pietro Solari was known, like the rest of his family, as "the Lombard" (Lombardo), from his birthplace near Lago di Garda. He worked in Padua before coming to Venice and setting up his large practice there, in which he was supported by his sons Tullio (c. 1455–1532) and Antonio (c. 1458–c. 1516), and Tullio's son Sante. There was no formal profession of architect in Renaissance Venice, so it lacked a guild. The architect was part of the stone-carvers' scuola, and even the best of them (e.g., Sansovino) might share the roles of sculptor and architect. Pietro himself graduated from decorative reliefs to tomb architecture to entire church structures (like Santa Maria dei Miracoli). But he was always best known for his decorative style, which used classical elements in a rich Gothic weave of forms on the surfaces of stone—a paradoxical combination of restraint and profusion that was copied in the paintings and the frames of Giovanni Bellini and other artists. His sons were more exclusively devoted to sculpture than to architecture—Tullio as the greatest Venetian creator of statues between Rizzo and Vittoria, Antonio known for the bronze statues in the Capella Zen of the Doge's Palace. Pietro and his sons collaborated on many of their projects, and returned to Padua to do the reliefs around the altar of Saint Anthony. Sante, by contrast, was an architect, not a sculptor, responsible for the rear elevation of the Scuola Grande di San Rocco.[17]

3. THE BELLINI FAMILY

The Bellini family had the deepest roots in Venice, where they were *cittadini originarii*. The founder of the school was Jacopo (1400–c. 1470), whose illegitimate brother Giovanni was also a painter—and after whom Jacopo's son was also named Giovanni (c. 1430–1516). Jacopo's son Gentile (c. 1429–1507) was named after his father's teacher, Gentile da Fabriano. Gentile Bellini became the great artistic entrepreneur of the family, the man put in charge of painting the Larger Council hall, and the one sent by the republic on a diplomatic mission to Constantinople. Andrea Mantegna (1431–1506) married into the family in 1429, as the husband of Jacopo's daughter Nicolosia. The Bellini shop had a long span that extended to Giovanni's adoptive nephew, Vittore Belliniano.[18] Its prestige was such that it was besieged by those desiring instruction in it.

> The acclaim and prestige of Gentile's and Giovanni's instruction was such that apprentices came from as far away as Rimini, Parma, and Bergamo, and members of the Venetian patriciate demanded that they take on their protégés. Elisabetta

Morosini Frangipani, for instance, wrote her brother Marco from the isle of Vegli (or Krk) asking him to arrange for his friends, the Bellini, to teach her chaplain "the right way of drawing." Later, another Morosini, Cipriano, discovered a talented youth drawing in the workshop of a smithy, and sent him to Giovanni. The lad showed great promise, but he died young, and Cipriano was obliged to pay a pension to his mother, a widow. Given the reputation of the Bellinis' teaching, Vasari probably gives way to exaggeration, without strict regard for fact, when he says that Titian and Sebastiano del Piombo achieved their stature because of Giovanni.[19]

Jacopo, though a cittadino, was born of a tinsmith father and a mother whose father was a boatman, and he inherited no estate. But he managed to be apprenticed to Gentile da Fabriano when that master of International Gothic style worked in Venice. Jacopo became a very successful artist, but almost all of his paintings have been lost. He is now known mainly for the two large books of drawings he compiled for use in his bottega. The drawings are experiments in fantasy, in the manipulation of space, and in unexpected twists on customary iconography. Here buildings proliferate out of each other almost as Piranesi's prisons fold in on each other. The detailed yet dreamlike structures of Carpaccio's works seem to have their basis here—evidence that Carpaccio studied in the Bellini shop. There is a teasing and exploratory mind at work in the books—as when Jacopo tucks little figures of the principal narrative in unexpected nooks or corners or distances.

The books went to Jacopo's oldest son, Gentile, who was a member of and adviser to the Scuola Grande di San Marco, as well as the primary artist for the sequence of paintings in the Scuola di San Giovanni Evangelista. The government's trust in this citizen-artist was shown when he helped seal a tense peace with the Turks in 1478. He gave Mehmet II one of his father's drawing books (the more expensive one, on parchment, now in the Louvre) as a lavish expression of trust. The other book, the one on paper now in the British Museum, Gentile left to his brother Giovanni, in return for Giovanni's finishing the painting Gentile was engaged in for the Scuola Grande di San Marco, *Saint Mark Preaching in Alexandria*. This large work represented Mark's Alexandria in terms of the Constantinople he had visited. Gentile, who was knighted by Mehmet II in Constantinople, includes his self-portrait on the left side of the picture, as he had on the right side of *The Miracle at the Bridge of San Lorenzo*.

Giovanni is the brother now revered as the greatest Venetian painter of the second half of the fifteenth century, the one from whom all later artists of the city descend. He gave Venetian art its atmospheric richness, enveloping his figures in an outer glow that

FIG. 76
Gentile Bellini,
Saint Mark Preaching in Alexandria

FIG. 62
Gentile Bellini,
The Miracle at the Bridge of San Lorenzo

symbolizes their radiant interiority. His figures respond to inner promptings that evoke a kindred hush in the onlooker.

4. THE VECELLIO FAMILY

Most of the painters of Venice came from the artisan class, even such cittadini originarii as the Bellini and the Tintoretto clans. Titian (Tiziano Vecellio, c. 1487–1576), though an outsider from the Alpine town of Pieve di Cadore, had professional ancestors (lawyers and soldiers), and entertained aristocratic aspirations. These were satisfied for his own person when Charles V made him Count Palatine of the Roman Empire, but Titian strove as well to promote his priestly son, Pomponio, to lucrative benefices and his painter son, Orazio, to imperial distinctions. Family members who worked in his shop included, besides Orazio, Titian's brother Francesco, his second cousin Marco Vecellio and his third cousin Cesare Vecellio.[20] In the Vivarini or Bellini or Lombardo shops, we can trace artistic developments from generation to generation; but Titian lived so long (his son died with him in the plague of 1576), and underwent such profound developments himself, right up to his death, that all the Vecellio work is absorbed into his large output.

Though Titian probably had some experience in the Bellini shop, the most profound influence on him came from another man who had been apprenticed there, Giorgione (c. 1477–1510). Giorgione is the almost-missing link between Bellini and Titian. Despite his obscurity in history and the small body of his securely attested works, Giorgione was a painterly genius who somehow absorbed the lessons of Leonardo da Vinci at an early age.[21] The soft bloominess of his shapes and colors gave Titian his starting point. But Titian added drama and energy to the Giorgione dreaminess.

Much of Titian's work was done for well-cultivated foreign courts. In the vernacular satirist Pietro Aretino, Titian had an international propagandist who advanced his own career by advancing Titian's. The large Vecellio operation—numbering as many as thirty assistants at a time—sent copies of his masterpieces to different countries or courts. Since so much of his work went to outside markets and catered to outside tastes, his relations with the government in Venice were sometimes touchy. He worked slowly, and fell behind on commissions. Other artists were favored as a rebuke to him. But his unquestioned greatness meant that he could always win back favor when he cared to.

5. THE ROBUSTI FAMILY

Jacopo Robusti (1519–1594), known as a "tinterling" (Tintoretto) since he was the son of a clothes tinter, broke with his first master, Titian, and developed his own shop with his sons Marco and Domenico, his daughter Marietta, and his son-in-law Sebastian Casser. Working to emerge from Titian's shadow, Jacopo undercut the competition, schemed for commissions, and had fewer grand patrons, for a long time, than either Titian or Veronese. He was a favorite of the *scuole piccole*, particularly those of the Blessed Sacrament, of which he had formed a deeply mystical conception.

While Titian quietly competed with Michelangelo in the rivalry (*paragone*) of painting with sculpture, pitting his color shapes against the Florentine three-dimensionality of draftsmanship (*disegno*), Tintoretto tried to combine the virtues of both approaches, making his colorful figures spiral in flight or dance out their emotions like decorously animated statues. His was a dramaturgy of virtue and vice. According to his biographer, Carlo Ridolfi, he drew from "flying" wax figures he hung from the roof or posed in shadow-box toy theaters, studying how to make human figures both inhabit and conquer space.[22] Titian's champion, Aretino, denigrated Tintoretto as a man too impatient to achieve perfect finish in his work, and it is true that he was an action painter *avant la lettre*—furiously dashing off images with long sweeps of the brush that could leave the paint vulnerably thin on his canvas. Ridolfi spoke of his "frenzy to create."[23] But he opened up new fields of vision not traveled by Titian or by anyone else before him—as we saw by comparing his and Titian's treatments of *The Rape of Lucretia*. As he aged, Jacopo came to rely more and more on Domenico, who executed, for instance, his grand scheme of the *Paradise* in the Larger Council. He also acquired court patrons elsewhere, especially Rudolph II, the Holy Roman Emperor at Prague.[24]

PLATE XX
Jacopo Tintoretto,
Paradise

6. THE NEGRETI FAMILY

Jacopo Negreti (c. 1480–1528), born near Bergamo, acquired the nickname Palma— and when his grandnephew, another Jacopo, became successful, he had to be referred to as the Elder Palma (Palma Vecchio). The original Jacopo painted, in the soft Giorgione style, lyrical religious pictures and bust-length portraits of "goddesses." A member of St. Mark's Distinguished Brotherhood, he completed *The Storm* for that scuola. His painter nephew, Antonio, married the niece of another painter in the shop, Bonifacio of Verona.[25] Antonio's son, Jacopo, was the Younger Palma (Palma Giovane, 1544–1628). A magnificent draftsman but slavishly imitative of other painters, he became—like Tintoretto—a great favorite of the scuole piccole, especially those devoted to the Blessed Sacrament, and a contributor of major canvases to the Doge's Palace.

7. THE CALIARI FAMILY

Paolo Caliari (1528–1588), called Veronese from his birth in Verona, was originally apprenticed to his father's trade of stone cutting; but early promise as a painter made his father turn him over to his painter uncle. Paolo's style was thus formed before he came to Venice at the age of twenty-two, but he adapted quickly to Venetian fashions and won major commissions in the Doge's Palace and Sansovino's library (where one of the judges assigning him the project was Titian). His courtly approach to large ceremonial scenes made him a favorite of Titian's elite patrons, and of families like the Barbaros, whose villa at Maser he decorated with a cycle of frescoes that were forerunners of work by the Tiepolo family (Giovanni Battista, Giovanni Domenico, and Lorenzo) a full century after his death. In that sense, this man from Verona helped forge the continuity of Venetian style through and beyond the Renaissance. A link in that continuity was the activity of his shop after his own death, when his brother, two sons, and a nephew worked together under the proud title of Paul's Heirs (*Heredes Paoli*).

8. THE DI BERTO (OR DA PONTE) FAMILY

In 1464, a tanner named Jacopo di Berto went to Bassano del Grappa, on the Brenta River, and set up shop beside a wooden bridge over the river—whence his nickname, James by the Bridge (Jacopo da Ponte). His son, Francesco, the first painter of the family, became known in time as the Elder da Ponte (da Ponte Vecchio), to distinguish him from his grandson Francesco, the Younger da Ponte (Francesco da Ponte Giovane). The first Francesco was trained (perhaps in Vicenza) to work in the Bellini manner, but his son Jacopo (c. 1510–1592) went to Venice to study with Bonifazio de' Pitati. Though he returned to Bassano, thirty miles outside Venice, to set up his shop (under the name Jacopo da Bassano), he remained popular in Venice, and *his* son the younger Francesco (1549–1592) was commissioned to do five major paintings in the Doge's Palace after the fire of 1577—four battle scenes for the ceiling of the Larger Council hall, and one work for the Alexander III cycle in the Sala.

Jacopo Bassano brought a feeling for rustic landscapes and domestic animals to Venetian taste, at a time when life on terraferma was being taken up by more patricians. His son devoted himself to the same taste. After the suicide of this younger Francesco in 1592, Leandro (1557–1622), one of the three remaining painter sons of the family, took over the shop and distinguished himself as a portrait painter, carrying the Bassano name well into the seventeenth century.

The conception of painting as a family's joint endeavor reaching over the generations has contributed to the idea that Venetian art was conservative. If that means a refusal to reject the past, as opposed to building on it, then the idea has some truth—and not only in the sphere of painting. Venetian politics, too, aimed for a seamless connection with the past. One symbol of that is the gerontocratic bias of the government. Age was trusted, not suspect. Even more basically, the government itself could be looked on as a family business. Since the "Lock-Up" (Serrata) of the ruling families in a continuing relationship, the political activities of the republic were the result of recurring family combinations: "With slight exaggeration, one may say that assemblies of the Great Council amounted to the congregation of large, interlocking family complexes based on both lineage and affection, *parenti e consorti*" (F 89). The same could be said of the family and student and collegial relations among the artists licensed by the state through their guilds. Each workshop upheld the honor of the family's name.

Even the profoundest developments in Venetian art caused no clear break with what went before. Giorgione developed latent aspects of Bellini's work, as Titian did of Giorgione's. No Venetian painter who came after Bellini failed to be influenced by him, no matter how individual his own contributions to the tradition. For those who think, with Jacob Burckhardt, that the essence of the Renaissance was individualism, this puts Venice almost at odds with (or outside) the Renaissance. But Burckhardt himself understood why Venice had to be different. Its precarious imperial outreach demanded a solid base: "An enterprise so contrived could maintain itself only by keeping its inner elements peacefully at one."[26] Venetian art was imperial by virtue of the peace kept between the generations, making of all the city's arts one large joint project. Individual rivalries and tension raged within, but were contained within, this overall conservatism. As so often, continuity was, at the core of it, a form of comity.

CHAPTER FOURTEEN

Outsiders

*L*IKE ATHENS, VENICE BOASTED that it accepted outsiders fearlessly. Pericles claimed, in his Funeral Oration as reported by Thucydides, "We keep our city open, not expelling foreigners to prevent their seeing something whose exposure could be useful to an enemy."[1] The Venetian diarist Girolamo Priuli echoed that confidence: Venice "was open to foreigners, and all could come and go everywhere without any obstacle" (F 33). And in 1527 the favored visitor, Pietro Aretino, addressed Doge Andrea Gritti this way:

> Venice opens her arms to all whom others shun. She lifts up all whom others abase. She welcomes those whom others persecute. She cheers the mourner in his grief and defends the despised and the destitute with charity and love. And so I bow to Venice with good reason. She is a living reproach to [papal] Rome.[2]

It is true that both Athens and Venice, as hubs of extensive empire, had to encourage the flow of information, diplomats, merchants, and labor. These passed from one part of their holdings to others through the central point, and foreign traders had to be brought within their network. These small city-states needed outsiders, so they made special provision for useful ones to dwell with them. Athens' very term for such people was "dwellers with us"—*met-oikoi*, conventionally Englished as "metics." Venice allowed certain foreigners (*forestieri*) to become *cittadini*, giving them higher rank than native *popolani*.[3] Other foreigners were not advanced to citizenship, but they could do business in the city, work at trades, fight in the galleys, form their own clubs (*scuole*).

The attitude toward foreigners shifted with the city's fortunes. When plague or war made Venice feel the need for extra hands in its Arsenal or in the fleet, the city welcomed people from the city's imperial holdings, its ports or islands, to perform tasks that went beyond its available manpower. Some of these tasks were too sensitive to be entrusted to slave-captives, so the aid of free foreigners had to be recruited. (Athens also used metics in the fleet.) After the supreme ordeal of the War of Chioggia

(1378–1381), when a lack of men and money was felt, the city had to replenish even the patriciate, by letting wealthy new families into it (the only time this was done on a large scale in the Renaissance). At this juncture Jews were allowed to stay in the city overnight, since their financial help was needed—previously they had been expelled at nightfall, after trading on the Rialto, sent to their homes on terraferma.

Nonetheless, despite professions of openness and accessibility, both Athens and Venice were suspicious of foreigners, not only in themselves but as the occasion of corruption for the internal population who came into contact with them. The internal surveillance of the ruling class by the ruling class led both cities to expel members of the elite who showed too much friendliness with outside forces—by ostracism in Athens, by decree of the Ten in Venice. To prevent contamination of the government, Venice forbade foreign representatives to meet privately with the doge or senators. This made diplomacy difficult, as we shall see: Henry Wotton, King James I's ambassador from England, could only communicate with parts of the ruling body through intermediaries, encountering each other by feigned accident in church or palace or marketplace.

Even when foreigners were not suspected of approaching the government, they were kept under official observation. Merchants who entered the city had to be licensed before they could engage in trade, and the license required frequent renewal.[4] Outsiders were encouraged or compelled to live with their fellow nationals in manageable clusters. When people from the Eastern cities of the empire (Dalmatians, Albanians, Greeks, Turks) came to Venice during the fifteenth century, they tended to congregate in the parish of San Moise, since it was a cheap (if dangerous) place to live, a slum.[5] When Jews were admitted to the city, they clustered on the left side of the Grand Canal, near the Rialto, where their financial trading was done.[6] German merchants, on the other hand, stayed near the Rialto on the right side of the canal.

Anything that emphasized the outsiders' difference from Venetians was encouraged. Apparent indulgences helped keep foreign groups compact and manageable. The city built, for instance, a large German Commercial House (Fondaco dei Tedeschi), where Lutheran services could quietly be performed for the merchants. Though it fronted on the Grand Canal, the Fondaco's busy life went on in its inner court, and the nationals could be observed more readily since they operated from this center. Turks were allowed to open an Arabic school, to act as a magnet for drawing others around it. Greek Orthodox services helped mark off the eight thousand Greeks who were in the city by the end of the fifteenth century. Henry Wotton brought an Anglican priest with him, to perform religious ceremonies within the confines of the English ambassador's palace.

Outsiders who were Western Christians had their own scuole, with their assembly points at altars, like those of the native brotherhoods. The Florentines, for instance, had an altar in the Franciscan basilica (Frari), for which they brought to town their own great sculptor, Donatello, to create the statue of Florence's patron saint, John the Baptist. At another point in the Frari, the Milanese put up a painting of their city's patron, the bishop Ambrose, begun by Alvise Vivarini and finished by Marco Basaiti. In 1506, the Germans had a magnificent altarpiece painted for their altar in the Church of Saint Bartholomew by their national painter, Albrecht Dürer.[7] This *Feast of the Rosegarlands* shows the Emperor Maximilian I kneeling on the left, at his coronation in Rome by Pope Julius II. Here the child on the Virgin's knee crowns Maximilian, while Mary herself crowns the figure on the right—presumably Pope Julius II in the days before he let his beard grow. (The painting lost favor two years after its completion, when Julius formed the League of Cambrai, with Maximilian and others, to drive Venice out of its land holdings.)

FIG. 107
Donatello,
Saint John the Baptist

More ambitious than these foreigners' altars in Venetian churches were the scuole of their own built by ethnic groups in the city—e.g., the Dalmatians, Greeks, and Albanians in the eastern part of the city. Carpaccio painted his brilliant cycles for the Dalmatian and Albanian brotherhoods.[8] The competitive display of foreign identities was welcomed by the city. The more marked the differentiation of outsiders, the more secure the identity of Venetians.

JEWS

The most significant mark of difference, of course, was the yellow garb mandated for Jews—as theirs was the most significant corralling, into the Ghetto. This occurred during one of the periods in which Venice reinvented itself, as a reaction to war with the League of Cambrai (1509–1516). The gains foreigners made as a result of the War of Chioggia were more than reversed by the moral panic at the temporary loss of its land holdings to the League. As in times of plague, there were loud calls for moral purification of the city. The doge, Leonardo Loredan, encouraged these calls in order to steel the people for wartime sacrifices. Franciscan preachers at the Frari denounced the corruption of the city by "heretics, schismatics, witches, wizards, and Christian women who have amorous flirtations and sexual congress with Jews."[9]

This urge to purify the city went with plans to create a new sacred space at its heart, the geographical midpoint or umbilicus marked out by legend as the site of the Church of San Salvador.[10] This was a project advanced by the prior of the San Salvador church-monastery, Antonio Contarini, who would soon become the patriarch of Venice.[11] Foreigners were cleared away from the area between the nodes of Venetian life—the Piazza on the east and the Rialto on the west. The Greeks and Dalmatians, previously clustered in the parish of San Moise, were moved off, farther east than San Marco, to the island of Castello.[12] And Jews, once near the Rialto, were moved to the northwest, to a thinly settled part of the Canareggio sector.

The first proposals were to move the Jews entirely off the main cluster of islands—to Murano or to Giudecca.[13] But on those islands they would have easy access to boats, for mingling with the population after nightfall. A sealed-off area was desired, with no outlet but by a single gate, which could be easily guarded by the authorities. There were only three such isolable quarters in the city—the Arsenal, self-contained for security reasons; the Lazaretto, where lepers were contained; and the New Foundry (Ghetto Nuovo).

The original brass foundry (*getto del rame*) had been established in the fourteenth century, when its walls went up to keep military operations secret. (A foundry is named for the jets—*getti*—of molten brass poured to make cannon.) By the beginning of the fifteenth century, a small island created by canals all around it was annexed to the foundry for future expansion and called the New Foundry, even though no factory was ever put up there. A single bridge crossed the canal to this annex. Since the island was uninhabited (it had been used mainly as a hunting and fishing area), it was not part of the parish system, though there was a monastery on the site opposite the foundry. When the foundry's operations were moved to the Arsenal, both its original site and its undeveloped annex were auctioned off in 1434 to Marco Ruzini, who began converting the factory buildings of the old site into rental homes. The island went undeveloped until it was separated from the original foundry and bought by the da Brolo brothers, Costantino and Bartolomeo, in 1455. Their family built houses all around the perimeter of the island, keeping a large open campo inside this cincture of apartment buildings. Three wellheads were created for the apartment dwellers' water supply—the da Brolo arms are carved on them, a shield with three lions, misinterpreted after the Jews moved there as a reference to the Lion of Judah.[14]

This island was seen as the ideal place to contain the Jews being moved out of "sacred" spaces. It had that rare thing in Venice, a large campo without a parish church. It was completely surrounded by water, so its one gate was easily guarded by a Christian watchman. The high apartment buildings that had been developed by the da Brolos could be turned into a walled circumference by sealing up the outside windows. Christians living in the buildings were expelled in 1516, and Jews were moved in—they had to rent the buildings, since they were not allowed to own real property. The Jews of this first settlement in the so-called New Ghetto were referred to as "the Germans," since many came from the North (though there were Italian Jews among them from the outset, and their numbers would grow).

Those on the island were free to leave it when the Piazza Campanile's great bell ("Marangone") rang for the Arsenal staff to begin the workday, but the Jews had to wear their identifying yellow tunic and hat (the hat was added since the yellow tunic could be covered by a cloak), and they all had to be back on the island by nightfall. An exception was made for Jewish doctors, much in demand for their skills, who could be called out by patients needing their services at night. (The Venetians' university at Padua graduated many Jewish doctors.)

During the day, Christians patronized shops and booths inside the Ghetto. Jews were not allowed to compete with the guilds by making their own fabrics, gold, or jewelry, but they could buy and sell used goods, often of very high quality, though for legal reasons they had to be called "rag stuff" (stracciaria, Venetian strazzaria.)[15] The Jews became known as such connoisseurs of high-quality products that they were called in to decorate the Doge's Palace for festive occasions, and to decorate the doge's ritual barge (Bucintoro).[16] Going to the shops in the Ghetto was a developed skill. Guides (senseri) directed people to the kinds and grades of items they wanted. More of these senseri were Christians than Jews, presumably because those being guided would trust one of their own. People with a taste for the exotic went to the Ghetto as fashionable people went to Harlem nightclubs in the 1930s. Gambling was available in the Ghetto. In fact, the learned rabbi Leon da Modena had a lifelong addiction to gambling.[17]

In the course of the sixteenth century, a new set of Jewish relations was forced on Venice. The spread of Turkish power into the Mediterranean denied whole areas of trade to Venice, unless the republic worked through Jews of the Levant, who had become intermediaries of exchange between the Turkish and Christian worlds. Since these Jews were, technically, Turkish subjects, they could be admitted to Venice as protected aliens. But that raised the problem of their relation to Jews in the Ghetto. Agents of the new arrangement working in Venice could not be treated as entirely different from their coreligionists, yet they could not just be consigned to the same Ghetto. For one thing, overcrowding had already begun in the Ghetto, which, since it could not be built out, had to be built upward. Storys were added to the old buildings, which reached six or seven levels in height, putting a strain on inadequate foundations. Holes for new windows were punched irregularly into the walls, and rooms were added or lofts created inside existing levels.

To accommodate the Levantine Jews, therefore, the original Ghetto (Ghetto Vecchio) was annexed to the island—reversing the order of the original acquisition (island annexed to foundry). This new residence in the old Ghetto was less circumscribed than the first residence in the *new* Ghetto—the original foundry walls had come down over the years—but the relatively self-contained nature of the buildings still suggested the original layout, and if the Jews there were less policeable than on the island, they were also more privileged in general, reflecting higher financial standing and greater usefulness to the empire.

The different treatment given Levantine Jews can be seen from the fact that a different body of the government administered their precinct—the Five Trade Experts (Cinque Savii alla Mercanzia), not Officers of the Income (Ufficiali de Cattaver). And there were distinctions within the Levantine community itself. Some of the Levantine Jews had originally fled from Spain or Portugal after undergoing forced or feigned baptism, in accord with the coercive measures of those states. If they now reverted to Judaism, that made them not only infidels but heretics, subject to the Inquisition, which had a branch in Venice. The republic was willing to grant the Levantines an exemption, as Turkish subjects, but how were they to distinguish these Marranos (baptized Jews) from others coming directly to Venice from Spain or Portugal, or from European points between, without the cover of Turkish jurisdiction?

The complexity of Venetian relations with Jews of the Levant can be represented in the opposed examples of Joseph Nasi and Daniele Rodriga, one a great foe of the republic and one its great friend.

JOSEPH NASI

Nasi belonged to the Mendes family, wealthy bankers of Lisbon and Antwerp. Joseph was born in Lisbon, probably around 1520, where he was baptized as João Micas.[18] But he was raised by his aunt, the powerful Gracia Nasi, who was determined to return to her ancestral faith. When her husband died in 1536, she took the sixteen-year-old Joseph with her to the Antwerp branch of their business. Handsome, athletic, and well educated, Joseph quickly became a popular banking agent throughout Europe, which he traveled with a large entourage. When his aunt, unwilling to hide her Jewish faith, had to flee from Antwerp to Venice, she was arrested by the Venetian Inquisition. Joseph intervened with the Turkish authorities to get her released, and followed her to Constantinople, where he became a favorite counselor to Suleiman the Magnificent, and to Selim, his heir.

Selim, on his succession to the throne in 1566, made Joseph the Duke of Naxos, an island just wrenched away from the Venetians. Nasi, with his eye on a bigger prize, supported the sultan's war on Cyprus, hoping to become the island's king. The prize seemed within his grasp when the Venetians were expelled from the Cypriot city of

Famagosta (the occasion of the infamous flaying of Marcantonio Bragadin). But Nasi's dreams were dashed by the almost immediately ensuing defeat of the Turks at Lepanto. Some Turks blamed Nasi's anti-Cyprus campaign for the disaster, and there was a decline in his influence. But he had been, for decades, what Riccardo Calimani calls him—the most powerful Jew in the world, feared or admired throughout Christian and Turkish lands. A lost German play, *Joseph, the Jew of Venice*, probably drew on his career, and may have resembled Thomas Dekker's lost play, *The Jew of Venice*. Certain of Nasi's traits appear in Christopher Marlowe's *The Jew of Malta*, whose protagonist has a banking empire strikingly like Nasi's (4.1.68–74):

> In Florence, Venice, Antwerp, London, Seville,
> Frankfurt, Lubeck, Moscow, and where not,
> Have I debts owing [me]; and, in most of these,
> Great sums of money lying in the banco.

Nasi's later enmity toward Venice shows how much damage a Marrano could do to the republic if he had a sense of grievance. The Venetian government had tried to conciliate the Mendes family—the charge brought against Gracia in Venice had been lodged by another Mendes. But Joseph followed the feelings of the outraged Gracia, who became a tireless defender of Marranos from her privileged position in the East.

DANIELE RODRIGA

Daniele Rodriga's is an entirely different story.[19] Baptized Daniele Rodrigues, he too became a wealthy financier, working from a Dalmatian base in Ragusa, which was being used as a link between the East and non-Venetian ports in Italy. Rodriga proposed opening a new route to the East by way of a port in Spalato (modern Split). Though he offered to put up much of the money for constructing the route, he needed the protection of the Venetian fleet at the port end of it. He pointed out the many advantages to Venice in this arrangement, at a time when its trade was being cut off. There was powerful resistance to his plan in the Venetian higher councils, because it involved using a strong network of Rodriga's fellow Marranos to service the route— including an influx of more Levantine Jews at Venice's end of it. When he had at last convinced Venice's Five Trade Experts of the wisdom of his course, he submitted a petition that would extend to Ponentine Jews (those coming to Venice straight from Spain) the privileges given the Levantines. This was accepted in 1589, ending the problem of discrimination between Jews from Spain and those from the Levant.

The financial advantages of Rodriga's new route were great, and Venice could rejoice in cooperative relations with Jewish financiers and diplomats serving their interests. This did not please the Inquisition in Rome; but the Venetian government put the Inquisition under its control within the empire. Brian Pullan points out that the Venetian Inquisition always had misgivings about pursuing Marranos in more than token ways, since that would often mean cooperating with the Inquisition in other nations, whose governments were not to Venice's liking. How, for instance, could one establish the baptismal record of a suspected heretic without calling for documents from Spain or Portugal—which might lead those countries to make reciprocal demands inconvenient to Venice. Venice would, instead, decide on its own which merchants deserved protection, based on their usefulness. Theology was all right in its place; but commerce came first, as Riccardo Calimani rightly concludes from Rodriga's brilliant dealings with the Venetian authorities.

MODUS VIVENDI

Jews of diverse origin came together to form a United Board of Jews (Università degli Ebrei), whose committees carefully balanced membership among the Germans, Levantines, and Ponentines (and among factions within those groups). The aim was to make sure one or other group did not gain advantage at the cost of the rest. There were always matters for negotiation. German Jews were more heavily taxed, for instance, than the Levantines. But the Levantines replied that the Germans did not have foreign trade, so they did not pay duties—Levantines would be doubly penalized if they paid the regular tax *and* their considerable duties. The issue of favoritism arose again in 1633, when crowding in the older two ghettos led to the opening of a third area (called the Newest Ghetto, since that term now referred to Jewish enclaves, not foundries). This gave space to the Levantines and Ponentines, but did not relieve the crowding of the Germans. The divisions in the community are reflected in the fact that five synagogues, three in the New Ghetto, two in the Old—along with three yeshivas—were needed to accommodate the different "nations."

By the end of the sixteenth century, a relatively peaceful modus vivendi had been arrived at between Christians and Jews. It was to the state's advantage to maintain a cooperative atmosphere. The danger of anti-Semitic outbursts was always there, but the government sealed in the Jews during celebrations (like the liturgy of Christ's death) that could lead to violent aggression against them. When Turkish merchants complained of the lack of accommodation for them in 1573, they asked for a ghetto of their own.[20] The stable arrangements in Venice made Jews from more volatile cities seek out the Ghetto.

Hebrew scholars worked there. Venetian printers competed to publish their books.

The Germans, the first to live in the Ghetto, were always the least protected, since their moneylending was done face-to-face, in close quarters, at home in the city. The technicalities of usury were brought up over and over by preachers, especially the Franciscans, who felt that charity toward the poor should be a Christian act, maintained by their own interest-free loans at the so-called Pity Crests (Monti di Pietà). Though these were technically interest free, there was a service charge levied for what we would call overhead at the lending and pawning centers. Dominicans called even this exaction a form of usury. The war between Jewish lenders and the Monti was engaged more fiercely on terraferma than in the lagoon, since the *scuole*, guilds, and other social services for the poor were better organized in the city. But the thunderous preaching against the Jews by a pious but fanatical Franciscan like Bernardino da Feltre reached Christian ears in Venice and stirred trouble.

It might seem surprising that anti-Semitic campaigns had been supported, in the fifteenth century, by the early humanists. But a greater Greek figure, Cardinal John Bessarion (an important figure in Venetian history), came to the Jews' support in 1463. He had been sent to Venice by Pope Pius II to gain the republic's support for a crusade against the Turks. He took the occasion to write a defense of cooperation with Jews for the doge, Cristoforo Moro, and the document remained a charter of enlightened policy through subsequent lapses and struggles.[21]

Finally, in 1573, the state undercut the rivalry of Christian and Jewish lenders by imposing a uniform loan rate on them all—five percent. Though Jews could only sustain that rate by increased sale of strazzaria or by investment in their fellows' overseas trade, the benefit of the flat rate was clear to Rabbi Simone Luzzatto. Looking back in 1638, he contrasted the lot of Jews in Venice with that of their fellows elsewhere:

> Usury makes them unpopular with all the orders of a [non-Venetian] city; by engaging in crafts, with the lesser people; by the possession of property, with nobles and great men. These are the reasons why the Jews do not dwell in many places. But these circumstances do not arise in Venice, where the rate of interest is only five percent, and the banks are established for the benefit of the poor and not for the profit of the bankers. The Jews cannot engage in crafts or manufacture, nor can they own real property. Hence they do not seem burdensome or threatening to any estate or order within the city.[22]

Much pain is hidden in that forgiving retrospect. But Venice's genius for pragmatic adaptation is evident in this tragic area as in others. Enlightened leaders like

Rodriga were able to make a case for cooperation, despite the cruelty of past theory and practice. There was an ugly eruption of anti-Semitism around the middle of the sixteenth century, and some Marranos were expelled; but by 1573 Rodriga was interesting the Five Trade Experts in his vision of new relations for the future.

GHETTO NUOVO SYNAGOGUES

The Ghettos still exist, along with their five synagogues. A bridge at the original gate leads to an underpass (*sottoportego*) through the ring of apartments and out onto the campo. An iron bridge now exists on the other side of the island, ending its isolation; but those who enter by the original gate are taken back in time to an amazingly well-preserved part of the Venetian past. The image of the Lion of Judah is still on the *pozzo*. The houses' irregular windowing reflects the need for subdividing the limited spaces behind them. The three synagogues on this campo are all nested in pre-existing buildings, and it is not easy to pick them out until you look for a row of five windows on the second story—a symbol of the five books of the Law (Pentateuch)—and spot the cupola of an architectural lantern letting in light from above. Internally, all three rooms retain their original shape, but they were redecorated in the seventeenth and eighteenth centuries (with some nineteenth-century restoration) and the most impressive things in them—their elaborately carved and gilded bimahs (pulpits) and arks (the *aaron hokadesh* for holding the Torah)—are later creations.

1. *Scuola Grande Tedesca.* The oldest of the three, dating from 1528, is the Germans' Distinguished Brotherhood (they were allowed to use the honorable Venetian title *scuola grande*). This synagogue has been changed more than any other. When an ornate bimah was substituted for the original, its weight was too great to place it in the original's position, in the middle of the room (where an octagon on the floor marks the first site). It had to be moved to the wall at the end of the room. The lantern that stood above the octagon has been covered over. The irregularity of the room's rectangular walls is disguised by the projecting oval of a woman's gallery looped around the upper part of the room. The delicate railings on this curved balcony, the gilt screen meant to hide the women's faces above the railings, the slim piers (with Corinthian capitals) behind the gallery, the oval inset to the ceiling sustained by those piers—all give the room an attractively frilly air that must be quite different from its first appearance.

2. *Scuola Canton.* The second oldest synagogue is tucked into the acute south angle of the campo, which might have given it its mysterious name (from *canton,* Venetian dialect for "corner").[23] Since its five windows cannot be seen from the campo, only the cupola of its lantern gives it away, but inside it has a nineteenth-century portico at the foot of its stairs, and its eighteenth-century bimah is the most beautiful in the city, with wood columns carved to look like intertwined vines. The most original feature of the present room is a frieze of paintings that tell Bible stories without using human or animal images—manna falls from heaven, the seas part, and so on, in ways that claim not to break the ban on representation.

3. *Scuola Italiana.* The latest synagogue on the campo shows by its name that the Italians had distinguished themselves from the Germans by 1575. It has an external portico and a warm wooden interior of rich browns, without the gilding of the other two, which gives it a more sober majesty.

GHETTO VECCHIO SYNAGOGUES

The same bridge that takes one into the original Ghetto leads out to the site of the original foundry, a rectangular plot of land with three asymmetrical blocks of buildings penetrated by two streets meeting at connected little squares (*campielli*). Its two synagogues are larger and grander than those on the other side of the bridge, and they are the ones in which services are held for the current community (the celebrations alternate between the two). They were both rebuilt in the Baroque style of Baldassare Longhena in the seventeenth century, which means that they fall outside the time limit of this book, though their opulence is a testimony to the success of the Ghetto residents.

1. *Scuola Grande Spagnole.* This was originally the Scuola Ponentina, founded in 1584. It has an oval women's gallery like that of the Scuola Grande Tedesca, but it is far larger and grander.

2. *Scuola Levantina.* This is the first of the synagogues to meet in a building raised just for the purpose of worship. Its bimah and aaron are massive pieces of architecture in themselves. The Jews of Venice, working against great obstacles, had reason to be proud of their achievements. "Intellectually as well as architecturally, the Venetian ghetto was outstanding; before the development of Amsterdam, Venetian rabbis were recognized by other Jewish communities of the West as the most authoritative" (L 305).

PART THREE

Imperial Piety

CHAPTER FIFTEEN

Christ's Blood

MPORTANT AS SAINT MARK WAS to Venice, one patron clearly stood even higher in the devotions of the city. The Feast of Corpus Christi, better known in Venice as Corpus Domini, was one of the principal events in the Venetian calendar, the occasion for pageants that, as Muir puts it, "turned religious drama to a political end," presenting the doge and his government as protector of the Body of the Lord— sometimes even protecting it against the pope (M 221–22). A long white canopy of honor was raised on Corpus Domini day, through which a procession carrying the Eucharist wended its way around and into San Marco, a passage that could take hours (five hours, for instance, in 1506). The importance of this feast to Venice is confirmed by the fact that Venice had the oldest known Corpus Domini procession, dating from the year 1317, and the oldest known church dedicated to Corpus Domini, from 1366 (S-L 105).

It used to be said that the Venetian emphasis on the Eucharist reflected the definition of transubstantiation by the Council of Trent in 1551. But the feast of Corpus Domini long preceded the sixteenth century, as did the many chapels devoted to the Sacrament, and the dozens of religious brotherhoods formed to maintain those chapels. As Maurice Cope says, "the development of the chapel of the Sacrament begins before the Counter-Reformation defense of the Sacraments, before the Council of Trent, and even before Luther nailed his theses on the door of Wittenberg Cathedral."[1] In fact, a far more important date than 1551 for grounding the Venetian attitude toward the Eucharist was 1204, the time of the Fourth Crusade, in which Venice conquered Constantinople.

THE RELIC

Like most of the city's prominent devotions, the Eucharistic cult had as one of its bases a prized relic. The Fourth Crusade had brought back, as part of its spoils from

Constantinople, a vessel containing some of the blood shed by Christ in his agony in the garden.[2] So central to Venice was this relic that the doge, in the liturgy of Holy Thursday (the day when the agony in the garden was commemorated), wore a long cassocklike robe, buttoned up to the neck, that was deep red in color to honor the blood of Christ.[3] Christ himself is wearing the *corruccio* in the huge Tintoretto painting of Paradise at the front of the Larger Council hall in the Doge's Palace. It is by virtue of his redeeming blood that Christ welcomes a saved mankind to eternal peace—and the sign of that blood, contained in the vessel of the Venetians' treasury, is the very robe that the doge wore, year by year. As Muir points out, this canvas presents Christ as "the celestial, eternal doge" (M 272).

The fact that Jesus is wearing the corruccio in the *Paradise* has been noticed, but not, I believe, an earlier use of the same garb by Tintoretto—in the *Agony in the Garden* of the Scuola Grande di San Rocco (P-R 2.205). In this scene, the soldiers being led by Judas advance through night's shadows—through "taciturnities of a tactful moon," as Virgil says.[4] The sleeping disciples are lit by the same moon, though over them it is not diffused through branches. Peter stirs at the clatter of armed men approaching, and his bald pate catches the light as he lifts it. But Jesus, sphered in an entirely different scheme of light above them, ponders the cup of suffering offered him—*and he is wearing the red corruccio.* Few painters found a dignified way to paint the copious shedding of blood in the gospel—"his sweat streamed to the ground in splashes (*thromboi*) of blood" (Lk 22.44).[5] But Tintoretto can get the right effect through the corruccio, with its Venetian associations.

The angel appears in apocalyptic and bloody-sunset spheres of light, and holds a scarlet-gold chalice that is itself a kind of blood reliquary. The red of the atmosphere the angel moves in tinges his gray garments and tints the leaves around Jesus, in a way that contrasts sharply with the moonlit effects on the other persons in the scene. The event's surreal character is underlined by its lack of topographical logic, a device Tintoretto had already used in the *Crucifixion* on this floor of the scuola—Jesus is not rooted in the solid geography of the scene, but is rapt up in the privacy of his agony. Among other things, the use of the corruccio here confirms that the blood in the Venetian relic was shed on Holy Thursday in the garden, not on Good Friday from the cross.

Elsewhere in the Scuola Grande di San Rocco, Tintoretto created a series of three pictures that are, in effect, meditations on the sacred blood. Over the doorway into the boardroom (*albergo*) of the scuola—above the inside pediment, where the board members would see it as they looked back from their dais opposite the door—there is an

Ecce Homo ("Behold the man"), the scene in which Pilate offers Christ to the judgment of the crowd (Jn 19.5). Most often, in this scene, Christ is standing, crowned with thorns, a rough mantle thrown over his scourged shoulders—the Gospel of John says that he "came out" (exēlthen, vs. 5), presumably on his feet, wearing a purple robe. Tintoretto's Christ is incapable of motion. He has collapsed under his tortures, and blood runs from the thorn-crown and the wounds of his scourging. Partly, no doubt, this posture is an adaptation to the cramped space above the doorway—though Pilate and the

soldier-torturer who flank Jesus are standing (in the side spaces, where the pediment subsides). Jesus could have been put to one side, replacing the soldier, if Tintoretto wanted to show him standing. Instead of a purple mantle, Jesus has an all-white one, thrown open by an attendant to show that it, too, is smeared with his blood. The attendant above Christ is garbed in red, and the cloth he sprawls on is red. Pilate's robe and the hosiery of the soldier are variations on the same color. Moreover, the armor of the soldier has red clasps and is reflecting a banner with red facings. The shadow the soldier casts across Christ's arms and the cloth beneath him deepens their crimson glow, almost as if liquefying the cloth. We look at the whole scene through a mist of blood. This is a drama of redeeming and condemning blood, all the more powerful because no overt violence is shown. The blood is a medium of vision, as in the cry of Marlowe's *Doctor Faustus* (5.78): "See, see, where Christ's blood streams in the firmament!"

In the picture to the right of this one (as one faces the doorway), where Pilate washes his hands,

PLATE XXII
Jacopo Tintoretto,
Ecce Homo

FIG. 53 (ABOVE)
Jacopo Tintoretto,
Christ Before Pilate

there is a dramatic change in Christ's appearance. Though this scene comes after the *Ecce Homo* (Mt 27.24), Christ's robe is now wrapped around him again, showing all white, and he stands upright, with only a halo in place of the thorn crown. He is the judge of his judge, not by dramatic gesture or by menace in his bearing, but by the quiet power of innocence. He is a pale flame of unwavering rectitude in a scene where everyone else is pliant or contorted. Pilate turns away from Christ, in a physical act of rejection, as he washes his hands of the case. He is seated with his legs turned to his left, which means he must turn the upper part of his body back to the right in order to hold his hands under the pitcher of water. Yet he keeps his head averted from what his hands are doing. The triple torque of his pose—legs to the left, torso to the right, head to the left—reveals his interior division. Try as he may to dismiss the judgment of his silent accuser, his official chamber is marked with the blood that no longer shows on Jesus. His own garb—like that of his attendants (all but the scribe, who prefigures the Evangelist recording the scene)—is red. There is a furled red flag behind Jesus, echoing the slim white line of his body, and the veins of the marble upholding Pilate's chamber look like blood smears. No water but that of baptism could cleanse this house of the sin Pilate is committing in his attempt to avoid commitment.

FIG. 54
Jacopo Tintoretto,
Way to Calvary

On the other side of the door, Christ is toiling up Calvary, along a higher diagonal, which is crossed by the other two condemned men moving, in the opposite direction, up a lower diagonal. This motion in two directions, one in the foreground and the other farther back, is a regular device of the cinema—a famous case is the Alpine scene in Abel Gance's *Napoleon*, where Napoleon sweeps suddenly across the screen while his army, on another level, is moving slowly in the opposite direction. There is something very cinematic about this painting—it may reflect the processions the scuola mounted on feast days, reenacting gospel mysteries, with attendant banners and marchers. Christ, who is being dragged by a rope around his neck, now wears a scarlet tunic with a blue swath of cloth around his loins, and blood is again streaming down his face from the thorns in his brow. The Roman flags waving above him are tinted pink by a setting sun, as if rinsed in blood. The city's dedication to its precious blood relic received no more striking expression than this trilogy of red-filtered paintings.

The role of Christ's blood in Venetian piety and politics was bound to be adverted to in the Doge's Palace, since the doge was the official keeper of the relic. In the Senate hall, another huge Tintoretto painting shows the dead Christ's body upheld by angels and streaming its saving blood down toward the dais (P-R 2.222). The work belongs to the genre known from German scholars' study of it as the Engelpieta, "angel *pietà*" (S-L 99). The usual pietà (lament) is that of the Virgin holding (or otherwise caring for) her son's dead body—the most famous example being Michelangelo's statue of Mary with Christ in her lap. The Engelpieta shows the dead Christ supported by angels—sometimes, as in Tintoretto's Senate painting, suspended in the air; at other times, as in Giovanni Bellini's painting at the Correr museum, held upright in his tomb (T 196–97); or even supported by angels as he stands in a giant chalice.[6]

FIG. 55
Jacopo Tintoretto, *Dead Christ Between Angels*

In Tintoretto's Senate picture, the five angels holding up the lifeless body of Christ signify, mystically, his five wounds, all prominently displayed. In the Engelpieta, there is sometimes an angel with a chalice catching the blood that spurts from Christ's body, as the angel does in Giovanni Bellini's painting of the unsupported Christ in London's National Gallery (T 194). The Engelpieta was, therefore, a eucharistic motif, most often shown on the door of a tabernacle or above an altar, where the Eucharist was regularly consecrated. The blood of the image flowed, as it were, into the consecrated elements on the altar. The presence of the angels is explained by the ancient rite of the Mass, in which the priest said: "Bid these gifts be carried *in your devoted angel's hand* up to your exalted altar, subject to your divine majesty's gaze" (emphasis added). Saint Gregory the

Great commented: "What believer can doubt that, at this moment of offering, the heavens open at the priest's call, and the angelic chorus attends the sacrament, mingling depths with heights, terrestrial with celestial, uniting visible and invisible?" (s-l 100). A comparatively recent practice of the Renaissance church—the elevation of the host and chalice at the consecration of the Eucharist—reenacted this elevation of Christ's body by the angels, seen just behind the lifted elements at the Mass (s-l 106).

It is a mark of the sacredness of politics in Venice that such an image would be placed, not only on many altars, but also on the wall above the seat of the Senate's officers. The connection of the Engelpieta with politics was emphasized not only in the Doge's Palace. A particularly striking use of the formula is on the tabernacle door of San Marco, in the former place of eucharistic reservation behind the main altar (where tourists now

FIG. 56
Jacopo Sansovino, tabernacle door of San Marco

go to look at the Pala d'Oro). A relief by Sansovino on this door shows the angels collecting Christ's blood as it streams from him, and dancing in a bacchic revel, enacting the pious belief that mystic ecstasy is a way of being drunk on the blood of Christ (s-l 104)—a conceit repeated in Lorenzo Lotto's Engelpieta, now in Vienna.[7] An even more overtly political use of the symbol of Christ's blood is a painting by Domenico Tintoretto, Jacopo's son, which shows three jurists of the state (avogadori) being blessed by the risen Christ while a personified Venice takes the place of the angel who collects the blood flowing from him in a chalice (s-l 218).

SCUOLE DEL SACRAMENTO

Given this official devotion to the eucharistic mystery, it is not surprising that religious clubs (scuole) devoted to the sacrament were so numerous in Venice. Their mission was to adorn the altar where the sacrament was kept (between Masses) with paintings and statues, to attend with tapers the Eucharist when it was carried to any sick or dying member of the scuola, and to march with the Eucharist in processions. "On Good Friday 1515, [the diarist] Marin Sanudo commented on the sixteen large candles and four hundred torches which were carried by members of the Scuola del Santissimo Sacramento through the parish of San Cassiano."[8] There was at least one such scuola in every parish:

Between 1500 and 1539 there were 78 in Venice that we know of, and possibly many more. There were, indeed, so many companies that it was necessary to establish one single procession for the entire city for the feast of Corpus Christi, and leave to the initiative of the individual companies the repetition of it on other Sundays.[9]

Tintoretto was the favorite painter of the Scuole del Sacramento, which accounts for the large number of *Last Suppers* in his work. But his piety toward the Eucharist seems to have been personal as well as the result of these commissions. He put his self-portrait into a deposition from the cross that serves as an altarpiece in a lower chapel of San Giorgio Maggiore (P-R 2.234)—Tintoretto's is the figure supporting Christ's shoulders. The lowering of the body toward the altar is a common motif, and in this picture Tintoretto shows the blood flowing down Christ's limbs as if into the priest's chalice as he celebrates Mass at this altar. The painting, completed shortly before Tintoretto's own death, holds a place in his body of work like that of Titian's highly personal *Pietà* in the Accademia, which also contains a self-portrait of the aged artist.

FIG. 57
Domenico Tintoretto,
*Christ with Venice
and Chalice*

Many of Tintoretto's *Last Suppers* were of a large lateral format, meant to be hung on the side wall of a sanctuary of the Sacrament, with a matching picture on the other side of an Old Testament forecast of the Sacrament (usually the descent of manna from heaven). An especially powerful example of this schema is the *Manna–Last Supper* pair in the upper-church sanctuary of San Giorgio Maggiore (P-R 2.234). The pictures are meant to be viewed from the communion rail, where the Christian becomes a participant in the Last Supper. When one stands there, it becomes clear that the pictures are currently mounted on the wrong sides. The viewer's left is the privileged right side of the altar that faces us. That is why it was the New Testament side, where the gospel was read from one pulpit. The altar on this side was the more privileged one as well—it was often dedicated to the Virgin. The readings from the Old Testament were from the other pulpit, on the altar's left side. The readings moved from the Old, which is meant to be replaced, to the New—and that is the motion that should be imagined with these two paintings.

The Old Testament scene should be on our right, which fits better with the perspective lines of the painting. Moses sits in the lower corner nearest us, and the gesticulating man near him directs his attention (and ours) into the depths of the picture,

FIG. 58
Jacopo Tintoretto,
Last Supper

which recede off from us to the glittering crowd under the distant sky in the far upper corner of the painting. Since Moses is a forerunner of Christ, he has his features, and the horns of light from his encounter with God on Mount Sinai are still darting out from his halo. Despite this manifestation of his spiritual authority, the people are rebelling against him. The shining bits of manna are scattered on the ground, but the people disregard them. They are packing up to abandon Moses, who keeps luring them on in their long journey with only the "daily bread" of manna, what appears each morning only to melt during the day.

The scene is one of a people who reject the assistance of God, illustrating Numbers 21.5: "But on the way they became impatient and spoke against God and Moses. 'Why have you brought us up from Egypt,' they said, 'to die in the desert where there is neither food nor water? *We are heartily sick of this miserable fare*'" (New English Bible, emphasis added). The man who addresses Moses is pointing to the distant crowd already assembled for their departure. (They are stopped, later in the biblical account, only by a plague of fiery serpents.) It has been suggested (P-R 2.234) that this scene presents not only the Jewish rejection of Mosaic leadership but the writings of sixteenth-century reformers who were denying the reality of Christ's presence in the Eucharist. Moses can do nothing to stop the rebellion—only an intervention by God will accomplish that, in the form of the deadly plague.

On the other side (it should be our left side) we look once again up a long perspective line that originates near us in the lower corner of the picture and rises toward the distant upper corner—this diagonal is the dramatically slanted supper table. At our end of it, there is a spookily fuming oil lamp. Suspended from the ceiling, it blazes with a halo of translucent spirits around it. Other angels ghost in toward this table serving "the food of angels." They fulfill the words quoted earlier from the canon of the Mass. Christ is not passive, like Moses, but active in the midst of the crowd that recedes from us, moving to dispense the food of heaven, a server (*diakonos*) of it. The mystically glowing darkness, as S. J. Freedberg says, makes the whole scene one of transubstantiation: "Light turns substance and appearance into spirit."[10]

FIG. 59
Jacopo Tintoretto,
Manna in the Desert

In Tintoretto's *Last Supper* at San Polo Christ is thrusting his arms out as they will be stretched on the cross, identifying this sacrificial meal with the death it commemorates (P-R 2.194) Tintoretto might almost be illustrating lines from Chesterton's "The Ballad at the White Horse," where a Saxon chieftain responds to a Danish warrior, one who had mocked Christians as broken men. Colan of Caerleon says:

> Oh, truly we be broken hearts,
> For that cause, it is said,
> We light our candles to that Lord
> Who broke Himself for bread.[11]

FIG. 60 (BELOW)
Jacopo Tintoretto,
Last Supper

In Tintoretto's picture we actually see Christ breaking himself on the cross in the act of giving out his fragmented body.

SCUOLA GRANDE DI SAN ROCCO

PLATE XXII
Jacopo Tintoretto,
Ecce Homo

Even when Tintoretto is not painting *Last Suppers*, he gives a eucharistic sense to some of his canvases—as we saw in the *Ecce Homo* in St. Roch's Distinguished Brotherhood (P-R 2.190). When Tintoretto added a cycle of paintings to the large upper hall of this club, he covered the totality of salvation history, traced in the countertypes of the Old and New Testaments; but the dominant theme throughout is that of the Eucharist. The story begins at one end with Adam and Eve eating the food of death, and the

Eucharistic motifs quicken and reach a climax at the other end of the room, where the bread of life was administered from the altar.

Tintoretto not only painted all the ordinary symbols of the Sacrament—Moses striking water from the rock, Elijah being fed by angels, the fall of manna, the sacrifice of Isaac, the Passover meal, the multiplication of the loaves and fishes, the Last Supper. He added other episodes little known or used—Elisha multiplying loaves or Samson drinking from the jawbone of the "sacrificed" ass—that are included for no other reason than to maintain a running insistence on the Eucharist as the central mystery of faith.

So important is this theme that I think it should be recognized where people have consistently missed it. The first picture at the albergo end of the hall, close to the *Fall of Man* on the end wall, displays Christ's temptation in the desert (P-R 2.206). Christ has been fasting in a makeshift hut (we look up through its rickety latticework, as we do through the roof of the barn on the other side of the room, where Christ's birth has occurred). A muscular angel soars up toward Christ's lonely perch, offering either stones or loaves to Jesus. It is customary to say that Tintoretto has here, for the first and only time, depicted the devil as an angel of light, the better to work his temptation. The angel would then be saying, "If you are the son of God, tell these stones to become bread" (Mt 4.3). This certainly fits with the context of the painting—where Adam and Eve fell when given a food test, Jesus passes the test. The devil is disguised as a serpent in the first picture. Why should he not be disguised as an angel in this one?

FIG. 61
Jacopo Tintoretto,
Temptation of Christ

But the oddity of this interpretation is not confined to the unparalleled form given the devil. What we are given is the devil's demand, not the Lord's rejection. We do not see Jesus overcoming the devil, which is the climax and point of the whole story. Jesus is passive here, not the agent that he is in all representations of his acts before the chosen passivity of the Passion narrative. His gesture might even seem a welcoming one, hardly an argumentative or resisting one.

There are clues, inside this very cycle and in other parts of Tintoretto's work, to indicate the real meaning of this painting. There is another flying angel bringing food to a man in the desert in this very hall—he swoops down on Elijah with a pitcher of water and bread (P-R 2.204; the painter follows the Vulgate text of III Kings 19.6). This angel is a brother to the one in the picture of Christ's temptation—and to Tintoretto's other winged athletes in this hall, like those who wrestle off the tomb cover in the scene of Christ's resurrection (P-R 2.205). These narrative devices make us look to the end of the tale of Christ's temptation, where it is said that angels came after the devil was dismissed and "acted as his servers" (*diēkonoun*, Mt. 4.11), bringing him food to break his fast and end his stay in the desert. Adam and Eve failed the food test and were expelled from a garden of plenty to labor in penury. Jesus passes the food test and can leave a barren place to carry on his work of salvation.

This scene, like the feeding of Elijah, is an archetype of the Eucharist as what Thomas Aquinas called "the food of angels," picking up the theme of the angels' ministration characteristic of an Engelpieta. Proof of this can be found in some of Tintoretto's treatments of the Last Supper, where a loaf of bread resembles the "stones" in the angel's hands in the *Temptation*. Look, for instance, at the loaf being passed to the beggar in the *Last Supper* of San Polo, already referred to (P-R 2.194). As Rona Goffen remarks, a stone "is what Venetian bread looked like." In fact, the closest parallel to the angel in *The Temptation in the Desert*, who comes with loaves in his lifted hands, is the figure of Jesus in the San Polo painting, who offers the broken bread in hands exuberantly thrust out at arms' length. Christ comes to end the long fast of mankind, starved for spiritual sustenance, just as the angels had ended his own fast in the desert by acting as his servers (*diakonoi*) in Matthew 4.11. The body and blood of Christ permeate Venice's piety-polity.

FIG. 60
Jacopo Tintoretto,
Last Supper

CHAPTER SIXTEEN

Christ's Cross

THE TIE BETWEEN VENICE and Christ extended beyond Eucharistic devotion. The city's founding date, after all, the Feast of the Annunciation, was the date of Christ's incarnation as a human being. Bernardo Giustiniani, writing in 1423, developed the consequences of this founding act:

> This was the day when the highest and eternal wisdom—that is, the Word of God—descended into the breast of the most chaste Virgin, becoming a man to hide in the depths of a pitiable obscurity, so that he could eventually be raised to the joyous conclave of celestial spirits. Indeed, there are no limits to the divine wisdom. For He who chose the Virgin on that day for the redemption of the whole human race looked to her humility—and He decided that on the same day, in a place the most humble, with a people most humble, should begin the rise of our present Empire.[1]

In this comparison, the humble Mary and the humble site of Venice are equated, and the rising Empire and the ascending Savior are the natural concomitants of that equation.

What is more, March 25, the date of the Annunciation, was also the traditional date of the Crucifixion. These two aspects of the date are frequently mentioned together in accounts of the city's origin.[2] The city identified itself with the suffering and saving God. It is not surprising, then, that one of the city's six regions is called Holy Cross, after the ancient church of Santa Croce, once a Benedictine and then a Franciscan monastic church.[3] But no one church could monopolize devotion to the cross, since relics of the True Cross were so important to various communities.

FIG. 62
Gentile Bellini,
*The Miracle at the Bridge
of San Lorenzo*

THE TRUE CROSS

Though slivers from the cross were abundant in Italian cities, several such relics had earned special regard in Venice. One of high repute was brought back with the booty from the Fourth Crusade, where, in the fourth century, Saint Helen had deposited the entire cross.[4] Another famous fragment from the East was brought to Venice and donated to the Scuola Grande di Santa Maria della Carità by Cardinal Bessarion. The reliquary holding the fragment is a masterpiece, with enameled pictures of the Passion of Christ—it stands in the Accademia near a portrait of Bessarion holding it. The painting, by Giannetto di Cordeghliaghi, is one of several based on cartoons by Gentile Bellini, who did the original of this work, which was lost after someone stole it from the Carità in 1540.[5]

But the most famous Venetian relic of the Cross was the treasure of a different scuola grande, not the Carità but St. John the Evangelist's Distinguished Brotherhood. This relic was given to the scuola in 1369 by Philippe de Mézières, Grand Chancellor of the Venetian island of Cyprus. A representative of one of the historic patrician families, Andrea Vendramin, was the scuola's Guardian Grande (Principal Protector), who received the relic. Mézières and Vendramin are standing at the altar of the Church of St. John the Evangelist in a painting that records this event, Gentile Bellini's *Donation of the Relic* (s-n 110). This is one of ten works dedicated to the relic in the *albergo* of the scuola (the eight surviving ones are now in the Accademia). Two of the paintings showed miracles associated with Andrea Vendramin's Protectorship. In one of them (now lost) Pietro Perugino painted Vendramin praying in a dream that his ships at sea would be rescued from storm—and the relic flew off to work that miracle.[6] The other miracle is recorded in a painting by Gentile: While the newly acquired relic was being carried by scuola members in a procession over the San Lorenzo Bridge, its bearer tripped and dropped it into the canal. Though several people jumped into the canal to retrieve the relic, it skittered away from them all, darting about over the surface of the water beyond anyone's capture, until Vendramin, wearing the white robes of a scuola member, jumped into the canal—and the relic glided into the hands of its protector.[7]

Andrea Vendramin's fourteenth-century connection with the miracle-working cross was a matter of such pride to his sixteenth-century descendants that Titian painted members of the family in prayer before the reliquary shown in Gentile's painting. For this image Titian removed the relic from the scuola and placed it on an idealized outdoor altar of the mind (though one with winds whipping the candle flames on either side of the relic, w 2.33–35, 147). Here another Andrea Vendramin, a descendant of the earlier one, is seen bowing in his ermine-lined state robes before the relic, while his father kneels near it, and his son stands behind him. Thus three generations, arranged so that their heads are on a level, gaze at this symbol of family pride, while younger members of the line fidget or look out at us.

One of Gentile Bellini's other paintings for the miracle series in Saint John's club is the huge and hugely famous depiction *Procession in the Piazza San Marco* (s-n 102). This is such a valuable record of the appearance of the Piazza San Marco in 1496 that few viewers advert to the fact that it is the tale of a miraculous healing—and in fact Bellini has almost hidden the beneficiary of the miracle, a Brescian merchant in red garb who kneels under the slanted candle just behind the canopied reliquary, where he successfully asks that his son be healed. The fact that this is the Feast of Saint Mark, celebrated at the basilica of St. Mark, emphasizes the importance of the cross to Venice's political life. The relic is aligned with the principal portal of San Marco. The other scuole have already passed out of the foreground of the picture, and the doge's

PLATE XXIII
Titian,
The Vendramin Family

retinue is still approaching it on the right. The ornate reliquary is carried on a gold platform, and its bearers march under a canopy from which hang emblems of all the Distinguished Brotherhoods. The emblem of St. John's Brotherhood is a red tracery in the

FIG. 63
Gentile Bellini,
*Procession in the
Piazza San Marco*

shape of the reliquary, and each member of the club has it emblazoned on the breast of
his white robe. The city founded on the day of the crucifixion is expressing its inmost
nature here.

THE SAN ROCCO CRUCIFIXION

PLATE XXIV
Jacopo Tintoretto,
Crucifixion

One of the most powerful expressions of devotion to the cross is in the albergo of St.
Roch's Distinguished Brotherhood, the panoramic work of Tintoretto that covers the
entire wall behind the governors' dais in that room (P-R 2.189–90). The horizontal
shape of this huge canvas posed severe problems of composition—how to include
enough incidents to fill forty feet of lateral space, without letting the picture fall into
disjunct segments? The proportionately short height of the picture is compensated for
in several ways. Only one of the three crosses is in the vertical position, and it is truncated. The top of the cross—the section of it that normally holds the inscription nailed
there by Pilate's order—is outside the picture. Thus the large circular halo around
Christ's body (not just his head)—like a stricken and fading sun, as Ruskin thought—
is cut off before it completes more than its lower semicircle.[8] Christ's arms outspread

on the cross are at the top edge of the painting, which continues their horizontal reach, directing our attention outward to events taking place as if under Christ's wings.

A second compositional device, described by David Rosand, arranges the crowd of onlookers in the shape of a large horizontal oval that is completed only below the lower edge of the picture, including us viewers in its sweeping compass.[9] We are part of this crowd. As the missing head of the cross and the uncompleted halo at the top extend the picture above its vertical strictures, so the uncompleted oval of the crowd carries it beyond its lower edge.

Other features drive the picture into our space. One is the diagonal thrust of the platform on which Christ's cross stands. Its wedge shape comes at us, as S. J. Freedberg says, like a plow.[10] Second, the other crosses are not placed on the platform with Christ, but in holes dug or being dug out in front of it, near us. One cross is still being wrestled into its hole by the men who lean out at us or draw back on the rope that continues its line toward us, so we are almost lifting the thief's cross ourselves if we stand on the left side of the picture. The Guardian Grande of St. Roch's Club, the man on the white horse, reinforces the line of the rope with his pointing arm, bringing us into his contemplation of the scene. On the other side, one man is just beginning to dig the hole for the bad thief, who—up on the platform—is about to be pinned to the cross as it lies on the ground.

All these elements of the painting move out toward us through Tintoretto's artful manipulation of space. If we look at the picture only from Christ's torso upward, he will seem on the forward plane of the picture, flush with its upper edge. Then, when we look down, we see that there is a vast range of actions occurring *in front of* the platform on which Christ's cross is raised.[11] On the left, the members of the scuola are as much in our space as in that of the platform. Not only are the comforters around the swooning Virgin on our side of the platform; so is the woman (Mary Magdalene) standing behind them. And on the right, the Roman and Jewish officials on horseback are in the space of the man beginning to dig his hole for the third cross—while soldiers huddle beyond him, but still at the edge of the platform, to gamble for Christ's robe.

So Christ is literally displaced, near us in the timeless upper zone, but thrust back from us by complex intervening actions at the lower part. We can approach him only up the lines of force that are raising the good thief. Christ is only partly in this our world, as the interrupted halo around him indicates. Could we see that glory's upper half, it would be bright with the radiance of another realm. Christ at this culminating moment is in time but also in eternity. The flat stretch of his arms resembles the level arms on Byzantine paintings that showed Christ as literally reigning from the cross, in royal robes and with a crown of gold, not of thorns. Once we realize this, we can look again at the figures around the base of the cross. They hide the actual socketing of the cross in the earth—is it really on the platform or just in front of it? In either case, it rises just at the forward point of the platform's "plow." Its literal place on earth is hidden from us. Despite all the realistic detail of human strain and bodies' torque, the quiet Christ floats free of earthly logic, "sprung" from the picture's confines.

The painting's lateral extent is also bound together by the great diagonals of the flanking crosses, one surging upward, the other slanting off at an angle as it lies on the ground. These, along with the ladders and ropes, are counterpointed against the wedge-thrust of the platform. The cross's struggle upward on our left looks back to the reason so many ladders are included in treatments of the Passion. Medieval artists showed Christ *climbing* the cross, using a ladder, to show his voluntary acceptance of death.[12] Christians were urged to rise with him, like the good thief, who gazes with acceptance at Christ—and he returns the gaze. The other thief, by contrast, has been dragged to the scene with the ropes held by the red-capped man on horseback and the muscular man on foot (one rope is still tied around the thief's arm). This criminal has his back turned to Christ and is resisting the cross that should be his salvation.

Early church fathers began a tradition of seeing the cross itself as a ladder, or a lifting apparatus—a scaffold or a crane—to take people to heaven with Christ. The strenuous raising of the good thief's cross recalls Ignatius of Antioch's words early in the second century: "You are lifted on high through the scaffolding of Jesus Christ, which is his cross—you are winched upward by the Holy Spirit."[13] Hippolytus in the same century spoke of the cross as a mast on the ship of the church, to let Christians climb up into the rigging of heaven.[14] Methodius said the cross is a construction crane that lifts Christians up as living stones to be built into the city of God.[15] Similar images were used by Justin Martyr.[16] Tintoretto would later paint, in the large upper hall of St. Roch's Club, the Hebrew Scriptures' supposed typology for this elevation—the raising of a healing serpent-sign in the wilderness in Numbers 21.9: "As Moses exalted the serpent in the desert, so must the Son of Man be exalted" (Jn 3.14).[17] All the scurry and effort of this picture are fulfilling a plan. Its swarming energies are contained in a cyclone of providential inevitability.

The idea that Christ is reigning as a judge on the cross picks up a frequent arrangement of people in treatments of the crucifixion. The sympathetic are bunched on Christ's right hand, the side of the saved in *Last Judgments*. That is the side, here, where the members of the Scuola Grande di San Rocco are grouped. On a rise in the distance stand the women followers of Jesus, while people closer to the cross look on and gesture in horror at what is happening. The mysteriously hooded figure on the far left who points to the cross represents the prophets who foretold this event. Other people are coming out of the gates of Jerusalem, moving from the Old Testament to the New—in contrast with the Romans and Jews on our right hand (Christ's left), who are distanced both from the Holy City and from the person whose death they look on with equanimity.

It is true that the soldiers on the "saved" side are crucifying the good thief, but they are unconsciously performing a service, and they are at least industrious. They have put down their crossbow arrows and are functioning as a team at their difficult task, five of them straining every nerve to work the cross into its socket. The soldiers on the other side are remiss—they let the work lag as they huddle to gamble under the ledge of rock. Rosand noticed that the great oval that arcs around to include us moves from the left to the right—toward Christ on the saved side, away from him on the condemned side. The Final Judgment is already being anticipated.

Tintoretto's canvas holds a theatrical pageant with a tremendous inwardness of spiritual meanings. One can enter it at many levels and not exhaust its implications. The artists in the cycle at St. John the Evangelist's Club painted only the miracles worked by the cross. Tintoretto gave the members of his scuola the miracle that *is* the cross.

CHAPTER SEVENTEEN

Venetian Annunciations

I MPERIAL PIETY IN VENICE, directed first toward Christ, was only slightly less intense in its devotion to the Virgin Mary—of necessity. After all, the source of both devotions was the same, the founding day of Venice, the Annunciation. As one would expect, the Venetians had not only a special fondness for this New Testament episode, but special ways of showing it. We have already seen this in the reenactments of the episode that took place during the Feast of the Marys. There are also special touches in the way Venetian painters presented the Annunciation. This is specially apparent in Tintoretto's great picture of the mystery for the Brotherhood of St. Roch (P-R 2.225).

TINTORETTO

Here there is no hushed appearance of the divine messenger to a cloistered young girl. A whole squadron of angels peels off like fighter bombers to strafe the rather ramshackle building where a seated housewife, far from glamorous, has recently been at her chores—her spinning wheel is still on the table, its thread dangling. She is startled (as well she might be) by this incursion, and drops the book she was reading, throwing her hand back in discomposure. Her husband does not notice the dive bombers, but continues working in his lumberyard just outside the house. All these elements make this the quintessential Venetian Annunciation.

To see how idiosyncratic is this approach to the tale, one has to contrast it with the radically different formulae adhered to by most Renaissance painters. There the angel, splendid of wing and decorous of bearing, salutes a young girl who is seated or kneeling in prayer. Since theologians taught that Mary is the "second Eve," called to reverse the harm done by the first woman, she is presented with all the human perfection that would have existed before original sin. Her garden, often glimpsed behind or beside her

PLATE XXV
Jacopo Tintoretto,
Annunciation

house, is a second Eden, blooming with pristine flowers (March 25 is a spring day, when nature is renewed). The woman has a control and serenity unravaged by the passions that entered history with Eve's sin. Symbols of her purity are present—a clear vessel, which light penetrates without violating, a flower or flowers in a vase (exegetes said that Nazareth, her home, means "flower" in Hebrew), doves, a limpid fountain, the enclosed garden. Her house is, in Italy (though not in northern versions of the tale), a simple but elegant home, spotless as she is. In fact the chamber she prays in is a symbol of her own body, filled with light and peace.

And if the house in general is her body, the withdrawn bedchamber, often visible behind her, is her womb, unrumpled by this act of spiritual impregnation. There is usually a pillar between her and the angel, a symbol of her unapproachability by any but the Spirit. In fact, several barricades or thresholds are offered to demonstrate her remoteness from all contact but God's grace, which streams toward her as a supernatural light, emanated from the Father or his Spirit (in the form of a dove). She is herself a sealed garden (*hortus conclusus*), and she often crosses her hands on her breast as if closing herself within herself. But she is also the gate of heaven (*janua coeli*), which explains the way her chamber opens onto vistas of unspoilt (unfallen) nature. Her isolation is emphasized, not a sterile separateness but an expression of her own plenitude of grace. From this moment, as John Donne put it, she harbors "Immensity cloistered in thy dear womb."[1]

Turn now from those scenes, the normal ones, to Tintoretto's stormy picture. No neat garden here, but a junkyard clutter of scrap lumber. No perfect enclosure in portico or chamber, but a rotted wall—plaster is flaking from its brick substrate; the base is all that is left of an ornamental pilaster; a structural upright has wood with slots in it for missing cross beams. Here are no spare but perfect furnishings, but a chair with its straw seat raveling out. No silvery dawn of a new day, in the blue of a Tuscan sky; but a livid smear of sunset behind the lumberyard. Another source of light, unexplained, strikes the dilapidating pillar and shines on the broken chair, leaving Mary in shadow.

Gabriel does not pause respectfully on the other side of a pillar, but penetrates her space in a barrel-roll rush of his veering wings. The putti accompanying the sacred dove skim up and over the remaining cross beam of the door, which stands free of the shattered wall. Mary, who was facing us as she sat with her book, is violently twisted round by the flutter over her shoulder of arriving wings. And this is no porcelain princess. If not exactly coarse, she is earthy, more like a pagan earth mother than the holy dove's little doll bride as painted by Fra Angelico. In fact, Tintoretto's scene suggests the showering seed of Zeus over Danae, that Venetian specialty of Titian, more than the Virgin's cool poise in Florentine pictures of the Annunciation.

What is Tintoretto up to? Is he just secularizing or sensationalizing, as some detractors have said of him? It is hard to believe that the officers of the scuola who commissioned the work would accept such a result, in this building put up for pious use and communal worship. Tintoretto's companion pictures on these walls have deep theological justification for their daring, and we expect the same from this painting. To justify those expectations, we need to consider carefully two clues to Tintoretto's purpose—the ruined house, and the working husband. Take first the house's peeling plaster and exposed brick. This is, we should notice, a Venetian structure typical of modest palazzi—light brick on a wooden frame, with a thin coat of plaster facing. Grand edifices could be built on the muddy Venetian lagoon, but only by sinking thick bundles of piles below the mushy surface to provide a base. Even then, as the many tilting bell towers remind us, the footing was difficult. Less pretentious buildings took exactly the form Tintoretto has given us.

Where, in the iconography of the Virgin, do we find architectural ruins as a regular feature? Not in Annunciations but in Nativities. If Renaissance artists show us the divine child laid in a manger, the manger is incongruously pitched inside the shell of a disused and moldering classical temple. This was to indicate that the new age brought to birth in Bethlehem would supersede the old law of Rome or Jerusalem. (Medieval legend claimed that the Capitoline temple was toppled at Christ's birth, just as the veil of the Temple was torn across by his death.) Since the Renaissance had just rediscovered the ruins of Herculaneum and Pompeii, artists were given patterns for the depiction of an old order sunken and displaced. Prints of the ruins near Naples provided elements that entered into paintings throughout Italy.

Though Tintoretto uses here a Venetian palazzo, not a Roman temple, it is clear that he is thinking of Mary at the Nativity, as we can see by the elements of transience in the picture. The Mary of conventional Annunciations is at home in Nazareth, in her perfect chamber with its adjacent perfect garden. But the house in Tintoretto's picture is a home for the homeless, like the Bethlehem of Nativity pictures. Though the Venetian house has seen better days, as we can tell from its richly coffered ceiling and the grand canopy over the bed, it is not—with its bare frame of a door standing where no wall remains—a fit place for permanent habitation. It cannot keep out the bad weather coming. The cloth Mary had been working on with her spinning wheel—it spills off the table toward us—will be needed in the days ahead.

The carpenter's yard of Joseph might suggest a permanent workplace, but it too is disordered and in the open, not the neat quarters of a Venetian *squero*, where craftsmen built *gondole*. It is unusual to have Joseph present at all. We have seen that Mary's inaccessibility was emphasized in the normal Annunciation. In fact, the gospel account does not have Joseph living with Mary at this time. He only takes her as his wife when the angel assures him that the child in her womb is not begotten by another man. Then why does he show up here? It helps to consider his place in the picture—to the left and in the background. In some other treatments of this story, that place was reserved for a symbolic scene, the expulsion of Adam and Eve from Paradise by the angel with a fiery sword.

This is an appropriate parallel for Gabriel's mission to Mary. As one angel had driven out the original parents for their sin, another brings news of the parentage that will redeem a fallen mankind. In pictorial accounts of Genesis (like that on the ceiling of the baptistery in St. Mark's basilica (D 2.116–17), the scene that follows on this expulsion is that of Adam and Eve forced to labor as a result of their expulsion, Joseph with a hoe or spade, and Eve with a distaff. In Tintoretto's picture, Joseph is seen laboring with a saw instead of a spade, since the gospel calls him a carpenter. As the second Eve, Mary was pictured by Byzantine artists holding a distaff when Gabriel brought her the news. In Tintoretto the distaff has appropriately fallen when Mary turns suddenly toward the angel—she is about to end the curse of Eve. In Venice, brides went back to their father's house on the eighth day after the wedding to receive a distaff.[2] The eighth day stood for the fall of man, after the six days of creation and the seventh day of rest. Mary in this picture is closely related to Venetian life.

It is clear then that Tintoretto has not simply contaminated the Annunciation formulae with realistic detail, but has complicated the iconography by blending in two other conventions—the picture of Adam and Eve at labor (from Genesis) and the Nativity set in a temporary and deteriorating world. He has shown, that is, not the second Paradise that will result from this descent of the Spirit into mankind, but the moment *before* that rescue occurs. This is still the world of fallen human beings, who must cope with decay and toil and shadow. There is as much warrant for this reading of the Luke passage as for the one that stresses Mary's exemption from the effects of sin. Before the moment of resignation when Mary says, "Let it happen to me as you say," she was "thrown into turmoil" (the Greek is very strong, *dietarachthē*; in Latin, *turbata est*) by the news that she will bear a child, since she is a virgin. Only when the angel assures her that the impregnation will be miraculous does she submit her will. This shows that, at this stage, she is not exempt from human passions of bewilderment and anxiety.

The violent reaction of Mary to the new order breaking into her world recalls another aspect of the Annunciation. As the remaking of human nature, it shows Mary as the reverser of order in the fallen world. The angel's greeting to her is, in Latin, *Ave*, "Hail," which exegetes liked to point out is *Eva* reversed. In the original creation, the Spirit of God overshadowed the disorderly waters of inchoate matter and brought order into them, and then Eve was drawn (without a mother) from Adam's side. In this picture, the Spirit descends on the chaos of a sinful world and places in the womb of a woman a man (without a human father) who becomes the first human being of the restored world. The squalor of Tintoretto's setting is what has to be refashioned by the newly conceived being. Even the sour light fading in the distance is a sign, like the decaying house, that the end of a sin-blighted time is at hand. Which brings us to the unexplained illumination coming from our (the viewers') side, which strikes the peeling wall. Light from two sources—one natural, the other supernatural—is a common device in pictures of miracle. In this case, the light shines past the decay to make Gabriel's wind-whipped robe sparkle in the gloom of the chamber he enters. His own face has moved ahead of the light; it is still left in shadow, like the figure of Mary. This is the moment before the incarnation occurs, and the light should be seen as moving *with* Gabriel's speeding figure. He literally brings light with him, trailing it behind him on his rapid errand. It will strike her as the act of will seals the compact between God and man. The flare of light on the structural decay is a last moment of sin's reign, ending even as we watch.

This is an Annunciation fitted to the purpose of the Scuola Grande di San Rocco, which was formed to bring light into the chambers affected by plague and poverty (Saint Roch was the patron of plague victims). It is a picture for those who felt that the light of Christ must continually beat back darkness. The laboring Adam and Eve were models for a Venice that put great store by labor and discipline, no longer as the penalty for sin but as part of the effort to rebuild the orderly world of restored mankind. It also reflects a belief that human struggle is rewarded by God. The Spirit that broods over chaos has wrought a new kind of order, reflected in the "common people" who will be present with the Magi in the next picture of Tintoretto's series in the Club—Mary in a hovel herself, with servants voluntarily bringing their offerings to the child.

VERONESE

The Venetian painters favored the perturbed Mary over the serene one. She is often spun around, with a wrenching of her body, by the angel's appearance from behind her—a theme the painters took from the twelfth-century mosaic in the north transept of their beloved San Marco (D 1.132), which shows the angel interrupting Mary as she is taking water from a well.[3] In the early 1560s Veronese painted a ceiling Annunciation in oval form, one now seen in the restored Rosary Chapel of the Church of Saints John and Paul (P 1.213–14). Mary turns again at the dramatic incursion of the angel, who drops straight down from heaven as if his wings were acting like a parachute. The abruptness of his plunge lifts the skirt of his gown up his calves, swirling it out into columnar form—echoing the heavy and twisting baroque columns on either side of the picture. Mary is framed in a soaring arch between the columns, a stunning use of Mary's symbol as heaven's portal (*janua coeli*). The suddenness of the Virgin's turn has swirled her robe out, too, in a columnar shape. Speed and architectural form blend in a

FIG. 64
Paolo Veronese,
Annunciation

paradoxically *constructive* moment of sudden drama. Both of Mary's hands are thrown out with a responsiveness that blends surprise and acceptance. The columns' busy swirls are interrupted in the middle by a band of bas-relief that gives a pause and permanence to their drama, as if these reliefs were "wombs" of quiet within the restive columns' writhing—expressing what is about to occur in the agitated Virgin's womb. In Veronese, much of the meaning of any picture is carried by its architecture. Here, by literally giving Mary no "grounding," we see an architectural complex built in air (appropriate to a ceiling painting), an adumbration of the heavenly Jerusalem glimpsed through the janua coeli.

TITIAN

Slightly before Veronese's painting, early in the 1560s, Titian had created the *Annunciation* that hangs in the Church of San Salvador (w 1.71–72). Here, too, Mary turns sharply about at the angel's entry. She has been kneeling at her prie-dieu, facing to our right, but she closes the Bible on her finger, lifts one knee from the prie-dieu, and pulls up her veil—all in one quick movement—to look back toward the angel. But the real action here is not that of the angel, who crosses his arms on his breast in the gesture often given Mary in older Annunciations. This angel is less a messenger than a witness, in awe of what is occurring—because above Mary the Spirit is descending (as a dove) in a lava flow of white light through fiery golds. The whole picture is a perfect example of Titian's hyperbolic claim that he really needed only three colors, white and black and red.[4] The white-hot purity of the dove kindles everything else in this quivering scene to endlessly nuanced reds glowing in the darkness of the Virgin's room. Titian, unlike other painters, represents this as a night scene—Mary was about to retire to the bed that is no longer visible at the darkened right edge of the picture.[5]

The angel's robes are a paler version of the clouds through which the dove is driving. The putti who careen crazily about the clouds wave a red cloth that is a symbol of pious ardor—and it perfectly matches the tunic worn by the Virgin. The flowers in the translucent vase of water at her feet are not so much flowers as little patches of local fire

FIG. 65
Titian, *Annunciation*

anomalously feeding on the water's purity (they were actually represented as jets of flame in an early engraving of this work).[6] Everything in the picture expresses the motto in the lower right-hand corner, IGNIS ARDENS NON COMBURENS—"a burning, not a consuming, fire," taken from the description of Moses' burning bush (Exodus 3.2), which burned bright red yet was not consumed (*rubus arderet et non combureretur*).

The ardent flame-reds of this picture recall the use Titian made of this color in his first great success, nearly half a century before the San Salvador painting—the colossal *Assumption of Mary* over the Frari church's high altar (w 1.74–76). The ascent of Mary is visible as a rising flame all the way down the long nave. This picture's contrast with the serenity of earlier treatments of the Assumption of Mary at her death is like the difference between a Fra Angelico *Annunciation* and Tintoretto's. An *Assumption* ordinarily showed a tranquil Mary, her hands folded in prayer, being lifted up by angels in the form of a *mandorla*—the almond-shaped body halo that suggests the intersection of two spheres of reality.[7] Titian, by contrast, has Mary spiral up in rapt ecstasy, reaching her arms out in longing toward God. The two men below who wear garments the same color as hers form with her a triangle of red, with her at the apex. One man stretches out his arms toward her with an ardor to match her own. She is not enfolded in a mandorla but carried within a semicircle of angels and clouds. If the dove's white heat lit the underworld in the *Annunciation*, here her own warmth seems to tinge the heavens along the top arch of the picture with the glow of her love. This is a very human and passionate virgin, one whose passion has spread to her followers. Rona Goffen shows that the Franciscans commissioned this painting to illustrate their favorite (and embattled) doctrine, of Mary's immaculate conception (without original sin), which supposedly freed her from human passions.[8] Yet it is the passion of Titian's woman that prevails.

FIG. 66
Jacopo Tintoretto,
Mary (Church)

AVE/EVA

A continuing emphasis in the theology of the Annunciation is the contrast between Mary's obedience to the call of the Spirit and Eve's disobedience to the divine command.

As the angel's greeting, "Ave," is the reverse of *Eva*, so Mary undoes what Eve did. This close association, it seems to me, explains the mysterious two paintings that flank the altar at the end of the lower hall in St. Roch's Club. These are two moonlit landscapes with a river running through them, and a lone woman seated with a book on each canvas (P-R 2.226). Since the most famous female hermits are the repenting prostitutes, Mary Magdalene and Mary of Egypt, those are the names commonly given in catalogues.[9] The palm tree in the right-hand picture is taken as a reference to Mary of Egypt's locus—but that is the only positive point of identification given for either figure.

It is hard to tell why these two women should be present, in a theological sequence carefully planned, where they have no apparent function. Mary of Egypt is a rare figure in Venice, one totally unconnected with the mission of St. Roch's Club, and the Magdalene is not given any of her common attributes—long hair, a cross clutched to her breast, signs of a fast, seminudity. In fact, neither figure has the typical hermit's rags or hair shirt or haggard look. They are, rather, well dressed ladies in urban clothes. Nonetheless, Hans Tietze suggested they were originally part of a series of hermits planned for another site, to be paired with male hermits like the one in Tintoretto's sketch, now at Princeton, where the landscape plays as prominent a role as in the Saint Roch paintings (P-R 2.220). But that work seems to display Saint John the Evangelist on the Isle of Patmos, writing his Revelation. There are pen and ink beside him, and he is consulting several books—Tintoretto's customary way of presenting the evangelists as they compare New Testament events with Old Testament prophecies. (See, for instance, the evangelists in Santa Maria del Giglio, P-R 2.166–67.)

FIG. 67
Jacopo Tintoretto,
Eve (Synagogue)

It is often the case, when two books or two sets of books are juxtaposed in Renaissance art, that one thinks immediately of the Christian linkage between the Old Testament and the New. Is that what we have here? The books are the only attributes of the women. Otherwise, their geographical orientation is the most obvious difference between them, one looking back up the river as it flows by her, one looking down along its flow. And the one looking downriver is on the Gospel side of the altar, while the one looking back upstream is on the Old Testament side, where readings from it had their special pulpit.

The principal women of the two Testaments were, obviously, Eve and Mary. Are those the two figures here? It might be objected that Eve should not have a halo—though, as we shall see, Old Testament figures are regularly treated as saints in Venetian art. But Eve is a great sinner, isn't she, not a saint? Not according to the Byzantine treatment of the anastasis, the freeing of Adam and Eve when Christ "descended into hell." This theme was a powerful one in Venetian art—in the mosaics at Torcello and San Marco, on the Pala d'Oro, and in Tintoretto's own "harrowing of hell" in the church of San Cassiano (P-R 2.194).[10] One might rather think of the figures as the Old Testament and the New Testament personified rather than as Eve and Mary. But the normal way of making that contrast was to show a personified Synagogue and Church, as in the mosaics in the arch on one's right as one enters San Marco (D 1.254, 259). It seems far more appropriate to end the San Roch cycle in the lower hall just as its story began in the upper hall. Above, Eve in Eden was juxtaposed with Mary in Bethlehem. In the lower hall, Eve looks back at the old Jerusalem while the water rushes by her. Mary looks to the future, to a fulfillment of the stream of revelation running from the prophecies onward toward the Parousia. Mary of the Annunciation is present even in this idyllic scene.

PLATE I (ABOVE)
Saint Mark's Body Carried into the Basilica, Byzantine mosaic

PLATE II (LEFT)
Apparition of the Relics of Saint Mark (left half), Byzantine mosaic

PLATE III
Apparition of the Relics of Saint Mark (right half),
Byzantine mosaic

PLATE IV (BELOW)
Vision of Saint Mark,
San Marco mosaic

PLATE V
Giovanni Bellini,
Leonardo Loredan

PLATE VI
Titian,
Doge Andrea Gritti

PLATE XI
Judgment of Solomon

PLATE XII
Antonio Rizzo,
relief, Scala dei Giganti

PLATE XIII
Jacopo Sansovino,
the Loggetta of the
Campanile of San Marco

PLATE XIV
Ca' d'Oro façade

PLATE XV
Giovanni Bellini,
Virgin Between Saints Nicholas,
Peter, Benedict, and Mark

PLATE XVI (BELOW)
Vittore Carpaccio,
Ursula United with Ereus

PLATE XVII
Pietro Lombardo,
Santa Maria dei Miracoli

PLATE XVIII
Jacopo Tintoretto,
Adoration of the Shepherds

PLATE XIX
Titian, *Sacred and Profane Love*

PLATE XX
Jacopo Tintoretto, *Paradise*

PLATE XXI
Jacopo Tintoretto,
Agony in the Garden

PLATE XXII (BELOW)
Jacopo Tintoretto,
Ecce Homo

PLATE XXIII
Titian, *The Vendramin Family*

PLATE XXIV
Jacopo Tintoretto, *Crucifixion*

PLATE XXV
Jacopo Tintoretto,
Annunciation

PLATE XXVI
Lorenzo Lotto, *Annunciation*

PLATE XXVII
Santi Giovanni e Paolo,
window

PLATE XXVIII
Vittore Carpaccio,
Vision of Saint Augustine

PLATE XXIX
Giovanni Bellini,
Ecstasy of Saint Francis

PLATE XXX (BELOW)
Titian,
Presentation of the Virgin

PLATE XXXI
Andrea Palladio,
Il Redentore façade

CHAPTER EIGHTEEN

The Vulnerable Mary

ALL ITALIAN CITIES SHOWED great devotion to the Virgin. Many (but not Venice) dedicated their most important church (the duomo, or cathedral) to her—Florence, Siena, Milan, San Gimignano. They made her a queen or an empress. Florence, for instance, painted the Virgin as Her Majesty (Maestà)—seated, apart from God the Father and the Holy Spirit, in the air, suspended by angels whose fluttering wings hold up her throne. Three magnificent examples of this genre are in the first room visitors enter at the Uffizi gallery in Florence—by Cimabue, Duccio, and Giotto. The same treatment of Mary as Her Majesty can be found in other cities, often in their public palaces, making her a political ruler as well as a religious icon—the *Maestà* by Simone Martini in Siena, for instance, or by Lippo Memmi in San Gimignano.

Since this type came from Byzantium, where the empress at court was a glorified figure, one would expect it to show up in Venice, with its strong Byzantine background. But it did not. One reason for this may be that the Venetians had no feudal tradition into which the type could be absorbed. We got the feudal logic behind the Maestà in the earlier-cited declaration of fiefdom to Mary by the mayor of Siena in 1260—just one of five recorded formal deedings of Siena to Mary (s-L 52). Forgoing the Maestà, the Venetians expressed their early allegiance to Mary in ambitious pictures of her coronation in heaven. Instead of her being seated holding the infant Jesus, facing out at us, on a throne before we which we are to bow, she is seated sideways beside the adult Jesus, who crowns her, with the Father and the Son above them. Here there is an even larger throne structure than in the Maestà; but it is a vast tiered work of architecture into which all the saints are integrated—prophets, patriarchs, fathers of the church, evangelists, virgins, martyrs. Mary represents the church that upholds her, and the entire mystical body of Christ is crowned in her as its representative. As Staale Sind-ing-Larsen argues, "The essence of the iconography of the Coronation was ecclesiolog-ical, and the motif was directly connected with the concept of the salvation of mankind" (s-l 46–47).

The great exposition of this theme in Venice was the *Coronation* by Guariento that covered the whole wall behind the dais in the Larger Council hall—where Tin-

FIG. 68
Tullio Lombardo,
Coronation of the Virgin

toretto's *Paradise* is now installed. It was not till 1903, when the Tintoretto was moved for preservation work, that people realized the Guariento fresco, faded and damaged, was still there behind it. Removed into a nearby room, it has a sweeping grandeur even in its ruinous state. The first room visitors enter at the Accademia has two large can-vases modeled on Guariento's fresco—the Corona-tions by Jacobello del Fiore (s-l 46) and by Michele Giambono (s-n 46–47), where the serried ranks of the saints are built up as "living stones of the Spirit's dwelling" (1 Peter 2.5).[1] More modest Coronations, in this same room of the Accademia, have the same theological purport—see especially those by Paolo Veneziano and Carino (s-n 30, 36).

TULLIO LOMBARDO

A *Coronation of the Virgin* of 1500–1502 also identifies Mary with the church, but in ways so startling that it is easy to miss the point, or the multiple points, being made. This is Tullio Lombardo's altarpiece relief for the Bernabo Chapel of the Apostles in San Giovanni Crisostomo (p-h 2.424). Here Mary is not seated beside Christ in heaven. She kneels before him on earth, as he places a crown on her head. The two figures are not surrounded by choirs of angels and saints, by tiered ranks of martyrs and fathers of the church. Instead, twelve apostles all in a row (to whom the chapel is dedicated) are arranged across the surface, as in the friezes on ancient sarcophagi, six on either side of the two central figures. Christ is not taller than the two most prominent disciples, Peter and Paul. He is not splendidly robed as in the heavenly Coronations. He has no halo.

His clothes do not differ from the other men's. The whole scene is deliberately stiff and archaizing, a bold departure from the normal iconography of the Coronation.

> Many scenes from the New Testament could readily be represented *all'antica*, and transposed into the language of imperial art. But this scene of Christ, the Virgin and the Apostles was not among them, and the prospect of portraying this most mystical of scenes as an event in space and time would have daunted an artist less intoxicated with antiquity. (P-H 2.330)

But Tullio was going back to early Christian as well as classical art, and the treatment was deeply Venetian after all. Sarah Wilk demonstrates that the scene is an adaptation of an early Christian motif. It represents the founding of the church by institution of its laws (Traditio Legis). There is, in the Treasury of San Marco, a thirteenth-century imitation of an ancient relief sculpture representing the Traditio Legis, a relief that Tullio knew and imitates here. (He probably accepted the frieze as an authentic survival from early Christian art, since it reproduces that period's poses and clothing and style.)[2] In the San Marco frieze, the apostles are lined up across the surface, just as in Tullio's work, but the Virgin is absent. Instead, Peter is genuflecting where Mary knelt, and Christ, turning to his right as in the Tullio scene, gives a document to Peter as he gives a crown to Mary. The document is the New Law he has come to institute in his church. The parallel is with God giving the Old Law to Moses on Mount Sinai. The fact that God as man gives his legislation, on flat earth, to a circle of disciples—rather than God as mystery giving law, on the mountaintop, to a single person—shows the meaning of the Incarnation, of the God who has come among his creatures as one of them.

Tulllio has replaced Peter with Mary, since the crowning is, as Sinding-Larsen put it, an ecclesiological subject. Mary personifies the church to which Christ gives his New Law. She receives honor as such while kneeling on the earth, rather than seated in heaven, to show that she is with the struggling church here below, as its representative, the "earthly" Mary that Tintoretto and other Venetians liked to paint. Wilk goes further. She claims that Mary is also Venice. The personified female Venice was often identified with Mary, as well as with Justice—which is why Jacobello del Fiore had the Archangel of the Annunciation, carrying the lily of the Annunciation, address Venice as if she were Mary in the Accademia painting mentioned before. There was a polemical meaning in substituting Mary for Peter. After all, "the Traditio Legis is a papal theme *par excellence*," so ousting Peter from the central spot in it cannot be seen as innocent of political intent.[3]

> Venetians openly disputed the theoretical basis of Rome's primacy. They espoused
> the Orthodox interpretation about the equal status of the Patriarchates, and asserted
> that Venice herself was the center of an apostolic see . . . Thus Venice confected the-
> ological justification to support her opposition to Papal rule. As part of this hostility,
> Venetian historians condemned ancient Rome. Venice openly derided the Pope. One
> of the ambassadors brashly warned the Pope [in 1509] that if he were to continue
> opposing Venice, the government would reduce him to a petty village priest.[4]

Tullio used a frieze in San Marco to make one of those continuing declarations of independence that Venice bristled with. Here is Mary as both church and Venice, and she is crowned in a church dedicated to the Greek church father Chrysostom. Let Rome make of that what it will.

TINTORETTO

When fire in the Larger Council ruined Guariento's huge fresco of the Coronation of Mary, Tintoretto won the contest to replace it with a work on canvas. Although he was supposed to keep to the earlier theme, he greatly altered the emphasis and meaning, so that his work is rightly called a Paradiso, not a Coronation. As in Tullio's frieze, Mary is not seated beside Jesus. She is on a lower level, kneeling to him. And he does not reach over to place a crown on her head. His right hand is held low, in a generally welcoming gesture, while his left hand rests on the crystal globe that is his symbol as the World's Savior (Salvator Mundi). Mary and Jesus have haloes that intermingle, though hers circles her head in a decorous ring, while his shoots out from him like fireworks going off. This is not a demotion of Mary so much as part of the emphasis on Christ in the council halls that was described in Chapters 14 and 15. There was a deepening awareness that the city must be a vicar of the Christ brought into being on its birthday, the Feast of the Annunciation. That is emphasized, as we saw earlier, by the cloak Christ wears in the picture:

> In Tintoretto's Paradiso in the Great Council Hall of the Ducal Palace, Christ, dressed
> in the corrucio the doges wore on Holy Thursday, figures as the celestial eternal doge:
> the terrestrial, mortal doge, who would have stood in front of the painting, was seen as

Christ's vicar. In this manner the conceptual distinction between the doge and the dogeship was ever before the patricians during their political assemblies. (M 272)

This association of Christ with the doge supports Wilk's claim that Mary here, as in Tullio's frieze, is a personification of Venice.

By her close identification with Venice, Mary was both exalted and brought low. She is the church, crowned by Jesus. But she is also brought close to ordinary Venetian life, as we saw in Tintoretto's *Annunciation* in St. Roch's Club, where she is a woman of the working class, interrupted at her chores. In the *Nativity* of the same club's upper hall, she is in need of help from others, who are not as poor as she is on this night. The vulnerability of Mary is stressed even more dramatically in Tintoretto's *Crucifixion*, where she does not stand stoically by the cross as in the medieval hymn *Stabat Mater*, but is totally unstrung and falls in a limp heap. Others, though grieving themselves, turn aside to comfort her. Here Tintoretto follows the gospel of Saint John, which makes Christ tell Saint John to care for the bereft woman in her need (Jn 19.27). Mary is not only a comforter, but one who needs comfort. There is an intimacy, almost a familiarity, felt for Mary in much of Venetian art.

GIOVANNI BELLINI

No one better caught this intimacy than Giovanni Bellini in his many pictures (at least eighty known ones from his workshop) of the Virgin and Child. These are based on the formulae of Byzantine icons. In the icons, Mary is seen at bust length, with a gold halo around her head; she is wearing a dark blue mantle with a stylized gold line along its hem, and she is often pointing to her son as the Way (the Hodēgētria pose). Bellini softens the face, makes the halo diaphanous or removes it entirely, and achieves the bust length not by arbitrary (timeless) abstraction of a part of Mary's body but by placing a parapet before her waist—a normal device for portraits in Venice, one that implies a narrative (historical) setting, not the timeless sphere of the icon. In these ways Bellini humanizes the type. But his deepest change is spiritual. Bellini's Virgin gazes either at the child or into space, not challenging us as the icons do, but drawing us into her own interior meditations.

The child is often absorbed in anything but her—sometimes looking out at us, sometimes up to his Father in heaven, in a different realm from the time that envelopes Mary. Occasionally, the baby lies stretched out in her arms (T 162–64, 206), and the two figures take on unconsciously a pose that we know awaits them in the future, that of

PLATE XXV
Jacopo Tintoretto,
Annunciation

PLATE XVIII
Jacopo Tintoretto,
Adoration of the Shepherds

PLATE XXIV
Jacopo Tintoretto,
Crucifixion

the mother with her *dead* son in her arms, the Pietà. The melancholy young girl of these pictures is less a queen than a quiet sister in the house (these paintings were made for private devotion, not public ceremony). Her face is not an idealized type, but neither is it a realistic portrait, but something in between. She does not have the conventional beauty of a Florentine Madonna—except when assistants are at work on the picture, as in the Trivulzio Madonna of the Castello Sforzesco in Milan. Bellini's oval-faced young women are too solemn to be anything so trivial as pretty. He varies the basically similar features, giving each picture its specific expression, sometimes more "grown up" (early twenties), sometimes with the baby-fat softness and double chin of a teenager. The face is lengthened sometimes, or given a more pointed chin.

That the girlishness of Bellini's Madonna does not rob her of profundity is proved in the Accademia picture of her between Saints Catherine and the Magdalen. The picture is steeped in a rich and contemplative darkness, goldenly lit from the left side, as if

FIG. 69
Giovanni Bellini,
Madonna and Child with Saints

these faces were swimming up at us out of some remembered tragic time. This is one of Bellini's rounder-faced Madonnas, pensively looking off toward the side where the light comes from. Catherine, as befits an Eastern queen, wears a richly damasked robe, with pearl edging. Other pearls are intricately wrought into her hair. The Magdalen has plain and disheveled hair, as in the seminude treatments of her by Titian and others, but she still wears the jewel-encrusted dress from her days as a prostitute. These touches of a former splendor set off the plain Mary in the middle, who has no jeweled garment or head-dress, only the blue mantle of the Byzantine icons, with a simple blouse underneath. Though patrician women were not bound in Venice by the black dress code of their husbands, there is a patrician plainness to this Mary pondering her great son's course. Between two exotic women, she is a somber Venetian.

The Virgin of these pictures has eyes half closed or glancing to the side, as if deflecting sorrow; or they stare wide open at the enormity of things. She might be someone looking out the window at the enigma and menace of passing events that will lead her child to his fate. There is time in her eyes. The fact that time is passing would be emphasized when Bellini painted the actual *Pietà* implied in some infancy pictures. The woman in the Accademia *Pietà* of c. 1505 (T 166–69) is not the eternally young Virgin of Michelangelo's sculpted *Pietà*. She is middle-aged, and worn by sorrow. In some Pietàs, her face is almost feral with the agony it is undergoing (T 94–95). She does not collapse, like Tintoretto's Virgin, but she is being torn apart before our eyes.

The intimacy Bellini achieved in his Madonnas for private devotion was carried into the public paintings of Mary enthroned above several attendant saints—in pictures called "sacred conversations" (*sacre conversazioni*), though everyone in the picture is communing with his or her own self, not with any other. The baby pays no attention to his mother or to the saints—a clear contrast with other artists' conversazioni, where he is made to bless with his regard some donor of the picture or founder of a religious order. What sets Bellini's works apart is the intensity of each figure's personal engagement with mystery. Only Benedict in the Frari triptych (T 136–38) breaks this absorption. He holds his Bible open for others to read, and directs a searching gaze at us—are *we* sufficiently intense as we contemplate this challenge of God incarnated in a child?

What unites these figures, who do not converse with one another? It is the rich Venetian atmosphere and light that Bellini sheds on them, uniting them in a specific time and place. Mary of the *Maestà* was timelessly enthroned in heaven, with angels supporting her chair. The Mary of these pictures is in a local church or shrine, identifiably Venetian in its style. The golden mosaics of the half-dome in the apse are reminders of St. Mark's mosaics. The columns and capitals in the pictures are carved with that paradoxical combination—of lush organic reliefs on simple forms—that is the trademark of Bellini's collaborators, the Lombardo family. In the Frari triptych, the outer columns of the real frame are seen as part of a colonnade in the painted scene. Light comes in from the left, where the colonnade is open, and its mystery makes the apse mosaic glow like a vast halo for Mary and the child.

PLATE XV
Giovanni Bellini, *Virgin Between Saints Nicholas, Peter, Benedict, and Mark*

The tie with the Lombardo sculptors is made express in his San Zaccaria painting (T 170–73), where the throne on which the Virgin sits has as its acroterion a mysterious grotesque from the choir carvings of the Lombardo Church of the Miraculous Mary (Santa Maria dei Miracoli). In all these scenes we are given a Venice transformed, an earthly spot of ineffable beauty, but nonetheless a real place on earth. The angels who play music in the Frari triptych or the San Zaccaria "conversation" stand firmly on the ground, unlike the angel musicians who fly through the air about the Virgin of the *Maestà*. The music played here, we may be sure from the attitudes of those who stand within its harmonies, is very quiet and contemplative, not triumphal—"chamber music" in the deepest sense, to yearn its way through the chambers of the mind. Only the Venetians' confidence in their city's intimate bond with the Virgin could make them give her such a "local habitation and a name."

FIG. 70 (ABOVE)
Giovanni Bellini,
*Madonna and Child
Enthroned with Saints*

PLATE XXVI
Lorenzo Lotto,
Annunciation

LOTTO

For the most vulnerable Mary painted by a Venetian, we must return to the Annunciation genre. Lorenzo Lotto worked in many places, but he was born and trained in Venice (perhaps in the Vivarini workshop, perhaps in that of the Bellini), and returned there to create some of his most important works.[5] The Venetian attitude toward the Annunciation is clear in his painting of that subject for a confraternity in Recanati (c. 1534). In this work, the announcing angel enters by a "back door," as it were, coming in from the garden shown in the background. But it is not true, as Peter Humfrey claims, that the picture "shows the angel approaching the Virgin from behind."[6] Her prie-dieu, at which she was praying when he approached her, faces away from us—he addressed her as she knelt at it, facing the garden. But she has turned completely around, in response to his words, and now faces us. The suddenness of this scuffling movement on her knees is registered in the strained fabric of the red robe that is still catching up with her motion.

She is trying to escape this frightening incursion. Her hands are spread ñot in acceptance but in dismay. She looks out at us for help. I thought, when I first saw the picture in an exhibition in Washington, of Jacqueline Kennedy turning to clamber out of her car when the tremendous blow fell on her in the Dallas motorcade. The Magdalen of Titian's late *Pietà* in the Accademia (w 2.122–23) has this same reaction when she turns from the horror of the dead Christ's body to run in protest and incomprehension toward us. Lotto's Virgin resembles even more closely Tintoretto's princess in peril who runs out of the picture toward our succor in the London *Saint George and the Dragon* (p-r 2.175).

FIG. 81
Jacopo Tintoretto, *Saint George and the Dragon*

If Mary is frightened by the angel, her cat seems electrified by him. No wonder the angel has a nonplussed expression at these reactions to his good news (*evangelium*). But the cat is actually put there to reassure us. The Ave of the angel is meant to undo the work of Eva in the garden, and Dürer's famous etching of Eve's subject showed a cat in the foreground dozing peacefully while a mouse pauses just in front of it. Dürer's Adam is about to eat the apple—upon which the goat in the background will fall off its cliff, the peaceful animals in the woods will flee each other, and the cat will snatch up its prey, the mouse. Death will enter the world along with sin. Cats were symbols of choleric temper in medieval bestiaries, their cruelty marked by the way they play with mice.[7] This trait made cats natural "familiars" (attendant spirits) for witches. What we see in Lotto's picture is a reversal of Dürer's scene—the cat fears the undoing of its fallen realm of predation and death. Its response makes us see that Mary's fear is unfounded. All will be well again when she says yes to the redeeming of the world. This explains the serene mood created, despite the cat's and the Virgin's violent reactions. The translucent sky is echoed in the cool blues of the angel's robe. The pink-fringed smock over Mary's red garment picks up the red robe and pink cloak of God the Father. We are encouraged to be amused by Mary's reaction—so the proper comparison is not, after all, with the tragedy in Dallas. This scene resembles more the comic fright of monks fleeing Saint Jerome's tamed lion in Carpaccio's painting for the Dalmatian Brotherhood (s 112–15). Lotto is familiar enough with the Virgin to rib her gently. The Mary of Venice is a winningly vulnerable woman.

FIG. 89
Vittore Carpaccio, *Saint Jerome and the Lion*

CHAPTER NINETEEN

Mark:
The Relic

T HOUGH CHRIST AND THE VIRGIN had to receive pride of place in
Venetian piety, and though the relics of Christ's cross and blood played a vital
role in the devotional life of the city, *the* relic of the polity was, of course, Mark's
body. His cult meets the definition of a supersaint as that was defined by the Jesuit
experts in hagiography, the Bollandists:

> A church here, an altar there, is dedicated to him; his feast is set in the liturgy; his
> relics are tended with devotion; his image is displayed for believers' veneration, repro-
> duced in various media, some of them costly; there are pilgrimages to his shrine; con-
> fraternities are formed in his honor, an institution takes him as protector; his name is
> given infants in baptism; there is a legend of his life and miracles—all these things
> must be weighed if one wants to form an impression of a saint's popularity.[1]

Mark's image was everywhere in Venice, and especially in the great basilica that was the
city's omphalos, radiating its spiritual energies throughout the whole urban fabric. San
Marco was all one huge reliquary. We have already seen how the relics of other saints
determined the patronage of churches, *scuole*, and altars in the city. This general trend
received its climax in the social rituals that were woven around the Marcan relic.

It is hard for a modern tourist to understand the devotion to relics. Of all the super-
stitions we find registered in the history, politics, and art of the Middle Ages, relics can
seem the most unconvincing, even the most absurd. It takes some historical imagination
to re-enter the value system that structured communities around these sacred items. To us,
the artworks celebrating Mark's body are far more precious than the relic itself. Few know
or care where or whether the relic is still present in the basilica named for it. (It is suppos-

edly in the crypt under the high altar.) Yet people made long and arduous pilgrimages to come within its force field. Asked what was the most important event in Venetian history, most modern visitors to the city would list many other dates before giving 827, the date of Mark's legendary arrival in the town. But Otto Demus was right to say that this was the coup which determined the ideological configuration of everything that followed upon it.

Wars were fought to retain or acquire relics. The True Cross, wetted by Jesus' blood, was such a precious relic that "in Jerusalem deacons stood guard to prevent the pilgrims who came to kiss the holy wood from biting off a sliver."[2] Saint Francis of Assisi's companions had to mount a guard over his body as soon as he died, to save it from raiders desperate to acquire some part of the holy commodity. The relic was a physical link with the spirit world—in the saints' case, a bodily stuff that would be reintegrated with its soul at the end of time. It was a kind of first step out of the realm of history and into the timeless sphere where the saint waited to reassume the body. At the Last Judgment, when the relic would be fired off like a rocket to its true home, its devotees hoped to be swept up in the energy of this ascent. Christians strove to be buried as close as possible to the place where the martyr's body lay.[3]

This began in early Christian times, when Mass was said over the bodies of martyrs. It was thought that history was about to end. A dead saint's corporeal component was resting behind only briefly, where it partly tore across the fabric of the mundane, opening a hole into heaven. So strong was this association of the worshiping community with its local forerunner into another realm that it became a liturgical necessity to have a relic of a saint in the altar stone wherever Mass was celebrated. André Grabar even argues that the whole of later Christian architecture grew from the martyr shrine (*martyrion*).[4] The relic and the Mass were intimately associated. As the second-century *Martyrdom of Polycarp* put it:

> Lifting his bones, more estimable than precious stones, more to be valued than gold, we put them in a place worthy of them, where, when we gather in grateful joy, the Lord will let us celebrate his death, to recall the others who have won this prize, and to prepare those who will contend for it in the future.[5]

The martyrion had to expand into the basilica in order to accommodate pilgrims to the martyr's shrine.

As Christianity spread beyond its places of origin, where martyrs were friends who had preceded other members of the community, it became difficult to meet the demand for saints' relics. The age of martyrs was over, the early saints were already lodged in places proud to retain them. The market for exchange in these precious items became highly competitive, leading to "pious thefts," as Patrick Geary calls them in his book *Furta Sacra*.[6] Even in early days, the market was skewed by different rates of martyrdom in different regions, especially in the Great Persecution of 303 to 324: "The number of martyrs was high, but their distribution uneven: the west was spared while persecution wreaked havoc in the east, in particular in Egypt and Palestine, under Diocletian, Galerius, Maximinus Daia, and Licinius."[7]

Peter Brown describes the dense weave of holy sites created by the distribution of relics as new shrines complemented the older sites:

> Translations—the movement of relic to people—and not pilgrimage—the movement of people to relics—held the center of the stage in late-antique and early-medieval piety. A hectic trade in, accompanied by frequent thefts of, relics is among the most dramatic, not to say picaresque, aspects of western Christendom in the middle ages. Only recently have medievalists succeeded in rendering this startling behavior intelligible.[8]

This odd black market in white magic worked somewhat as the underground trade in artworks does in the modern times. The same concern for authenticity of the object that we witness now was exercised with regard to relics. To quote Peter Brown again, "Whatever the modern historian may have done, if confronted with a relic, sixth-century men can be trusted to have looked their gift horse firmly in the mouth."[9] The modern purchaser submits the work to scientific tests by radiography or chemical analysis. The late-antique bishop performed his own experiments, putting the relic to an empirical test: Can it work miraculous cures? That is how Helena had established the authenticity of the True Cross, or how Ambrose, the Bishop of Milan, proved that he had found the bodies of Saints Gervasius and Protasius.

A saint's relic was thought to be so closely associated with the soul of the saint, from which it was only temporarily separated, that the relic was considered an active agent, as if sending out a benign radioactivity. In fact, relics actively resisted being moved by impious hands. There are tales of relics becoming too heavy to be lifted, or flying from pursuers. There were two examples of that in paintings for the Distinguished Brotherhood of St. John the Evangelist—first, in the picture of the True Cross relic flitting from the hands of all but its official protector; and second, where the same relic became too heavy

FIG. 62
Gentile Bellini,
*The Miracle at the Bridge
of San Lorenzo*

to be moved in the burial procession of a sinner. Part of the legend of Mark is that he attended in spirit the transfer of his body to Venice, stilling a storm that threatened the ship bringing it from Alexandria to Venice. That is why two Marks appear in pictures of the Transfer—the body itself and the soul that is its ghostly attendant.

This complex of beliefs about the historical status of the relic is celebrated in the artworks devoted to Mark in his own city. The various connections between the saint and his community called for extended narratives to bring out all their aspects. These narratives took three main forms, as cycles traced in every artistic medium (mosaic, enamels, medals, paintings, sculpture, tapestries). These are the Life (Vita) cycle, containing twenty-one canonical episodes, the Transfer (Translatio) cycle, containing seven episodes, and the Discovery (Inventio) cycle, containing two episodes. The middle sequence was the most popular, since it dealt with the pivotal event of Venetian history, the arrival of the relic.

THE TRANSFER CYCLE (TRANSLATIO)

1. Mark's body is identified by merchants and removed from its tomb in Alexandria.
2. The body is carried to the ship.
3. The Muslims investigate the cargo, but do not look below the unclean pork with which the merchants have covered it.
4. The ship sails.
5. Mark appears to save his body from shipwreck.
6. The ship reaches Venice.
7. The doge takes the body into his care.

It will be seen that most of this story takes place on shipboard, and the mosaic cycles of the Translatio accentuate the maritime aspect of the saint who safeguards the Venetian sea empire. It is true that the earliest version of the cycle—the eleventh-century enamels on the jeweled altar front in San Marco (the Pala d'Oro)—has only one sea scene, but the Translatio is covered in only three enamels of its narrative (as opposed to its seven for the Vita cycle). The painted cover for this jeweled Pala (the *Pala Feriale* by Paolo Veneziano) pays even less attention to the sea passage—but Mark's rescue of his own body on this Pala is the vividest picture of this event in all of Venetian art. San Marco's two mosaic cycles devoted to the Translatio focused most intently on the ship that brought Mark's body to Venice, associating the saint as closely as possible with the city's mastery of the sea. In the twelfth-century cycle—on the vault over the

Chapel of San Clement, to the right of the main altar as we face it—four of the seven scenes show a ship with the details of rigging that stirred Venetians' professional pride (D 1.65–69). And on the thirteenth-century lunettes of the façade, the original mosaics devoted, probably, seven of their eleven scenes to seafaring (D 2.192–206). Only one of these originals survives—later substitutes fill the other lunettes.

It is difficult for me to choose, from the many representations of this cycle, some favorite images. But if forced to, I would single out these:

1. The identification of Mark's body: Tintoretto's painting for St. Mark's Distinguished Brotherhood.

3. The Muslims crying, "*Kanzir!*" ("Pork!") as they recoil from the container with Mark's body: the mosaic in the Chapel of San Clement in San Marco (D 1.67). Three Muslims have come out on the harbor's pilot boat to inspect the cargo. One tends the skiff, another is climbing aboard, but the third already reacts to the news that there is pork in the midship area—under the sails that the two merchants are beginning to hoist. (In the next episode pictured, the sails, spread on the yardarms, are being lowered because of storm.)

FIG. 34
Jacopo Tintoretto,
The Identification of Saint Mark's Body

FIG. 71
San Marco,
The Ship with the Body of Saint Mark Being Searched by the Muslims

5. The apparition of Mark to save the ship: Paolo Veneziano's panel on the Pala Feriale (1345), now on the balcony level of San Marco next to the four bronze horses. The painter shows strong winds driving the ship into the Clashing Rocks (Symplēgades) from Homer's *Odyssey*. The mountainous red rocks are closing so rapidly that a sailor is scraped

FIG. 72
Paolo Veneziano,
*Pala Feriale of
Saint Mark*

PLATE I
*Saint Mark's Body
Carried into the Basilica,*
Byzantine mosaic

off the side of the ship. The crew has not had time to take in sail, but Mark stands with an easy poise on the stern of the ship, unaffected by the winds bellying the sails. His calm is contrasted with the desperately gesticulating seamen. The details of rope along the gunwale, and of the basket-fencing around the poop, are worked out with loving care, suggesting the control over chaos that Mark brings to the scene.

7. The doge receives Mark's body: the thirteenth-century mosaic on the façade.

A SECOND TRANSLATION: NICHOLAS

The coup that brought Mark's body to Venice was so great and influential that an imitation of it was used against Venice in the eleventh century, forcing the Venetians to stage a shadow Translatio mimicking and strengthening the main one. This relic war was waged with Bari, the city at the south end of the Adriatic that was challenging Venice's control of that sea. Bari decided to assert its right to the water lanes by bringing in a powerful and popular champion of its cause, Saint Nicholas, the Bishop of Myra, whose body Barian merchants stole from Myra in a sequence almost exactly paralleling the theft of Mark's body from Alexandria two centuries earlier.

To take the full measure of this challenge, we have to recall that the cult of Nicholas was widespread and intense at the very time when the raiders from Bari struck. In some ways Nicholas was the most obvious patron for merchants. One of the two miracles by which he was best known involved the rescue of a merchant ship from storm—the subject of many dramatic paintings (by Fra Angelico, for instance, in the panel now at the Vatican Pinacoteca). This miracle, performed for a merchant ship, not a war galley, made Nicholas the patron of merchants in general. For Bari to have a special claim on the saint automatically frayed his ties with merchants from rival cities. As Patrick Geary, the expert on holy thefts, put it:

> In the absence of such devotion to Nicholas throughout the Mediterranean world, the translation would have been meaningless and the proliferation of his cult in merchant communities would have been unthinkable. The religious basis of Nicholas's cult made the translation an important political and economic event throughout the West. Only his status as a great and important saint could have made the theft of his body appear to be an answer to the economic crisis in which the citizens of Bari found themselves at the end of the eleventh century. The secular importance of the translation was not something added after the fact, but rather logically and chronologically simultaneous with the religious devotion that led to the translation.[10]

The Venetians responded to this challenge by invading Myra themselves, early in the twelfth century, and carrying off what they claimed was the true body of Nicholas. The testing of a relic was, remember, an important step in validating holy plunder. Saint Helena had set the standard, making the True Cross perform a miracle before she would accept it—and Tintoretto's painting showed how Mark's body performed an exorcism to make its bona fides evident to the merchants who were risking its theft. Nicholas's relic was brought to Venice in great pomp and lodged in the sailors' church on the Lido. Now, "to make assurance doubly sure," the Venetians had Mark *and* Nicholas guarding their ships at sea.

FIG. 34
Jacopo Tintoretto,
*The Identification of
Saint Mark's Body*

Nicholas was incorporated into that most authoritative statement of official piety, the mosaics of San Marco, with four prominent representations of his image (D 1.32, 262 and 2.101, 193). A chapel to him was established in the Doge's Palace, to commemorate the sea feat of Constantinople's conquest in 1204:

> It became an obligation of the doge to offer prayers to Nicholas in order to retain the saint's favor. The Saint Nicholas chapel was the only one within the walls of the Ducal Palace that hosted an annual ducal ceremonial visit and thus had an affinity—

albeit a relatively minor one—to the doge's other private chapel, the basilica of San Marco. Of the ducal and ecclesiastical establishment Saint Mark and Saint Nicholas formed a "binomial mystery," a dual protectorship that signified Venetian independence and rights over the sea lanes. (M 98–99)

The teamwork of Mark and Nicholas at sea was given its most dramatic and important expression when they provided the doge with a symbolic ring to be used every year when he married the sea. The original of that ring was kept in the Scuola Grande di San Marco, where two large paintings (now in the Accademia) recorded the myth of the ring.

On the night of February 25, 1341, a fisherman was awakened by Saint Mark and asked to ferry him to the Church of San Giorgio Maggiore, where Saint George himself joined the party. Then they went to the Church of St. Nicholas on the Lido (where the relic of Nicholas was kept). A huge storm was now sweeping a ship laden with devils toward Venice—till the three saints stopped it in its track and made it disappear. Before the saints too disappeared, Mark gave the fisherman a ring and told him to present it to the doge. The first painting for the scuola—*La Burrasca* (Storm at Sea)—was begun by the Elder Palma. It shows the crisis of the scene, when the diabolic boat comes shuddering to a halt before the uplifted cross in Mark's hand. Palma had finished the ominous ship, and the huge shoreward wave it was pushing before it, when he died in 1528. Paris Bordon then added the modest boat to the right with the fisherman and the three saints. In the eighteenth century, the boat with naked devils cast out of the ship was repainted. (The nude figures are shown to be devils by their pointed ears.) In the nineteenth century, a blank in the lower right section of the picture, where a door had originally opened in the scuola, was filled with the painting of a large "Saint Peter's fish" (San Pietro, the Venetian name for a John Dory).[11]

The sequel to this painting, as we have seen, was Mark's gift to the fisherman of a ring for the doge. That makes up the subject of Paris Bordon's masterpiece, *Presentation of the Ring* (c. 1545–1550). This was completed after Sansovino's Serlian redesign of the Piazzetta, whose ideals are expressed in Bordon's classical staircase (taken directly from the 1545 edition of Serlio's *Architecture*) and the classical buildings whose perspectival recession echoes Serlio's theater sets. The picture shows how Venice could update its myths through successive eras and styles. The original cycle of paintings devoted to the ring legend was in the Doge's Palace, but it perished in one of that building's fires, leaving this as the major statement of the myth that underlay the most colorful of Venice's annual festivals—the one in which, on Ascension Day (Sensa), the doge went out in his ceremonial barge (the Bucintoro) to throw a copy of his sacred ring into the sea, thus marrying Venice to its partner in world domination.

The importance of Nicholas in this ceremony is expressed mythically by the fisherman's trip to his church on the Lido. That was demonstrated in the Sensa ceremony itself by the fact that the doge's galley went from the spot where he threw his ring into the sea

FIG. 74
Lorenzo Lotto,
Saint Nicholas of Bari in Glory, Saints Lucy, John the Baptist, and George Killing the Dragon

directly to Saint Nicholas's church. Muir suggests that the Bishop of Myra was thought of as officiating at the marriage service (M 98). We might imagine him blessing the marriage in the pose Titian gave him for the altarpiece of the Nicholas shrine in the Church of St. Sebastian (W 1.151–52). This image of his name saint was commissioned by Niccolo Crasso in 1563. The imperious male claim upon the (female) sea was adapted, for Christian purposes, from a pagan fertility rite. The Feast of the Ascension marked the beginning of the sailing season. The "marriage" was the equivalent of agrarian rituals that blessed the fields at the beginning of the sowing season, when the ground was to be "impregnated." Venetians expected a "harvest" of cargoes as the farmers prayed for a harvest of crops.

Since sailors clustered on the Lido near St. Nicholas's Church, the workers at this end of the Venetian island cluster were called "Nick-ites," Nicolotti, and they staged mock battles with the other maritime contingent, from the other end of the complex, the "Arsenal-ites," Arsenalotti. Saint Nicholas had the patronage role among Nicolotti that Saint Giulia in time assumed for the Arsenalotti.

Second only to the sailors in their devotion to Nicholas were the merchants. The Merchants' Brotherhood (Scuola dei Mercanti) specified in its charter (*mariegola*) that members must pray "that God and Saint Nicholas protect and save all the fleets and ships of this city on the open sea, with all who sail in them, and bring them safely to port."[12] In fulfillment of this duty, the scuola commissioned a painting for its Nicholas altar in the Church of Santa Maria dei Carmini—the first of four great altarpieces Lorenzo Lotto created for his native city. The painting is still in its original stone frame, as we can see by the spread of the saint's cope out at the level of the capitals on the frame. He is haloed with a nimbus of cloud, the symbol of his role as the protector of storm-besieged men. In the harbor landscape below his floating figure, we can see dark clouds being driven out at the right of the picture as a serene sky opens up on the left. In the part of the picture still dark with storm, Saint George battles the dragon. He is included, as is Saint John the Baptist above, because the officers of the scuola were, at the time of the painting's commission, a John-Baptist (Giovanni-Battista Donati, the Guardian Grande) and a George (Giorgio de Mundis, the deputy Guardian). The third saint in the picture is Lucy, who became popular in Venice when her body was brought to the city in 1244.[13] The sign of her martyrdom, the eyes struck out by torturers, rests above a cup that is placed on the cloud throne of Nicholas.

The transfer of Mark's relic was an event so charged with meaning for Venetians that there was an overspill of its significance into its doublet, the transfer of Nicholas's relic. The latter was the complement of the former, as if Venetians could not stop drawing consequences from their greatest coup, the holy theft on which the dogal religion of empire was based.

CHAPTER TWENTY

Mark: The Life

APART FROM THE TRANSLATIO myth of Mark's relic, which the Venetians had all to themselves, there were wider legends of Mark's life, most of which had been formulated elsewhere, and had to do with the evangelist's supposed activity in the Holy Land and Alexandria. Venice incorporated these into its general devotion to the saint, after supplying a connective link to them through the story of Mark's visit to Aquileia during his life, and of his stop at the Venetian lagoon, where he heard the forecast (*praedestinatio*) of his body's return there. This larger cycle of Mark's Vita had twenty-one episodes, occurring in five locales:

Rome:

1. Mark writes his gospel from Saint Peter's account of Christ's life.
2. Mark presents the gospel to Peter.
3. Peter consecrates Mark a bishop and sends him to spread the gospel in Aquileia.
4. Mark begins his Aquileian ministry by healing the leper Athaulf.
5. Mark baptizes Athaulf.
6. Mark baptizes Hermagoras.

Venice:

7. Taking Hermagoras back to Rome, Mark stops overnight in the Venetian lagoon, where a vision gives him the forecast (praedestinatio) of his final resting place.

Rome:

    8. Peter consecrates Hermagoras as bishop.

    9. Hermagoras is sent to Aquileia, where he will be martyred.

    10. Peter sends Mark to the Holy Land.

The Holy Land:

    11. Mark heals a demoniac.

    12. Mark is ordered in a dream to go to Alexandria.

    13. Mark sails for Alexandria.

Alexandria:

    14. Mark heals the wounded hand of the cobbler Anianus.

    15. Mark baptizes Anianus.

    16. Mark preaches in Alexandria.

    17. Mark causes the toppling of idols.

    18. Mark is suspended by ropes above the altar where he is celebrating Mass.

    19. Mark is thrown into prison, where Jesus appears to him.

    20. Mark is dragged through the streets by ropes, then martyred.

    21. A storm disperses the executioners, and Christians smuggle his body off to burial.

In most Venetian accounts of the Vita, the Holy Land interlude was dropped, since the Aquileia events were more important.[1] Few media could include all the episodes, so different emphases were developed. The oldest cycle (c. 1105), the enamels on the Pala d'Oro in San Marco, contains seven events from the Vita (those numbered 3, 8, 14, 15, 16, 18, 19, and 21, above), as well as three episodes from the Translatio cycle (D 1.59–60).[2]

There are two mosaic cycles devoted to Mark's Vita in San Marco, one from the twelfth century, one from the thirteenth. The earlier one (D 1.57–59) is on the vault above the Chapel of St. Peter (to the left of the main altar as we face it). It contains eleven of the seventeen episodes (those numbered above as 3, 4, 5, 8, 9, 13 through 16, 19, 21). The later cycle is in the barrel vault of the atrium, to our right as we enter the right hand door of the basilica (D 2.185–91). It contains episodes 1, 2, 6, 7, 8, 11 through 14, 18, 20, 21.

Some notable treatments of these events, chosen to show the range of styles and atmospheres in Venetian devotion to Mark over the centuries, would include:

PLATE IV
San Marco mosaic,
Vision of Saint Mark

7. The Praedestinatio in the Venetian lagoon: the atrium mosaic of the thirteenth century.

14. The miraculous cure of Anianus: Tullio Lombardo's relief on the façade of the Scuola Grande di San Marco (c. 1489). In Tullio's reliefs, people are bunched in abstract patterns of overlapping depth. Here the tight human drama involves three standing figures and the semirecumbent Anianus. The central turbaned spectator gazes with sympathy on the suffering cobbler. The standing man to our right cranes over the turbaned man's shoulder at Saint Mark as he works the miracle. Only Anianus himself breaks this rosebud knot of mutual attentivenesses by jerking his head away in anguish at the pain in his hand. The formal patterns are woven across the different depths of the relief—Mark's right arm and Anianus's left one are aligned. Anianus's right arm resumes the slant of the distant figure's shoulder and head. Three swags of clothing move across the upper part of the picture, and two larger ones across the lower. It is a marvel of concentration on the supernatural occurrence.

15. Mark baptizes Anianus: the pedestal panel on Tullio Lombardo's tomb of Giovanni Mocenigo (c. 1515, P-H 2.424). This tomb, on the other side of the west (entry) wall from the tomb of Mocenigo's older brother, done by Tullio's father, is more severe and classical than the earlier works of the Lombardo workshop.[3] It is also opposed to the crowded style of Tullio's relief on the façade of the Distinguished Brotherhood of St. Mark. The classical nudity of those approaching Tullio's baptismal pool (which projects into our space) is justified by the fact that Christians were originally unclothed before immersion in the waters. Mark leans forward, the sweep of his garment emphasizing the forward thrust of his right arm as it blesses Anianus. The turbaned figure behind Anianus locates the scene in Alexandria. The woman approaching the tomb modestly covers her breasts, a sign of the fall of humanity in Eve's offense, the original sin that baptism must expunge. The child's tug away from the pool dramatizes the resistance to grace by unredeemed human nature. The lightly sketched tree to the right, echoing the curve that runs down the arms of the woman and child, balances the forward lean of Mark on the left side of the scene. Though Tullio carved the whole scene in comparatively shallow relief, the gradations of space move backward in four steps— from the pool to Mark's arm to Anianus's body to the turbaned attendant. The skillfully

FIG. 75
Tullio Lombardo,
Saint Mark Baptizing

negotiated recessions in the main group of figures are balanced by the more fully modeled woman and child. And their rotundity, in turn, is contrasted with the tree that
recedes in aerial perspective, showing Tullio's ability to haze objects over as if he were a
painter. This scene alone would prove that the Renaissance had now reached Venetian
sculpture. In fact, Pope-Hennessy says: "No relief in Florence in the whole quattrocento
communicates the same feeling of nostalgia for Roman art" (P-H 2.328).

16. *Mark preaches in Alexandria:* the painting by Gentile and Giovanni Bellini for
the Scuola Grande di San Marco, now in the Brera gallery of Milan (T 220–30). A fire
in the scuola had destroyed a Marcan cycle of paintings in 1485, and Gentile was commissioned to replace it with the huge paintings of Mark's last sermon and his execution
(the latter now in the Accademia). When Gentile died in 1507, his brother Giovanni
finished the two paintings. Giovanni has supplied a portrait of Gentile—the figure in
red on the left, wearing the gold chain given him by the Sultan Mehmet II when Gen-

FIG. 76
Gentile Bellini,
*Saint Mark Preaching
in Alexandria*

tile went as an ambassador to Constantinople. The fact that Mark is giving his last
sermon (taken down by a scribe) is indicated by the presence of the executioner, who
stands by with his scimitar. Gentile has reinterpreted earlier pictures of Mark, which
showed him preaching when he *arrived* in Alexandria, as an event that occurred
between the dragging through the streets and the beheading of Mark. The exotic
Egyptian church in the background shows the structure of ancient belief that Mark
was unable to defeat, as does the crowd of Asians who listen to Mark but will not inter-

fere in his execution. This is in contrast with the earlier, simpler version of Mark's struggle with idols on the Pala d'Oro.

17. Mark topples the idols: one of the square enamels telling Mark's legend on the Pala d'Oro (c. 1105). The inscription in the blue border at the top says, "The blessed Mark destroys an idol." Mark in all the Pala scenes of his Vita has a blue halo circled with a thin gold line, to which a red-brown outer circle is added, to set the gold off from the gilt background of the scene. The architectural frame suggests economically the city of Alexandria. The pillar where the idol stood has beautiful spiral ornamentation. The armed god is seen in the act of falling—his spear is still upright as he struggles to keep his stance, but the shield's weight is pulling him down. He and it are both about to drop. These enamels all provide a maximum of drama in a minimum of space.

19. Jesus appears to Mark in prison: a panel in Paolo Veneziano's Pala Feriale (1345). The prison holding Mark is a very Venetian one. The *bifore* divided by a slender column in the attic are straight off the streets of Paolo's own time, as are the polychrome stone and the gilded balcony and capitals. The soldiers who crouch ignominiously before the prison, like the curious bypassers, are smaller than the sacred figures seen through the bars, with their large haloes of stamped gold in complex patterns. Real freedom breathes inside this prison, and the cramped and broken figures are outside it.

20. Mark dragged through the streets to his death: Sansovino's relief in the choir of San Marco (P-H 3.461, 1537).[4] Sansovino actually sculpts *rain* in this scene—the storm that will disperse the killers as soon as Mark dies, allowing Christians to smuggle the body off for pious burial. Though the tempest cannot prevent Mark's execution, it has already divided the crowd into opposite surges, one of which (Boucher argues) is modeled on the flight of Dacian troops on Trajan's arch in Rome (BB 1.59). The resigned massive profile of an unresisting Mark is contrasted with the excited gestures and expressions of the crowd, which are also out of keeping with the poised classical statues in the niches behind the storm.

21. Christians spirit Mark's body off for burial: Tintoretto's picture for the Scuola Grande di San Marco.

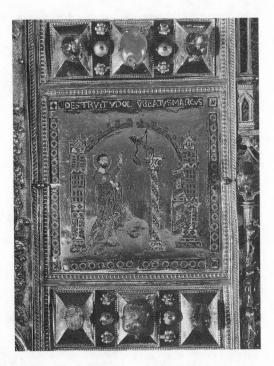

FIG. 77 (ABOVE)
San Marco, *Saint Mark Toppling the Idol*, detail from the Pala d'Oro

FIG. 72
Paolo Veneziano, *Pala Feriale of Saint Mark*

FIG. 33
Jacopo Tintoretto, *The Rescue of Saint Mark's Body*

FIG. 78
Jacopo Sansovino,
*Saint Mark Dragged
Through the Street*

To get some feel for Mark's omnipresence in Venetian consciousness, these samplings from the Life cycle have to be placed in the context of the Transfer and Discovery cycles, as well as with the many other forms his iconography took: his place among the four evangelists, his inclusion as the thirteenth apostle, the representation of his posthumous miracles, his emblematic appearances with his lion (or *as* the lion). These emblems were flown from the masts of the galleys that sailed out from Venice, or placed on the walls and gates of cities compelled into the Venetian empire. They appeared on house fronts, on missal covers, on illuminated manuscripts. They worked their way into the inmost recesses of the Venetian sense of identity.

CHAPTER TWENTY-ONE

War Saints: George and Theodore

BEFORE THE TRANSFER of Mark's body, Saint Theodore was the patron of Venice. His relic had come into the city's possession before that of the evangelist, and it had become the basis for the doge's original private chapel.[1] In the ninth century, Theodore was demoted to be Mark's adjutant, and the doge's chapel began its expansion into what we know as the basilica of San Marco. But Theodore was not entirely gone or forgotten. He was still important enough to be placed on the pillar next to Mark's lion in the Piazzetta, and to be paired with Mark in the protection of Venice. Yet he was more often paired, in popular devotion, with the warrior patron of the city, Saint George. The two had come together from the East, where they were important figures—as we can see from the original (Byzantine) sections of the Pala d'Oro, where George is represented on six different enamels and Theodore on three.[2] More important, when they arrived in Venice, they were companions in many representations—beginning with three joint appearances in the mosaics of San Marco (D 1.112, 113, 262). This is not surprising, since they were both martyr-soldiers of the Middle East who vanquished dragons. Theodore's legend is probably a variant on George's. But the relics of Theodore in the doge's chapel gave him an identity separate from George's. The two could be treated separately, therefore—especially George, who was immensely popular throughout the Christian world—but one would always suggest the other because of their shared iconography.

CARPACCIO'S SAINT GEORGE

Saint George was best known, of course, for slaying the dragon that had terrorized the city of Silena in Lybia, a Christian feat like Hercules' civilizing efforts against the primitive monsters of Hellas. It is significant that both Saint George and Hercules are portrayed in relief on the outer walls of San Marco.[3] George was an early favorite of Venetian devotees, including the Benedictines, who dedicated their monastery to him (the island of San Giorgio Maggiore). At first this complex named for him had no relic of George. The treasury in San Marco had bones from George's arm and leg (properly cased in knight's armor), but only in 1296—when the town of Fiore de Calabria was captured by Venice, and a cherished arm of George was carried off among the spoils—did the Senate decree that the church named for him should possess this new and acclaimed relic.[4]

Nonetheless, for the modern visitor to Venice, the relic of Saint George that left the clearest mark on Venetian culture belonged to the Dalmatians' Brotherhood of Saints George and Tryphon (now known as the Scuola di San Giorgio degli Schiavoni). The arrival of that relic in 1502 was the occasion for commissioning a cycle of three paintings of the Saint George legend by Vettor Carpaccio. As "Easterners," the Dalmatians had a reverence for George and Tryphon as culture heroes of Byzantium, but—like the monks of San Giorgio Maggiore in its early days—they had no relic of their principal patron. That was remedied by Paolo Valeresso, a patrician who received a valuable relic of George from the patriarch of Jerusalem and brought it back to his parish church of Sant'Angelo. In 1502, with the approval of the government, he gave this treasure to the Dalmatians. A great procession was formed, with trumpets and horns playing, to escort the relic to its new home, where Carpaccio would celebrate it.[5] Two of his three paintings devoted to Saint George prominently display bands of musicians celebrating George's victory and the baptism of the rescued princess with her fellow citizens—an echo of the music instruments that had conducted the relic to this site. (The event was very likely re-created in the musical masques of Carpaccio's patrons, the *compagnie della calza*).

The story of George took its canonical form in *The Golden Legend*. A dragon in Libya emerged from the lake where it dwelled, and killed those trying to enter or leave the nearby city of Silena. When citizens mounted the walls to watch its attacks on those outside, it raced to the walls and slew the people on them with its fiery breath. The Silenians, cut off from all supplies, from all intercourse with the outside world, placated the beast for a while by dropping two sheep over the walls for it to eat. When they ran out of sheep, humans were offered to it, chosen by lot. When the lot fell to the only daughter of the king, he tried to buy her ransom, but the citizens refused to let him make an exception of his family, and the princess was sent out, in her regal garments, to die. Just at this moment her rescuer chanced by, called on Christ's name, and drove his lance (shattered by the shock) through the dragon's skull.

The dragon, with its lethal breath, probably stands for the plague, the deepest-seated of the Venetians' fears, as we shall see in the next chapter. The beast's deadly realm, which fills the foreground of Carpaccio's painting, is a place where nothing grows. The trees near the clustered skulls on the left are not only twisted and dead— the most prominent one has its upper part wrenched away, not neatly as by a saw, but as if bitten off by the dragon in its indiscriminate rage. The principal human remains

FIG. 79
Vittore Carpaccio,
*Saint George and
the Dragon*

are those of a nubile woman and virile youth. Her genital area is gnawed away, and a lizard approaches to lick the entrails. The man's leg is snapped off by his scrotum, and a frog limps toward the stump. The hope of progeny, the fertile prospects of the city, are blighted at their source. The dragon's claws have wrenched off limbs and sucked the marrow from their bones.

Into this lifeless scene, the young armored George rides as a symbol of all that is vital in human effort and accomplishment. The artistry of his horse's harness and his own armor are statements of civilization's power to create new resources—as are the three beautifully crafted ships on the knight's side of the picture. The knight's horse bounds up and flings its mane in the wind—bearing down on the earthy monster, whose tail curls in a writhing kinship with the twisted and lifeless trees. Life is pitted against death. The tree that stands between the monster and the man is blighted on the monster's side, but puts forth new leaves out of the dead trunk on the man's side. The struggle that intertwines life and death is so intimate that the features of the dead young man and woman are pallider images of the live champion's and princess's faces. These figures are even arranged chiastically (in the rhetorical A-B-B-A order): dead *woman*, dead *man*, live *man*, live *woman*.

The second picture in Carpaccio's series, *Saint George's Triumph*, shows the inside of the walled city that was seen on the hill in the preceding scene. George has now led the dragon into the city, using the princess's girdle as a leash. He is about to kill the beast, who has frightened the two horses nearest it. (Why were the horses not sacrificed when the town ran out of the sheep it was feeding to the dragon?) On the scene's left the king and queen advance, mounted, while the princess walks along beside them, her hand in her father's, restored to him by her champion. The marching band of musicians is celebrating the victory.

In the final picture, Saint George, who has put on a red mantle over his armor, is baptizing the princess he saved, along with her father, the king. After them, the whole citizenry will become Christians (twenty thousand of them, according to *The Golden Legend*). The princess's mother stands ready to be baptized, wearing a sober dark dress, but with a jeweled cloak around her shoulders and an odd high hat of the sort she wore in the preceding picture. A wet nurse near her holds a baby (the princess's baby brother?), figurative of the whole new generation being brought into the church by Saint George. The drummer from the earlier picture is at the forefront of the musicians who have marched to the event, and over him three trumpeters have mounted a tapestried parapet to sound their energetic music for the festival.

TINTORETTO'S SAINT GEORGE

In 1552, Tintoretto painted a work to hang in the Palace of the Treasurers near the Rialto (PR 2.165). This work, now in the Accademia, was intended for the office of the Salt Magistracy, one of the principal financial institutions of Venice. It was commissioned by outgoing magistrates to commemorate their term in office—Giorgio Venier and Alvise (Venetian for "Louis") Foscarini—so it contains the men's two name saints, Saint George and Saint Louis of Toulouse (a popular saint, seen for instance in Giovanni Bellini's *Saint Jerome* for the Church of St. John Chrysostom). There was some complaint at the odd iconography of the work, which shows the princess as having ridden the vanquished dragon into the ground; but Tintoretto was just following the lead of *The Golden Legend*, which describes the aftermath of the dragon's conquest:

> Then he called to the maiden: "Have no fear, child! Throw your girdle around the
> dragon's neck! Don't hesitate!" When she had done this, the dragon rose and followed

her like a little dog on a leash. She led him toward the city; but the people, seeing this, ran for the mountains and the hills, crying out: "Now we will all be eaten alive!" But blessed George waved them back and said to them: "You have nothing to fear! The Lord has sent me to deliver you from the trouble this dragon has caused you. Believe in Christ and be baptized, every one of you, and I shall slay the dragon!"[6]

In this, the most common source of the legend, George does not kill the dragon at the first encounter, but subdues it, rendering it so weak that even the initially frightened princess can lead it on a leash as fragile as her own belt. This accords with other tales of saints who subdue animal passions—like Daniel in the lions' den, or Jerome taming the lion he leads into the monastery. Here we see the princess, who has overcome her fear, using the dragon almost as a rocking horse. Her Michelangesque body is relaxed, by contrast with the way Saint Louis draws himself stiffly up, clearing his garments of the beast, turning away from it with caution. The bishop's staff of Louis is played off against the broken shaft of the lance that projects off the ledge into our space and reminds us of the battle that preceded this scene.

The princess turns in confidence toward Saint George, her body counterpointed against the curled sinuosity of the dragon, the lift of her face contrasted with the collapse of its head—which also projects from the ledge, inviting us to overcome our fear more completely than Louis does. Her complete accord with George is suggested by her bright reflection in his black armor. George is seen at the moment of his exhortation to the crowd to have no fear. He offers the princess as a model for their trust. His white charger and black suit of mail proclaim his mastery of the situation. As the dominant figure in the tight little ballet of this scene, George is the patron of church and state, of bishop and princess—just as when he led Venetian troops into war.

There could not be a more complete contrast than that between the serene princess of the Accademia painting and the panic-stricken woman running toward us in the picture of George slaying the dragon now in London's National Gallery. This

FIG. 80
Jacopo Tintoretto,
The Princess, Saint George, and Saint Louis

was painted c. 1555–1560, probably for a private chapel in a palace of the Cornaro family (PR 2.175). There are points to compare with Carpaccio's painting of the scene—the corpse of one of the dragon's victims on the ground, the tree bitten off in this realm of death, the fabled city in the background. But Carpaccio's city is made legendary by his technique of magic realism—realistic details on unearthly structures, while Tintoretto

dissolves his city in the mists of romance. You feel you could walk on the solid ground Carpaccio has strewn with the meticulously observed but iconic body parts. Tintoretto's landscape, by contrast, undulates in the rhythms of a dream.

Both artists faced the problem that the legend of Saint George has a feel of pagan myth—it is uncomfortably close, for instance, to the story of Perseus rescuing Andromeda from the sea monster. Carpaccio handles the difficulty by making his George frankly heraldic, a flat and frontal emblem of a knight with ornamental armor, almost a statement of pedigree. Tintoretto, in the Accademia picture considered above, with the princess riding the dragon, recognizes and even emphasizes the fairy-tale quality of the story. But in the London picture he makes the scene oneiric, a place of misty distances, dreamy spires, and a wispy (almost translucent) knight on some archetypal quest. Only the fleeing woman—so different from the statuesque princess standing above the fray in Carpaccio's work— suggests that the dream might shift to nightmare.

The commentators on the National Gallery collection think that the iridescent epiphany in the sky may be introduced precisely to meet any objection that this is a pagan myth or fairy tale.

FIG. 81
Jacopo Tintoretto, *Saint George and the Dragon*

Many reforming churchmen were aware that some of the legends of the saints had no real connection with Christianity, and, as has been mentioned, George, whose cult was strong in Venice, was especially controversial. As unusual as the reduced prominence of George [in the London painting] is the miraculous presence of God the

Father, and it may have been that Tintoretto wished to emphasize delivery by the hand of God, rather than by a knight in armor.[7]

But if Tintoretto wanted to play down the mythical, he would hardly have introduced so many fairy-tale touches in the scene. It is the strength of Tintoretto that he can go *through* dream toward inner truths—a thing often seen in his treatment of spatial relations (not topographically chartable) and weightless bodies. The range of this picture—from fear to epiphany, from death to the maiden, from idyllic country to cloudy spires—reveals the psychic depths attainable in myth. His Saint George does not fall short of the real but takes us beyond the real.

THEODORE

Saint Theodore, known familiarly to Venetians as Todaro (emphasis on the first syllable), has his place of honor on the pillar in the Piazzetta next to the one holding Mark's lion. This awkward statue is a composite—an ancient head combined with a different ancient torso, to which limbs and shield and halo have been added.[8] He stands on a composite creature, too—the "dragon" made of a crocodile torso with a canine head. Put on the pillar in 1329, Todaro serves with the lion as part of an apotropaic (averting) pair guarding the entryway to Venice—to warn off the hostile and offer others admission through the portal formed by their pillars.

When Theodore is not paired with Saint George, as the twin warriors of the city in peril, he complements Saint Mark, suggesting the city's Byzantine past and its continuity with "the new saint in town." They appear together, for instance, on the Rialto Bridge. It has already been noticed that those approaching the bridge from one side see the angel of the Annunciation and Mary on the aprons of the bridge. Those coming from the other direction see, on one apron, Theodore seated in his armor and holding his spear, while on the other Mark is seated with his lion and his gospel. The two saints were also paired at the end of Sansovino's reliefs inside the iconostasis in San Marco, where tapestries of the life of Saint Theodore (probably designed by Sansovino) were hung on special feasts (BB 2.56).

FIG. 82
Statue of St. Theodore, original taken from the Piazzetta

These images prove that Theodore was not entirely extruded by Mark. In fact, his relics were moved to the Church of San Salvador, which had a special place in the myth of Venice. That is the church where an altar was originally blessed by Pope Alexander III in 1177, when he was rescued by the doge from Frederick Barbarossa. We have seen how that episode was used to declare Venetian independence from the pope. Manfredo Tafuri suggests that a new devotion to Theodore was meant to reinforce that point in the middle of the sixteenth century. Just in this period, when Constantinople was in peril from the Turks and then fell to them, a dogal procession in honor of Saint Theodore's relic was instituted, wending its way to San Salvador. This was a means, Tafuri thinks, of claiming that Venice was the new Constantinople, according to the ancient pattern of rule transferred to the west (*translatio imperii*).[9] He notes that the nearby church of another Byzantine saint, John Chrysostom, was also given new importance in the period, sacralizing the midspace between the piazza and the Rialto.

The campaign to promote Theodore led to the elevation of his scuola, which was housed near San Salvador. This had been a minor club (*scuola piccola*), but the government made it a *scuola grande* in 1552. The same emphasis on Theodore's status can be seen in Tintoretto's painting (c. 1567) *Madonna of the Treasurers* (PR 2.193–94), discussed earlier. Here Theodore sits in his armor on the top step of Mark's throne, while Mark reaches across his back in a gesture toward the treasurers. The rose-colored garment of Mark is stretched out as if to form a mantle over the black armor of Theodore. The two are part of a pyramid formed with the diagonal slant of the infant Jesus, a subordinate unit in the painting that expresses the partnership of Mark with Theodore for the guarding of Venice.

GEORGE AND THEODORE

Though Theodore could be seen as Mark's adjutant, he was still more often the companion in arms of Saint George. That is apparent in one of the most ambitious battle-monument complexes ever reared in Venice. I described in Chapter 4 the tremendous communal effort Venetians had made when three great powers joined forces against them in the League of Cambrai (1509–10). One of the leaders of that effort, the scion of a great military family, was the orator Giorgio Emo—whose name saint was George. Emo was a strategist who worked with stalwarts in the field, three of whom died in action—Niccolò Orsini, Count of Pitigliano, the captain general; Dionisio Naldi di Brisighello; and the courageous *condottiere*, Leonardo da Prato. Emo meant to pay these men honor in their death, and he provided for fitting monuments to them in the Church of Saints John and Paul, of which he was an official overseer. After arranging

FIG. 2
Jacopo Tintoretto,
*Madonna of the
Treasurers*

260

their solemn funerals in the church, he commissioned tombs for each of them—with life-size equestrian statues of gilded wood for Niccolò Orsini and Leonardo da Prato and a standing statue of Dionisio Naldi in gilded armor.

Lionello Puppi demonstrates that Emo meant to make the north transept of Saints John and Paul a pantheon to the heroes of the war with the League.[10] The monument to Orsini was put on the transept's western wall, and that of Naldi stood over a newly opened door to the church that made this area more grand. Most important, Emo got the Dominicans to commission a completion of the huge stained-glass window in this transept (1510–15). The priests had begun the window in the 1490s, filling its upper section with a theology of the church turning upon the Incarnation. This section was done by Murano glassblowers working to cartoons from the Vivarini workshop. Now a lower section was added, by the artist Girolamo Mocetto (who seems to have worked from cartoons influenced by Cima da Conegliano).[11]

The principal feature of this addition to the window is a row of four armored saints, two mounted, two standing. The mounted ones, on either end, are Saint Theodore (killing his "crocodile") and Saint George (rescuing his princess from the dragon). The two in the middle are the obscure martyr-soldiers after whom this church is named, John and Paul. (The common misconception that the church was dedicated to the apostles John and Paul is rarely corrected.) The combination of the new entrance and the new range of windows, with the gilded statue of Dionisio standing above the one and at the base of the other, along with the gilded statue of Orsini flanking the entrance, made this transept a blaze of honor for the fallen. The linking of Venice's warrior-protectors with the theology of the window's upper part unites their sacrifice with the whole mission of Venice. The warriors protect the city's physical existence, as the Dominican preachers in the trefoils immediately above them protect its spirit—and both are subordinated to the workings of divine providence in the scheme of salvation enacted through the Incarnation. There is no greater example of Venice's customary blending of patriotism with piety.

The monument to Leonardo could not be accommodated in this transept, since its eastern wall opens onto a preexisting chapel; but Leonardo's statue is right across the nave, at the entrance to the corresponding transept. As a condottiere, he ranks a bit below the two native Venetians; but he is united with them in the overall program, the "pantheon" of Emo. The place of highest honor is the statue of Dionisio, who stands between John and Paul in the window, armored like them, holding a spear as they do. The spheres of the heavenly and the earthly combatants overlap and reinforce each other.

PLATE XXVII
Santi Giovanni e Paolo, window

But why, if there are only three monuments to the fallen, are there four soldiers in the window? To understand that, we have to remember that a commissioner's name saint was often identified with him, could even be given his features. We saw that in the case of Saint Thomas, who bore Rangone's features, or Saint Anthony, who bore Milledonne's. Giorgio (Venetian "Zorzi") was a common name in Venice—whence the painter's name, "Big George" (Giorgione, "Zorzon"). A man named George might have his portrait painted with the attributes of the saint. One such portrait, by Tintoretto, is in the National Gallery in Washington, D.C. (P-R 1.103). The man holds a battle standard, suggesting service in a war, and the enemy is typified by the slain dragon seen in the left background of the picture.

Given these conventions, it is easy to identify the fourth warrior in the window, the figure of Saint George, with Giorgio Emo himself. He is present in spirit with the fallen men who were his comrades. And where George is, there Theodore will be, too. They fight together.

FIG. 36
Jacopo Tintoretto,
*The Temptation of
Saint Anthony*

CHAPTER TWENTY-TWO

Plague Saints

THE MOST FAMOUS OUTBREAK of plague in Europe was the Black Death of 1348. But plague was a constant presence, flaring up erratically, unpredictably, irresistibly, throughout the late Middle Ages and the Renaissance. And Venice offered almost ideal conditions for its spread—it was a warm seaport with high humidity, just the kind of place where the black rat flea (*Yersinia pestis*) flourishes. This flea preferred its original host, but it was so lethal that it killed the host population, proving more deadly to rats than to humans. Only when it had killed off the available rats did it settle for biting humans—carried into proximity with them upon clothes or other items. These items came from ships where the fleas had ravaged the rat (and some of the human) population on board. Since only the flea spread the plague, contact of human with human was not of itself contagious (though this was unknown at the time). That is why only one person in a home might be killed, and why people tending those already plague-stricken in the *lazaretti* usually survived. Isolation was an effective preventative only secondarily, if the flea was kept from other humans until it had time to die itself.

Because the plague struck so mysteriously, killing and sparing in patterns little explicable, the fear of it could be apocalyptic, especially when numbers of the unnoticed fleas struck large parts of the population. The plague of 1575 to 1576 killed 51,000 in Venice, almost a third of the population. Titian was one of the victims. Many saw in these catastrophes the punishment of an angry God, and turned to passages like Psalm 38.3 (37.3 in the Vulgate text used by the Venetians): "There is no health in my flesh, because of thy wrath: there is no peace for my bones, because of my sins."[1] Penitential services and public self-scourgings were meant to placate the Lord, and vows of reform were backed with promises to raise new altars or churches.

Special saints were called on for assistance—especially saints Sebastian, Roch, Job, Christopher, Cosmas, and Damian. One painted invocation of the plague saints seems particularly ominous now, since we know that its artist would later succumb to the blow his picture was trying to ward off. Titian painted his *Saint Mark Enthroned*, now in the Church of the Salute, during the epidemic of either 1505 or 1510, over half a century before the one that would kill him (w 1.143). Even without that consideration, it is a somber work, with the city's suffering suggested by the dark shadow thrown over Mark's

FIG. 83
Titian,
Saint Mark Enthroned

face (recalling the plague-stricken Job's lament, "My eyes are dim").[2] We know the source of Mark's sorrow from the marshaling of plague saints before Mark's throne—the doctor saints Cosmas and Damian, Saint Roch pointing to the plague mark on his own thigh, and Saint Sebastian with his arrows. The last named was the principal champion against plague.

SAINT SEBASTIAN

Sebastian was a fourth-century Roman soldier who secretly ministered to tortured Christian prisoners and the plague stricken. Taken by the Roman authorities, he was put before a firing squad of crossbowmen who—according to *The Golden Legend*—"shot so many arrows into his body that he looked like a porcupine."[3] But he miraculously survived this barrage, and was later martyred by being beaten to death. So there were two reasons to call on him for help against the plague—his ministry to the sick, and his own survival of multiple wounds. This latter point was given greater focus by the association of Job's sores with arrow wounds in Job 6.4 and 16.13: "For the arrows of the Lord are in me, the rage whereof drinketh up my spirit . . . He hath set me up to be his mark." Job's sores were equated with the marks (bubos) of the most common (bubonic) type of plague (the other two being septicemic and pneumonic).[4] Sebastian was thus the victim of plague spots, and the survivor of them, and a protector from them. The latter role was dramatically presented by Benozzo Gozzoli when he painted an apotropaic (averting) picture during the 1460s plague in San Gimignano—here the saint's mantle is spread out over the citizens like a huge canopy, and the arrows of God's wrath are splintering on it, unable to reach their targets under the sheltering garment.[5]

Sebastian's wounds were so associated with plague spots that the arrows directed at him were made to hit the points where the bubos of the plague were most common—especially the lymph glands in the throat, armpits, and groin. These are the main targets, for instance, in Giovanni Bellini's Saint Sebastian panel in his early *Polyptych of Saint Vincent Ferrer* at the Church of Saints John and Paul (T 88–93). One arrow hits the throat gland, another is in the upper right arm, and a third stabs through the loincloth into the saint's groin. In most pictures of the saint, church decorum made artists tactfully insert the groin arrow in the upper thigh. That is where Tintoretto directs the arrow in his large Saint Sebastian painted for the Scuola Grande di San Rocco (P-R I.102) He also puts an arrow in the upper arm (the left one this time), but not in the neck. Instead, he wounds the saint in the forehead, since pneumonic plague caused facial blotches (we saw one in Tintoretto's *Search for the Body of Saint Mark*).

SAINT ROCH

Roch ("Rocco" to Italians), an obscure man born (apparently) in France in the fourteenth century, exploded onto the Italian scene in the fifteenth century, when a series of miraculous plague cures was attributed to him. His "biography" suspiciously resembles the pattern of other pilgrim saints, who spend some time in the desert, are fed miraculously, and then cure others rather than receive cure at the place they sought in pilgrimage. After the Second Vatican Council, he was (like Saint Christopher) removed from the official calendar of saints.[6]

Roch was revered with special ardor in Venice. The scuola devoted to him began with a chapel in the Church of San Giuliano, for which Antonello da Messina painted an altarpiece in 1475, with panels containing three plague saints—Sebastian, Christopher, and Roch (only the Sebastian panel survives, in Dresden).[7] The scuola wanted to expand into its own building, and the plague of 1485 gave it the opportunity. In that

FIG. 84
Jacopo Tintoretto,
Saint Sebastian

year, when many plague-stricken cities were calling on Saint Roch for protection, the Venetians, with typical enterprise, stole his body from its tomb in the terraferma city of Voghera. (In a hotly competitive field, the Venetians were probably the champion body snatchers.) The government gave custody of the relic to the scuola devoted to him, which did not have a place of its own to lodge it in. The body was kept for a time at the Church of San Giminiano, then at that of San Silvestro. But in 1590 it was brought to

its own new Church of San Rocco, where it rests over the high altar. Tintoretto and assistants, who would create the biblical cycle for the adjoining scuola building, painted Roch's life in the sanctuary area of the church.

Roch was, according to his legend, born in Montpellier, the son of rich parents. After giving his possessions to the poor, he set off on pilgrimage to Rome. But at Piacenza he was moved by the misery of plague victims, and ministered to them—the subject of Tintoretto's first painting in the sanctuary (P-R 2.158), where Roch leans over a man who has lifted his leg to show the bubo on his inner thigh (the place where Roch himself will be afflicted). Roch contracted the plague from those he comforted. In most pictures that show him standing, he draws up his pilgrim's cloak to show the bubo on his upper thigh. Unable to suppress his groans of agony, he withdrew into the wilderness in order to spare other patients the sight of his pain. Left alone there, he was fed miraculously by a dog who brought bread from its master's table—the subject of Tintoretto's second painting in the sanctuary (P-R 2.218), which has a beautiful landscape by his assistant, Flemish Paul (Paolo Fiammingo).[8]

Cured of the plague himself, Roch became a curer of others, not only of humans but of animals as well. In the third painting of this series, Tintoretto has the lion of

Saint Mark lead an exotic herd to Roch's lair, one that includes a camel and a unicorn (P-R 2.193). When Roch left the wilderness, he resumed his pilgrimage to Rome, where he cured a cardinal of the plague. In a painting that was originally a panel for the organ, but which is now placed in the rear of the church, Tintoretto shows the cardinal presenting Roch to the pope, the curve of whose tiara is echoed in the rotunda behind the scene and in the mitres of the cardinals in attendance (P-R 2.224–25). According to the story, Roch cured a bubo on the cardinal's forehead by making a sign of the cross over the mark, and the cross traced there stayed in place as a token of his cure. The mark does not show in this painting (perhaps because a restorer thought it was an accidental stain), but it is clear on the painting Tintoretto did for the high altar of the adjoining scuola's upper floor, *Saint Roch in Glory*.[9]

After his Roman sojourn, Roch returned to France, where he was arrested as a spy at the Battle of Montpellier, the subject of Tintoretto's painting for the side wall of the nave (P-R 2.220). For the sixth and final painting in this cycle, we return to the sanctuary, where Roch is seen in prison, being comforted by an angel (P-R 2.192–93). The explosion of light around the angel and the saint is set off by the dark scene of suffering, which represents the anguish of the plague stricken who turned to Roch for succor. This cycle, painted to honor the body of Roch as it lay in the sanctuary, called members of the Scuola Grande di San Rocco to their task of comforting the plague afflicted.

SAINT JOB

Venice acquired in its early days the Byzantine custom of treating "Old Testament" heroes as saints. That is why we find churches of Saint Moses, Saint Jeremiah, Saint Zachariah—and of Saint Job (San Giobbe). Job became a plague saint because of the sores that he suffered:

> My flesh is clothed with rottenness and the filth of dust,
>   my skin is withered and drawn together.
>
> In the night my bone is pierced with sorrows;
>   and they that feed upon me do not sleep.
> With the multitude of them my garment is consumed,
>   and they have girded me about as with the collar of my coat.
> I am compared to dirt,
>   and am likened to embers and ashes. (Job 7.5, 30.17–19)

Though God let Satan test Job with such trials, he was restored to health and wealth after his ordeal—which made him the perfect patron for sympathizing with his clients' suffering and for offering hope of recovery. This made him the patron of lepers as well as of plague victims. In Constantinople, both the churches of Saint Job were connected with hospitals (McA 134), and San Giobbe in Venice began as a hospital chapel attached to a hermitage of Observant Franciscans.

FIG. 86
Giovanni Bellini,
*Virgin and Child
Enthroned with Saints*

In the later fifteenth century, Doge Cristoforo Moro decided to expand the Venetian chapel to Job into a full church, where he and his *dogaressa* would be buried. He did this in part to honor the Franciscan preacher, Bernardino of Siena, whom he had met during the latter's visit to the hermitage—Bernardino was canonized quickly after his death. This complex of events forms the background for the most famous celebration of Job as a plague saint, Giovanni Bellini's San Giobbe Altarpiece, now in the Accademia, though it was commissioned for the Church of San Giobbe (T 124) in response to the plague of 1478 (S-N 72). Large as the painting seems in its present site, it lacks the grandeur of its original size and setting. Almost two feet have been cut away from the picture's height since its removal from the high marble frame that is still in the Church of San Giobbe. It should be higher than its current position in the Accademia, as the coffering of the barrel vault in the picture shows—we are looking *up* at the figures. Bellini painted the architecture to look as if the picture were a chapel opened up within the arch of the frame. The mosaic of the concave apse, with its Byzantine archangels, suggests that this is a companion site to San Marco.

The saints around Mary's throne are neatly arranged, three on each side, but the two most prominent bodies, startling for their nudity in this decorous setting, belong to the plague saints Sebastian and Job. Though Job is not shown with his sores, his older and drier skin makes a dramatic contrast with the youthful flesh of Sebastian. His gaze at the introspective Sebastian presents him as the forerunner of the Christian era's suffering figure. In this context, even Saint Francis's display of his hands with their stigmata can be read as referring to the plague wounds. The saints are turned out in force to battle the city's affliction.

The other saints are less often called on, though Cosmas and Damian were natural patrons, given their profession as physicians and the presence of their relics (both men's hands) at San Giorgio Maggiore.[10] Saint Christopher was a general averter of menace, placed as an apotropaic figure at entryways (see Titian's large fresco over the door in the Doge's Palace, w 1.131), so it was natural to take him as a warder-off of plague as well. The Virgin of the Misericordia (who spreads her mantle of protection over her devotees) was also invoked to shelter people from the plague.[11] Despite this range of resources, the workhorses of plague protection in Venice were Sebastian, Roch, and Job, pictured singly, in pairs, or all three together.

CHAPTER TWENTY-THREE

The Other Lion: Jerome's

S AINT JEROME (C. 350–C. 420) was born near Venice's mother city of Aquileia and lived there for some time. He was a patron of learning, of monastic life, and of asceticism. But Venetians felt a special bond with him mainly because his iconography included a lion, as Mark's did. If you came to Venice with a lion, they had to take you in. Jerome's lion is seen as the congener of Mark's—sometimes it appears to *be* the lion of Venice. One such place is in the Doge's Palace, on the ceiling of the Gilded Chamber (Salotto Dorato) at the top of the Golden Staircase. The octagonal painting at the center of the ceiling is by Tintoretto (P-R 2.186). It shows Doge Gerolamo Priuli (1559–1567) kneeling before the personified Justice who often represented Venice. She is giving the doge a sword with her right hand, while holding the scales of justice in her left hand. The use of just force (the sword) is underscored by the presence of Peace behind Justice, wearing an olive branch around her arm. Hovering over the whole scene is a bald and naked figure with a book, the customary depiction of Jerome as a desert hermit. Yet the presence of the lion behind the scales of Justice made people identify the presiding saint as Mark, and some modern scholars have followed that tradition.

FIG. 87
Jacopo Tintoretto,
*Doge Priuli with Venice
and Saint Jerome*

It is understandable that people would feel that this scene calls for Mark's presence. It is an official ceremony, by which the doge is invested with the sword of power and the admonitions to peace. Who better than Mark could set the seal on such a procedure? One scholar even asserts that "his [i.e., Mark's] presence is indispensable in any scene reflecting an investiture ceremony" (S-L 239). Palluchini agrees (P-R 2.186). But it is not only the iconography that establishes Jerome's identity here.[1] The vital clue is the fact that Jerome (Jerolamo, or Girolamo) was Doge Priuli's name saint. Sinding-Larsen objects that with the use of the doge's own patron "the painting would have taken on a more private character than is compatible with the position it occupies on the top landing of the Scala d'Oro" (s-L 239). But Jerome was not just a private protector. His special standing in Venice, and the lion he shared with Mark, made him a public patron as well. The link between his lion and Mark's is emphasized in the Younger Palma's painting of Christ in heaven for the Senate chambers in the Doge's

Palace. Both Mark and Jerome are in that picture, and their lions are the same size and are a replica, each, of the other (SMR 141–42).[2]

JEROME THE MONK: CARPACCIO

Jerome was depicted in several ways—as a hermit, a scholar, father of the church, a cardinal. The pictures of him as a scholar regularly show him in a monastic cell, but the monastery complex, with its community of brethren, is rarely presented. It is seen in the only surviving picture from a cycle of paintings created in the fifteenth century for the Scuola di San Girolamo, which was attached to the Church of St. Jerome—the death of Jerome by Bastiani.[3] But for a deeper treatment of Jerome's monastery we must go to Carpaccio's two paintings of it in the Dalmatians' Brotherhood of St. George (Scuola di San Giorgio degli Schiavoni). Its members were naturally devout to a fellow Dalmatian, though its two original patrons were Saint George and Saint Tryphon (the latter a patron of the Dalmatian town that some scuola members came from). Though the altar in the scuola's ground floor now has a late painting of the Virgin over it, that place was filled in Carpaccio's time by a triptych dedicated to the three club patrons, George, Tryphon, and Jerome.

Those, then, were the three saints Carpaccio had to celebrate. The surviving paintings—three of George, one of Tryphon, and three of Jerome (along with two scenes from the life of Christ)—may not be all that were originally completed. An early inventory indicates there were other works, and they were probably arranged on both floors of the scuola, not just on the ground floor, as at present.[4] We cannot conclude anything, therefore, from the present arrangement of the nine paintings, or know if Carpaccio conceived them as a united cycle. But there are some suggestive continuities, other than the Eastern setting of all the episodes. Carpaccio gives the scenes his customary magic atmosphere, as of a fairy tale, and he is helped to do that in this case by the exotic animals involved in each saint's miracle—George's dragon, Tryphon's basilisk and Jerome's lion. All three stories give us a saint who overcomes demonic or bestial nature—Christian civilizing myths like those of the Greek conquerors of monsters, on the Heracles model.

I have already discussed the Saint George paintings. The Tryphon tale is of a saint so famous for holiness in his youth that he was summoned by the Roman ruler of Bithynia, whose house was in disgrace because his daughter had become possessed by a demon. Tryphon prayed for the girl, who is shown standing before her father with her hands folded in prayer. The devil, cast out of her, takes the form of a fearsome basilisk, which Tryphon renders helpless by his prayer. The parallels with Saint George are obvious. Both saints rescue a princess, both stabilize the reign of the princess's father, both do this by controlling an inhuman power that takes animal form. How does Jerome fit into this sequence?

The story that Jerome controlled a fierce lion by taking a stone or thorn out of its paw has both classical and Christian antecedents. It was told of two Palestinian ascetics before it became fixed in Jerome's legend.[5] The miraculous nature of the taming is indicated in what may be Giovanni Bellini's earliest surviving picture, which shows Jerome in effect anesthetizing the lion, before operating on his paw, by tracing the sign of the cross over him (T 192). In the legend elaborated around Jerome, the saint introduced the lion into his monastery at Bethlehem, where the monks, after initially fearing it, taught it to perform useful chores for them. In the most famous episode of this legend, the lion was given the task of guarding the ass that carried the monks' firewood. One day the lion fell asleep, and a merchant caravan riding by seized the ass for its own use. The monks thought the lion had eaten the ass, and made him bear the firewood. Months later, however, the lion saw the merchants' caravan coming back. He roared them into submission and shepherded the whole caravan onto the monastery grounds, where the merchants begged Jerome's forgiveness and promised to stop their caravan, whenever it passed the monastery, to replenish its oil lamps.[6]

FIG. 89
Vittore Carpaccio,
Saint Jerome and the Lion

That is the background for Carpaccio's two paintings of Jerome's Bethlehem monastery. In the first, Jerome is bringing the lion onto the sacred grounds. It lifts its wounded paw, a kind of mirror-reversed image of Carpaccio's lion of Venice that lifts its right paw to hold Mark's gospel. Frightened monks dash off like the deer behind them. Their black-and-white garbs become ornithological markings as two of them fly like starlings up the stairs in the background. Skirts not only fly up but stretch out to suggest the blur of speed that is lengthening their very limbs in the takeoff effort that rockets them away. Nothing as wild as a lion belongs, they obviously feel, in this peaceful community of work, with its Venetian frescoes on the outer wall of the church, its monks' habits hanging out to dry along the right-hand wall. The keys and the writing boxes hanging from the monks' belts suggest the secure and settled ways of these men, who work with Jerome on his scholarly translations of the Bible. This is a place that will find work even for a lion.

In the next picture, the dead Jerome is laid out on the ground, his head pillowed on a stone, for the austere burial of a monk. In the right middle ground, the lion roars its sorrow, in contrast with the contained discipline of the monks. In the left middle ground

FIG. 90
Vittore Carpaccio,
Burial of Saint Jerome

the recovered ass grazes. The horse starts at the lion's roar, and so does the horseman with an Asian head-dress—is this one of the merchants returning to supply lamp oil, who is reminded of the lion's dreadful roar when he forced the caravan onto these grounds?

Jerome's body lies in a frame that has no architectural use. The narrow strip of flooring under him has a beam high over it, and pillars to hold the beam, but grass grows on either side of the platform underneath. It is as if the entire group on the platform were lifted out of everyday reality, fixed in timeless mourning over the dead body. Carpaccio is using one of the theatrical pavilions that the *compagnie della calza* commissioned for just such emblematic presentations. This detachment from the rest of the scene prepares us for the next picture, in which Jerome's soul, freed of the body here, laid out, streams light into a scholar's study, where a dog pricks up its ears at this sign of supernatural life, forming a contrast with the lion who sees only the saint's dead body.

This third painting was for centuries taken to be a depiction of Saint Jerome in his younger days, though the man at the desk has laid a bishop's mitre on the altar, not a cardinal's hat (Jerome was neither bishop nor cardinal but was thought to be the latter). The person represented is Jerome's contemporary, Saint Augustine, who (according to legend) was beginning to write Jerome a letter, asking about the nature of the Trinity, at the very moment when Jerome died. A great light streamed over him and Jerome's voice spoke out of it, saying he could ask him directly about the Trinity, now that his soul was freed to gaze on God's mystery.[7] It is a supernatural light that shines on Augustine's uplifted face, after passing through the astrolabe (symbolically, *through* the created universe, from beyond it). We know this light's special character from the contrast with natural light, which enters from the opposite direction to shine on the apparatus in the recessed cabinet.

PLATE XXVIII
Vittore Carpaccio,
Vision of Saint Augustine

We have seen that a man commissioning a picture of his name saint might have his own features given to the saint. More broadly, when a scholar-saint was depicted with books surrounding him in his study, the features of a famously learned man were given to him—as in the paintings of Saint Jerome by Jan van Eyck and Antonello da Messina, or of Augustine himself by Botticelli.[8] Is that true here? Many scholars have thought so, at least since 1955, the year Guido Perocco reported a resemblance between the *mandorla*-shaped seal on the document so prominent in Carpaccio's foreground and the heraldic seal of the Eastern cardinal Bessarion.[9] Bessarion had a close connection with the scuola, since in 1464 he had delivered a papal indulgence for devotions carried out there, and he was close to the Valaresso family, patrons of the scuola (Paolo Valaresso gave the Dalmatians a relic of Saint George).[10] Perocco suggested plausibly that the document to which Bessarion's seal is attached is the papal indulgence of 1464, which would have been carefully preserved in the treasury of the scuola. If that is so, then the document flanking it is probably a new indulgence from Rome delivered in the very year (1502) when Carpaccio was beginning work at the scuola.

Augusto Gentili thinks that the deliverer of this latest indulgence, Angelo Leonino, must be the model for Saint Augustine, but Gentili admits that we have no idea what Leonino looked like or even how old he was at the time he came to Venice.[11] Bessarion's features were well known—his snub nose, his black beard (the only one worn by a cardinal in the West, since Bessarion kept the custom of his Eastern origin). Bessarion was famous in Venice. A portrait of him by Gentile Bellini was included in one of the history paintings of the Larger Council hall. Another of Gentile's portraits is now in Vienna, and a copy of it is in Venice, at the Scuola della Carità (Accademia).[12] An important friend of Bessarion in Venice was a Jerome—Jerolamo Valaresso. Fortini Brown suggests that the Jerome series may have been commissioned as a joint celebration of Bessarion and Jerolamo by the latter's nephew, Paolo.[13]

John Bessarion, the Byzantine archbishop of Nicea, had come to Italy in 1438 to attend the Council of Ferrara (transferred to Florence). This meeting was meant to heal the schism between East and West. The effort foundered on the East's refusal to accept papal supremacy; but Bessarion threw in his lot with the West and went to Rome, where he was rewarded with a cardinal's hat by Pope Eugene IV, who was a Venetian *cittadino*. When Bessarion came to Venice on a papal mission in 1461, he was honored with a great procession and made an honorary patrician, entitled to sit in the Larger Council. His warm ties with Venice made the pope send him back to the city in 1463, to raise money and troops for a crusade against the Turks. This is when, as we have seen, he pled successfully for kinder treatment of the Jews in Venice. He was also made a member of St. Mary of Charity's Distinguished Brotherhood, to which he donated a prized relic of the cross that he had received from the patriarch of Constantinople. The painting of him holding that relic is still in the Scuola (now the Accademia).

During this stay in Venice (1463–1464), Bessarion lived as a pious monk in the monastery of San Giorgio in Isola, to which he donated the library he had brought with him from the East, with many precious Greek manuscripts. He later transferred the gift from the humble monastery to the care of the doge, who could better protect it. Bessarion admired the intellectual freedom of Venice and feared the censorship of Rome, where anti-Platonism might have jeopardized his precious manuscripts, the best collection then in the West.[14] It was for this collection that Sansovino would build his great library on the Piazzetta. Bessarion's patronage of learning makes him an appropriate model for Augustine in Carpaccio's painting, with its many volumes, open or in closed ranks. Michel Serres had the interesting idea of counting the books—there are ninety-four of them, exactly the number of his own works that Augustine listed in his *Reconsiderations (Retractationes)*.[15] This suggests that Carpaccio had the advice of a scholar—or, more likely, scholars—in the creation of this iconographically rich and detailed work.

The same conclusion emerges from the music manuscripts opened in our direction. These have been read and found to represent two forms of music, sacred and profane, reflecting the combination of Christian and classical (pagan) artifacts in the room, suggesting the range of Augustine's (and Bessarion's) knowledge.[16] A statue of Venus stands among the Greek vases on the shelf, while a statue of the risen Christ is on the altar. The seraph in the Venetian apse mosaic suggests the vision of God that seraphs are supposed to enjoy, a divine vision that Jerome is mediating to Augustine at the moment. On Augustine's writing shelf by the window there is a seashell, referring to another legend associated with Augustine. He is supposed to have been pacing by the sea, meditating on the Trinity, when a child playing in the sand asked what he was doing. The little boy, an angel in disguise, took the shell up and said he could as easily put the ocean inside it as Augustine's mind could contain the mystery of the Trinity.[17] The shell brings us back to the content of Jerome's message to Augustine, which was also about the Trinity.

JEROME THE HERMIT: VITTORIA

The most common way of depicting Jerome was as a hermit, and this was confused with his much later life in a monastery. He had gone to a desert in Chalcis, during his late twenties, to repent of his youthful sins—an episode described in his most famous letter (Letter 22), where he talks of fighting off temptation with extreme self-torture:

I was shapeless in my hairy sack, my rough skin blackened like a Negro's ... When peremptory sleep overcame my resistance to it, I dislocated my bones by banging them down on the bare earth ... Visions of dancing girls swarmed around me, keeping the mind in my frozen body fiery with sexual yearning. To a body all but dead, lust presented its human nature seething with evil flames. (22.7)

FIG. 91 (LEFT)
Alessandro Vittoria,
Jerome, Frari

FIG. 92 (RIGHT)
Alessandro Vittoria,
Jerome, Santi Giovanni
e Paolo

This desert passage was sometimes applied to Jerome's much later life, when he lived in Palestine with a set of holy women disciples and male amanuenses, working on his biblical translations. That is why the pictures of him as an ascetic show him with a long white beard, still beating his breast with a stone to drive off visions of lust. The fact that he is supposed to have found his lion in the *desert* and led it immediately into the *monastery* sealed this iconographic conflation of the separate periods in his life.

Though Jerome speaks of his body as emaciated and all but dead in Letter 22, admiring devotees later treated his asceticism as a regimen that strengthened him, gave his body a champion's power to do spiritual battle. Even as an old man, he is muscular, with the sinews of body and spirit that equipped him to wrestle free of the devil's grasp. That is the commanding presence set before us in Alessandro Vittoria's great statues of Jerome. The first (c. 1565), in the Frari, was part of an ambitious altar complex commissioned by Girolamo Zane for his name saint (P-H 3.512–13). Much of the altar was lost (including two saints and an altarpiece in high stucco relief) in the eighteenth century, when it was moved from its site in the Frari to make way for a new altar there. This Jerome, a restless intellectual athlete despite his age, has just sprung to his feet from a seated position, startling the lion reclined by his side, who throws its head back in surprise, to see what his master is up to. Jerome in the desert had often been depicted as seated on a rock, as in the early Bellini painting. Here Jerome, struck by a passage he has just read in the Gospels (probably the crucifixion, since he is normally seen contemplating the cross), has surged up in a motion that tenses his thigh and calf muscles—it is the same rising motion that Michelangelo gave to Christ in the Sistine *Last Judgment*. The energy of his action is seen in the way his beard is swept back as he jerks his head to the left. He strikes his breast, as he rises, with the rock he uses for self-punishment. Action is stamped on every inch of the marble surface. The lightning of inspiration is playing through his limbs, through the finely traced nerves and sinews of both arms and hands. Here, as Virgil puts it, brain permeates the bulk (*mens agitat molem*—Aeneid 6.727).

FIG. 93
Titian, *Saint Jerome*

Vittoria's second statue of Jerome, completed two decades after the first, is a contrast in every way with the earlier work (P-H 3.513). Here, too, Jerome is reacting to the passage in Scripture, but instead of leaping up, he is sinking to his knees on a stone outcropping, with the rock of his self-castigation hanging in his limp arm, as if there were no penance he could do that would be equal to the great suffering of Jesus that he (as a sinner) caused. The face is melancholy and resigned, rather than fixed in the determi-

FIG. 94
Titian, *Pietà*

nation of the first state. The lion lies undisturbed beside him; this is a picture where all action is useless. The only thing to regret is not regretting. (Jerome, the great celebrant of virginity, had to admit that he had lost his own as a dissolute young man.)

It seems likely Vittoria drew inspiration from the great Saint Jerome paintings completed by Titian toward the end of his life (w 1.133–36), since the canvases combine both the impulses captured separately in the statues. In the Titian at the Brera in Milan (w 1.135), Jerome is collapsing on the rock near which his lion sleeps, but it is a collapse that is also a lunge up toward the crucifix that inspires him. He seems to climb while kneeling, a beautifully choreographed expression of the concept that humility is a form of spiritual advance. Titian's Jerome is also an aging athlete, but here the skin is loosening as he nears death. The furnishings that are often emphasized in pictures of his cell—the books, the skull, the hourglass—lie behind him as if no longer needed. He has reached his goal, and is in effect rising from a life of suffering to the final reward.

A similarly terminal feel pervades the *Pietà* of the Accademia, where Jerome also yearns toward the dead Jesus, whom he is now allowed to touch (w 1.122–23). Titian has given this figure, no longer athletic, his own aged features, suggesting that he came to identify with Jerome in his own old age, and in this highly personal picture. Vittoria was not the only one to be moved by Titian's intense tributes to Jerome. The Younger Palma, in his picture for the Senate chamber already referred to, copies exactly the kneeling supplication of Titian's *Pietà*—and no wonder: Palma put the final touches on Titian's painting, after his death.

FIG. 80
Jacopo Tintoretto,
*The Princess, Saint
George, and Saint Louis*

JEROME THE SCHOLAR: BELLINI

When Jerome is presented as a scholar, the greatest biblical expert of the early church, he is normally seen in a book-filled study, just as Augustine is in Carpaccio's painting in the Schiavoni. That was not a favorite device in Venice. But the scholarly note was struck in other ways. Giovanni Bellini, for instance, combined the scholar in his study with a picture of Jerome in the desert when he painted his 1513 altarpiece for the Church of St. John Chrysostom (T 180–83). This was such an unusual bit of iconography (Jerome's lion is missing) that some scholars have thought the figure must be Saint John on the island of Patmos, where he is supposed to have written Revelation. But the red cardinal's cloak is one indication that Jerome is intended. An even better proof is Tintoretto's imitation of Bellini in his own treatment of Jerome in the painting (now in the Accademia, P-R 2.166) commissioned by magistrates called Andrew and Jerome (Andrea Dandolo and Girolamo Bernardo). He is seminude, but with a Bible on the book stand, combining the scholar and the penitent in the desert. Even the positioning of the legs is similar in this work executed almost four decades after Bellini's great picture.[18]

Bellini was able to create the aura of the scholar around Jerome without having to place him in a book-lined cell. In his altarpiece for a Saint Jerome altar in the Church of San Zaccaria, he shows him in the cardinal's robe he was normally given in such conversation pieces.[19] Despite the indignities suffered by this great work (taken off by Napoleon, truncated above and below, transferred from panel to canvas with loss of paint in the Virgin's and Child's faces), the power of Jerome's concentration is unparalleled in depictions of absorption in a book. This is a man who carries his scholarly setting about with him.

FIG. 95
Giovanni Bellini, *Saints
Jerome, Christopher, and
Louis of Toulouse*

PART FOUR

Imperial Learning

CHAPTER TWENTY-FOUR

Franciscan Learning

S AINT FRANCIS WAS A SAINT popular throughout Italy, but he had an especially strong presence in Venice, where there were many Franciscan monasteries
and churches. The first such complex was raised on the lagoon island of Saint
Francis of the Wilderness (San Francesco del Deserto), just south of Burano. This is
the place where Saint Francis was thought to have visited the lagoon in 1220, where he
spoke to the birds, and where a handful of Franciscans still tend the remaining church
and cloisters. But the main Franciscan church in the urban complex of present-day
Venice is the Church of Santa Maria Gloriosa dei Frari (the Friars' Saint Mary Raised
in Glory), whose importance to Franciscan ideas about the Assumption in Glory was
discussed earlier. In this Gothic church, created in the fourteenth century, visiting
preachers of the order swayed huge crowds. The monastery adjacent to the church is
now home to the city's vast archival collections.

The Frari was the home of the Conventual Franciscans, those who argued for a mod-
ified observance of Francis's strict approach to poverty and asceticism. Early in the sixteenth century, the stricter Observant Franciscans were split from the Conventuals, and
the pope gave the Observants the original Church of St. Francis in the Wilderness. With
their great fervor, the Observants founded or detached from the Conventuals a number
of smaller but important churches and monasteries—St. Job, St. Francis at the Vineyard,
St. Clare on Murano, St. Clare in Venice proper, the Holy Sepulcher, St. Francis of the
Cross, and the convent of Claretian nuns at the Church of the Miraculous Mary.[1]

BELLINI

All these institutions guaranteed that devotion to Francis would thrive in many forms,
from many centers, and that the expressions of love for the saint would take many artis-

PLATE XXIX
Giovanni Bellini,
Ecstasy of Saint Francis

tic forms. But the most moving picture of him created in Venice is, I believe, Giovanni Bellini's of c. 1480, now in the Frick gallery in New York (т 112–15). This did not, apparently, come from a church or monastery. It was first mentioned in 1525 as displayed in a private home, and its unusual iconography seems to reflect the personal devotion of a patron for whom Francis was the name saint, and whose portrait may explain the departure from the traditional physiognomy of Francis. We see here the prominent nose of an individual. The painting is mysterious, with a hushed and rapturous quality, as if the whole landscape were listening for a divine message (like the alert rabbit peering out from its crevice near Francis's shelter).

There has been a great deal of argument over the work's interpretation—argument not easily resolved, since roughly eight inches have been cut from the top of the picture. Did the customary seraph of the crucifixion appear in the lost upper corner of the painting, making this a stigmatization scene? But the convention of stigmata pictures was to show a kneeling Francis with his upturned palms lifted high, accompanied by the companion who witnessed the miraculous piercing of Francis's hands, feet, and side. That is the way Bellini himself had painted the stigmatization in a predella panel of his *Coronation of the Virgin* in Pesaro (т 96–101), and the way his father presented the scene in his book of drawings (now in the Louvre). In the Frick painting, by contrast, Francis is standing, he holds his hands below his waist, the stigmata are inconspicuous (none in the feet, at least in the picture's present condition, and there is no opening of the garment for Francis to receive the wound in his side), and the companion is missing.

Many critics, nonetheless, think there is some kind of miracle occurring, signaled by what they see as two sources of light, one on the background landscape, the other shining through or on the leaves in the upper left corner of the picture in its current state. John V. Fleming, in a book devoted entirely to the painting, claims that this work expresses the Franciscans' belief that their order's founder was a new Moses being addressed through the burning bush—that is why, like Moses, he has removed his sandals before the tossing leaves of the tree.[2] But Francis is not gazing at the tree, which is placed too far back from the foreground for his line of sight. Francis seems to be looking higher, and toward the light that throws a strong shadow behind him and *partly away from us*—which puts the source of light on our side of the picture plane. This, too, militates against the idea that the upper half of the painting could have held a crucified Christ. If such a cross is the source of light, then it is outside the picture.

Millard Meiss, in another book devoted to the painting, thinks that it is a kind of soft stigmatization by the beauty of nature, the transport of a poetic spirit.[3] One thing that would support this view is the widely opened mouth of the saint. That usually suggested suffering (as in the Laocoön) or singing (as by angelic choirs). Is Francis singing his own "Canticle of the Sun"? The text of it may be on the sheet of paper tucked into the rope around his waist. But Meiss's humanistic crucifixion without the cross is not quite what the Franciscans had in mind when they compared Francis with Christ. The spread of the saint's hands in a gesture downward is the gesture of patronage, most familiar in pictures of the Virgin's Misericordia pose, in which she spreads her mantle to cover her kneeling clients. The same pose is taken by other saints—as in Bartolomeo Bon's lunette of Saint Mark protecting the members of his club on the façade of the Scuola Grande di San Marco. The pose of the Frick Saint Francis is replicated in Titian's Pesaro altarpiece at the Frari, where the family kneeling in the lower right hand of the picture is placed under the protection of the saint's spread arms.

FIG. 31
Titian,
Pesaro Altarpiece
of the Frari

The problem with taking the pose as one of patronage in the Frick painting, of course, is that there are no clients kneeling under his gesture. But there may be an implied patronage. In fact, there are two possibilities, either or both of which would explain the picture's pose. If the light source is on our side of the picture plane, then we viewers are implicitly included in the scene. In fact, the family or patron who commissioned the painting would, if placed in front of the saint's figure, be in exactly the same relationship to it as the family included in the Pesaro painting.

But a more conventional kind of patronage may be more important here. The organizing principle of the picture is the contrast of the stark landscape around the saint, barren and rocky and lit with an eerie green luminescence, with the warmer and softer brown world of vegetation and civilization in the background. The barren tree in the middle foreground shows how arid this part of the picture is—as does the effort with which Francis had to coax a small garden into existence, in its rocky flower box with his watering pitcher beside it. (One flower shoots up above this garden, its slim profile echoing that of Francis.) This contrast of barren foreground with fertile background is present in works that show a heroic sacrifice or labor, performed in the harsh space, protecting or benefiting a more prosperous area of human life. The two worlds, that of struggle and that of the rewards won by the struggle, are juxtaposed.

This is the strategy of several Bellini Crucifixions, most notably perhaps the one of c. 1500–1502 in Prato (T 209), which was brought to Venice for the 1999 exhibit on Venice and the art of the North.[4] Here Christ's cross is wedged into the hard ground where five skulls litter its rocky surface. The site is part of a cemetery with stunted and dying trees. Jewish headstones are tilted here and there in untended disarray. But the landscape in the distance has trees and full foliage, an orderly urban life with churches and homes and farms, all made safe by Christ's sacrifice for its salvation. As Bernard Aikema says, "The upper part of the picture corresponds to the *salvatio* and is bathed in warm light."[5] The picture might be an illustration of Chesterton's lines:

> Yet by God's death the stars shall stand,
> And the small apples grow.[6]

FIG. 79
Vittore Carpaccio, *Saint George and the Dragon*

Bellini's painting thus belongs to a broader category, that of the civilizer-hero, whose labor or suffering rescues a populace. The labors of Hercules were of this type, as was the ordeal of the Christian Hercules, Saint George. In Carpaccio's painting of George, the hero encounters his dragon on a plain strewn with the decomposing bodies of its victims. Writhing snakes and lizards emphasize the desert quality of this drear arena. A dying tree is placed between the saint and the monster, and only palm trees can flourish along the water that divides this plain from the city on the far shore, where normal foliage and beautiful structures show what is at stake in this contest. In works of this genre, civilization is held in the balance awaiting the outcome of the heroic contest. The preservation of life for the rest of us is the theme of works that celebrate such heroic deeds. As Thucydides makes Pericles say of the fallen Athenian heroes, "The valor of these men and their peers gave the city her beauty."[7]

In the case of the Frick *Saint Francis*, the hero does not slay a dragon or die on a cross, or even receive the marks of the cross. His achievement is the ascetic life of prayer and sacrifice that intercedes for less heroic humans, who need the blessings of God called down on them by their champion and advocate. A person of such heroic sanctity can, as it were, exorcize the demons from our ordinary world—as Saint Francis is seen expelling the devils from the city of Arezzo in the Giottesque painting on the upper level of Francis's church at Assisi. Chesterton said that the effect of Francis was to purify a tainted world: "The flowers and stars have recovered their first innocence. Fire and water are felt to be worthy to be the brother and sister of a saint. The purge of paganism is complete at last."[8] That purifying effect is what bathes the whole picture by Bellini in such a glowing sense of wonder—both his own ascetic realm and the world of nature and culture that benefit from his prayer and purpose.

Though Bellini painted Francis only once in this hero-civilizer genre, he had used it several times for the hermit life of Saint Jerome (T 192, 226), and each time with the contrast between the lonely wilderness in the foreground and the civilized world in the background. This was a natural way to present Jerome, since he had been a self-professed hermit who struggled with monstrous temptations in the desert, like Saint Anthony—the spiritual equivalent of George's contest with the dragon.[9] A lonely struggle by a vulnerable single combatant was at issue in such cases. Francis does not quite fit this pattern, since he was not a hermit alone with tempting devils but a man who lived his world-renouncing life in a brotherhood. Bellini skirts this problem by making his Francis stand alone, without companions, while not presenting him as a hermit. Hanging in the leaves of his shelter is a bell, whose cord is looped on one of the slender supports of his shelter. The bell implies a community, since it is used for calling the brothers together in prayer.

Francis's mendicant life of wandering is suggested, too, by the temporary nature of the flimsy shelter. It is not a real cell. The sandals put aside for the moment have the same purport. Francis did not want his friars to be settled in monasteries, but to move with the Spirit and live on what they could beg. That is why the lone ass stands so prominently within the picture's ascetic area. Some have treated this as the donkey Francis rode up Mount Avernus just before the stigmatization—but Francis is not standing on a mountain here, and Fleming rightly notes that the animal is neither shod nor bridled.[10] It is wild. The most important scriptural reference to a wild ass is at Genesis 16.12, where it is said that Ishmael "will be a wild ass," the founder of a Bedouin tribe of wanderers. Ishmael, abandoned in the wild but cared for by an angel, is a perfect type of the freely roving Francis and his followers.[11] This Francis will be moving on, like the ownerless ass, loose in the world he paradoxically stabilizes. The Book of Job, too, celebrates the lonely freedom of the wild ass:

> Who hath sent out the wild ass free,
>> And who hath loosed his bonds?
> To whom have I given a house in the wilderness,
>> And his dwelling in the barren land?
> He scorneth the multitude of the city
>> He heareth not the cry of the driver. (Job 39.5–7—Douai-Challoner)

The way Francis's isolation helps others live in community is suggested by the presence of the rabbit in the rocks. Fleming, in accord with his Mosaic interpretation of the picture, thinks this refers to the way Moses was hidden in a rock so as not to be overcome by God's splendor (Exodus 33.22).[12] But if Francis is, in Fleming's view, the new Moses, how can the rabbit be Moses too? Fleming does not enough reflect on the fact that Bellini regularly put a rabbit in his pictures of Jerome as a hermit (T 51, 192, 226–7). The rabbit was known principally for its fertility. By putting one in the desert, where it does not belong, Bellini suggests the spiritual fertility of the physically celibate ascetic. The heron, too, does not belong in a desert—but its freedom to soar is like that of Francis.

The strong link between Francis's wandering life and the settled town of the Frick painting is emphasized by the way the saint's golden-brown habit, strangely architectural, with a stiff linearity reminiscent of Bellini's brother-in-law Mantegna, is lit and shaded just like the golden-brown tower to the left of the city. Francis is a moving pillar of life, giving the conventional rampart its solidity. The Giottesque artist in Assisi had painted the dream of Pope Innocent III, in which Francis with arched back and structural clothing is a pillar that upholds the collapsing church. Bellini makes his monumental Francis, back arched in ecstatic prayer, a supernatural support for the entire natural world.

ZORZI

The patron for Bellini's work was probably a devotee of the Observant Franciscans in Venice—perhaps a relative of a man named Francis who had joined or worked with the Observants. Though even the Observants lived in friaries in the fifteenth century, and were not itinerant beggars, they were more true than were Conventuals to the ascetic life of Francis indicated in Bellini's painting. In Renaissance Venice the most holy and learned Observant was the superior of the monastery and church of St. Francis by the Vineyard (Francesco della Vigna), Francesco Zorzi (or Giorgi), and Zorzi collaborated with the doge Andrea Gritti to create two spheres in Venice—one of them a private realm of prayer and charity, the other of political life both busy and stable. These correspond to the two sectors of Bellini's painting, and the Zorzi-Gritti axis was meant to make the two Venetian areas, despite all their contrasts, just as mutually supportive as the two spheres of Bellini's painting.

This was part of that "urban rebirth" (*renovatio urbis*) of the 1530s that Manfredo Tafuri has analyzed—a project to renew Venetian pride and confidence after it was badly shaken by the temporary loss of the city's terraferma empire during the war with Julius II's League of Cambrai. I have already considered one part of the Gritti program, the Loggetta of Sansovino, which reasserted patrician virtue against the dogal presumption of the Scala d'Oro. Why would a doge be part of this implied rebuke to the growth of power in the dogate? Gritti knew he had to assuage misgivings about his own status while building up confidence in the whole ruling class. As Muir puts it, "The arrogant bearing of Gritti had caused him significant political harm, as witnessed by the popular demonstration against his election and the frequent votes against his projects by the Experts of the Convention (Savii del Collegio)."[13]

Gritti not only supported the public elevation of the patriciate's symbols in the Loggetta, but engaged in what Tafuri calls a "showy humility" (*ostentazia di modestia*) in the rebuilding of his family palazzo during this time.[14] In fact, he coordinated the entire area of his private world in deliberate contrast with the ambitious reworking of the public arena. His house, in the Castello region, was a place where charitable institutions were clustered, close by San Francesco della Vigna. The Observants were rebuilding their church in the 1530s to express their ascetic ideals. Gritti entered enthusiastically into their project, recruiting for it the same architect, Jacopo Sansovino, who was reshaping the environs of the doge's public palace.

Zorzi, the presiding spirit at San Francesco, was a mystical philosopher of international renown. Following the lead of Marsilio Ficino (1433–1499) and Pico della Mirandola (1463–1494), Zorzi forged a spiritual combination of Neoplatonism, Pythagoreanism, and the Hebrew Kabbalah. In his masterpiece, *The Harmony of the Universe* (*De Harmonia Mundi Totius*, 1525), he strove for the collaboration of all philosophers (*concordia omnium philosophorum*) that Pico had proposed.[15] The *Harmony* was a multilevel text applicable to harmony not only in the universe, but in the Franciscans' revived order, in the Venetian state, and in the proportions of the Church of San Francesco della Vigna.[16] The church thus became part of the program for a renewed church and state occupying the minds of Zorzi's intellectual circle, which included not only Gritti and Sansovino, but the architect Sebastiano Serlio, the humanist Fortunio Spira, and the painter Titian.

In 1533, Sansovino's architectural model had won the contest for construction of the new church, meant to express the lofty ideals of the Observants. But Gritti asked Zorzi to write a subsequent memorandum (*memoriale*) on the proper proportions for such a church. Rudolf Wittkower, who made this memorandum available for modern study, thought Zorzi was called in to settle a dispute over Sansovino's plan; but Tafuri argues persuasively that Zorzi was cooperating with Sansovino and Gritti to justify changes in the plan that would a) explain in terms of pure number the omission of the originally conceived dome, and b) vindicate the extension of the church onto land that members of the Contarini family had claimed.[17] To cinch this validating function of the memorandum, Serlio, Spira, and Titian were called on to give it public approbation.

The church was built to Zorzi's cosmic proportions, echoing the music of the spheres, the measurement of the temple of Solomon, and the magic of the Kabbalah. Everything in the church is exfoliated from the number three, which is both the number of the Trinity and the only perfect number (because it alone has a beginning, a middle, and an end which are also a matter of simple progression: one-two-three). Three squared is nine, and nine by three is twenty-seven.[18] On those numbers all aspects of the church are constructed. Its nave is nine *passi* (paces) wide and twenty-seven passi long. Its ten side chapels are three passi wide. The façade that Palladio would eventually add to the church is twenty-seven passi wide.

TITIAN

PLATE XXX
Titian, *Presentation of the Virgin*

The coordination of the two spheres represented by the San Francesco area and the Piazzetta is a manifestation of the extraordinary gift Venice had for integrating apparently discordant elements into the continuum of its myth and its needs. Here learning combined with asceticism, politics with mysticism. The interaction of these motifs is expressed in a painting that Titian was working on at the very time when he and Serlio were consulting with Zorzi and Sansovino on the measurements of San Francesco della Vigna.[19] The *Presentation of the Virgin in the Temple* (1534–1538) was one of the few paintings Titian did for a scuola grande—in this case, that of the Carità (now the Accademia). According to David Rosand, Titian helped change the fenestration of the club's boardroom (*albergo*) to throw just the right illumination on the Virgin's progress up an impressive set of stairs to the Temple of Solomon, where the high priest awaits the young girl.[20]

According to the popular *Golden Legend* (on which all the painters drew for the early life of the Virgin), Mary was brought to the Temple at the age of three to live there as a perpetual virgin. Though only a toddler, she "mounted to the top [of the stairs] without help from anyone, as if she were already fully grown up."[21] Actually, according to the *Legend*, after she completes her thirteenth year of life with the young virgins in the temple, the high priest will order her return to her parents for marriage. It is clear that Titian is interpreting the story in terms of mystical numbers of the sort deployed by Zorzi at San Francesco. The sacred number nine is evident in the two rows of four Corinthian columns, with the girl herself as the ninth (she is aligned to complete the first row of columns, and the blue of her gown picks up the blue veins of the columns' precious stone). Serlio, one of the experts who endorsed Zorzi's memoriale, had written in his *Treatise on Architecture* (which praises Titian) that the column is modeled on the human body, and that the Corinthian, the most feminine column, is appropriate for churches dedicated to the Virgin.[22] Titian's picture puts this whole doctrine in symbolic form.

The painter is using sacred numbers even more pointedly in the articulation of his staircase. *The Golden Legend* says that Mary went up fifteen steps, corresponding to the fifteen Psalms of Ascent (the so-called "graduals"), and that is the number often shown

FIG. 96
Jacopo Tintoretto,
Presentation of the Virgin

in pictures—as in Tintoretto's organ panel at Santa Maria dell'Orto (P-R 2.164–65). But Titian changes the number to thirteen, since Mary will complete her thirteenth year in the temple, and he breaks the stairs into two flights, one of eight steps, the other of five. As Meyer Schapiro pointed out to David Rosand, eight to five is one of the commonest ratios in the so-called "golden section" discussed by Serlio as an ideal of proportion.[23]

SANSOVINO

The right side of Titian's picture is feminine—the Corinthian columns harmonizing with Mary's gown, backed by the diaper-patterned bricks of a building resembling the

Gothic Doge's Palace, and a receding line of façades arranged as in Serlio's stage perspectives for a Roman theater. The left side of the painting, by contrast, is male—with strong pillars broken by a rude kind of Ionic capital, and a solid obelisk, and the majestic board members of the scuola. This arrangement expresses the combination of values being shaped by Sansovino in the Piazzetta, where, as Tafuri notes, the right side of the space (as one enters it through the twin pillars that are a kind of arch of triumph) is delicate and Greek—the diaper-patterned palace, the gilded Porta della Carta, the Byzantine San Marco—while the left side is a careful crescendo of Sansovino's Roman effects, moving from the squat and rusticated Mint, through the Ionic orderliness of the Library, toward the Corinthian grace of the aristocrats' retreat, the Loggetta.

The fortress aspect of the Mint (Zecca), with its sweaty foundry and guarded treasury, would have been more obvious before the top story was added to Sansovino's design. The rough, undecorated stone of the Mint loosens into the half-engaged sculptures of the Library and leads to the fully detached statues of the Loggetta. This move from war and labor to intellectual effort, and then on to refinement, is recapitulated, as John Onians says, in the left-to-right progression of the Loggetta's own statues—from armed Minerva to the archer Apollo, and from orator Mercury to the final figure of Peace.[24] There are layers on layers of intellectual gradation in Sansovino's three buildings on the Piazzetta, reflecting not only the different uses of the buildings but the different users of them, as Onians has remarked:

> All these variations represent consistent modulations on Serlio's scales from *sodo/semplice* to *delicato/gentile*, matching the consistent increases in refinement of the buildings' occupants and the activities with which they are associated, from lower-class people involved in physical labor, through middle- and upper-class people doing commercial, intellectual, and administration work, to the nobility doing nothing but displaying themselves. The same consistency is found in the application of another scale referred to by Serlio, that revealed in the number of steps leading up to a building. He says of a church that "the more its floor is raised above the ground, the more dignity (*maestà*) it will have." Again, in Book V, "I will always be of the opinion that every building, or rather its pavement, should be raised above the ground by several steps and that the more it is raised the better it will be." If Sansovino's buildings are viewed in the light of this rule, it can be noted that the Zecca had originally only one step up to its front arcade, the Libreria building three, and the Loggetta five.[25]

We have returned to the staircase of Titian in this circling around of proprieties called for by the cosmic harmonies of Serlio and Zorzi. Since the Piazzetta faces the three Roman structures of Sansovino with the Byzantine-Gothic gracefulness of the structures to the right of our entry into Venice—the Doge's Palace, Porta della Carta, and San Marco—Tafuri is justified in seeing here a combination of a Roman forum's function, as public gathering place, and a Greek propylaeum's function, as forecourt to the "temple" of San Marco.[26] The city was being shaped, in this vast project, to express the ideals and relationships of those who lived and worked in it—and through each part runs the music of Zorzi's numbers, of the Franciscan mysticism that these great artists honored.

Dominican Learning

WE LOOKED EARLIER—WHEN considering Giorgio Emo's pantheon of heroes from the war with the League of Cambrai—at the great colored window in the Dominicans' Church of Saints John and Paul. The upper part of that window, it was said then, offers a theology of the Incarnation of the Word of God in Jesus. The clover-leaf (quatrefoil) window panel at the top shows God the Father, with the dove of the Spirit below him. Yet, though he wears the triangular symbol of the Trinity as a halo, the second person of the Trinity is not in the quatrefoil.

PLATE XXVII
Santi Giovanni e Paolo,
window

That is because he is already being dispatched to earth on his redemptive mission. On the right of the Father is the sun, on the left the moon, reversing the normal positions of these cosmic symbols. The sun is usually on the right, the favored side. The explanation for this departure is that the sun's rays shine out from its own glass compartment and reach the lower panel, where Mary of the Annunciation is kneeling. Since she is usually on the viewer's right in Annunciation scenes, the sun has been displaced to her side—the sun's rays passing through glass were used as an analogy in Thomist theology for the ability of the Son of God to pass into Mary's womb without violating her body. Therefore, as we should expect, the angel of the Annunciation is on our left side (the moon's side). The moon attends on the sun, as the angel pays court to Mary. It is a crescent moon, signifying that the earthly course of Jesus' life has just begun.

In the quatrefoils between the angel and Mary are the two prophets who were thought to have predicted the Incarnation—Moses with his horns of light, and David with his crown and psaltery. Under this tier of the window, as a border for the next level below, there are four trefoils, with a "sea thiasos" of putti and dolphins in the middle two. There is a Nereid with fish tails in the left trefoil and a Triton with fish tails in the right one. These Roman sepulchral motifs indicate that Jesus entered the mortal realm as he "came down" to earth.[1] The next-lowest rank of figures puts Mary in the center (with the incarnate Jesus) beside John the Baptist (forerunner of the Savior's earthly career). They stand in little shrines, with the richly polychromed architecture that the Lombardo family was making popular in Venice during the 1490s. Mary and John are flanked by Saint Paul on our left and Saint Peter on our right, as the apostles of the church founded on the Incarnation.

Paul's figure is smaller than the other three, and he stands in a more severe shrine. Serena Romano reasons that the first campaign to complete this window ended before his addition, and that the resumption of the project, under Giorgio Emo's inspiration, had to supply this panel before adding the lower part of the window.[2] This lower section moves down through two rows of four quatrefoils. The top row presents the four evangelists holding their Gospels—John with his eagle, Mark and the lion, Luke and the ox, Matthew and the man. These are the bearers of the church's message out beyond the apostles, and they pass their charge on to those in the second row of quatrefoils, the ancient fathers of the western church—Ambrose with his whip (as the scourge of heretics), Gregory the Great with his papal crown, Jerome with his cardinal's hat, and Augustine with his bishop's crook.

In the trefoils above the warriors' panels are four Dominican saints, men of the Order of Preachers (Ordo Predicatorum, O.P.), founded at the beginning of the thirteenth century by the Spaniard Saint Dominic (Domingo de Guzmàn). The four Dominicans pass on the gospel that descended from the apostles to evangelists to fathers—Saint Vincent Ferrer with a preacher's open book, Dominic with a lily, which stands for purity of doctrine, Peter Martyr with the sword blade that ended his life, and Thomas Aquinas with the sun of knowledge blazing on his breast.

Aquinas was the culminating theologian of medieval scholasticism, and his teaching informed the most famous and most surprising book to have come out of this church and its adjacent monastery, *Poliphilo's Dream-Combat of Love* (*Hypnerotomachia Poliphili*), published anonymously in 1499 but almost certainly the work of a Dominican priest, Francesco Colonna, who was an official of Saints John and Paul when the great window there was being completed.[3] Many have doubted that a priest could have succeeded in getting an erotic work like the *Dream Combat* published and yet stayed on in his order. But Francesco Colonna did more scabrous things than that, and continued to win his way back into the friary despite periodic exile from it and recurring scandals. Admittedly, the monastery he belonged to was itself a scandalous one, which the government had, at times, to punish and reform by outside monitoring. But the puzzle of a priest-pornographer is not so great if we look at the book in terms of the learning and the philosophy—in fact, the Thomism—informing it.

The *Dream Combat* is the oneiric fantasy of a voyage into the self. It has forerunners and models, from antiquity (Apuleius), the middle ages (Dante), and the Renaissance (Petrarch and Boccaccio). But it is entirely original in its use of architecture to structure the tale. Traveling down into dream, and then into dreams within dreams, the hero of the tale is seeking his beloved, Polia (Manifold)—the hero's name, Poliphilo, means not only Polia-Loving, but Manifold-Loving as well, and also Polis-Loving. He is chased or lured into building after building (their architecture described in loving detail), led on, often, by nymphs who tease and tempt and arouse him. But he or they break off every flirtation before there is any sexual intercourse. The whole tale is one of *concupiscentia interrupta*. Through each stage of this journey, Poliphilo's senses and taste are being tuned to subtler and more refined awarenesses.[4] The sensual experience becomes intenser yet more delicate, music and odors and flowers enriching the appeal of the architecture. He is being made worthy of the woman he at last reaches. Then, after having trouble recognizing all of her manifold beauties, he is joined to her in a holy ceremony on Venus's isle. But even then there is not a consummation. A second part of the tale (perhaps written earlier) acts as a further dream within the dream, telling of his earlier meetings with Polia and of her death before the ceremony on Venus's isle could be completed. The consummation recedes forever before him, like the "fleeing shores" that Virgil seeks in the *Aeneid*. Only the purification of endless approach remains.

What sets this story apart from the writings of Francesco Zorzi—and sets Franciscan learning apart from Dominican—is the fact that Zorzi wanted a Platonic escape from the senses into the realm of pure mind, while Thomas Aquinas taught that the senses are the source of all knowledge in the mind.[5] For him, there was no such thing as immaterial thought for humans on this earth. Our very self-knowledge, like our knowledge of the rest of the world, begins with sensation.[6] Even Saint Paul's ecstasy (2 Cor 12.2) was not a direct knowledge of God, just a higher use of the evidences for God contained in the world.[7] For Thomas, then, asceticism is not an escape from the senses but a proper control and use of them—just what Poliphilo is being forced to achieve as he moves through the manifold sensual solicitings of his dream voyage. The maxim repeated to him often is "Make a leisurely haste," *Festina lente*. He can reach true joy only by suppressing a too-hasty pleasure, "saving himself" for Polia. At the crudest level, then, the story is one long effort to avoid premature ejaculation. Even after he has found Polia, he must be purged from his animal precipitancy before he can reach union with her, a spiritual union if not a physical one. This almost drives him mad at one point, and she has to cool him off by sending him to the intellectual equivalent of a cold shower—another tour of a classical building:

> I recognized that I was battered beyond every imaginable or contrivable torture, and this in the presence of my healer, who could apply her remedy on the spot—she was my healer-in-chief—yet I was mightily dumbfounded to see that she, reversing right order, was precisely what was poisoning and destroying me: her every graceful move, each cultured phrase, each piercing glance, close as they were, just held me farther off from the alleviation I needed. I grew evermore convinced that I ought to show myself grateful for this convenient opportunity, and brave in taking it—a haughty claim fit only for vile seducers. I quivered like a mad and barking dog running down its pretty quarry on the Alpine heights—such was I, crazed with desire for my sought-after prey, which was trapped at last. Though by now I was used to perishing from love, I did not see what suffering would come of this ravenousness, and so felt any encroachment, however vicious, was acceptable. But Polia, with poise, diagnosing this insane state of blind love, to quench such a raging fire and entirely snuff it out, assisted me, my last-minute rescuer, and told me gently, "Poliphilo, whom I love so, I know how eager you are to gaze on antique works. So while we spend this time waiting for the arrival of Cupid our master, you may go, at leisure and without check, to admire as you like that deserted sanctuary, ruinous, fallen in, dimmed with age, wasted by fires, and ravaged by the course of time. By yourself you can admire the noble remains, which are worthy of your highest appraisal. I will sit here, happy to wait for the arrival of our master, who will lead us to his mother's holy and longed-for realm."[8]

The humor of this scene—the "mad dog" blithely trotting off to the temple as to its kennel—is typical of the comic humiliations Poliphilo undergoes. His spiritual testing is often indecorous, like that of Lucius in Apuleius's *The Golden Ass*. Lucius is turned into an ass as he journeys toward his final transformation into a votary of Isis. Poliphilo enters odd buildings shaped like animals and moves through their artificial intestines as he sets off on the pilgrimage that will make him a votary of Venus.[9]

Though the story's titillations make it hard for some to see the spiritual discipline involved, the logic of the tale is simply a more "sexy" way of putting Saint Augustine's recognition that one travels to God through lower sensual pleasures that beckon us toward higher ones:

> What, in loving you, do I find lovable?—not, surely, the body's splendor, nor time's disciplined successions, not light's kindly aptness to the eye, nor sweet linkages of variable melody, not soft fragrances of flower, oil, or spice, not honey or heaven-bread, not limbs intermingled in embrace.

This is a dizzying evocation of circumambient sensual buzz, like that in Poliphilo's dream. Yet even in moving beyond this swarm of sensations Augustine recognizes some use for them, framing his conception of God by analogy with them.

> These are not what in loving you I love, my God. And yet I do—*do* love a kind of light, a kind of song or fragrance, food or embrace—in loving you, who are my light and voice and fragrance, food and embrace, all of them deep within me, where no light fades, no song ends, no fragrance is dispersed in air, no taste blunted with satiety, no embrace ended in exhaustion.

That last phrase suggests the perfect *Festina lente*, a coition with no depletion. Augustine can only develop his meaning by turning back again to the world of the senses:

> That is what, in loving my God, I love—yet what can I call this? I interrogated the earth, which said: "I am not it," and all its contents gave the same testimony. I interrogated the sea, its depths with their slithery inhabitants, and they informed me, "We are not your God. Go higher." I interrogated the shifting winds—and the entire atmosphere, with its flying things, said, "Anaximenes was wrong, I am no God." I interrogated the cosmos—sun, moon, stars—which replied, "No more are we that God you are in quest of." So I addressed the entirety of things thronging the portals of my senses: "Tell me then of the God you aren't, tell me *something* at least." And, clamorous together, they came back: "He is what made us." My interrogation was nothing but my yearning, and their response was nothing but their beauty.[10]

Colonna's book is famous for its numerous woodcut illustrations, combining energy and elegance. But in one sense they are misleading. By their nervous line drawings in black and white they misrepresent the text, which is Venetian in its love of polychrome effects. Take, for instance, the portal Poliphilo goes through early in his journey, severe in its woodcut representation, but more like Santa Maria dei Miracoli in the text:

> According to the harmonic proportions of the structure, all its elements were deftly fitted to each other—and the colors of the marbles were correspondingly disposed, conspiring with the overall effect. Here was porphyry, ophite, Numidian marble, alabaster, mottled-red, serpentine, wavy-veined white marble, coal-black flecked with white, and other variously blended colors.[11]

This first and partly ruined archway leads on to gems like this one on the island of Venus:

> I concentrated on a study of the overwhelming project of this gateway. It was of oriental stone from Armenia, in which bright glints of gold were scattered as in a starry sky, matching the purest gold of the columns' bases and capitals. Of the same stone were the architrave, frieze, cornice, acroterion, threshold, forward columns, and all subordinate elements. The interior of the arch was of ophite, with entry columns of porphyry, followed by alternating ones of ophite and porphyry.[12]

The book's colors show a Venetian taste formed on the flicker and iridescence of San Marco's mosaic and silky stone surfaces. Venus of Seething Nature (Venus Physizoa) has a temple lit inside by a translucent hanging lamp, from which burning alcohol casts shifting lights around, throwing out "rainbows that not even the sun can paint in the air after a rain."[13] These stroboscopic lights make it seem that the statues in the chamber are in motion.

Where color is concerned, art and nature mingle their interactive hues. When Polia sends the "mad dog" off to contemplate a temple or two, Poliphilo must extract himself from the bower of flowers they are in: "All around the honeysuckle was painting the ground with its odorous blossoms. Flowering jasmine overtwined us with its dark sweetness of shade, richly showering down on us white blossoms at the peak of their fragrance."[14]

Needless to say, when Poliphilo encounters his love, she combines all the shapeliness, color, and fragrance of both art and nature—just as Augustine's God does. Her limbs are soft polychrome columns, completing the anthropomorphic view he takes of architecture throughout the book:

Now and then, when soft breezes parted the silk tunic floating over her virginal limbs, her slim white legs winked out, beautiful, shaped perfectly, and I can honestly swear that they were of a crimson more delicate than was ever drawn from dyes of the Peloponnese, only tempered with creamiest white and odoriferous musk-tan.[15]

The coming and going of colors at touch shows how bodies interact:

I was full of wonder at how and by what measure the warm red pulse in her wrist's palpability did not remain, at my pressing it, but showed white as milk.[16]

When Polia finally dissolves from his dream, it is as a flare-up and fading of rich colors:

While she clung to me in soft embraces, I saw an adorable blush bloom and diffuse itself over her snow-white cheek, and on her limbs a roseate pink mingled with a soft glow of ivory, radiant with the most graceful beauty. And at the height of her ecstasy small tears welled up in her shining eyes, with the translucency of crystal and the shapeliness of pearls, more beautiful than those Euryale shed or than the dawn distills at morn on roses. This divine image evanesced like a mist, breathing the rarest perfumes of musk and ambergris that dissolve into the atmosphere.[17]

Descriptions like that rightly call to mind the colors of Titian's Venuses, and the whole polychrome world of Venice that exists only vestigially now—all the frescoes and gilt ornament on façades, the painted statues, the brightly decorated ceremonial barges, the processional flags and floats. The colors of Colonna's novel are structural, not just dabs put on the surface of things. Buildings and persons articulate themselves through blendings and borderings of hue. If one looked just at the woodcuts in the novel, you would think oneself in a world of Florentine *disegno*, the defining lines of anatomy, plan, and perspective. But turn to the novel's words and the Venetian world of *colorito* floods over you. And this is appropriate to Colonna's Thomistic world of sensation.

Thomas Aquinas defined beauty as the splendor of inner being (*claritas formae*).[18] It is not just a trick of light falling on an outer surface, but the effulgence of intelligible form. He compared it to the splendor of the transfigured Christ or the glory of risen bodies in Paradise. In Florence, drawing came first, and color was applied to it. The great Venetian colorists built up their bodies in layers of color, creating an embodied glow of each thing's precious reality. The contrast between the two approaches calls to mind another Thomist distinction, between a thing's whatness (*essentia*) and its is-ing (*esse*).[19] The single continuous charge of God's *esse* is individuated by multiple essences, but pulses through them all alike—as the sun coming through the great window of Saints John and Paul is a single light that gives each separate form its specific glory. Colonna's naughty novel is not so far from the rogue priest's church setting after all. And the window is itself very close to the great last works of Titian, where a single energy vibrates through all the colors of the picture, giving a molten unity to scenes like *The Flaying of Marsyas* or the final *Pietà*. Many efforts have been made to connect the woodcuts of the *Dream-Combat* with the work of Carpaccio or Bellini or Giorgione; but the real connection is in the text, where a single light comes through flower and temple and female limbs. Here, supremely, there is nothing in the mind that was not first in the senses.

PLATE VIII
Titian,
The Flaying of Marsyas

FIG. 94
Titian,
Pietà

CHAPTER TWENTY-SIX

Book Learning

C OLONNA'S *HYPNEROTOMACHIA POLIPHILI* WAS the greatest book put out by Venice's greatest printer, Aldo Manuzio (Latinized in his print editions as Aldus Manutius). It has been called the most beautiful book printed in Italy during the Renaissance. But Manuzio probably did not want to enter into the vast labor that produced it. Colonna, the author, had brought his religious order into conflict with the Venetian government, and he might bring trouble to the printer's shop, too. Authorities were keeping a careful eye on Manuzio in 1498. While succumbing briefly to the plague, Manuzio had made a rash vow to become a priest if he recovered. When he became healthy again, he asked for a papal dispensation from his vow—which was granted, on condition that Venetian authorities encourage him to go do good works through his printing projects.[1] Many would not feel that the printing of a graphically illustrated erotic tale fell into the category of good works.

But Francesco Colonna had powerful friends (this helps explain his survival of so many scandals, which somehow never ended his priestly career). Leonardo Crasso from Verona was the sponsor of the *Dream-Combat*, and he was part of a Venetian circle that both patronized and published with Manuzio. So, whatever his misgivings, Manuzio threw his resources (and Crasso's money) into the production of this lavish volume. It entailed two artists for designing the illustrations, three engravers to do the woodcuts, and type designers to make the attractive layout.[2] The text was varied by ornamental capitals at the beginning of each chapter (the letters of the acrostic revealing Colonna's name), by interspersed summary paragraphs in capital letters, and by artfully shaped chapter endings in which the letters take on the form of a chalice or some other design.[3]

But the revolutionary thing was the use made of the 171 elegant woodcuts. These were not bunched together, as was often the case with preceding illustrated books, but placed artfully in conjunction with the parts of the text they illustrate. Giovanni Pozzi argues that the illustrations were not just added to the text, but the two were conceived together, with the pictures sometimes posing a question that the text then goes on to answer, or the text leaving something inexplicit that is then spelled out in the picture. The two elements are interactive, one first leading the other, then reversing that order.[4] Besides, there was a division of labor between the two, one that reverses normal expectation. Woodcuts would generally be used for *description* in books where they were introduced—in, for instance, anatomical or architectural books, where they could present details or relationships hard to make clear in words. But the heavy burden of description is left with the words in Colonna's book:

> Two hundred pages out of 370 are exclusively devoted to architectural descriptions. No fewer than 78 of the first 86 pages are occupied by the painstakingly minute detailing of the *boschetto*, the palm grove, the giant pyramidal building, the bridge, the octagonal baths, and the palazzo. Indeed, the great pyramidal building alone monopolizes almost 50 pages; and of these, 5 pages, in turn, record nothing but the measurements of the triumphal arch that serves as its entrance. The temple of Venus fills an additional 18 pages, the *nymphaea* and the aquatic labyrinth 12, the ruins 35. Description of various landscapes and the gardens run close to 60 pages.[5]

If description is expected in the plates, dialogue and personal interaction are expected in narrative fiction. But little of the text is devoted to this, the meat and potatoes of a novel: "A mere 30 pages at most are left to the actual action of the love story, to its dialogue and inner monologue, and to the devices usually associated with the genre."[6] The pictures take up the slack, devoting a highly disproportionate number of plates to the human story, to Poliphilo's relations with the all-female (except for Cupid) cast of goddesses, nymphs, and women he encounters. The static text is driven forward by the engravings, which kick-start the story over and over. As Pozzi puts it, the book *draws* with words and *narrates* with drawings, setting up a dialectic relationship that teases the mind back and forth between word and image.[7] One keeps sending you to the other, as the shrewd Polia sends her overheated lover to contemplate a building. The tug of fleshly desire against ideal form is re-enacted in the push-pull play of words against images. They re-enact, as it were, the drama of desire fighting contemplation But which is which? The designs are fleshly, the paragraphs ideal—at least some of the time. The paradox is repeated at many levels. The static verbal descriptions are a riot of color, while the passionate love story is picked out in austere black-and-white plates. This is another dream "that has no bottom."

The book was not an instant success. It puzzled as much by its language, a surreal mix of Latin and Tuscan and Venetian, with scraps of Greek and Arabic and Hebrew thrown in, as by its multimedia presentation. But artists and scholars soon grew enamored of its riddles, which tease us still. It entered into the legend of Venice's great power of the press—for Venice, a latecomer to the Renaissance in Italy, became a symbol of it to the North. This was mainly accomplished through the spread of the Renaissance from Venice's many printing firms.

When classical scholarship was restricted to finding, interpreting, and discussing manuscripts, Venice took a back seat to Florence, Rome, and Naples. In the fourteenth century, while Petrarch, Boccaccio, and others were reviving classical learning, Venice was building its commercial empire. Though Petrarch spent some years in Venice while fleeing the plague in Milan, and promised to leave his library there, he found no circle of leisured humanists such as could be found at feudal, princely, or papal courts. A symbol of Venetian backwardness is the way the city let Cardinal Bessarion's 1468 gift of manuscripts—752 of them, 482 in Greek—lie unused for almost half a century. Bessarion had assembled his library to represent the best extant texts of Greek philosophy, rhetoric, drama, and history and to bring it to the West after the fall of Constantinople. The collection included the principal manuscript of Homer (*Venetus A*) and one of the major texts of Aristophanes (*Venetus V*). It was "the best and most comprehensive range of Greek codices available anywhere in Western Europe."[8]

We have seen how Venetians honored Bessarion, from the time when Gentile Bellini put his portrait in scenes painted for the Doge's Palace to the time when Carpaccio featured him as Saint Augustine. Yet most Venetian humanists were not curious enough to find out what they possessed in the boxes Bessarion shipped to them from Rome. The Venetian elite constituted an engaged political and military class. Some of them were interested in classical texts, and in the Aristotelian philosophy taught at Padua, people like Ermolao Barbaro or Gasparo Contarini. But they had to carve out time for their literary pursuits from active diplomatic or military careers. The best men were not trained to be scholars, and the severe imperial atmosphere did not attract courtiers who had time for philology. The ironic thing is that Bessarion had given his library to Venice because he was suspicious of the censorship and academic narrowness he had observed in various courts and universities in other parts of Italy—yet Venice's very freedom from those concerns went with a lack of scholarly zeal in dealing with his gift.

It is typical of this commercial realm that it only became a leader in the European Renaissance when that became a good business proposition for the empire. It was still not aware of the possibilities the new technology of printing was opening when, in 1469, it gave the first German printer to come to town, John of Speyer, a five-year monopoly on the trade. Luckily, Speyer died within a year, and his heirs were not allowed to inherit his monopoly rights. A swarm of freelance printers moved into this trade not foreseen or regulated by the guilds. Venice also had the advantage that it was readier to defy Rome's censoring efforts than were other Italian cities. Within thirty years of John of Speyer's arrival, there were 150 presses operating in Venice, and they had turned out 4,500 different books. There was a kind of "gold rush" of printers into Venice, with an average of ten new firms starting up every year between 1480 and 1500.[9]

That a world market was being exploited is clear from the fact that Venice, in this period, printed twenty times more books than it had inhabitants. That statistic gives us a clue to Venice's success. Its skill was not simply for printing but also for shrewd distribution. Other cities had more and better scholars, at least at first, to sort and correct Greek and Latin manuscripts for scholarly printing. They could master the techniques of printing as rapidly as Venice did (for the creators of Renaissance medallions, the casting of type was an easy assignment, once its usefulness was pointed out). What gave Venice its advantage was the scope of its imperial trade, with the intelligence-gathering this entailed. Knowing the market was a matter of having far-flung agents who could determine what books would sell to which universities, or wealthy patrons, or struggling scholars. Venice knew the climates of opinion as well as of sailing seasons.

CENSORSHIP

The printers' first bestsellers were textbooks, aimed at the four universities within the orbit of Venice (Padua, Bologna, Pavia, Ferrara)—mainly in law, but also in disciplines like medicine.[10] Aristocratic patrons continued, for a while, to prefer beautifully copied old manuscripts to "vulgar" mechanical products. But students were grateful for cheaper and cleaner copies of texts that had been sealed up in libraries or stingily passed around. The next most profitable items were Bibles and religious tracts. Though Protestants are credited with the creation of an "apostolate of print," the Catholics of Venice were busily making profits from the idea before Luther ever posted his theses on the door at Wittenberg.

It was only a matter of time before Venetian printers realized that the new demand for classical texts was moving out of the manuscript market and into the print domain.

The key date here is 1489, when Aldo Manuzio came to Venice to set up his own press. He was the first printer who was a humanist scholar. He had been a successful teacher of the classical languages, trained at the court of Ferrara. He was acquainted with such prominent humanists as Pico della Mirandolo and Poliziano. Almost forty when he arrived in Venice, he quickly established the program of what would become known as the Aldine Press, though he was at first a subordinate partner to Andrea Torresani and the protégé of a patrician sponsor, Pierfrancesco Barbarigo.

The great advantage Manuzio had over his competitors was a metal-casting and aesthetic genius, Francesco Griffo, "arguably the most important single figure in the establishment of the Aldine company."[11] This is the man who created the Aldine Press's Latin, Greek, and Hebrew fonts. I said above that casting type characters was not a difficult matter for craftsmen of the Renaissance. But designing clear letters for them to cast, letters legible and aesthetically pleasing, meant all the difference in weaning people away from the beautiful handwriting of the manuscripts. Griffo was so successful that the designs for his letters are still being used today. Among other things, he created cursive figures that approximated the handwritten letters in manuscripts—we now call it italic. And because reading a large folio page of such curlycued letters was difficult, Manuzio reduced the page by folding his sheets into eighths, creating the octavo (or pocket book).

But the real challenge for Griffo was the creation of Greek characters, and on this Manuzio's reputation as the great early printer of Greek classics would be built.

> The type-font was always the most expensive item in a printer's capital equipment, and a Greek font posed particular problems. First there was the question of finding a craftsman competent to design it: then there was the matter of the language itself. Greek uses "oxytone" or "perispomenon" accents on all words except enclitics, and "rough" or "smooth" breathing symbols over all initial vowels. These symbols had either to be designed and cast along with the appropriate letter-form, in every possible combination, or cast as entirely separate type-sorts which could then be set in place by the compositor above the vowel they were to accent. The first solution vastly multiplied the number of types needed, and consequently the expense incurred: Victor Sholderer calculates that the font used by Laonicus and Alexandros in Venice during the mid-1480s must have contained over 1,400 separate letter forms. The second [solution] made the compositor's task much slower, and meant a wider spacing of lines to leave room for the accents: the books therefore took longer to produce, needed more paper, and were naturally more expensive.[12]

Griffo solved the problem by inventing a system of "kerning" that supplied the accent as each vowel was set.[13] Because of this economical maneuver, Manuzio became the champion printer of Greek texts just when the demand for them was growing. "Before he started his career as printer in 1495, only three books in Greek had been printed in Venice, one in 1484 and two in 1486."[14] Of the twenty-four Greek authors printed during his career, Manuzio was responsible for eighteen—including his large five-volume edition of Aristotle. After he established a near-monopoly on Greek publishing, he asked for and won government protection of an actual monopoly, to strengthen Venice's position in the international competition for Greek texts. But this made it impossible for Griffo to take his handiwork to any other printer, which apparently contributed to other frictions between Manuzio and Griffo, who parted ways after a decade or so of creative partnership.

Once it became clear that classical texts were being authenticated and turned into print at Venice, scholars (including Erasmus) left the courts of earlier patrons and came to this source of the new learning. A leading example of this process is the return to Venice of Pietro Bembo. He was a patrician of the city whose father had been a diplomat in foreign courts, where Bembo absorbed a love of classical learning and the vernacular poetry based on it. When he launched his own career as an author, he moved from the d'Este court in Ferrara (where he was a courtier to the duchess, the former Lucrezia Borgia) to the Montefeltro court at Urbino (where he was made a leading interlocutor in Castiglione's famous dialogue *The Courtier*), to Caterina Cornaro's court at Asolo (where he wrote his famous dialogue *Gli Asolani*), and then to the court of the Medici pope Leo X, in Rome (where he served as the pope's secretary).

After that pope's death in 1529, he finally returned to his native city, as its official historian, and was put in charge of the new library to be built for Bessarion's manuscripts, the Biblioteca Marciana. In these roles he worked closely with the Aldine Press, and with other scholars now clustered around it. He published his own works there, and helped edit a Petrarch manuscript he brought to Manuzio.[15] Venetian pride had at length been engaged in the business of learning, as its books coursed out through a far-flung commercial network. The Aldine trademark, a dolphin curled around an anchor, became a worldwide symbol for the publishing of scholarly and aesthetically pleasing books. Bembo himself gave Manuzio the Roman coin (from Vespasian's reign) containing the dolphin and anchor emblem, from which Jean Grolier drew the printer's device for Aldine books. The design, which was perhaps a tribute to Poseidon on the original coin, was interpreted by Manuzio as combining his firm's speed (dolphin) and steadiness (anchor). This was another application of Poliphilo's maxim, *Festina lente*.

The awakened interest in manuscripts suitable for printing brought Bessarion's gift back to people's mind, and Doge Andrea Gritti included it in his concept of Venice's classical revival, arranging for Sansovino to build a library for these manuscripts. The architect would draw on the scholarship of Sebastiano Serlio, who had been attracted to Venice as the printing center for illustrated architectural books of the sort he was preparing. Woodcut illustration opened up a whole new era of architectural learning. The only extant ancient treatise on architecture, by Vitruvius, had few original illustrations, and they had been lost. Reproducing illustrations by hand in a manuscript was not a practical idea. Scribes were trained to form letters, not to be draftsmen or artists whose impressions could be trusted. Later, Masonic guilds were secretive about their processes, and accustomed to use models, not outlines on paper, in the process of their work.

With the Renaissance introduction of printed (correct) illustrations to editions of Vitruvius, and to original works produced by Renaissance artists, the basic language of the architectural profession changed. It would henceforth think in terms of plans, elevations, and sections. Mario Carpo argues that the Renaissance is different from most other eras of architectural innovation. New techniques or materials in the actual building often caused those changes—the arch in Rome, the counterstresses of Gothic, the arrival of poured concrete, steel, glass, and so on. The Renaissance made no such technical or material change. What it added was a new way of envisioning buildings from woodcuts and books, creating what Carpo calls "the typographical architect."[16] In this revolution, Venice was clearly the leader. Though it did not print the first Renaissance treatise on the subject—Leon Battista Alberti's *Art of Architecture* (*De Re Aedificatoria*) was published in 1486, in Florence—it swarmed all over the subject in the sixteenth century. Alberti's book was written in Latin, and was not illustrated, which limited its audience to humanist scholars. In 1511, the Venetian philologist Fra Giovanni Giocondo corrected the corrupt text of Vitruvius, the only ancient Roman to have left a treatise on architecture. Moreover, he took the important step of including printed woodcuts of the various designs in the book. The illustrations no doubt explain the quick demand for two new editions, but in the smaller octavo format.[17] A whole new scholarly resource had been created.

The key date in Renaissance architectural scholarship may be 1527, when Sebastiano Serlio came to Venice with his own architectural drawings based in part on those of his master, Baldassare Peruzzi. Serlio was soon part of the circle devoted to Doge Andrea Gritti's renovation of the city—the publicist Pietro Aretino, the painter Titian, the Franciscan mystic Francesco Giorgio, and, above all, the architect (and sculptor) Sansovino. Serlio continued making his drawings for an ambitious work to be published in many books. These were seen by the Aretino circle, and they began at once to influence the works of Titian and Sansovino. In 1537, Serlio published the first part of his great work—it would be Book IV in the later and larger publication. This was not only illustrated, it was written in the vernacular. Working architects not classically trained (most were not) would no longer be sealed off from the text by a linguistic barrier. Serlio had set another precedent, to be followed most famously by Palladio.

Most important of all, Serlio here created the grammar of classical architecture for the rest of history, since this was the book that first named as "orders" the four classical schemata that worked out the mathematical relations between columns and their bases and entablatures. He even added a fifth order, of his own devising, that became part of the canon, the "composite." Now the floodgates were opened for Venetian works on architecture, with these landmarks:

1540: What would be Book III of Serlio's final treatise appeared.

1546: Alberti's Latin work was published in Pietro Lauro's translation to the Venetian dialect.[18]

1547: A program for intensive study of Vitruvius, formulated earlier in Rome, was published in Venice.[19]

1554: Pietro Cataneo published *Four Introductory Books to Architecture*, in the vernacular and with illustrations.

1556: Daniele Barbaro, the aristocratic patriarch of Aquileia, brought out a translation of Fra Giocondo's Vitruvius, this time with illustrations. He was helped in preparing the woodcuts by Andrea di Pietro della Gondola, who had taken the name Palladio when he moved up from stonemason to architect. Barbaro was one of Palladio's patrons, for whom the architect created the famous Villa Barbaro.

1567: Barbaro's book was printed in a new edition, with expanded commentary, the fruit of Barbaro's scholarship and Palladio's experience.

1567: Cataneo published *The Architecture of Pietro Cataneo from Siena*.

1570: This busy trade in architectural scholarship was crowned, in 1570, with Palladio's own *Four Books of Architecture*. This is the book that would sweep

Europe. It even become, in time, Thomas Jefferson's architectural "Bible." The whole neoclassical movement would bear a Venetian stamp because of this man who was born and worked in the city's terraferma.

Classical ideals already enunciated by Albert and Serlio would now be credited to Palladio alone. The seminal work of Serlio faded from people's memory. There are several reasons for this, including an unjustified attack on him for plagiarism in Giorgio Vasari's influential *Lives of the Most Eminent Painters, Sculptors, and Architects* (1568).[20] Serlio also suffered from his decision to go to the court of Francis I in France after publishing just two books of his major work in Venice—the rest were published in France. This took him out of the mainstream of architectural theorizing and practice. And though he built some civic buildings and chateaux in France, he did not have the large body of great buildings that Palladio created—his three churches in Venice, civic buildings and the classical theater in Vicenza, and villas along the Brenta River for Venetian aristocrats. Besides this, even after his death Palladio had a champion in Vincenzo Scamozzi, an architect who continued and publicized his work. The leader of the Palladian movement in England, Inigo Jones (1573–1652), came to Italy after the death of Palladio, but in Venice he got to know the aged Scammozzi, who gave him some of Palladio's unpublished drawings.[21]

The triumph of Palladianism was a victory for Venetian book learning, but also for the city's cultural imperialism in a larger sense. It imposed its vision on Europe not only by the books it printed but by the buildings it put up, Palladio's primarily. Yet Palladio was preceded by the great Renaissance architects who brought Alberti's and Serlio's pages to life along the canals of Venice.

CHAPTER TWENTY-SEVEN

Learned Architecture: Codussi

J OHN RUSKIN ENDED HIS three-volume architectural history, *The Stones of Venice*, in the fifteenth century, since he thought only Byzantine and Gothic styles were great. He abominated the Renaissance in general and Palladio in particular. That still left him a good run of Gothic history to cover, since the Renaissance came late to Venice, in architecture as in other things. During the first half of the fifteenth century, when Brunelleschi, Michelozzo, and Alberti were creating works modeled on antiquity—in Milan, Florence, Rome, and Rimini—Venice was still elaborating its old Gothic forms. Bartolomeo Bon, Antonio Rizzo, and Pietro Lombardo added some classical references to essentially Gothic structures, but not a single Venetian building was created in an entirely Renaissance style until the eighth decade of the century, when the Church of San Michele in Isola was completed (1479). This was raised by the creator of Venetian Renaissance style, Mauro Codussi, who appeared, according to John McAndrew, "as suddenly and brilliantly as a comet" (McA 232).

Codussi did not come to architecture from sculpture, as did Bon and Rizzo and Pietro Lombardo, who moved out from an initial interest in ornament. Codussi, like Palladio after him, was trained as a stonemason, with a sense of structure as a whole that responded to classical ideals of volume and harmony. He was born near Bergamo, and traveled in the north of Italy, where he saw work by Brunelleschi and Alberti. His genius was recognized, though he was still in his twenties, when he did some work for the Camaldolese religious order in Classe (on the outskirts of Ravenna). When the Camaldolese monastery in Venice wanted to build a new church, the monks consulted the head of the order in Classe, who recommended Codussi, despite his youth.

CHURCHES

1. *San Michele in Isola* (1468–1479). The monastery of San Michele had rich patrons—many of its members came from prominent families—so it could afford to support an architect calling for the best in materials, deployed in a church not large by the standards of preaching orders. What Codussi gave them was clearly classical. It was the first Venetian church with an all-white stone façade, unlike the brick fronts of the Gothic buildings. It had two rows of engaged columns, each with its entablature. The Roman custom of placing Latin inscriptions on the entablatures is followed. The door is classical, though too small for the façade—McAndrew argues plausibly that the monks presented Codussi with this completed unit from another commission. The statue placed above the pediment is needed to match the height of the old Gothic door to the adjacent monastery.

Despite this overall classical schema, Codussi or his patrons seemed to realize that one reason the city had clung to Gothic so long was Venetian conservatism, which preferred to emphasize continuity rather than novelty in projecting its serene republican identity. So the architect "Venetianizes" the classical idiom. The tall central section flanked by two lower wings repeats the Gothic reach of a lofty nave with lower roofs over the side aisles. The narrow round-headed windows in Codussi's side units recall Gothic lancet windows. The scallop-shell patterns in the quadrant curves of the side wings, and in the round top, recall the apse patterns in traditional shrines. And the *paterae* (thinly sliced disks of precious stone) used in the upper section refer back not only to Lombardo buildings or the Ca' d'Oro but to San Marco itself. The placement of these paterae is not coordinated with the round window in the rectangle where they occur—indeed, that window is not centered in its space. These touches of "regular irregularity" suggest Gothic asymmetry rather than classical balance.

The most surprising thing about the façade is the rustication of its fine stone. Rustication (marked separation of rough stones) was prescribed for coarser kinds of buildings—fortresses, workshops, foundries. What is it doing on a church? Vitruvius recommended finer and more delicate styles for a temple. The answer is that this is not only a monastic but a Camaldolese church. The order had begun as an eremitic one, with the monks living in separate huts. Though they became more cenobitic with time, they looked back to their origins as giving them a special ethos. The rough stone seems to be a reference back to the hut era, as is the comparatively low façade, rounded off and returning to earth.

The interior opens up the closed system of Gothic, where thick piers had lined both sides of the nave, making the side aisles separate entities. The Western liturgy demanded processional gradations and divisions in a church—not only the separate aisles and transepts, but a nave which kept the laity outside a rood screen, while the section beyond the screen was divided between a choir and a sanctuary. Classical style shunned divisions that obstruct the comparison of a structure's harmonious volumes. So Codussi replaced thick piers with high long-striding arches, which break down the separation of nave and aisle.

One division of the nave had to be retained, for monastic purposes. The monks here did not sing their office in a choir before the sanctuary. Instead they had a perch above a *barco*, a transverse screen running right across the nave and holding above it a platform (or "bridge") where the monks assembled and sang the canonical hours. This was designed to let the monks file onto the bridge from a corridor on the second story of the adjacent monastery. At the height of the Renaissance, it held about sixty clerics performing their prayer duties. Codussi gives the screen a proper classical colonnade, on either side, with high-pedestaled Ionic columns under a large entablature.

2. *San Zaccaria* (1483–1500). We met this church earlier, since it is the wealthy convent church of the Benedictine nuns who gave a papal crown to the doge, the reason for the government's annual visit at Easter (M 221–22). It was also one of the churches treating an "Old Testament" figure as a saint, in the Byzantine manner, which suggests that the original church, of the ninth century, was Byzantine, with a Greek cross plan. But it had long been replaced with a Gothic one, whose latest apse was still being decorated by Antonio Vivarini in the fifteenth century—we see it now as the Chapel of San Tarasio, a kind of crypt under the present church. The convent was wealthy and important enough to call for a new structure in 1458. This was in the period, following the Turk-

ish conquest of Constantinople (1453), when Venice was refurbishing its image as the new Constantinople, asserting its imperial status with a grand building program. San

FIG. 98
Mauro Codussi,
San Zaccaria façade

Zaccaria, because of its intimate connection with the doge and his nearby palace, had to be "upgraded."[1] Antonio Gambello was appointed to build the new church. This was still not a Renaissance church, but an expanded Gothic one, as we can see from the French-style ambulatory around the apse, the only one in Venice. Enough of this was built to give Codussi, who was called in after Gambello's death in 1481, the problem of vaulting the fan of chapels around the apse with classical arches and not the more easily folded-in groin vaulting of Gothic.

On the church's exterior Gambello had built, before his death, the first two courses of the façade—which launched, from the ground level, a huge upward thrust of four massive buttress-piers. These retired slightly, at the second level, into more modest piers with niches in them. McAndrew chides Codussi for thwarting this vertical emphasis. But McAndrew admits that the scallop-shell shrines lined up ineffectually across the second level have no organic connection with what is below. The design was losing its sense even this early. What Codussi did was insert a third level that would neutralize what is below. He broke the pier succession with free-standing columns. Then he used a Venetian window scheme of three lights in the center and two single openings on the sides. This in effect called a halt to whatever was going on below. In the new game this makes possible, he now capped the design with a monumental variant of his San Michele façade—curved quadrants buttressing a center section that mounts to a hemispherical crown. The vertical ambition of the base could not have found any completion, on Gambello's scheme, except in some Gothic upward reach. That would not fit with the Renaissance alterations Codussi was bringing to the interior. The rough Gothic ardor of the lower course had to be tamped down and changed by tour de force into a horizontal scheme that curved energies back into a self-contained pattern. McAndrew points out that this led Codussi to be far more three-dimensional than he was in works that were his from the outset, where he preferred a flatter plane with subtler undulations of recess and projection. Here he shapes light as he molds forms, in a flurry of distraction from what he is interrupting. It is showier than he liked to be, but as a kind of heroic one-upping of the problem he was given.

The interior has the high-pedestaled columns, with wide airy arches, that Codussi had experimented with at San Michele. The tracery of light grays on pearl walls, the austere scheme of Brunelleschi, has been betrayed by later ages that covered the walls with Baroque paintings, arresting the continuous flow of attention from one interior space to another, dividing the building into scenes you must advert to separately. But the restraint Codussi imposed on Gambello's flamboyant apse and ambulatory still gives them great power.

3. *Santa Maria Formosa* (1491–1504). We have met this church before, too. As the earliest one in Venice devoted to the Virgin, it played an important role in the Festival of the Marys (Marie). Supposedly founded in the seventh century, when the shapely (*formosa*) Virgin appeared to Bishop Magnus, the church was rebuilt in the twelfth century, still keeping the Greek cross design of its Byzantine origin. In 1487, Antonio Bragadin, a devotee of Mary, left his considerable fortune for a new church, which Codussi was commissioned to build. Codussi followed the original plan of the church, using as much of the old foundations as possible—a practice generally followed in Venice, where the sinking of successful foundations was an operation not to be unnecessarily repeated.

The use of the low central dome here takes a long stride toward the openness and lack of mystery that classical design aims at. The main dome is echoed in the shallow saucer-domes of the areas between the arms of the Greek cross. The low piers and wide arches of these arms let one constantly compare the volumes of each, in spaces shaped by gentle curves and intersecting arcs, almost as in John Soane's eighteenth-century buildings. Even the side chapels communicate with each other, through *bifore* in their walls. It was a mistake, after an earthquake brought down the central dome in 1688, to put the new dome on a drum that lifted it higher. That made it impossible to see its relationship with the ancillary domes, since the main one was not visible from some interior angles. It was almost a stroke of luck that an Austrian bomb destroyed the replacement dome in World War I. A fine restoration after the war adhered to Codussi's original scheme.

The lightly suggested groin arches of the nave seem to spring out of the wall, with only small corbels to act as their pseudosupport. The tracery of gray stone articulates an abstract scheme drawn above and around one in an artificial heaven of ideal spaces. McAndrew's description of the subtle result cannot be bettered:

> Everywhere in the restored S. Maria the spare stone membering, limited to verticals, horizontals, and arcs of circle, is set off in a Brunelleschian way against smooth areas of plaster, flat below and curved above, in sections of cylinders or spheres. The stone parts combine to form a delicate but firm, cagelike armature, while the plaster does no more than bound the interior volumes of air, showing where they come to their ends. They do not show themselves as the face of massive masonry (which, of course, is what they actually are). The vaults of the nave and transepts, resting apparently on small corbels, appear to float weightlessly, not like lids but only as surfaces lightly indicating the top of the interior air. The profiles of the various moldings are everywhere immediately clear and geometrically pure and, like the large forms, they are generated only by straight lines or perfect arcs, never irregular curves or angles. The delicate armature could never really hold anything up—and the weightless vaults pretend that they do not have to—for they just act out in pantomime what the supporting forces would be doing if we could somehow see them. (McA 298)

Codussi died before he could put a façade on the church—though the exterior shape of the triple apse shows his design. The beauty is all within.

4. *St. John Chrysostom* (1497–1504). This is a another Greek cross plan—all Codussi's churches except San Michele were originally Byzantine. John Chrysostom was himself a Greek father of the church, and Mass is still celebrated here in the Greek liturgy on his feast. The façade of the church, hard to see in the narrow street, repeats the basic scheme of San Michele without the white Istrian stone (this was a poorer parish church, not a wealthy monastery). Curved quadrants prop up a center section crowned with a hemisphere. The interior has the same interplay of spaces as at Santa Maria Formosa, but the logic of a Greek cross within a square building is clearer in this smaller version, which lacks the ring of outer chapels at Santa Maria. The arms of the cross all have barrel vaults, except for the sanctuary arm, which has a flat ceiling. McAndrew convincingly supposes that the vault there was replaced to make room for windows to light the altar—a local effect destructive of overall form. Tullio Lombardo worked on

this church with Codussi, an experience that helped convert him from his father's style to the Renaissance clarity of his own mature work (as at San Salvador).

TOWERS

1. *San Pietro Campanile* (1482–1490). A campanile being built for San Pietro di Castello, the patriarch's seat, was toppled by lightning in 1474. The patriarch had trouble raising enough money to begin construction again, but by 1482 he was able to commission the bold new architect in town to build a classical tower. Codussi created another building all of white Istrian stone, in marked contrast to the brick structures, all over the city, that imitated San Marco's campanile. The tower is massive, yet somehow delicate, as a result of the lightly indented panels that run up its side, and of subtle modulations in width as it rises:

FIG. 99
Mauro Codussi,
Campanile at
San Pietro in Castello

The whole is fastidiously tapered, but so little that this is sensed rather than consciously noted. Also, the upper half, above the middle cornice, starts out a bit narrower than the top of the lower half on which it rests—another refinement felt rather than recognized, though here more easily discernible if looked for. (MCA 267)

The tower has, as it were, a waist, making it a bit sturdier below and more refined above. On the top cornice, with its giant dentils and egg-and-dart pattern, the bell chamber sits, reconstructed after another lightning strike, to Codussi's design but probably a bit shorter than the original (according to a representation of it on the famous city plan engraved by Jacopo de' Barbari in 1500). The octagonal structure above the lantern is not Codussian.

2. *The Clock Tower* (1496–1499). The Torre dell'Orologio has already been described in Chapter 5. But it is worth comparing it to the Campanile, to show how Codussi could adapt his classical gateway to Venetian colors, paterae, and figural art. The frame of diminishing pilasters contains the profusion of details in a classical grid.

PALACES

1. *Palazzo Zorzi* (1470–1490). This palace's long front along the Rio di San Severo posed the problem of imposing Renaissance order on the foundations and walls of a huge Gothic palace (perhaps two palaces conjoined).[2] To achieve this, Codussi made three equal arched water entrances, one central and one at either end of the long run. The horizontal reach of the united façade could not be denied by adding a tall central section, Instead, Codussi achieved a central emphasis by giving the normal three-light central window of a Gothic palace a heroic treatment. The middle window, set off by double pilasters on either side, is immediately flanked, to right and left, by double bifore (four lights in all), each framed by single free-standing columns. This screen hides the fact that some of

FIG. 100
Mauro Codussi,
Palazzo Corner-Spinelli

the windows are filled in because of the engagement of beams with the wall behind them (part of the former building Codussi was given to work with). The solution to the problems of the site is unique, and shows once again Codussi's desire to meld Venetian Gothic with new Renaissance forms.

2. *Palazzo Corner-Spinelli* (1490–1510). By the Sant'Angelo stop on the Grand Canal, this building has a four-square feel to it. Every arched opening is contained within a rectangular frame, and the wide panels between windows suggest rectangular piers running up

through the top two floors. The high entry level and mezzanine are rusticated, suggesting the humbler offices of lower stories in Venetian palaces. The two top floors are both *piani nobili*, the same size and with the same fenestration (the upper one looks higher because of the frieze above it). The trilobate balconies at either end of the lower floor form the only distinction between them. The widows use arches in a way that cleverly

FIG. 101
Mauro Codussi,
Palazzo Loredan

323

refers to Gothic trefoils of the sort found on the Doge's Palace or the Ca' d'Oro. Springing from the columns on either side of each bifora, a large arch circles the whole. But from the same columns smaller arches reach to a column in the middle. Then a circular form is put between the large arch and the smaller ones, touching all three. This is a form that had been envisaged before—Carpaccio used it on his striking building-as-triumphal-arch in the Saint Ursula cycle (*The Terms Accepted*). But no one before Codussi had made it a striking motif for a principal building.

3. *Palazzo Loredan* (1502–1509), also known as Palazzo Vendramin-Calergi. Near the San Marcuola stop on the Grand Canal, this is the grandest palazzo of the early Renaissance. It begins with a modest (though not rusticated) ground floor with pilasters placed exactly under the ten columns on each of the upper floors. The central three-light opening is observed here below. The middle arch is plain, while the flanking ones deploy Codussi's clever tracery of Romanized Gothic—as do the ten bifore above. All these arched windows are the same size, on all three floors. On the two identical piani nobili, there is no central emphasis—in fact, the middle bifora is the only one flanked by single (rather than double) columns. The impression is of two open arcades and *no wall at all*. The great heavy cornice gives an imposing skyline, completing a design that is simple yet monumental. The inscription on the ground floor, NON NOBIS DOMINE—the first part of a famous verse, "Not to us, Lord, be the glory, but to your name"—demonstrates the need of patricians to proclaim that even their proudest edifices were meant to glorify the state and its religion.[3] Anything even apparently imperial had to pay deference to the *religion* of empire. The building has a colorful history (Wagner died while living here) and it is now the city casino.

Codussi did other work, including colossal stairways for two scuole (San Marco and San Rocco). But the churches and palaces are his most conspicuous claims to the title of first master of the Venetian Renaissance. Not as theoretical or learned as Sansovino or Palladio would be, he intuited the essence of Alberti's classical thinking and made it acceptable to conservative Venetians by his way of infusing its spirit into forms familiar to the city. He broke down most of the resistance to the new.

CHAPTER TWENTY-EIGHT

Learned Architecture: Sansovino, Palladio

T HERE WERE MORE IMPORTANT Renaissance architects in Venice than I can deal with here—Michele Sanmicheli, for instance, and Giorgio Spavento, and Antonio Abbondi ("Lo Scarpagnino"), and Sante Lombardo. But I think it is safe to say that the big three are Codussi, Sansovino, and Palladio. Sansovino was the most important builder of public structures, as we saw in looking at his work with Andrea Gritti for the renewal of the city—the Mint, the Library, the Logetta. His other civic projects include the Poor House (Ca' di Dio) and the New Shops (Fabbriche Nuove) for the Rialto—two long and narrow buildings that bend to follow the canals they border. His huge and uncompleted Scuola Grande della Misericordia has already been mentioned. That leaves two other areas of his creativity—churches and palaces.

SANSOVINO: CHURCHES

Three of Sansovino's churches no longer exist—San Geminiano, destroyed by Napoleon to create his ballroom on the piazza, the church for the Syphilitic Hospital (degli Incurabili), and Santo Spirito in Isola, built for an abolished Augustinian monastery. That leaves one monastic and three parish churches he designed.

1. *San Francesco della Vigna* (1534–1582). We have already encountered this church, for which Doge Andrea Gritti had Francesco Zorzi draw up his memo on the numerical ratios of the structure. Sansovino worked from the sanction given that memo by Titian and Serlio. Not only was Zorzi followed in the matter of "cosmic harmony" in the church. He also urged that the simple Doric order be used for the columns, in keeping with the Observant Franciscans' austerity, and that the walls be kept plain white, with modest gray for the columns and modeling elements.

The example of other Observant churches was followed in two ways. First, the lower aisles that run along the sides of the nave in Gothic churches were omitted, leaving the nave one great meeting space for all the congregation. Chapels are placed along both sides of the nave, where the aisles would normally be, containing memorials to families of the monastery's patrons. You look in on them through the wide gray arches articulating the nave, and they are sealed off from each other.

The second characteristic of the Observant church is the removal of the choir space to the rear of the altar. The community here was large, and a choir before the altar would distance the congregation too far from it. The extended chancel-cum-choir equals the nave's length. If the church had transepts, it would form a Greek cross. But the transepts were eliminated along with the aisles. What stands in their place is just a cleared area the depth of the chapels that come to an end here.

The high arches of the crossing make one expect a dome, but we have seen that the committee eliminated that, perhaps in keeping with Zorzi's desire to make the church plain—yet the very simplicity of the design, with its wide gray arches and simple attic above them, gives the place its majesty. The austerity is abated somewhat by the fact that the families tending the side altars were able to exalt their pride with great works of art. The Giustiniani chapel flanking the altar space has some of the Lombardo family's exquisite reliefs, including a delicate *Paradiso* on the chapel's altar front. The Capella Sagredo has ceiling frescos of the four evangelists by Tiepolo, with Mark's lion looking very wise, a philosopher lion.

2. *San Martino* (1553–1566). This small parish church in the Arsenal area was designed by Sansovino, though probably not built by him. It is a Greek cross church, and Sansovino treats its interior spaces much as Codussi had. But now the clear articulation of central and subordinate spaces is obscured by a trompe l'oeil ceiling and eighteenth-century paintings on the walls. Space is broken up and broken through, destroying the whole genius of the design. The façade is also a tribute to Codussi, with curved semiscrolls where Codussi's curved quadrants propped up a central section. The central window even has a variant on Codussi's Renaissance version of Gothic tracery.

3. *San Giuliano* (1553–1580). This is the church on whose façade Sansovino put the statue of Tommaso Rangone, who patronized the rebuilding of the church. The interior is the simplest of all Sansovino's surviving churches—a plain open box with orders only at its end, where two engaged Corinthian columns hold up the arch over the altar.

The façade (hard to see as a whole in the cramped street) belies this simple interior. It suggests a tripartite plan, a nave with aisles, by putting the statue of Rangone in a central block with two rows of four columns, and adding side sections ending in pilasters. Vittoria completed the façade after Sansovino's death.

SANSOVINO PALACES

There are only dim traces left of Sansovinos's huge Palazzo Moro at San Girolamo, so that leaves only his two Grand Canal palaces by which to judge his domestic architecture.

1. *Palazzo Dolfin-Manin* (1538–1547). Near the Rialto Bridge on the Grand Canal, this first of Sansovino's Venetian palaces was completely rebuilt inside for the last doge of Venice, Ludovico Manin (1789–1797), but the façade remains true to its original design. Zuanne Dolfin, a great merchant, wanted his palace to stand at the water's edge, but he could not obstruct a public way running across the front of it. So he had Sansovino build an arcade, open at either end, roofing the passage. That meant that his water-level storehouses had to be recessed back of the public space, though the upper stories extend over it. It was natural, then, to make the arches of this arcade rest on workmanlike Doric pilasters. The

FIG. 102
Jacopo Sansovino,
Palazzo Dolfin-Manin

six openings are high, wide, and bold, and the number six precludes a central member, which fits the undifferentiated public passage below. But Sansovino achieves a central emphasis above, since the wide intervals of the two bays on either end are repeated in the two levels above, and each of these has an arched window exactly half the width of the lower arch, and placed over its center. That leaves room for four windows of the same size to be aligned over the two central arches, as a four-light window. And the bold piers below give way to slender Ionic engaged columns above, and then to even slenderer engaged Corinthian columns. The height of each floor decreases as well, revealing a more feminine grace as one rises from the workaday world of the public passage and the warehouse entrances. Though the palace is marginally smaller than the huge Gothic Palazzo Bembo next to it, its members are larger, bolder, and more regular, as if the Renaissance were quietly but authoritatively correcting the fussiness and detail of the Middle Ages. The building now houses the Banca d'Italia.

2. *Palazzo Corner, or Ca' Grande* (1545–1556). This huge building, now the Venetian Prefecture, is by the Santa Maria del Giglio landing on the Grand Canal. The brother of Queen Caterina Cornaro owned the famous Gothic palace, known as *la bella casa*, that stood on this site till a fire destroyed it in 1532. His son Jacopo asked Sansovino to create something as grand as the lost mansion, and he produced what Vasari called "perhaps the finest palazzo in Italy."[1] The façade begins with a huge rusticated entry-cum-mezzanine, its three central arches lacking any classical order. But engaged Doric columns framing the lateral windows are topped with segmental shell pediments. There is both strength and delicacy in the combination of columns, themselves rusticated like Sansovino's at the Mint, with the delicate low curve of the pediments.

Above these come the mezzanine windows between large volutes (also resembling those on the Mint). The two piani nobili form a continuous arcade of seven openings in each, and they would lack any central emphasis were it not for the massive three arches below and the fact that the balconies for the central three windows are continuous, while the lateral arches have separate balconies for each window. The double columns marching between the windows progress from Ionic on the lower story to Corinthian above. The openings have antique emblems—torsos, armor, spoils—in the spandrels on either side of the arch, and lions' heads at the keystone of each arch. The oval widows in the attic resemble those on Sansovino's Library, and the dentiled cornice finishes off the whole with quiet dignity. For understated elegance it would be hard to match Sansovino's masterpiece. Casina Rossa, the "little red house" in the

garden adjacent to the palace, is famous as Canova's workshop in the eighteenth century and Gabriele d'Annunzio's Venice home in the twentieth.

PALLADIO'S CHURCHES

Palladio, as Andrea di Pietro della Gondola is known, was born (in Padua) and lived
(in Vicenza) on the Venetian terraferma. Yet his work for Venice was bifurcated. He
built no churches outside the city of Venice and no palaces inside it. His urban palazzi
and country villas were done for aristocrats who did not feel constrained by the Venetian palazzo style. We have seen that Codussi and Sansovino—and, as well, people like
Sanmichele—respected Venetian traditions even while updating them. They retained
reminiscences of the tripartite Gothic façade, its fenestration, even its traceries, while
creating decidedly classical buildings. Palladio was at the same time more radical and
more predictable than they. He favored putting "temple fronts"—pedimented column
orders—on everything, even his "ornamented farms" (villas). That was more than the
Venetians were willing to countenance on their "main street" of the Grand Canal.

On the other hand, his churches were too radical for the terraferma, which enjoyed
only part of the city's freedom from Roman control of liturgical reforms. Though the
Council of Trent did not prescribe architectural forms, promoters of its decrees did—
men like Cardinal Carlo Borromeo of Milan.[2] They wanted Western cruciform
churches with hierarchical divisions in the functional areas, suitable for preaching to the
laity and for processions devoted to the Eucharist (in defiance of Protestant denials of
the real presence of Christ in the consecrated elements). Some Catholic reformers also
wanted a withdrawal from pagan forms in Christian art. Nothing could be farther from
Palladio's desire to Christianize the pagan temple. Not only his temple-front pediments
but his *rotonda* floor plans (harking back to the Pantheon) were bound to raise objections to his ecclesiastical architecture—as they did, even in the city of Venice, when his
"round plan" for the Redentore was rejected. Despite these problems, he was able to
create one Venetian church façade and two complete churches by the end of his life.

1. *San Francesco della Vigna Façade* (1562). This church, begun in 1534 by Zorzi, Gritti,
and Sansovino, still did not have a façade thirty years after construction began. This
pace of construction was not unusual for a large building, but it was unusual to take the
job of creating the façade away from so distinguished a man, and one so identified with
the project, as Sansovino (who would not die until 1570). But by the 1560s both Zorzi
and Gritti were dead, and the Grimani family had become the principal patrons of the

church, with a chapel inside and the intention of turning its exterior and interior façades into family memorials. Giovanni Grimani wanted to put the tomb of his grandfather, Doge Antonio Grimani, on the front of the church. He also wanted something more grand than the Doric order and the simple tetrastyle that Sansovino had planned, in accordance with Zorzi's call for austerity. (We know Sansovino's planned elevation from a representation of it on a commemorative medal struck when the project was commissioned.)[3] So Grimani became the first Venetian daring enough to let Palladio engage in church architecture within the city (though the communities at the Scuola Grande della Carità and San Giorgio Maggiore had let him do cloisters for them by the 1560s). The architect was able to move Grimani away from putting an actual tomb on the façade. Instead, he took this first opportunity to create the double temple front that would mark his other churches.

Rudolf Wittkower formulated the idea that Palladio created a high temple front flanked by the ends of a lower one, whose completion is to be imagined in phantom reality as intersecting the high one.[4] His concept has been criticized, on the grounds that an architect who thinks in three dimensions would not create a fictional "interpenetration" of two forms that had no actual realization. But we shall see him multiplying phantom forms on the façade of the Redentore. It has often been said that Palladio invented this device to cover the high nave and the lower side aisles of the typical Western church. But San Francesco, as we have seen, had no side aisles, just rows of chapels, whose height and depth are far less than the pediment ends that Palladio is supposedly using to "cover" them.

It is clear that Palladio was thinking only of the relation of his lower "temple" to the higher one. It "enters" the high temple's form precisely at the juncture of the main engaged columns with their capitals, and it reaches its imagined apex at the center of the cornice on which the high pediment is based. This is a self-contained harmonic system, and it says nothing about the church to which it is attached. That is confirmed when we look back to the Zorzi memorandum, which said that the outside should use the same Doric order as the inside, and should "correspond to the inside of the building, and from it one should be able to grasp the form of the building and all its proportions."[5] The Sansovino elevation, found on the commemorative medals, had Doric columns, and the fact that they are lifted on high pedestals indicates they were probably of the same height as the interior Doric pilasters. Furthermore, the façade is of uniform height, with no flanking lower sections, revealing that the church has no aisles. So the one thing cited to show Palladio was following Zorzi's thought—the fact that his front is twenty-seven paces wide—is really beside the point. Sansovino's façade, truer to Zorzi, was narrower. The Latin inscription across the entablature shows that there were two different schemes involved here—DEO UTRIUSQUE TEMPLE AEDIFICATORI AC REPARATORI (To God, who began one temple and completed another).

The front is decidedly odd, odder than later imitations of it indicate. The actual door is not carried by stairs up to the height of the formal door, which rests on the level of the columns' pedestals. So the real entry is cut through the middle by the pedestal level, and the fact that the real door is so low means that the formal door needs a fan arch placed *under* the door's entablature to fill up the space. This arch is echoed in the thermal window reaching from the cornice over the door to the entablature over the major order (four engaged columns with composite capitals). The shorter engaged columns of the lower "temple" are the same size as the two beside the formal door, suggesting they are a continuation of the phantom temple's order—but they are placed forward of its line. This is not a serene construct. It seems to be wrestling with its own meaning.

2. *San Giorgio Maggiore* (1565–1610). The work Palladio had already done on this monastery's refectory and cloister apparently led to the commission for this, his first church in Venice. Because it is a monastic church, he put the choir behind the altar, as Sansovino had at San Francesco della Vigna. Since there were many processions to San Giorgio on the feast days of saints with relics in the monastery's extensive treasury, a long nave with side chapels had to be included in the plan; but Palladio gave the crossing area the feel of a rotunda by rounding the transepts into apses. The whole interior is flooded with light from the rows of thermal windows resting on the entablature of the composite columns. The white walls and gray trim, without any decoration but the structural elements themselves, make undistracted communion with the spaces the only proper aesthetic response. The huge inner columns stand on high pedestals, and have

FIG. 104
Andrea Palladio,
San Giorgio Maggiore

high entablatures, like those of the major order on the façade. And, as on that façade, the minor order of pilasters stands on a low base.

Wittkower criticizes that placement of the façade's two orders on different levels. He feels that those who completed the façade, after Palladio's death, must have deviated from his elevation.[6] But the lower setting of the pilasters solves some of the problems created by having a door placed lower than the pedestals of the major order. The line of those pedestals still bisects the lower door, but the pilasters beside the door no longer start from the higher (pedestal level). They seem to be partners of the lateral pilasters, and this appearance is confirmed by the way the entablature of this lower temple runs right across the front, as if behind the engaged columns—the columns look as if they stood forward on a portico. The swaths between the capitals also make it look as if the columns were free-standing (though the placement of the real door would make no sense in a portico format).

This playing with space, illusionistic and schematic, proves to James Ackerman that Palladio liked to give his façades a two-dimensional quality, to be read as if they were pages in his *Four Books*. He wanted them to be looked at from dead center (he arranged for his villas to be approached that way, down long perspectives), so all the balancing elements will be seen in equipoise. "From this distant frontal position and from none other we grasp a proportional system."[7] Though the building exists in tangible stone, it remains in some way a building of the mind, an almost disembodied concept. Lit artificially at night, seen across the water on its island, the façade seems to hover, a paper vision under a paper moon, unearthly. Something of this quality lingers about it even by day: "The impression of two-dimensionality is sustained by the absence of chiaroscuro contrast; the façade looks toward the north and is never illuminated by direct sunlight."[8]

3. *Il Redentore* (1577–1592). Here Palladio was blessed with another site that allows his church to be seen across the water and approached straight on. This votive church was deliberately built to be the goal of a procession, every third Sunday in July, and the bridge of boats that led up to it gave Palladio an *allée* more romantic than he could contrive for any of his villas on land. The church was an urgent civic project. During the crushing plague of 1576 to 1577, the one that killed fifty thousand Venetians, the government had to do something spectacular for morale. In September 1576, Doge Alvise Mocenigo arranged for three days of processions to San Marco for prayer, and on the third day he announced that the city would pledge itself to an annual celebration of the Redeemer on

his feast, at a church to be built especially for that purpose, in thanksgiving for ending the plague. The government appointed a committee to identify the best site for this new church—preferably one outside the parish structures, and one where a religious community could care for it during the year, when it was not being used for the procession. By November 17, the committee had identified three possible sites, giving costs, accessibility, and maintenance provisions. On November 22, the Senate chose a site by the Capuchin monastery on Giudecca. The very next day Palladio was commissioned to make two models, one circular (his preference), the other rectangular. They were completed by the beginning of February 1577, and the Senate picked the rectangular plan. On March 3 the cornerstone was laid. The Capuchins had a relic of the True Cross that would be made the formal goal of the annual procession's reverence, confirming again Venetian ties with Christ's blood and cross that were described in chapters 15 and 16.[9]

The function of the church was very similar to that of San Giorgio Maggiore—a choir behind the altar of the monastic community, a high visible altar for exposure of a relic, and a nave with side chapels for solemn procession. Palladio came even closer, however, to his circular ideal, even in this rectangular design, by suppressing the transepts and giving the area between nave and chancel an oval form, as if the apses of the San Giorgio transepts had been drawn together before the altar. Then a complementary curve was given to the exedra of columns arcing around the back of the altar, acting as a choir screen. The purity of the space is emphasized by a continuous entablature, simpler than the one he had used at

FIG. 105
Il Redentore interior

San Giorgio. Renaissance openness, publicity, and illumination are divorced, here, from any reliance on mystery or secrecy. The awe must come from mere harmony of parts, from sheer scale of ordered control.

The exterior façade solves, at last, the problem of having a real entry at odds with an ideal one set on pedestals. Here the pedestals are removed, and the real door is lifted up by a flight of stairs, so that it coincides with the columned door—which now holds a pediment on top, without the need for semicircular filler below the pediment. What's more, this pediment over the door sits on the cornice line of the phantom pediment, interlocking these three lower triangles. But the fugal action has just begun. Over the highest entrance pediment there is a rectangular attic, which itself holds a triangular roof echoing the pediments below. And it, as it recedes, melts into the triangular roof of the whole building, in effect putting five pedimental shapes in play. The rectilinear attic and the curved dome exhaust this exploration of possible figures. Though Palladio has still not given us a real portico, the attic suggests a pronaos before the temple cella—a sequence of imaginary chambers through which one moves to the inner place of light and calm. This is the most illusionistic front of all—and therefore the most Palladian.

CHAPTER TWENTY-NINE

Learned Sculpture

BECAUSE OF THE CONTINUITY of artists' family shops in Venice, we can trace the blossoming of he Renaissance in particular families. What was only a faint move toward classicism in Antonio Vivarini (1415–1476) was full-blown in his son, Alvise (1456–1503). The same development can be seen from the work of Jacopo Bellini (1400–1470) to that of his son Giovanni (1433–1516). In sculpture, which lagged behind painting at first, the move is from the protoclassical tombs of Pietro Lombardo (1438–1515) to the Roman friezes and nude statues of Tullio (c. 1455–1532). As we have seen, Tullio turned even the *Coronation of the Virgin* into a classical frieze, with Christ and Mary standing on the ground, not throned in heaven. The same classicism is at work in the reliefs done by Tullio for Saint Anthony's tomb in Padua. The best way to survey the effect of Venice's look back to ancient Rome is to compare some of the nude male figures created at the turn of the fifteenth to the sixteenth century.

TULLIO LOMBARDO (C. 1455–1532)

By the end of his life Antonio Lombardo could create such classical figures, with toga and contrapposto, as his *Saint Peter* in the Capella Zen of San Marco. But it was his son Tullio who made the Renaissance fully at home in Venetian sculpture.

> In the field of sculpture, it is above all Tullio Lombardo who stands as the first major Venetian artist to involve himself thoroughly in the absorption and transformation of classical imagery as regards both content and style . . . [He] collected antique mannerisms and used them as the core around which he developed a personal style.[1]

Tullio was considered so expert on antique style that he restored ancient statues with missing parts, as Marcantonio Michiel recorded in 1532.[2] He was familiar with the classical collection of Cardinal Giovanni Grimani, who donated it to the city. (Vincenzo Scamozzi created a Statuario Pubblico for it in Sansovino's Library, where it is now the core of the Archaeological Museum.) Debra Pincus has even identified one of Tullio's restorations in the collection—the Muse of Philiskos, altered to make her a Cleopatra. This ancient statue, as reworked by Tullio, is closely associated with the Adam that Tullio carved for the Vendramin Tomb in the Church of Saints John and Paul.[3]

Tullio's Adam was meant to be paired with an Eve in the lower niches of the tomb, but he never carved the Eve. The prospect of a woman as nude as this Adam standing in the church may have given the Dominicans, even those of Francesco Colonna's lax house, some misgivings. Warrior figures were placed in the niches instead, and Adam had to find sanctuary in the Vendramin palazzo, built by Codussi (with Tullio giving some assistance on the building). For a time this Adam stood in the palazzo's garden, with an Eve that had been supplied as his partner. But in time the Adam made its way to the Metropolitan Museum in New York. Pope-Hennessy thinks that the Metropolitan statue combines a body based on the Apollo Belvedere (slim and soft limbs) "with a head based on the Capitoline Antinous" (P-H 2.323). Adam puts his hand on a support of the kind common in Greek statues.

Pincus notes how characteristic of Tullio is the handling of Adam's head—the open mouth revealing his teeth (as in the marital busts we saw earlier), the heavy but symmetrical locks of hair, the hint of a frown in the brows, the upturned eyes with their refined carving:

FIG. 106
Tullio Lombardo,
Adam

The lids are finely and cleanly indicated, with a rather precise overlapping of the upper lid over the lower at the outer corner. Part of the life of the expression comes from handling the eye as distinct from the skin envelope. The eye is shaped as a rounded form hovering behind the outer skin container. Pupil and iris are distinctly marked.[4]

Adam is holding the fruit in his hand. Is he caught pausing at the temptation to eat, or just after he has yielded? The suggestion of a tentative step in the posture would indicate the former. The fig leaf might indicate the latter. If he is still being tempted, he would resemble the Adam of the Doge's Palace's corner, who puts up his right hand in a last show of resistance. If he has just tasted the fruit, he would be in the moment of Rizzo's Adam on the Arco Foscari, just realizing what he has done. Since the fruit is intact, he must be pausing before the plunge, and the fig leaf is a concession to church sensibilities rather than an expression of narrative logic in the work. In any case, the somber expression on Adam's face means that fatality has begun to shadow the natural beauty and Edenic form of man.

SANSOVINO (1486–1570)

Great as was Jacopo Sansovino's contribution to Venetian architecture, it should not make us forget his leading role as sculptor to the city. We have seen his great sculptural program on the Loggetta, his *Giganti* on the doge's staircase, his reliefs in San Marco. One of his early Venetian statues (c. 1533–1534) brought him praise throughout his lifetime—*John the Baptist* in the Frari (BB 2.323–24). The Baptist was important to all of Italian art, since his likeness was often shown, in stone or mosaic or fresco or canvas, in the baptistery of any church. Statues, moreover, could be put over holy water stoops as well as on baptismal fonts. In fact, Sansovino's John was created for the holy water basin at the entry to the Florentine scuola's chapel in the Frari.

Here Sansovino was up against the toughest imaginable competition, since Donatello's great wood sculpture of John originally stood in the same chapel. Though carved a century before, it was still "modern," then as now. Two statues of John were done for the Florentine chapel, since John was the special patron of Florence. Donatello's countrymen in Venice did their city proud by commissioning these works for this site. The sculptor's polychrome terra-cottas are familiar (e.g., those in the Louvre), but a wood statue as brightly pigmented as this is startling—a gesture, perhaps, to the Venetian love of color. The brilliance of the saint's tunic makes for dramatic contrast with the austerity of its wearer. John's starved figure, his gaunt face, his shaggy hair (wild as the rough pelt he wears) all speak of the penitence to which he calls others by so obviously exemplifying it. He has lifted his eyebrows (and, no doubt, his missing index finger) to recognize the coming of Jesus that is proclaimed in the scroll that unrolls,

FIG. 107
Donatello,
Saint John the Baptist

without his noticing it, from his left hand—enough of its writing is seen to show that *Ecce* begins the sentence, "Behold the Lamb of God." The moment John has been prepar-ing himself and others for has arrived—Jesus has come into sight. The scene most often used in painting John is the moment when he bap-tizes Jesus—here is the look of recognition that precedes that event. John has fasted himself into a mystical state of worthiness to know what is before him.

What could Sansovino do that would not look trivial beside so powerful an image? He went back to an even earlier stage of John's life in the wilderness. Here he is seated, studying prophecies of the coming of Jesus—no doubt in Isaiah ("Prepare a path for the Lord, straighten the avenue of his coming," Mt 3.3). He looks up in an inspired realization of what such words portend. This John is younger than Donatello's, with hair not grown out to the length of the earlier statue's. But, young as he is, his body is already wasted, his seminude upper torso shows the effect of fasting and severity through openings in the shaggy goat skin he (like the other John) wears. The torque of the body shows the impact of sudden inspira-tion, as does the awed expression on the youthful face. He has lifted his head to the right while thrusting the scroll aside to the left (the position of the feet shows that he would have been reading, just a moment before, with the scroll on his lap).

Though the rock John sits on was designed to emerge from a holy-water basin, the statue was given a new base, turning it into a baptismal font, when it was moved to a different part of the church. Then it was moved again to its present site, the Corner chapel. Somewhere along the way it lost its right arm, which was restored in a different marble. The work is no longer viewed in con-junction with Donatello's, as it should be. They complement rather than compete. Sanso-vino's John was worthy of such exalted company.

FIG. 108 (ABOVE)
Jacopo Sansovino
John the Baptist

FIG. 91, 92
Vittoria, *Jerome*

FIG. 32
Jacopo Sansovino,
San Giuliano façade

VITTORIA (1525–1608)

Alessandro Vittoria crowns the era of Renaissance sculpture in Venice. We have already looked at his powerful *Saint Jerome* (in two versions), his portrait of Tommaso Rangone. Trained in Sansovino's shop, he did the two giant caryatids for the entrance to his Library. He was also famous for his stucco ceilings (he did that on the Golden

Staircase of the Doge's Palace), and for the medals he cast. An early work of his (1551) continues, as it were, the conversation between his master Sansovino and the preceding century's Donatello. This is the marble *John the Baptist* now in the holy-water stoop of San Zaccaria.

The work reverses the progress of Sansovino's statue from holy-water stand to baptistery. Vittoria's work was intended for the baptistery of San Geremia, but ended up on the holy-water stoop of San Zaccaria. The patron who commissioned it for the first church died before it was completed, and Vittoria refused to deliver it to the church because he claimed he was not being paid what it was worth. The matter was finally adjudicated in 1553, when Vittoria paid back what he had received so far and retained the statue himself. Since this was his finest work to date, he kept it in his shop throughout his life, where it was praised by many. In his will he left it to the Church of San Zaccaria, with a proviso that he be buried near it—as his master Sansovino had intended to be buried near his own *John the Baptist*. Eventually, Vittoria changed his mind, and created his own memorial, with a self-portrait bust, to be placed elsewhere in San Zaccaria (on the north wall).[5]

Vittoria returns to the standing John of Donatello, but he reproduces the youth and the rapt expression of Sansovino's seated figure. The seminude upper torso is gaunt but not wasted, and it has the same animal pelt over the shoulder that Sansovino's figure does. Vittoria's John has stepped barefooted into the river, pulling back his cloak with his left hand. With his right arm, he completes a pouring gesture with the bowl he uses for baptizing. Lorenzo Finocchi Gherhsi says he is preparing to scoop more water into the emptied cup, but that seems too prosaic an act to justify the intense expression on his face. He seems awed with what he has just done, so we must imagine that he has poured the water over Jesus, who would have bowed low as in Tintoretto's *Baptism* in the Scuola Grande di San Rocco (P-R 2.204–5).

John is still dazed at the thought he expressed as Jesus approached: "I am the one who should be baptized by you—so why come to me?" (Mt 3.14). Vittoria's John is torn between stepping forward to obey Jesus' reply ("Agree to it for now," Mt 3.15), and recoiling from the tremendous irony, the reversal of positions with the one he calls the Lamb of God. No wonder Vittoria kept this statue by

FIG. 109
Alessandro Vittoria,
Saint John the Baptist

him. It was here that he learned he could express a jumble of complex emotions by deployment of every element of the figure's torso and limbs and face.

Thirty years later Vittoria did a very different John, this one in bronze, for another holy-water stoop, at San Francesco della Vigna. This John is older, but more robust—his asceticism has made him an athlete, as it had Vittoria's Saint Jerome. He is now performing a heroic act, as we can see from the fact that his body is twisted like that of the Discobolos and his right arm is thrown up in the gesture of Laocoön. A feeling of unworthiness gives the torque to this exertion of the will. He was originally facing to his left, but he has twisted his body around to perform the act of pouring on his right—he looks down and away from what he is doing, as if unable to take in the enormity of *his* baptizing Jesus. Christian humility is paradoxically expressed in terms of pagan heroics. Classical learning is "mastered," in several senses—achieved by Vittoria, yet subordinated to a higher goal.

CHAPTER THIRTY

Learned
Politics

THE NEW BREED

I N THE LAST HALF OF the sixteenth century, the Venetian sea empire was con-
tracting. A new generation mobilized its resources to cope with that fact. This
involved a renewal of learning (more science, less scholasticism in the Venetian
university at Padua), deeper piety (with a strictly Venetian emphasis, by contrast with
the Counter-Reformation being organized from Rome), concentration on control of
the terraferma (to compensate for dwindling sea income). The opposition to Rome
went along with a fear of its ally in the Counter-Reformation, the Spanish-Austrian
empire of the Hapsburgs. The Hapsburgs pressed on the terraferma from two directions—on the north from Austria and on the west from Milan (a Spanish holding).
Jesuits were seen as circulating everywhere to promote the pope's schemes—their
house of studies in Padua was resented as a challenge to Venice's university there.

With the terraferma in such peril, hardheaded younger Venetians progressively
called for a renunciation of the sentimental attachment to the sea empire, insofar as
that weakened realism about the city's land holdings.[1] We can see now that Veronese's
1575 Collegio painting in the Doge's Palace was a visual manifesto of this movement:
Neptune, as a symbol of the past, is honorably fading on the right of the picture, while
the vigorous warrior on the left, armed for war on horseback, is offered as the leader of
the future. New laws were passed to consolidate Venetian control over land holdings,
especially those of religious establishments.

The leaders of these efforts came to be known as the New Breed (I Giovani),
opposed to the ways of the Old Guard (I Vecchii). Daring to defy the gerontocratic ethos
of Venice, the Giovani met informally at the homes of various members—at that of Paolo

PLATE VII
Paolo Veronese, *Mars
and Neptune*

Paruta in the 1560s, and later at the house of the Morosini brothers (Andrea and Nicolò) on the Grand Canal. They also gathered at the Merceria tavern called Ship of Gold (Nave d'Oro). This group included the ascetical diplomat and future doge Leonardo Donato (usually called Donà), scientists like Galileo (who came over from his professor's post in Padua), the visiting philosopher Giordano Bruno, political writer and future doge Nicolò Contarini, and Fra Paolo Sarpi, the former prior general of the Servites (Servants of Mary). William Bouwsma describes the dedication of this "new breed":

> The *giovani* were a peculiarly devout generation, combining the spiritualized ecclesiology and individualism of the Evangelicals with the austerity and moral rigor of Jansenism or the Puritans. The peculiar piety of the *giovani*, so different now from what prevailed elsewhere in Italy, enabled them to preserve that cool perspective on the external history of the church which had for some time served to strengthen the Venetian case for ecclesiastical autonomy. From this stance, still fiercely committed to their own ideal of reform, they also continued to stand in judgment on the Roman church, which appeared so different from their own.[2]

Gaetano Cozzi, too, notes the "intense spirituality" of the Giovani, whose reform was not of the northern or the Roman sort, but involved a revival of the values implicit in the religion of the empire itself. The future doges from this insurgent group, Leonardo Donà and Nicolò Contarini, took oaths of celibacy to consecrate their lives to service of the republic.[3]

> Those reclaiming this tradition were men like Leonardo Donà, his brother Nicolò, Francesco and Nicolò Contarini, Andrea and Donato Morosini, Ottaviano Bon. Only in and through that tradition can we understand such men—or even, I might say, such a troubled soul as Friar Paolo Sarpi. Their faith—and I believe this can be said of Sarpi, too, at least till the beginning of the seventeenth century—was (or tried to be) Catholic, as was their piety.[4]

Despite their idealism, these were practical men who knew the state had to reform its governing machinery if it meant to survive in the changed conditions of the late sixteenth century. The republic had responded to the growing crisis by turning over more power to the secretive Council of Ten, including tighter control of state money. The Giovani challenged this arrangement in 1582—a thing that others would not have attempted, given the Ten's power of retaliation. But these patricians of unchallengeable integrity brought off the reform in 1588.[5]

THE INDEX (1596)

Having taken on the Ten in their own government, the Giovani now defended that government against Roman intrusion in its affairs. The Venetian book trade had long been opposed to the various editions of Rome's Index of Forbidden Books, enforced by the Roman Inquisition. The republic also resented these, as challenges to the lay leadership of its own religion of empire. The Roman Inquisition was admitted to the republic only on condition that Venetian laymen be included in all its deliberations.[6] The republic also used its own (lay-dominated) Inquisition to make the Roman one otiose. Thus the Indexes published in 1549, 1555, and 1559 had little effect in Venice, where the government suggested, among other things, that Inquisitors must first buy any books they wanted to burn. Rome chafed at this defiance, and a papal nuncio was sent to break it in 1557—Fra Felice Peretti da Montalto (the future Pope Sixtus V). He was so resented that a member of the Donà family spat in his face when he entered the Collegio chamber of the Doge's Palace. When Peretti's patron Pope Paul IV died in 1559, he had to flee Venice, and the city informed Rome he would not be readmitted to its jurisdiction.[7]

But in the 1560s Venice began cooperating with the Roman Inquisition—for a number of reasons. The bookmen themselves needed Roman authorization to print profitable liturgical and other texts, and they smarted from boycotts of their wares in Roman-controlled territories. The republic needed Roman help in various endeavors. But, principally, Venice was as wary of Protestantism, the main target of the Index, as was Rome. The reformers, after all, attacked the cults and saints, the ceremonies and symbols, of Venice's religion of empire. Nonetheless, the Venetians kept up a show of independence by doing much of what Rome wanted under its own authority, by ameliorating measures that hurt Venetian printers—and by tolerating a brisk black market in banned books.

There was always friction between Rome and Venice over the control of the press. The state had to oppose enforcements of the Index that made printing profits fall off too sharply, or that threatened the success of its university at Padua. Sometimes, as well, Venice wanted to allow more Hebrew publication than Rome was allowing, in order to maintain its profitable relations with the Jews.[8] Increased control of the terraferma also ran up against Inquisition activities there. These tensions increased in the 1580s, with the Giovani criticizing the political costs of repression.

The government wanted to remove Jews from the jurisdiction of the Holy Office because a civil court was more likely to keep in mind that the delicate rapport with the Turks partially depended on benevolent treatment of the Jews. Gradually, a series of ad hoc initiatives took on the character of policy.[9]

These struggles came to a head in 1596, when Pope Clement VIII issued a new Index, which the republic refused to accept. The Index demanded an oath of loyalty and the printers' prior submission of manuscripts to Rome; it allowed bishops to add books to the list at their discretion. Venice objected to each of these points, and refused to promulgate the Index until they were removed. But one of their own number, a member of the great Priuli family who was serving as patriarch of the city, promulgated the document without the government's permission. Donà, the leader of the Giovani, who would later (as doge) wage an even greater campaign against Rome, moved swiftly:

> The Venetians were enraged. The Collegio ordered the bookmen under pain of death to disregard the Index, and summoned the patriarch, his vicar, and several priests, to justify their actions. At one pont Donà asked the vicar what respect he had for the prince [doge]. The vicar answered that he respected the prince's authority very much, but as vicar he also owed allegiance to the church. Donà pounced on him: You say that you respect the prince very much? I say that he is everything, and that all other powers are accessorial.[10]

Rome, backing down, had to issue a concordat modifying the Index. "Thanks to Venetian intransigence and papal mishandling, the bookmen and the Republic achieved a clear victory."[11] But the battle was not over; it was just beginning. Donà's friend and ally Paolo Sarpi had been engaged in the struggle, and he called into question the very institution of the Index. He deepened the tendency of the New Breed to make learning a tool of politics.

THE INTERDICT (1605–1607)

As part of its determination to impose tighter control on the terraferma, the republic decreed in 1604 that no religious structures could be built there without the government's permission. And then, in March, 1605, subjects of Venice were forbidden to donate land to religious use. This was done to prevent encroachment by religious orders loyal to Rome, and the pope predictably called the provisions an assault on the freedom of the church. Then new grievances were added, in March of 1605, when two clerics, arrested for committing crimes on the terraferma, were hauled before the Ten for their trials. One of these men, the canon Scipione Saraceno, had smeared with filth the house of a noble kinswoman who rejected his advances. The other, the Abbot of Nervosa, Marcantonio Brandolin, Count of Valdemarino, was accused of poisoning members of his family to cover up other crimes.[12] The papacy had permitted the Venetians to try some clerics in the past—but only before the Council of Forty, for egregious crimes, and with ecclesiastical representation. It called the Ten's assertion of full jurisdiction a usurpation of ecclesiastical authority over Rome's clergy.[13]

A new pope was installed in Rome two months after the clerics were arrested—Paul V, a stickler for canon law and papal prerogative, a man who had served on the Roman Inquisition. And in Venice a new doge would be installed in January of 1606—Leonardo Donà, the aging (seventy-two) Giovane who had defeated the Index ten years earlier. Paolo Sarpi wrote that Paul V meant to crush Venice, but Sarpi knew that his friend Donà was the last man to let himself be crushed: "Above all his [the Pope's] anger was enflamed against the republic of Venice, since it alone maintained the dignity and efficacy of a realm independent [of Rome]—and also because it entirely excluded clergy from its government."[14] In December of 1605, the pope threatened to excommunicate the whole Senate and to place an interdict on the Venetian empire—a ban on dispensing any sacraments, even final confession, to the inhabitants. This was an ancient measure that had broken opposition in the past, since inhabitants of the condemned place feared going to hell unshriven.

Shortly after this threat was delivered, and before it could be answered, the old doge (Grimani) died, and a new man had to be chosen. It is fortunate for those interested in this period that the English ambassador in Venice was the witty and learned Henry Wotton. He had been sent by James I to convince the Venetians that the Jesuits had been behind the attempt on his life called the Gunpowder Plot (1605). He warned that all rulers should fear such plots against them—a conclusion the Giovani had already reached. Wotton's fascinated observations are a lively picture of the time. He was a great admirer of Donà, and he voiced impatience with the Old Guard's traditional fear of putting a powerful man in office:

> His merits were known, his wisdom confessed, and rather indeed amplified than
> denied by his adversaries; but great understandings were rather to be wished in

Princes that are absolute. . . . With these and the like speeches and murmurs they sought to weaken him: certainly not altogether out of cunning for the present, but from a true feeling of his greatness and eminence, which had been long, and (I may say), according to the nature of this State, somewhat strangely endured.[15]

As soon as Donà was elected, he let Rome know that he would not yield on any of its demands (canceling oversight of ecclesiastical construction, the ban on land donations to the church, or the surrender to ecclesiastical courts of the clerics Saraceno and Brandolin). The doge ordered canon lawyers at Padua and elsewhere to look into the legality of the pope's claims, and he brought Sarpi into the Doge's Palace with a salaried position as special counsel to the state on matters legal, historical, and theological. (This is ironic, since Sarpi, a Servite friar, claimed that the pope hated Venice for not letting clerics have a role in the government.)[16]

The threatened interdict brought Wotton out of his diplomat's palace on the Canareggio Canal, where he had shut himself up in protest at some Venetian fees on English trade. He bustled into this new fray with indiscreet glee, and would soon be egging on the doge and his own king to make joint war against the papacy. He wrote back to his diplomatic contact in England:

I must needs tell your Lordship, not in sport, but in very good earnest, that this breach hath put many kinds of men into work. The politiques [politicians], how to find delays; the canonists, how to find distinctions; the divines, how to find a new religion: which last point they divided into two resolutions, either to force their Latin priests to say mass after the excommunication, or to pass to the Greek [Byzantine] faith. Our new Prince [the doge is "our," so much does Wotton identify himself with the quarrel against Rome] is warm in the cause, and very well skilled in the Roman Court, where he hath been nine times in quality of ambassador.[17]

It excited Wotton no end to see with what firmness the Venetians were preparing to defy the pope:

Now, in the dependency of this business, many things have been done here provisionally; some in judgment, some in passion, some in earnest, some in sport, some in contempt, and nothing (that I have yet seen) in fear: which I will set down by way of rhapsody, like the very nature of the time itself.[18]

Jesuits, though they were accused of fomenting this strife, had both in Rome and in Venice tried to prevent the pope from reckless action, and hoped to heal the rift before it became final.[19] One of their priests, a native of Venice with ties to the governing class, asked the doge to let his order negotiate with the pope for some accommodation. Wotton rejoiced in the answer that was reported to him:

> He [the Jesuit] had from the Prince this noble answer, that "the State of Venice had never before used such instruments and would not now begin"; and therefore he told him "to forbear the employment of themselves either much or little in this matter, and rather to spend their time in considering that they had been already too busy in the world." And so he departed.[20]

In order to prevent the pope from threatening Venetians, the government ordered that no missive from the Curia be published, that clerics turn over any dispatches from the Curia unopened, and that no clerics suspend their sacramental tasks. The Jesuits had reluctantly to comply with the Interdict, upon which the Senate banished them from the realm, ordering "that an under secretary of the Senate, with a *Commandatore* or pursuivant, should take an inventory of their movables, not permitting them to transport with them anything but their quotidian habit, and their breviaries; which hath accordingly been executed here."[21] Galileo was in the city on the evening of May 9, 1606, when the Jesuits departed, and he described how they marched to the ships at eight o'clock, each man wearing a crucifix around his neck and carrying a lighted candle.[22] Sarpi said they wore the crucifix to show that they were taking Christ out of the city.[23]

Two other orders, the Capuchins and the Theatines, were also banished, along with the Observant branch of the Franciscans.[24] But the major Franciscan friary, the Conventuals at the Frari, submitted to the state, along with the Dominicans and the Benedictines. Wotton describes one method the Benedictines used for keeping themselves uninformed of Rome's instructions:

> The monks of St. Benedict (which draw 200,000 crowns of yearly revenue out of the Venetian Sate) have found a notable way to delude the Pope's authority, not yet daring to deny it, which is this: they have caused a chest to be made without a lock, fast nailed on all sides, and in the top thereof a little hole, into which they throw all letters that are directed to their convent without exception, lest they might receive

some prohibition from their General, and so mean to save their consciences by the way of ignorance: which point of subtle discretion is likely to be imitated by other orders.[25]

The religious orders were, of course, the clerics most dependent on Rome. The bishops on terraferma (nominated by the government and only approved by Rome) and the parish priests (elected by their leading parishioners) were generally loyal to Venice's religion of empire.

To show that religious life had not been interrupted, Venice put on a particularly splendid procession on the 1606 Feast of Corpus Christi, early in the days of the Interdict. The normal floats showing religious scenes were paraded along the way, but political ones were added—including the representation of a collapsing church upheld by Doge Donà with the help of the patron-founders of the Franciscan and Dominican orders, who were obedient to the empire, not to the pope. A Jesuit "intelligencer" [spy] in the crowd called this "a lamentable thing to behold" (M 230). Wotton attended this,

> the most sumptuous procession that ever had been seen here, wherein the very basins and ewers were valued in common judgment at 200,000 pound sterling . . . The reasons of this extraordinary solemnity were two, as I conceive it. First, to contain the people still in good order with superstition, the foolish band of obedience. Secondly, to let the Pope know (who wanteth not intelligencers) that notwithstanding his interdict, they had friars enough and other clergymen to furnish out the day.[26]

It was not only at solemn festivals that religious observance went up in Venice during the Interdict. Even Cardinal Bellarmino had to admit that more people than ever were going to Mass—though he said they only did it to spite the pope.[27]

The Curia in Rome attacked Doge Donà as an enemy of the Christian faith (a charge echoed in Ludwig Pastor's propapal history), but few in Venice shared that view. In fact, a political opponent of Donà had to admit:

> This Donato enjoyed the greatest authority, from his long exercise of it at the highest levels, from his learning, his prudence—and besides he had conducted himself in all his dealings with a tenor of life incorrupt and restrained, applying his severity more to himself than to others, since he was approachable and humane to all. He was always strict on himself, never yielding to grandiosity, impulsiveness, or lack of disci-

pline. He despised riches, turned away bribes, shrank from indulgence—in short, he aspired to the reputation of Cato for austerity, of Fabritius for poverty.[28]

This foe of Paul V was more like the ideal of a pope than any pontiff who had been seen for some time, and it was not hard for religious people in Venice to identify their cause with the Christian faith itself. Sarpi mounted a propaganda effort to seal this association. In the process he gave the Venetian myth something it had lacked before—a rigorously learned rationale. The efforts of Gasparo Contarini and others to explain the myth in terms of classical political theory had never gripped the Venetians at any deep level, since they left out the most important aspect of the myth, its grounding in Christian faith. The city of the Virgin and of Christ's blood was more important to them than were ideals of balanced government or republican liberty. Now Sarpi would talk their language, and do it with expert deployment of Scripture, of church councils, and of canon law.

PAOLO SARPI (1552–1623)

Sarpi, fifty-three when the Interdict crisis began, had unconsciously been preparing all his life for the role he was about to play. Born a commoner in Venice, and baptized Pietro, he was so small that people called him Peterkin (Pierino) in his youth.[29] He lost his father at the age of eight and was taken into the care of his uncle, a friar in the Servites, who ran a school attended by patricians. Sarpi's fellows there included his future New Breed comrades, Nicolò Contarini and Andrea Morosini.[30] Sarpi was a child prodigy with a gift for science who conceived an early desire to imitate his uncle and become a Servite. Despite discouragement by that uncle, he was allowed to become a novice at age eleven, taking the religious name of Paolo (Saint Paul would always be his favorite biblical authority). At age fifteen, attending a general chapter of his order in Mantua, he defended 318 theses in philosophy and theology, so successfully that he was asked to repeat the performance in Bologna before that city's cardinal. He was so famous three years later that Guglielmo Gonzaga, Duke of Mantua, made this boy wonder his court theologian.

Returned to Venice at age twenty-two, Paolo was ordained a priest, and then Carlo Borromeo, the reforming Archbishop of Milan, asked him to come help him train priests in his diocese. He was called back to Venice to become prior provincial of his order at age twenty-eight, then prior general at age thirty, and procurator charged with reforming the order in Rome at age thirty-three. In Rome he became a friend of

Roberto Bellarmino, the famous Jesuit theologian. During his forties, spent in Venice, Sarpi was deeply involved in scientific studies, with Galileo and others, and in the reform programs of the Giovani, who tried to nominate him several times for a bishop's post, but Rome was too cautious to advance this brilliant and original man to such an office in the restive Venetian empire.

When Doge Donà called Sarpi into the Interdict battle, the scholar and scientist began a whole new career as public polemicist, a calling for which he had rhetorical skills to match his learning and mental discipline. His outpouring of pamphlets during the crisis attracted a worldwide audience. The papal apologist Ludwig von Pastor had to admit:

> Sarpi's assertions caused an enormous sensation throughout Europe and started a controversy which, in the years immediately following, seemed likely to go on indefinitely . . . Through him Venice, already in decay, became for a last time the center of world politics and once more riveted all eyes on itself.[31]

To refute Sarpi, Rome called on its two greatest scholars—the Oratorian cardinal Cesare Baronio, a chronicler famous for his answers to Lutheran versions of church history, and Bellarmino, who would become famous for his answers to the theory of absolute monarchy enunciated by James I of England.

By instant consensus, Sarpi ran rings around these prestigious adversaries. Before broadening his argument out to the whole issue of religion's role in Venice, Sarpi addressed the specific points covered in the interdict. In his first brief on the government's position (*Advice on Maintaining Two Laws of the Most Tranquil Republic*, January 14, 1606), he began with the law forbidding land donations to the church. This was directed not at clerics but at laymen, and was based on the state's general protection of its own territory. Since it told Venetian subjects not to spend Venetian resources needed for the city's prosperity, it reached only to what the church did not yet have. Since the church could not own the land before the subjects donated it, it could not be deprived of what it did not possess.[32]

Moving on to the law against church construction without the government's permission, Sarpi said that the republic was the custodian of its own territory, and he compared its right there to what would come to be called the power of eminent domain: just as the state had "the right to build forts, to lay out streets, to divert rivers," it could decide when and where the people were best served by religious constructions.[33]

In his second pamphlet for the state (*A Treatment of the Force and Validity of Excommunications*, January 28, 1606), Sarpi took up the power of the church to issue its interdict. Going back to the penalties issued by Peter in the New Testament, he established the criteria for just excommunication. It must be directed a) at a specific sinner for a specific sin, and b) to a sin that is grave and committed knowingly, and c) to a sin that the church has warned the sinner against by way of counsel and kindly efforts at reform. Only when such efforts at persuasion have failed can the church resort to the drastic "medicine" of excommunication, a medicine dispensed in the degree and on a schedule that would bring the sinner back into the community. For the pope to excommunicate the whole Senate of Venice is not to address the sin of a specific person after using persuasion—and an interdict imposed on a whole people is even less justifiable. This is not medicine but aggression. "Do we want to see if an excommunication is valid? Let us see if Saint Peter would have imposed it. And if we see it standing far off from that apostle's love and non-assertiveness, we cannot believe that it has the force of apostolic authority."[34]

And what did the republic do to merit the pope's action? Has not a state the right—rather, the duty—to order all its resources for the good of its subjects?

> As for an unjust Interdict, imposed because a sovereign has performed the tasks God enjoined on him—the maintenance of tranquility in his realm, the protection against foreign aggression, the contrivance of good law for the subjects' peace and prosperity, having as its goal the public good and the private convenience—one should have no hesitation in making a proper estimate of the Interdict, and in opposing force to an ecclesiastical aggression masked under claims of reason and justice, the same force God sanctions for the defense of a state against any external aggression.[35]

God has entrusted the temporal order to temporal rulers—and crimes like those committed by the two clerics are offenses against the rights of subjects, whose protection is the responsibility of the state. To let some external authority check or eliminate the duty of the sovereign to protect his subjects would mean that the ruler cannot rule.

> I cannot help saying that no deeper wrong can be inflicted on a realm than to limit its primacy, its sovereignty, or to subject it to alien rule. A sovereign is a sovereign, whether over a large or a little portion of the world's territory. Romulus [in primitive Rome] was no less a ruler than Trajan [in the high Roman empire], and Your Tran-

quility [Doge Donà] is no more a ruler now than were your predecessors when their empire did not extend beyond the lagoon. To take away part of a ruler's territory is to make him a ruler of less but no less a ruler. But to subject a ruler to another's law, or to try to make him a subject, even if he should hold on to all of Asia, deprives him of the essence of rule.[36]

If Sarpi stopped here, he would be making the large claims for temporal sovereignty that were just being elaborated by Jean Bodin and others in France.[37] But Sarpi is going to vindicate the *Venetian* order, in which the doge is not only a temporal but a spiritual leader, the head of that religion of empire that is the subject of this book. So in his third pamphlet (*Advice on Trying the Crimes of Clerical Personnel*, January 28, 1606), Sarpi maintains:

It is obvious that, in the early church, all the faithful took part in electing pontiffs and priests, and in governing the church. But now all the government is in the hands of the clergy. This is not the place to go into this reversal, but I mention it only to point out that if the entire body of believers used to have a say in the spiritual order, then pious Christian emperors, as leading members of the church, made many of its laws, judged many of its cases, even those having to do with the ecclesiastical structure. Such were Valentinian, Valens, and Gratian in their writing to the bishops of Asia and Frisia. Such were Gratian, Valentinian II and Theodosius in the laws telling "all the people" what should be the Creed. Such were Honorius, Theodosius II and Justinian in their *Updatings*. And many other rulers after them made laws deciding how many clerics should be assigned to each church, or the duties, age, and qualifications of bishops, or the punishment for clerical offenses, or the manner of fulminating excommunication.[38]

Venice, then, has kept up a living memory of the primitive church at a time when it was growing corrupt elsewhere, and especially in the papal states.

If it be asked what role the church plays if the state has so much responsibility for earthly life, Sarpi would answer that bishops in ordinary life, and councils of bishops in special crises, cooperate with rulers in serving God—as early ecumenical councils met in cooperation with Constantine and other emperors. The bishops carry on the study of Scripture, the conducting of worship, the administration of the sacraments. It is the pope who had intruded into *both* the emperors' and the bishops' spheres, trying to hold a temporal power above that of the sovereign and a spiritual power above that of the bishops.

> No one should let himself be swayed by the maxims we find in some canon lawyers' books:"The Pope is another God. The Pope is God on earth. The Pope is greater than Moses and the Apostles. In the Pope we find heaven's decrees. The Pope's will supplants our reason. The Pope's and God's are one and the same tribunal." What labels such words deserve I shall not bother to say—let them be their own condemnation.[39]

But in the very next sentence Sarpi cannot resist a little private needling of cardinal Bellarmino in this public document. He does not name the cardinal, but he knows he will remember what he said twenty years earlier, when Sarpi was on easy terms with him in Rome:

> I remember the year 1588, when I was a delegate on a Roman commission containing five Cardinals, a great number of bishops and more theologians and canon layers, where it was asked if the Pope could give a dispensation to the Prior of Toulouse to take a wife, since this former younger son of the Joyeuse family had become the head of the family by the eldest son in the Anna branch. Some canon lawyers then trotted out in quantity such sayings [as"The Pope is another God"]. There was a man of the greatest orthodoxy, justly made a Cardinal since then, who leaned over to me as I sat near him and said,"This is the kind of thing that has lost us Germany and will someday bring Italy to the brink of ruin."[40]

Protestants throughout Europe took Sarpi's attacks on the Roman Curia as a sign that Venice was ready to join the reformers. Wotton, who was not allowed as an ambassador to meet privately with government officials, set up a line of communication with Sarpi through the embassy's Anglican chaplain, who met regularly with the Servite under cover of giving him English lessons.[41] From his chaplain's reports Wotton conceived a belief that Sarpi was a Protestant at heart. But attacking the pope was nothing new to Venetians, and the religion Sarpi defended was very far from the churches of Luther or Calvin. He stood for the traditional religion of Venice, with its cult of the Virgin and the saints, its relics, its vivid pageantry and sacred images. It has become a commonplace to say that Sarpi lacked the initiative to act on his own best instincts and go all the way in revolt against Rome; but the convictions he shared with pious Giovani like Donà and Contarini were never Protestant ones. He had no more desire to be subject to Reform theology than to Roman doctrine. He was defending the Venetian religion of empire. And modern liberals cannot make a claim on him either. He was an absolutist. He attacked Rome, which subsumed politics into religion, by praising the Emperor Constantine, who had subsumed religion into politics.

The year and a half of the conflict with Rome became a war of nerves. Who would back off first, and what formula could be contrived for doing so? Diplomats of various countries tried to decrease tensions, which threatened to bring on a war that could engulf a number of countries. Preparation for such an eventuality was draining Venetian resources; but meanwhile the prestige of the papacy was declining with each new attack by Sarpi. As Pastor concedes, "There can be no doubt that Paul V seriously misjudged the effect of the Interdict."[42] Henry IV of France, who had secured his throne by a timely conversion to Catholicism, a move supported both by Rome and by Venice, wanted to make peace between his old allies. He sent François de Joyeuse, a cardinal and his relative, to conduct shuttle diplomacy between Rome and Venice.

Joyeuse, taking messages back and forth, deftly gave the impression to each side that the other was yielding more than, in fact, it had. Venice said it would readmit the banished religious orders—but not the Jesuits. Paul insisted that the Jesuits be included, but the Jesuit general asked that this demand be dropped. He did not want his men to be blamed if the negotiations failed.[43] Venice would not rescind the property laws for terraferma, but Joyeuse told the pope it would not enforce them. The two priests in prison were given over to French custody, to be tried in French courts (ecclesiastical ones, as it turned out, though that was not specified in the deal), while Venice retained the right in principle to try such offenses.

Doge Donà was ready to let Rome save some face, to bring the crisis to an end. But Sarpi insisted that no principle he had enunciated could be surrendered. He put up a hard resistance to accepting absolution from Rome, as if there were any sins to be absolved. Joyeuse assured Rome he had delivered such an absolution, since he blurted it out at a Mass without having got the Venetians' acceptance for it.[44] The settlement was a great defeat for Rome, which had to take what it could get to stop the attrition of Roman pride under Sarpi's attacks. When Sarpi was attacked by would-be assassins four months after the settlement, Rome's fury seemed to be expressed in the three stabs to his face and head, even if the Curia did not expressly order the attack. Sarpi not only survived—itself an affront to Rome—but made all Europe laugh with the pun he made on *stilo* as both style and stiletto, saying, "I get the Roman Curia's point." He went on to deal an even heavier blow against the papacy with his wildly popular *History of the Council of Trent*. Pope Paul V's successor, Gregory XV, would later say that the Interdict crisis had been "the inspiration of a man of genius for evil who exerted greater influence through his tongue and his friends than by reason of his position [on the issues]."[45] The Venetians, by contrast, thought he was just voicing their own historical attitude, now made stronger by his learning.

CHAPTER THIRTY-ONE

Learned History

SARPI AFTER THE INTERDICT

AFTER THE INTERDICT CRISIS, Sarpi's position in Venice was a delicate one. He had been excommunicated during it, and he refused to receive any absolution, yet he continued to act as a priest. The Venetian government was certainly not going to disown him, and its leaders felt grateful for the way he had championed their cause. Yet to celebrate that service too ostentatiously would be a way of rubbing Rome's face in the dirt and prolonging the tensions that had been eased by the ambiguous settlement of the Interdict. It would also stoke the fires of revenge that the Curia in Rome felt after its drubbing by the troublesome priest-genius of the Servites. Therefore, though Sarpi printed a few quick pamphlets in the aftermath of the struggle, he was discouraged from pursuing the controversy further. Unable to publish a history of the whole course of the Interdict under his own name, he wrote one nevertheless, to be used in the running anti-papal history (*Historia Sui Temporis*) being written in Paris by his Calvinist friend Jacques-Auguste de Thou. But by the time Sarpi found a way to smuggle the manuscript to Thou by diplomatic pouch, Thou had died.[1] Sarpi's *History of the Interdict* would be published posthumously (1624), reigniting controversy and making good on his threat that he would be an even greater foe to Rome in death than he had been in life.

Sarpi wanted to do more thorough historical research on points he had touched on in the heat of battle. The whole dispute over temporal control of a sovereign's realm, for instance, occasioned by the Venetian laws for ecclesiastical restrictions on terraferma, led him to write his *History of Benefices*, tracing the way real property had made popes become stockbrokers for a market in lucrative church holdings. This book, also published posthumously, gave a cooler historical basis for the more heated Protestant attacks on episcopal and monastic venality.

While he was engaged in these historical labors, including the even greater one, his *History of the Council of Trent*, Sarpi could not give up his political activity. But this political scheming had to be conducted in secret, in correspondence with those able to influence the Protestant powers. Convinced as he was that Roman authorities had suborned the attempt on his own life, he did not assume that Rome had taken its setback over the Interdict in a forgiving spirit. It looked forward, he believed, to revenge not only on Sarpi but on all of Venice. That proud republic had, after all, used his polemic to reduce ad absurdum the pope's vaunted weapon—never again did Rome try to use an interdict after the way it backfired with Venice. The Curia, Sarpi felt, was just biding its time for the day when it could redress the losses inflicted on it by the declining republic.

A plausible scenario was that Rome and Spain would organize a new crusade against the Turks' increasing control of the Mediterranean. A mobilization of the Christian countries could serve as the pretext either for coercing a depleted Venice to join this costly crusade, or for using its refusal as an occasion to conquer it. In that case, Sarpi said, Venice might have to be saved by the Turks. He wrote his French friend, Groslot de l'Isle, "We may be in such straits that we have to recite the litany of Monsigneur de Bourges, 'Holy Turk, deliver us [*Sancte Turca, libera nos*].'"

It was in his private correspondence with the Protestants of northern countries that Sarpi did most of his political maneuvering. He told them to anticipate aggression from the Curia and the Hapsburgs, abetted by Jesuit schemers trying to carry the church back into Protestant territory. This correspondence, separately published in two volumes during the 1920s, revived debate over Sarpi's theology—was he really a Calvinist in disguise, as had been said during his lifetime?[2] This was a view that the pope's defenders took, in order to convict Sarpi of hypocrisy in pretending to defend the Catholic faith of Venice. Reformers, too, found it useful to treat Sarpi as one of their own, forced by fear of Rome to postpone a full break with Catholicism. But Federico Chabod makes a very strong case that Sarpi's motives in this correspondence were political, to muster support for Venice against future attacks by Rome.[3]

The Servite showed as little interest in the niceties of Lutheran debate over the mechanics of justification, or in Calvinist subtleties of predestination, as in the scholastic quibbles of Rome's theologians.[4] His was a pragmatic and scientific bent, with its piety fed by the particulars of Venetian religion, which he compared to the primitive church, humble and submissive to its Christian emperors. Sarpi was pious, as his friend and biographer assures us, just as other Giovani were—Donà and Contarini and the rest, inheritors of the indigenous reform energies of Gasparo Contarini and other pious and patriotic sons of Saint Mark.[5]

HISTORY OF THE COUNCIL OF TRENT (1619)

During this period, when he was writing things he could not publish, Sarpi let one thing be smuggled into print, under a feigned name, in an English translation—and it is the thing he is remembered for now, a landmark in historiography, and the one undisputed prose masterpiece of the Venetian Renaissance, his *History of the Council of Trent*. Sarpi was born in the seventh year of the sessions that made up that council. He was eleven when the council finally ended. His biographer says he was interested from his precocious youth in the Counter-Reformation launched from Trent, which shaped the religious environment of his formative years. Even as an eighteen-year-old in Mantua he sought out Camilo Olivo, who had been a delegate to the council, for information on its inner workings.[6] Later, in Rome, his friendship with Bellarmino helped him gain access to the papers of Marcello Cervini, the pope's principal agent in the opening sessions at Trent, and a man who later became pope himself (Marcellus II).[7]

The *History* was instantly translated into the major European languages, after its appearance in 1619, and its reputation increased over the next century, making it a favorite text of Enlightenment figures like Lord Bolingbroke and Samuel Johnson (who planned to retranslate it into more adequate English).[8] The work was praised for its learning, shapeliness, and quiet drama. At a time when controversy between Reformers and Catholics was waged with verbal battle-axes, with hyperbolic denunciation of the other side's alliance with various devils, Sarpi showed how much deadlier could be the rapier of understated wit and apparent gallantry toward a foe. He relied on irony to make his points. It was a lesson not lost on Edward Gibbon. Here, for instance, are some samples of Sarpi's "character" writing, brief personality sketches of some of the popes referred to in his tale.

> Inasmuch as Leo X was born and brought up in the aristocracy, he came to the papacy with an abundance of gifts, including deep acquaintance with the best classical authors, sweet courtesy in his dealings with others, a charm almost beyond human capacity, and a patronage of writers and artists not surpassed or even equaled in recent memory of his office. He would have been an ideal Pope had he added to these

gifts any knowledge of religious matters, or any feeling for them. But neither the former nor the latter concerned him at all.[9]

Clement VII passed out of this world, to the exceeding delight of his court [the Curia], which, precisely because it admired his virtues (his grand bearing, his exemplary stinginess, his dissimulation), held in greater contempt his greed, stubbornness, and cruelty, which either increased or became more obvious as illness wore him down.[10]

Paul III, a prelate distinguished for good attributes, treasured none of these virtues more than his ability to deceive others.[11]

Paul IV, for all his magnanimity and profundity, was convinced that he could solve any problem by the sole exercise of his authority as pontiff, nor did he think he needed the help of any temporal ruler, since he listened only to ambassadors who told him that he was superior to their masters, that he needed none of their company, that he could overthrow regimes.[12]

Despite these deft needlings, Sarpi usually keeps a straight face as he presents both sides of debates in the council, paraphrasing the major speeches for and against each topic taken up. This was an amazing achievement, since the record of debates at the council was not public. Sarpi had to draw his information from a vast range of correspondence by those who attended the Council, from memoirs of participants, from reports to the embassies of various countries that had representatives at it.[13] Though he was bound to pick up afterthoughts, especially from people whose positions had been defeated, he could discern from their protests what arguments they had succumbed to.

The resulting book is oddly bloodless, with only the slightest ironic glances at personalities or political events. It is one sustained intellectual battle, with the same forces engaging now on one issue, now on another, the arguments ranged in order with an air of apparent balance. The *History* has, in fact, been called a Renaissance dialogue strung out to heroic length. It has also been compared to a scientific report, the experimental Sarpi testing each thesis as it was attacked or defended, letting the results emerge from mere statement of the case from so many angles.[14] Though the Jesuit cardinal Pietro Pallavicino was assigned to refute Sarpi, using Roman records that had been sealed to the Servite, his book had a less "objective" air than the Venetian's. In terms of wide acceptance, Sarpi won the battle for interpreting the council. Not till the nineteenth century did the Vatican begin the only effective way of countering Sarpi, by opening the archives that would let scholars verify facts for themselves.

Sarpi prevailed by organizing the chaotic events of those two decades of ecclesiastical squabbling in terms of a continuing clash of three different parties. He called this struggle the modern *Iliad*, and he achieved an air of detachment, as of an Olympian looking down on battles, by tracing the ironies that baffled each combatant in turn.

> After a period of eighteen years, when it was sometimes meeting, sometimes dispersed (for various reasons), the council's outcome was exactly the opposite of what those who proposed it had desired and what those who strenuously opposed it had feared—a clear reason for surrendering one's expectations to God and not relying on human plans. This Council, desired and brought about by devout men in order to reunite a church that was beginning to come apart, deepened the divisions and hardened the adversaries, making their embattled positions irreconcilable:
>
> [1] Conducted by secular rulers to reform the church's conduct, it caused the greatest church misconduct since the Christian name came into use.
>
> [2] Hoped for by bishops as a way of reclaiming a collegial authority that had largely been monopolized by the Roman pontiff, it caused their total loss of that authority, reducing them to even greater servitude.
>
> [3] Feared and avoided by the Roman court [Curia] as a tool for checking its overgrown power (which from small beginnings had by various stages reached an uncontrolled excess), it in fact so stabilized and confirmed that excess (over those still subject to it) that it has become greater and better entrenched than ever.
>
> It would not be off the mark, then, to call this the *Iliad* of our era.[15]

What gives shape to the narrative is the persistent striving of the battle's three forces after what repeatedly eludes their grasp. These forces can be listed alliteratively (following Giovanni Getto's lead) as princes, prelates, and popes.[16] Though Sarpi interweaves their activities, it is best here to take them one by one.

1. *Princes.* This means mainly Charles V, the Hapsburg ruler of Spain, Naples, the Lowlands, and much of Germany—though Francis I of France hovered attentively, ready to seize what advantage he could from the procedures. Charles, who was the principal

promoter of the council, saw Martin Luther's revolt from Rome as a threat to the unity of his empire. In order to prevent the Germans from splitting away from his secular authority as well as from Rome's spiritual rule, he wanted to use the council as a means of reforming a corrupt Vatican, removing the grounds for Protestant revolt, and reintegrating the restive parts of his realm into the whole. He repeatedly tried to get Protestant enclaves to send representatives to the council, to voice their concerns directly—he even tried to coerce them after he won his war with the Schmalkalden League. But the Protestants were too wary to step onto the pope's turf, no matter what assurances Charles gave them.

2. *Prelates.* Bishops wanted some measures of reform, especially *reformatio capitis,* "reform of the head"—meaning the pope and his Curia. They resented the money siphoned from their dioceses by an avaricious papacy selling indulgences, granting benefices, giving ecclesiastical exemptions from local duties to those paying money to the Vatican. They also wanted to reclaim their power in councils to control the pope. This power had been confirmed when a council had to reform the papacy during the Great Schism: the Council of Constance (1414–1418) deposed the three rival popes of the schism and installed Martin V, after extracting from him a promise to call another council in five years. But when that council met at Pavia, Martin undermined its independence, and his successor, Eugenius IV, did the same with a council held at Basle from 1431 to 1437. In subsequent councils (Ferrara-Florence from 1438 to 1445, the Fifth Lateran from 1511 to 1517), the pope controlled the efforts of bishops to act independently of his instruction.[17] Despite these papal victories over efforts at conciliar action, the risk of holding a council was still considered great, since Roman pontiffs were in the position of monarchs in that era, who resisted the summoning of their parliaments.

3. *Popes.* Why, then, did Paul III agree with Charles V to call the Vatican Council? His predecessor, Clement VII, had lost a war with Charles, whose troops sacked Rome in 1527 and imprisoned the pope. Paul needed to placate Charles in order to hold his own territories. Besides, he thought he could control the council if it met within his government's borders. Rome was out of the question—Charles would not accept that, since he still hoped to lure Protestants to the meeting—but Paul maintained that a northern Italian site like Bologna would be acceptable. It was not. Charles insisted on a German site, so Trent, in an Alpine pass just over the Italian border, was chosen. Even so, the pope sent his legates to Trent with a secret authorization to move the council

back to Italy if any plausible pretext for doing so arose—as in fact happened when plague was alleged to be menacing Trent. The papal delegates used this occasion to transfer the council to Bologna after all. But Charles's representatives, plague or no plague, stayed in Trent, where the others were forced to return in time.

Charles wanted the council to be a reform council, attacking church corruption. To blunt that effort, Paul wanted to turn it into a dogmatic council, to condemn the heresies of Luther and the other reformers. Charles planned to regather the rebels; Paul planned to thrust them farther off. Since Charles was absent on his wars and other projects, Paul's active legates prevailed in a long attritive struggle, baffling the last remaining hope of healing the rift within the Christian churches. Sarpi presents the pope's efforts to rig the council as almost entirely successful (despite Paul's own efforts to abort the process that was unexpectedly helping him). Modern historians realize that the process was not as simple as that.

For one thing, the papal legates were not entirely in charge of the council, and were not merely puppets of the pope. In terms used of later councils, we can call the pope's three cardinal-legates, who presided over the council, a conservative (Giovanni Maria del Monte), a liberal (Reginald Pole), and a pragmatist (Marcello Cervini). Del Monte would gladly have given the pope anything he wanted, but he was not effective with the fathers of the council, and the pope knew that. Pole was a reformer of the emperor's type, but he was too modest and retiring to steer things with energy. Cervini, trusted by the pope, realized that he could not prevail unless he persuaded the bishops to go along with him. Attempts to force them would drive neutrals into the camp of the imperial minority of bishops sent by Charles.

A pattern that would recur was established in the first fight of the council, over which agenda to take up first, the emperor's emphasis on reform, or the pope's concern with dogma. Cervini wrestled a compromise through the body of debaters—parallel discussion of both items, so that each decree in one area would be matched with one in the other. The pope was unhappy with this, but finally accepted it, as the best bargain he could get until he succeeded in transferring the council back to his realm.[18]

Sarpi also simplifies the position of the bishops (with whom he sympathized). Though they were ardent for *reformatio capitis*, they were in varying degrees sluggish about reform of the body of the church (*reformatio membrorum*), which included their own deficiencies—absenteeism, retention of plural sees, neglect of clergy training, refusal to take seriously their own teaching and preaching duties. Sarpi misrepresents, as well, the role of religious orders at the council. The generals of five mendicant orders and the abbots of major monasteries each had a vote in the council, and Paul sent Jesuits as his personal representatives. Sarpi, who hated the Jesuits, sees in the religious orders mere papal minions attacking the bishops. They were, in fact, a separate force.

Bishops resented the intrusion of the preaching orders into their domain—the Dominicans and Franciscans drew attendance, prestige, and money away from cathedrals and parish churches, since the friars were not directly subordinate to diocesan authority but to the Roman Curia's commissions on religious orders. Still, the mendicant orders had reformed themselves in many cases, and the new order, the Jesuits, had allied itself with reforming bishops like Charles Borromeo. So, though the religious orders supported the pope at the council, they put reform pressures on the bishops to reclaim their dioceses by residence, single sees, and renewed preaching disciplines in the parishes.

In one area, Sarpi comes across as disinterested and fair—the description of esoteric points of doctrine like the nature of grace and free will. Since he thought both sides equally fanciful, he could present their arguments fairly—as opposed to the arguments over practical reforms, about which he cared deeply. Of course, this had the eventual effect of trivializing the doctrinal debates. At times, his straight face broke into a restrained smile. Faced with the question "Does the will's primary goal act upon it, or does the will act upon the goal, or do both act on each other while being acted on reciprocally?" he could not resist adding: "Some wiseacres said that if astronomers, ignorant of what really moved the celestial bodies, had to introduce eccentric and epicyclic motions to save the phenomena, it was no wonder that those trying to save the phenomena of higher than celestial movements had to introduce eccentric ways of thinking."[19]

Despite the agreement to channel discussion of dogma and of reform on parallel tracks, they continually intersected. The question of bishops' absenteeism, for instance, presented itself at first as a straight matter of church discipline. But those arguing for episcopal residence buttressed their view with arguments that the bishops' authority comes directly from God—and the papal camp saw this as whittling away at the pope's authority, so the question became dogmatic: How does God impart power to the church? Similarly, the advisability of allowing vernacular translations of the Bible would seem a matter of church government, but defenders of Jerome's Latin translation (the Vulgate) argued that the translation was as inspired as the originals in Hebrew and Greek—otherwise God would not have allowed the Vulgate to be used by the church for so many centuries. The whole theology of inspiration was thus opened up. Others said that if the translator was not directly inspired, the council would be when it declared the translation inerrant.[20]

Sarpi observes such twists and turns with a wryly documentary air. His methodical observation even follows the process by which people on one side end up arguing in the terms used by the other side—as when the advocates of episcopal residency began to say this would actually *strengthen* the pope's authority, while the pope's men began to *defend* residency on grounds other than God's direct grant of their authority: "Neither the one side nor the other could argue on such grounds without letting their disingenuousness show, making clear the very goals they tried to hide. Everyone was wearing a mask, and everyone knew."[21]

If Sarpi agreed much of the time with the bishops, he agreed most of the time with the emperor, faulting him only for not being more energetic in his interventions. So it is no wonder that he (like the imperial delegates in general) looked with great suspicion on the fear of plague that let Paul's legates move the council back to Italian soil:

> Several of the bishops' attendants were conveniently sick at this time, either from overindulgence at Carnival [this was early Lent] or from an oppressive humidity that had lasted for many days. Del Monte had some of his aides inquire whether this illness could be contagious. Doctors, who always warn against the worst—if they turn out right, they are wise; if wrong, they are even wiser, since they take credit for cures and precautions—gave an ambiguous diagnosis, which was artfully represented; so that, taken up by the panicky, it spread to the credulous masses and to those who, already desirous of leaving, wished it to be true.[22]

No one would go to Sarpi, now, for the best historical judgment on Trent. Expectations were not as universally baffled as he made out in his exquisitely symmetrical account. Real reforms occurred, but at the price of deepening enmities. Perhaps the only way to begin rooting out deep defects in the Roman system was by mobilizing this as a means of resisting Protestant criticism. This may be an irony beyond even Sarpi's skeptical gifts—that reform was achieved out of hatred for Reformers. But Sarpi's book lives, nonetheless. The eighteenth century read it as a study in the psychology of error in retreat. For the purposes of this book, Sarpi's masterpiece should be recognized as the last grand statement of the myth of Venice.

It will surprise no one that the *History* is a kind of veiled replay of the Interdict crisis, with the Emperor Charles in the role of Doge Leonardo, the bishops at Trent acting as loyal prelates did in Venice under the Interdict. And the pope? He was, of course, the pope in each case. The view of the primitively virtuous church presented in the *History* confirms the Constantinian right of the state to rule its clergy, as it did before the rise of the papacy. That is not a position that will appeal to a modern audience, which fears totalist states more than grasping churches. If asked how secular power should be checked, Sarpi would not have allowed that the church should do it. He believed, instead, in the distributions of power that the Venetians achieved when they splintered government into a cluster of overlapping and mutually investigative committees, presided over by the doge as a symbol of unity—a unity more convincing to Sarpi than the pope's claim to unite all of human society in and under his office. The myth of Venice inspired many great works of art—not the least of which was the last great one, Sarpi's defense of the religion of empire in his *History of the Council of Trent*.

A Farewell to Empire

*I*T IS HARD FOR a modern liberal to admire Venice in her time of greatness. It was, above all, an imperial time—and empires prey on others. They exploit different cultures for the benefit of their own. No better example of this exists than the act that established Venice's empire as a major international force—the use of the Fourth Crusade as an excuse to capture Christian Constantinople and to absorb three-quarters of *its* empire, including the best parts (like Crete). Many of the most characteristic artifacts and relics around which Venetian identity congealed were taken from Constantinople in 1204.

The fragility of the empire, with its improbable base—a comparatively small population sealed up in a lagoon—called up the ruthlessness of people who felt they were fighting for their lives. The admirable discipline of the city was militaristic. Should we feel relieved, then, that the city lost its power to harm, when its empire shrank with the expansion of Turkish power into the Mediterranean and the shift of trade to the Atlantic? Moralists might urge us to feel content with that outcome, but it is hard not to look with sorrow at the fading of so splendid a thing—as people know who regret the decline and defeat of Athens, which was clearly just as ruthless and exploitative as Venice (and more deeply mired in slavery).

Does that mean we are willing to trade human suffering for great works of art? Empires, with their control of resources, including the resource of human talent, often do create cultivated forms of life. The Roman empire gave us the Augustan age. Because of such cultural achievement, imperialists say that they prevail by being superior in civilization as well as in power. And it is sometimes true that any sufferings they inflict were being inflicted already. It is not as if the imperialists imposed themselves on a pristine and pacific world. Modern imperialism gets its bad name because it takes away from colonized nations the right to self-determination. But the self-determining nation-state rarely existed in the past. Trading one monarch for another, or one code of law for a scramble of feuding ethnic groups, is not always a bad trade. The Roman empire had that to recommend it. But the danger in this approach is that it is always easy for an imperial power to justify its exploitation in terms of what the French called their "civilizing mission." Kipling called it the white man's burden. Hitler was bringing superior Aryan values to the world. Stalin was bringing it the blessings of communism.

Venice poses a special problem for Americans, since we sometimes criticize ourselves, or feel uneasy about, what has been called our "exceptionalism"—the belief that we are better than other nations, specially blessed, with a right to do things forbidden to lesser peoples. If that strain ever did exist in our history, it is infinitesimal next to the Venetian sense of superiority to other human beings. The whole myth of Venice is simply exceptionalism writ large. According to it, Venetians were the favorites of Christ, Mary, and Saint Mark. Their city's birth was miraculous. Their doge was a spiritual leader better than the clerics who conducted religious services elsewhere, and a temporal leader better than the monarchs who ruled elsewhere. He stood above popes and emperors—though not above the republic he served. That myth would become harder and harder to sustain as the empire fell away—Cyprus lost in the sixteenth century, then Crete in the seventeenth. Bravado tried to cover this decline with Baroque swagger, but the trappings of power call themselves in question when the reality of power is going or gone.

There was one tempering element to the Venetian exceptionalism: at least it did think of itself as the exception among nations, not as a model for them. It had no missionary sense that it should spread its values to other people. Americans believed that we should not be an exception but a pattern. Others should emulate us. Our man from the North, John Winthrop, said it in 1630: "He [God] shall make us a praise and glory, that men shall say of succeeding plantations, 'The Lord make it like that of New England.' For we must consider that we shall be a city upon a hill . . . "[1] Our man from the South, Thomas Jefferson, said it in 1801, calling America "the world's best hope."[2] Our man from the then-West, Abraham Lincoln, said it in 1854: "The succeeding millions of free happy people, the world over, shall rise up and call us blessed to the latest generation."[3]

Though Venice praised republicanism in general, a sense of its unique birth and circumstances meant that it never seriously thought there could be other Venices. It had this virtue in its megalomania, that it was not a redeemer nation, not a savior of others, only of itself. It was not out to convert or crusade, only to trade. It joined Crusades, for what was in it for Venice, but it could always strike a deal with the other side. Its very worldliness made it tolerant of anyone who could offer a market. Venice had no *libido dominandi*, only a *libido vendendi*, a vendor's compulsion. This freed it from a lot of pious bullying in the Kipling vein. If Venice dominated its imperial holdings, this was done only so far as domination could be made profitable. People's souls were left alone as the merchants of the Rialto went after their purses.

The Venetian air of separateness was not racially based. Though its Serrata "locked in" a small group of the pure-born, this was not a racial category but an administrative convenience, and those outside the magic circle were not genetically inferior, or even different. The city did not have the Athenian attitude toward others as lesser breeds, as *bàrbaroi*. There was no Venetian Aristotle to quote Euripides' line, "It is the norm for Greeks to rule barbarians," and add: "This means the barbarian is by nature a slave."[4] Though there was some slavery in Venice, and much slave trading in its empire, the slave was not a defective human. As a captive in war, anyone, given bad luck in battle, could become a slave. It was an equal-opportunity affliction.

Venice was not kept by moral qualms from massive dependence on slaves. As with most of their cultural patterns, the explanation was economic. Slaves were just not very useful to them. They did not, like Athenians, have silver veins to be mined by slaves. They did not, like the Romans or the Turks, have galleys in need of them for rowers. They did not, like Czarist Russia or antebellum America, have fields to be worked by them. Venetian guilds largely reserved labor for their own members.

Imperial Venice is not easy for modern people to understand, given our moral categories. It was not only extremely worldly but extremely religious. It was religious about being worldly. Saint Mark would not only rescue but reward Venice. It is characteristic of our own limits that we find it hard to see in a man like Paolo Sarpi the genuine union of religion and worldliness—we believe that when the latter invokes the former, it must be doing so insincerely. To think otherwise would be to defy not only the Christian claim that money is the root of all evil (I Tim. 6.19) but the classical Roman belief that affluence (*luxuria*) is the necessary enemy of virtue. Both these strains of thought united in Ruskin, making him unable to understand the most basic elements of Venetian history. He endlessly measured its buildings and described their setting, but its ethos was a total mystery to him. He kept trying to make the city fit his a priori certainty that religion must recede as worldly values prevail. For him, the empire fell because of a preceding moral failure.

In point of fact, the opposite is true. The loss of empire was more a cause than the effect of moral decline. It was the empire that instilled in Venetians their sense of common purpose, their confidence in divine guidance, their discipline of moral responsibility, their use of learning as a civic achievement. It was only when these energies were blocked, unstringing the nerves of state, that Venice became known as the world capital of frivolity—a reputation exaggerated, no doubt, but with a certain purchase on the truth. Sometimes, it seems, powerlessness may tend to corrupt, and absolute powerlessness, if that were attainable, could corrupt absolutely.

Lisa Jardine may help us understand the paradox of worldliness as a possible *opposite* of corruption, not its necessary cause or concomitant. In her book, *Worldly Goods*, she argues that the Renaissance broadened people's minds, increased their tolerance, taught them respect for other cultures, precisely by means of its trade in worldly goods from other places. Liberation, that is, was venality's unintended side effect. She seems not to realize that she is echoing Hume's "heretical" praise of *luxuria* as a civilizing and animating force, not a debilitating one.[5] She gives us a neat reversal of the puritan ethic that was supposed to undergird capitalism with asceticism. Call it the impuritan ethic.

> The world we inhabit today, with its ruthless competitiveness, fierce consumerism, restless desire for ever wider horizons, for travel, discovery, and innovation, a world hemmed in by the small-mindedness of petty nationalism and religious bigotry but refusing to bow to it, is a world which was made in the Renaissance.[6]

Whatever qualifications one might have to make of that as a verdict on the Renaissance in general, it sounds like a detailed description of the Venetian empire. So does Hume's claim that trade and industry promote "sociability."[7] In fact, the transition from imperial to postimperial Venice could not be better stated than in Hume's description of commercial failure in a state:

> In times when industry and the arts flourish, men are kept in perpetual occupation, and enjoy as their reward the occupation itself, as well as those pleasures which are the fruit of their labor. The mind acquires new vigor, enlarges its powers and faculties, and by an assiduity in honest industry, both satisfies its natural appetites, and prevents the growth of unnatural ones, which commonly spring up when nourished by ease and idleness. Banish those arts from society, you deprive men both of action and of pleasure; and leaving nothing but indolence in their place, you even destroy the

relish of indolence, which never is agreeable but when it succeeds to labor and recruits the spirits exhausted by too much application and fatigue.[8]

Venice built on its exceptionalism a paradoxical cosmopolitanism. Its empire had its victims, who should never be forgotten. But there is no calculus for balancing in Ruskin's moral ledger all the rights and wrongs of a complex human transaction like the history of Venice. Many of the city's moral claims were bogus. It was not even a republic, but an oligarchy. Yet the Florentine or Sienese republics, which had their own oligarchical aspects, did not last as long. Venice's was not an ideal state. It was just better than most of those around it—better able to sustain, over a long period, whatever ideals it had. It was ruthless, but was it more ruthless than the pious Emperor Charles V? It was worldly, but was it more worldly than the court of Pope Julius II? The imperial Venetians were not moral paragons, but they certainly were splendid achievers. The traces of their high accomplishments are discernible still in the record left behind them—in stone and pigment and glass and print. Perhaps the best that can be said for them, in all these forms, they said themselves.

Notes

INTRODUCTION, ATHENS OF THE RENAISSANCE

1. Italian text at Margaret F. Rosenthal, *The Honest Courtesan: Veronica Franco, Citizen and Writer in Sixteenth-Century Venice* (University of Chicago Press, 1992), p. 63.

2. Ruskin's views on Venice were spectacularly incoherent. While attacking the Renaissance as a great corrupter of the city, he admired extravagantly some of its leading painters—"John Bellini" (as he always called him), Veronese, Tintoretto.

3. Otto Demus, *The Church of San Marco in Venice* (Dumbarton Oaks, Harvard University Press, 1960), p. 20.

4. When Athenians had manpower shortages, they hired foreigners rather than use galley slaves. Lionel Casson, *Ships and Seamanship in the Ancient World* (Johns Hopkins, 1995), pp. 322–38. The Venetians had no slaves at the oars during their rise and early dominance (L 366–67). They had reluctantly to bring convicts to the task only when their power was declining (McN 282–83).

5. Aristotle, *Politics*, 1304 a22 (*nautikos ochlos*—a rower was a *nautēs*).

6. Vincent Gabrielson, *Financing the Athenian Fleet* (Johns Hopkins, 1994), pp. 106–7.

7. Thucydides, *The Peloponnesian War*, 2.63.

8. Ibid., 1.70.

9. Dennis Romano, *Patricians and Popolani: The Social Foundations of the Venetian Renaissance State* (Johns Hopkins, 1987), p. 134.

10. Karl Wittfogel, *Oriental Despotism: A Comparative Study of Total Power* (Vintage Books, 1981), pp. 12, 263.

11. Demus, op. cit., p. 45.

12. Ibid., pp. 19–20.

1. CONTRACT WITH MARK

1. Bianca Maria Scarfi, *Il leone di Venezia* (Albrizzi Editore, 1990), pp. 79–113.

2. The earliest form of this lion image had it holding the *closed* gospel of Mark in *both* its paws. See Giandomenico Romanelli, "Tamquam Leo Rugiens," in Scarfi, ibid., pp. 216–20 and the picture on p. 126.

3. Scarfi, op. cit., pp. 107–9. The lion originally carried on its back a standing statue of Sandon, the tutelary god of Tarsus in Cilicia (modern Turkey). Turkish Christians removed the lion's wings and horns to give it a new religious meaning (perhaps as "the lion of Judah")—religious significance alone kept it from being melted down. When Venetians seized it from Turkey in the twelfth century, they restored wings to it, making it a symbol of Mark.

4. Otto Demus, *The Church of San Marco in Venice* (Dumbarton Oaks, 1960), p. 20.

5. Anthony Hecht, "Venetian Vespers," in *Collected Earlier Poems* (Alfred A. Knopf, 1990), p. 231.

6. Patrick J. Geary, *Furta Sacra: Theft of Relics in the Central Middle Ages* (Princeton University Press, 1978), p. 89.

7. Demus, op. cit., p. 21.

8. Guido Tigler, "Le fonti teologiche del programma negli anconi del Portale Maggiore," in Bruno Bertoli, ed., *La basilica di San Marco: Arte e simbologia* (Studium Cattolico Veneziano, 1993), pp. 151–53.

9. Michael Jacoff, *The Horses of San Marco and the Quadriga of the Lord* (Princeton University Press, 1993), pp. 26–30.

10. Terisio Pignatti, "The Triumph of Christ," in Francesco Valcanover et al., *Titian, Prince of Painters* (Prestel, 1990), pp. 156–59.

2. DECLARATIONS OF INDEPENDENCE

1. Patricia Fortini Brown, *Venice and Antiquity* (Yale University Press, 1996). Irene Favaretto, "Arte antica e cultura antiquaria nelle collezioni venete al tempo della Serenissima," *L'Erma*, 1990.

2. Sarah Wilk, *The Sculpture of Tullio Lombardo: Studies in Sources and Meaning* (Garland Publishing, 1978), p. 46.

3. Diana Norman, *Siena and the Virgin* (Yale University Press, 1999), p. 3. The city was pledging fealty in gratitude for its 1260 victory at the battle of Montaperti.

4. Muir points out that the candle actually carried in ducal processions had a less honorable origin in fact (M 109).

5. Terisio Pignatti, in Umberto Franzoi et al., *Il palazzo ducale di Venezia* (Canova, 1990), pp. 233–42.

6. For a summary of what is known about the lost cycle, see ibid., pp. 247–56.

7. This painting, by Girolamo Gambarato, is thought to reflect the work of Giovanni Bellini that it replaced. The other paintings are worth a stroll down their range along the north wall of the council hall, if only to see how the legend of the Pact is reasserted. A summary of the information about them is in Wolfgang Wolters, *Storia e politica nei dipinti del Palazzo Ducale* (Arsenale Editrice, 1983), pp. 171–78:

   1) *Doge Ziani Greets Pope Alexander Disguised as a Monk*, by Carlo and Gabriele Caliari (sons of Veronese), with a good view of the Convent of the Carità.

   2) *Venetian Ambassadors Make Offer to Frederick Barbarossa*, by Credi di Paolo, based perhaps on a composition by Veronese.

   3) *The Pope Gives the Candle to the Doge*, by Leonardo Bassano. Doge Ziani is given the features of the doge ruling at the time the picture was painted, Marino Grimani.

   4) *Frederick Receives the Ambassadors at Pavia*, by Jacopo Tintoretto and assistants. The ambassadors are haloed by the niche behind them, containing a statue of Peace.

   5) *The Pope Gives the Sword to the Doge*, by Francesco Bassano. A strong composition in which the verticals—the admiral's lamp on the boat, the pillar with Mark's lion, the Campanile—mount upward to the left, while the foreshortened Doge's Palace comes forward on the right. The pope is taking the fleet out to capture Otto, Frederick's son.

   6) *The Pope Blesses the Fleet*, by Paolo Fiammingo.

   7) *Otto Captured at the Battle of Punta Salvore*, by Domenico Tintoretto. The quiet submission of the doge in the bow of the boat may reflect a composition from Giovanni Bellini's original painting of the scene.

   8) *The Pope Gives the Ring to the Doge*, by Andrea Vicentino. There are portraits of unidentified contemporaries among the bystanders.

9) *Otto Sent by His Father to Request Peace from the Doge*, by Palma Giovane. The statues behind Otto and the doge are of Peace and Abundance, the gifts of Venice to the emperor, who is thus in the republic's debt.

10) *The Pope Puts His Foot on Frederick's Neck*, by Federico Zuccari. The submission is made in a special pavilion erected before the façade of San Marco, with a view of the lion pillar and San Marco in the background. Zuccari's original sketch had the emperor kissing the pope's foot, but the finished picture shows him submitting *to the doge* while being humiliated by the pope.

11) *The Pope Gives the Umbrella to the Doge*, by Girolamo Gambarato.

12) *The Doge Thanks the Pope*, by Giulio Agnolo, known as Dal Moro. This picture was supposed to contain the other gifts of the pope, but how to show them all apparently defeated the skill of Dal Moro.

8. David Wootton, *Paolo Sarpi: Between Renaissance and Enlightenment* (Cambridge University Press, 1983), p. 53.

3. THE LION'S WINGS

1. There is a drawing of a lion with the same grin, presumably taken from the bronze lion, in Jacopo Bellini's Louvre sketchbook: Colin Eisler, *The Genius of Jacopo Bellini* (Harry N. Abrams, 1989), p. 83.

2. D. S. Chambers, *The Imperial Age of Venice, 1380–1580* (Thames and Hudson, 1970), p. 128.

3. Mark Twain, *Innocents Abroad* (Oxford University Press, 1996), pp. 228–29.

4. Rugiero Romano, "Economic Aspects of the Construction of Warships in Venice in the Sixteenth Century," in Brian Pullan, ed., *Crisis and Change in the Venetian Economy in the Sixteenth and Seventeenth Centuries* (Methuen, 1968), pp. 60–61.

5. Ibid., p. 62.

6. Frederic C. Lane, *Venetian Ships and Shipbuilders of the Renaissance* (Johns Hopkins Press, 1934), p. 193.

7. Ibid., p. 185.

8. Ibid., p. 186.

9. Ibid., p. 189.

10. Romano, op. cit., p. 59.

11. Lane, op. cit., p. 193.

12. For the paintings, executed after the fire of 1577, see Wolfgang Wolters, *Storia e politica nei dipinte del Palazzo Ducale* (Arsenale Editrice, 1983), pp. 179–85. The eight are these:

1) *Crusaders Take the Cross in San Marco*, by Giovanni Leclerc (replacing the treatment of this scene by Domenico Tintoretto after it was damaged by humidity). Dandolo, the blind doge, is in the polygonal pulpit near the choir screen of the basilica, inspired by his mission and oblivious to the scramble of departure below him (which includes a dog whose barking protest is beaten into silence—an apparent symbol of the breaking of ties as the men depart for the crusade).

2) *Conquest of Zara*, by Andrea Vicentino. This tributary city was retaken en route to Constantinople in order to help finance the expedition.

3) *The Keys of Zara Surrendered to Doge Dandolo*, by Domenico Tintoretto.

4) *Alexius IV Pleads for Doge Dandolo's Aid in Assuming His Throne*, by Andrea Vicentino.

5) *Threatened Siege of Constantinople*, by the Younger Palma.

6) *Successful Siege of Constantinople*, by Domenico Tintoretto.

7) *Baldovino of Flanders Elected (Frankish) Emperor of Constantinople*, by Andrea Vicentino.

8) *Coronation of Baldovino*, by Aliense (Antonio Vasilacchi).

13. John Julius Norwich, *A History of Venice* (Vintage Books, 1989), p. 255.

14. Fernand Braudel, *The Mediterranean and the Mediterranean World in the Age of Philip II*, translated by Sian Reynolds (Collins, 1973), Vol. 2, pp. 1089–1142.

15. Iain Fenlon, "Lepanto: Le arti della celebrazione nella Venezia del Rinascimento," in Vittore Branca and Carlo Ossola, eds., *Crisi e rinnovamenti nell'autunno del Rinascimento a Venezia* (Civiltà veneziana. Saggi 38, Olschki, 1991), p. 375.

16. Johann Wolfgang von Goethe, *Italian Journey, 1786–1788*, translated by W. H. Auden and Elizabeth Mayer (North Point Press, 1982), pp. 76–77. Goethe was impressed by the doge (Paolo Renier) who, though old and ill, "holds himself, for the sake of dignity, erect under his heavy gown."

17. Fenlon, op. cit., p. 392. When the fire occurred in 1867, Titian's most famous painting, the *Death of [Dominican] Saint Peter Martyr* (W 1.153–55) was there in temporary storage after being returned from Paris, where Napoleon had taken it. That work perished along with Tintoretto's Lepanto painting and Giovanni Bellini's *Madonna and Child* from the Scuola di Sant'Orsola. In the restored chapel that now exists, Veronese's Marian paintings from the ceiling of the Umiltà have been installed.

18. Among the other tributes to Saint Justine are two more works by Tintoretto—one that shows the city's treasurers being blessed by her for their financing of the fleet (PR 2.218), and another commissioned by Francesco Duodo, one of the fleet commanders, who had a picture of Justine with his own name-saint, Francesco di Paola, painted for the Church of Santa Maria del Giglio.

4. THE LION'S TREAD

1. Andrew Butterfield, *The Sculptures of Andrea del Verochhio* (Yale University Press, 1997), pp. 179–82.

2. Ibid., p. 173.

3. Ibid., p. 170.

4. Christine Shaw, *Julius II, The Warrior Pope* (Blackwell, 1993), p. 125: "Hostility to Venice, and the obsessive urge to recover the territory that she had taken from the Church, would be the fulcrum of his policy for the first six years of his reign."

5. A less serene Loredan is shown on his tomb in the sanctuary of the Church of Saints John and Paul, where his statue, by Girolamo Campagna, shows the doge rising from his chair to face the crisis represented by allegorical statues, on either side of him, of Venice and the League of Cambrai.

6. Rona Goffen, *Giovanni Bellini* (Yale University Press, 1989), pp. 208–9.

7. Umberto Franzoi and Dina Di Stefano, *Le chiese di Venezia* (Azienda Autonoma Soggiorno Turismo-Venezia, 1975), p. 423.

8. For "Titian's often-cited borrowing for the Gritti portraits of the massive hand in Michelangelo's Moses," see David Alan Brown, in Francesco Valcanover et al., *Titian, Prince of Painters* (Prestel, 1990), p. 254.

9. J. R. Hale, *The Military Organization of a Renaissance State* (Cambridge University Press, 1984), pp. 441–42.

10. Tintoretto treated the Marsyas myth three times (PR 2.1134–35, 139–40, 143–44). More important, because more public, was the myth's representation in the relief above Apollo's statue on Sansovino's

Loggetta in the Piazzetta. For other Venetian uses of the myth—by Bonifazio dei Pitati and Paris Bordon—see Edith Wyss, *The Myth of Apollo and Marsyas in the Art of the Italian Renaissance* (University of Delaware Press, 1996), pp. 113–19.

11. Poem 33 in the Saslow edition: James M. Saslow, *The Poetry of Michelangelo* (Yale University Press, 1991), p. 111.

12. Ibid., poems 51 and 94 (pp. 135, 219).

13. The skin on which the torso is seated was supposed for a long time to be Hercules' lion skin; but it is now recognized as the leopard skin of the Phrygian Marsyas. Gösta Säflund, by a study of the dowel holes in the torso, demonstrated that the figure had its arms bound behind it. Michelangelo's echoes of the fragment in his own paintings often involve twisting the arms behind his figures. Michelangelo's friend Vasari recognized the Marsyas myth on the Medici medallion, so Michelangelo, too, would have seen what it represented. Gösta Säflund, "The Belvedere Torso: An Interpretation," *Opuscula Romana* 10 (1975), pp. 63–83.

5. DISCIPLINES OF TIME

1. Priuli quoted by Alberto Tenenti, "The Sense of Space and Time in the Venetian World of the Fifteenth and Sixteenth Centuries," in J. R. Hale, *Renaissance Venice* (Faber and Faber, 1973), p. 33. In less optimistic mood, Priuli predicted the end of the republic.

2. Logan Pearsall Smith, *The Life and Letters of Sir Henry Wotton* (Oxford University Press, 1907), vol. I, p. 55.

3. Frederic C. Lane, "Double Entry Bookkeeping and Resident Merchants," in *Studies in Venetian Social and Economic History* (Variorum Reprints, 1987), vol. IV, pp. 177–91.

4. Otto Demus, *Le sculture esterne di San Marco* (Electa, 1995), p. 19.

5. The planets and their houses are depicted this way:

   1) Saturn, a seated old man with a piercing gaze who pours water from a large ornamental pitcher (Aquarius).

   2) Jupiter, a seated man in a merchant's drooping cap. The fish of Pisces are on his right, but he holds up a wand in his left hand as if directing the aim of the bowman to his left (Sagittarius).

   3) Mars, a standing warrior, with the sign of Aries on his right side and of Scorpio on his left.

   4) Sun, seated on a lion (Leo), holding up his own disk, but rays emanate from his head, not from the disk.

   5) Venus, throned on a bull (Taurus), looking at herself in a mirror.

   6) Mercury, seated as he reads a book out loud to three children, a girl on his right (Virgo) and two boys on his left (Gemini).

   7) Moon, standing in a boat, with her own crescent in her right hand, her left hand drawing a crab (Cancer) from the water.

6. John Ruskin, *The Stones of Venice, Volume II: The Sea Stories*, in *The Works of John Ruskin* (George Allen, 1904), vol. 10, p. 416.

7. Charles de Tolnay, "Tintoretto's *Allegories of the Seasons* and Giorgione's *Three Philosophers*," *Scritti di storia dell'arte in onore di Mario Salmi* (De Luca Editore, 1963), vol. 3, pp. 117–31. I reverse De Tolnay's assignment of Summer and Autumn, for reasons given in the text.

8. Andrew John Martin, "The Origin of the Milky Way," in Bernard Aikema and Beverly Louise Brown, eds., *Renaissance Venice and the North* (Rizzoli, 2000), p. 628.

9. De Tolnay, op. cit., p. 122.

10. For the Platonic reading, see Peter Meller, "I *Tre Filosofi* di Giorgione," in Rodolfo Palluchini, *Giorgione e l'umanesimo veneziano* (Civiltà veneziana. Saggi 27, Olschki, 1981), pp. 234–47.

11. Erwin Panofsky, *Meaning in the Visual Arts* (University of Chicago Press, 1955), pp. 146–48.

6. DISCIPLINES OF WORK

1. Otto Demus, *The Church of San Marco in Venice* (Dumbarton Oaks, Harvard University Press, 1960), pp. 117–18.

2. Antonio Manno, *I mestieri di Venezia* (Biblos, 1997), pp. 58–61. This capital is on the column nearest the corner sculpture of the Fall of Man, on the Piazzetta side.

3. Antonio Manno, *Palazzo Ducale: I Capitelli* (Canal e Stamperia Editrice, 1996), p. 43.

4. John Ruskin, *The Stones of Venice, III: The Sea-Stories*, in *Works* (George Allen, 1904), vol. 10, pp. 416–17.

5. Elisabeth Crouzet-Pavan, *La mort lente de Torcello* (Fayard, 1995), pp. 203–49.

6. Manno, *Mestieri*, pp. 39–43.

7. Demus, op. cit., p. 161.

7. DOGE

1. Rodolfo Gallo, *Il tesoro di S. Marco* (Istituto per la collaborazione culturale Venezia-Roma, 1967), pp. 193–98.

2. Solon 22 (Diehl), Aeschines 1.23 and 3.2, 4.

3. Demosthenes 54.1, 58.1, Lysias 7.29, 16, 20.

4. Scott Gordon, *Controlling the State: Constitutionalism from Ancient Athens to Today* (Harvard University Press, 1999), p. 141.

5. Kenneth Hempel, "A Technical Report on the Condition of the Porta della Carta and its Restoration by the Venice in Peril Fund," in S. Romano, *The Restoration of the Porta della Carta* (Venice, 1980).

6. Debra Pincus, *The Arco Foscari: The Building of a Triumphal Gateway in Fifteenth Century Venice* (Garland Publishing, 1976), pp. 246–48, 400.

7. For the attributes and appropriateness of the three archangels—Raphael, Gabriel, and Michael—see S-L 167–75.

8. The group is so brilliant that there has been vigorous debate about the artist good enough to have executed it. Some favor Bartolemeo Bon himself (WW 1.287-88), while others prefer Jacopo della Quercia (EA 20-52), though Pope-Hennessy says that Della Quercia is "the single attribution that is totally untenable." Pope-Hennessy suggests Nanni di Bartolo, working under the supervision of Bon (P-H 1.276).

9. Pincus, op. cit., pp. 232–48.

10. Pincus (op. cit., pp. 384–400) thinks this doge-lion pairing (now missing, torn down at the same time as the one on the Porta della Carta) was the original of this pattern, later copied on the Porta della Carta and on the side wall of the Arco Foscari—but it is hard to see why Foscari would have been celebrated on the Porta years after his death, given the disgraceful end of his reign.

11. It is hard to read the expression of Adam's face, since it was damaged and clumsily restored—though the open mouth and eyes and the upward angle say a great deal. Pincus, op. cit., p. 305.

12. For the friendship with (and influence of) Antonello, see Michelangelo Muraro, "La scala senza giganti," in *De artibus opuscula XL: Essays in Honor of Erwin Panofsky* (Princeton University Press, 1961), pp. 357–58, 368. For effects of aerial perspective on the stair complex, see SMR p. 113, and Muraro (p. 368) on Rizzo's Giorgionesque "shadowiness" (*sfumatura*).

13. Muraro, op. cit., pp. 365–66.

14. Muraro, op. cit., passim.

15. Muraro, op. cit., p. 361.

16. Muraro, op. cit., p. 352.

17. Muraro, op. cit., pp. 367–68.

18. There is a summary of the long tradition of aesthetic dismissal of the statues at BB 1.340. But Pope-Hennessy thinks Sansovino did not realize the statues would be placed where they are, and did not intend them for viewing in the round (P-H 3.243).

19. Muraro, op. cit., p. 368.

20. It might be questioned how the Loggetta could show an intention of lowering the prestige of the doge by raising that of the patricians, since it was a doge, Andrea Gritti, who worked closely with Sansovino on the Piazzetta's refashioning. But Gritti knew that restoration of confidence in the ruling class demanded from him a "showy humility" (see Chapter 24). And besides, Manfredo Tafuri, who has been the leading exponent of Gritti's "urban rebirth" program, admits that "A study of the Gritti era makes sense only if it can find in the events of the 1520s and 1530s a chain of processes with interconnected causation, one long in preparation. It must take account of actual realignments brought about by new influences applied to tendencies of longer duration. On that level, the name of Gritti can, in fact, play a role that is simply figurative, as the indication of a plurality, a constellation, of tendencies and intentions." Manfredo Tafuri, "*Renovatio urbis*": *Venezia nell'età di Andrea Gritti, 1523–1538* (Collana di Architettura, Officina Edizioni, 1984), pp. 26–27.

21. Deborah Howard, *Jacopo Sansovino: Architecture and Patronage in Renaissance Venice* (Yale University Press, 1975), p. 33.

22. The imagery of the standards, and their connection with the Loggetta, is well described by Patricia Fortini Brown in *Venice and Antiquity* (Yale University Press, 1996), pp. 265–68. The bases of the standards are shaped as giant candelabra, and they develop their iconographical program—just as the Loggetta does—in four superimposed layers. Though the details of Sansovino's lower panels are debated, Pope-Hennessy gives them as depicting a) Venus prevailing in the Dardanelles, b) Venus prevailing in Cyprus, c) the fall of Helle, and d) Thetis rescuing Leander (P-H 3.459).

8. PATRICIANS (NOBILI)

1. Vincent Gabrielson, *Financing the Athenian Fleet: Public Taxation and Social Relations* (Johns Hopkins University Press, 1994), pp. 6–7, 35–38.

2. A.R.W. Harrison, *The Law of Athens: Procedure* (Oxford University Press, 1971), pp. 208–11.

3. Donald E. Queller, *The Venetian Patriciate: Reality versus Myth* (University of Illinois Press, 1986).

4. Richard J. Goy, *The House of Gold: Building a Palace in Medieval Venice* (Cambridge University Press, 1992), pp. 229–31.

5. These early tombs are well studied by Debra Pincus in *The Tombs of the Doges of Venice* (Cambridge University Press, 2000).

6. Erwin Panofsky and Fritz Saxl, "Classical Mythology in Medieval Art," *Metropolitian Museum Studies 4* (1933), pp. 228–31.

7. Rona Goffen, *Piety and Patronage in Renaissance Venice: Bellini, Titian, and the Franciscans* (Yale University Press, 1986), pp. 57–58.

8. Ibid., pp. 125–27.

9. NOTABLES (*CITTADINI*)

1. Both Shakespeare and his source emphasize the nobility of the Bassanio figure.

> 'Tis not unknown to you, Antonio,
> How much I have disabled mine estate,
> By something showing a more swelling port
> Than my faint means would grant continuance.
> Nor do I now make moan to be abridg'd
> Of such a noble rate . . . (1.1.123–27)

The source is *Il Pecorone* (*The Big Muttonhead*) by Ser Giovanni of Florence (1558), translated by Geoffrey Bullough for his *Narrative and Dramatic Sources of Shakespeare* (Columbia University Press, 1964), vol. I, pp. 465–66:

> These nobles were highly delighted with Giannotto's bearing, his social graces, pleasantness and agreeable discourse. Everyone fell in love with him; the whole day was spent in dancing, singing and feasting at court in his honour; and all would have been pleased to have him for their lord.

2. Philip L. Sohm, *The Scuola Grande di San Marco, 1437-1550: The Architecture of a Venetian Lay Confraternity* (Garland Publishing, 1982), pp. 58–61.

3. Ibid., p. 22.

4. Ibid., p. 152.

5. Ibid., p. 10.

6. Manfredo Tafuri, *Venice and the Renaissance*, translated by Jessica Levine (MIT Press, 1989), pp. 80–81, 93–94.

7. Erasmus Weddigen, "Thomas Philologus Ravennas," in *Saggi e memorie di storia dell'arte 9* (1974), p. 17.

8. Ibid., p. 27. It is amusing to note that Shakespeare has a "County Palatine" woo Portia in *The Merchant of Venice*.

9. Ibid., pp. 15–16.

10. Ibid., pp. 44–45.

11. Ibid., p. 67. The bust is now in the Atheneum of Venice (by the Fenice theater), since San Geminiano was destroyed in the nineteenth century by the French, who replaced it with the Ala Napoleona

(now the entrance to the Correr museum). The design of the façade can be seen in Tintoretto's painting *The Rescue of Mark's Body*.

12. Pope-Hennessy (3.462–63) attributes the statue to Sansovino, but Weddigen (op. cit., pp. 64–65) and others (BB 1.116–17) make a strong case for Vittoria as the sculptor.

13. There were at least two prior examples of scholars' rooms sculpted in relief—on Dante's tomb in Ravenna (1480s, by Pietro Lombardo) and on Pietro Roccabonella's in Padua (1490s, by Bartolomeo Bellano and Andrea Riccio)—but they did not combine relief with a fully three-dimensional statue. For the Rocabonella work, see Dora Thornton, *The Scholar in His Study* (Yale University Press, 1997), pp. 62–64.

14. Weddigen, op. cit., pp. 29–30.

15. Weddigen, op. cit., p. 66. Just to complete the recondite display, there are inscriptions in the three learned languages, Latin, Greek, and Hebrew, dating his death according to three systems—from the birth of Christ in Latin, from the Byzantine date for the creation of the world in Greek, and from the Jewish date for it in Hebrew. The Latin inscription refers to the titles given Rangone by the doge, Defender of the Faith and Protector of Virtue. The Greek one praises his writings. The Hebrew one praises his work as a teacher.

16. Ibid., p. 69. The statue is now in the patriarchal seminary.

17. Ibid., p. 60.

18. Ibid., p. 57.

19. The tale was in the most famous thirteenth-century collection of stories about the saints. See Jacobus de Voragine, *The Golden Legend*, translated by William Granger Ryan (Princeton University Press, 1993), vol. 1, p. 246.

20. Francis Ames-Lewis and Anka Bednarek, "Decorum and Desire in Some Works by Tintoretto," in *Decorum in Renaissance Narrative Art* (University of London, 1992), pp. 121–23.

21. Peter Humfrey, "Andrea Odoni," in David Alan Brown et al., *Lorenzo Lotto: Rediscovered Master of the Renaissance* (Yale University Press, 1998), p. 164.

10. GOLDEN YOUTH

1. Maria Teresa Muraro, "La festa a Venezia e le sui manifestazioni rappresentative: Le compagnie della calza e le momarie," in Girolamo Arnaldi and Manlio P. Stocchi, eds., *Storia della cultura veneta* III (1982), p. 333.

2. Giorgio Padoan, "La commedia rinascimentale a Venezia dalla sperimentazione umanistica alla commedia 'regolare," in *Storia della cultura veneta* III, pp. 448, 464.

3. Muraro, op. cit., pp. 325–26.

4. Matteo Casini, *I gesti del principe: La festa politica a Firenze e Venezia in età rinascimentale* (Marsilio, 1996), pp. 301–2.

5. Muraro, op. cit., p. 321.

6. Casini, op. cit., p. 299.

7. Ibid.

8. Françoise Bardon, "La peinture narrative de Carpaccio dans le cycle de Ste. Ursule," *Atti dell' Istituto Veneto di Scienze, Lettere ed Arti* (Memorie 39, 1985), p. 106.

9. Michelangelo Muraro, "Vittore Carpaccio o il teatro in pittura," in Maria Teresa Muraro, ed., *Studi sul teatro veneto fra Rinascimento ed età barocca* (Olschki, 1971), pp. 7–19. Ludovico Zorzi, *Carpaccio et la representation de sainte Ursule*, translated by Jean-Paul Manganaro et al. (Hazan, 1991).

10. Françoise Bardon, op. cit. Sgarbi (S) 37–38. Giovanna Nepi Scire, *Carpaccio: Storie di Sant'Orsola* (Electa, 2000).

11. An engraving of the picture by Giovanni de Pian shows the missing column (Zorzi, op. cit., pp. 59–61) but places the prologue figure awkwardly.

12. See Zorzi, op. cit., p. 2,424, fn. 134. Zorzi himself thinks Carpaccio's *artistry* was being pointed out, since the candelabrum-column that is gone would have had the "necklace" of spikes around its base that form a *mazzocchio*, a showpiece of perspective drawing. Zorzi thinks the prologue figure is pointing to that, though the De Pian engraving does not bear this out.

13. Nepi Scire, op. cit., p. 27.

14. Bardon, op. cit., p. 71.

15. Jacobus de Voragine, *The Golden Legend*, translated by William Ganger Ryan (Princeton University Press, 1993), vol. 2, p. 258.

16. Stella Mary Newton, *The Dress of the Venetians, 1495–1525, Pasold Studies in Textile History* 7 (1988), p. 9.

17. Zorzi, op. cit., pp. 36–38. But Zorzi thinks that the preceding picture (Number 2) takes place in Anglia—despite its Lombard-style architecture!

18. Zorzi, op. cit., p. 81.

19. Zorzi, op. cit., pp. 116–19. The scroll has the initials N.L.D.D.W.G.V.I., standing for *Nicolaus Lauretanus donum dedit vivens gloria virgini inclytae*, or "Nicolao Lauredan, while still alive, made this offering to the famous virgin."

20. Newton, op. cit., p. 33.

11. COMMONERS (*POPOLANI*)

1. The church was dedicated to the Immaculate Conception, but not called by that title, since the name had just been given to another chapel raised in Venice to a miraculous image of Mary—Mary of the Fava Bridge (C-P 647–52).

2. The roof is a semi-ellipse, a hard shape for ordinary carpenters to deal with, which makes McAndrew think carpenters trained in the ship-building skills of the Arsenal were employed.

3. For Christian use of Nereids and Tritons taken from Roman funeral motifs, see Jan Bialostock, "The Sea-Thiasos in Renaissance Sepulchral Art," in *Studies in Renaissance and Baroque Art Presented to Sir Anthony Blunt on His Sixtieth Birthday* (Phaidon, 1967), pp. 69–74.

4. Including the grand structure, attributed to Longhena, for the launderers' guild (Scuola dei Laneri).

5. Antonio Manno, *I mestieri di Venezia* (Biblos, 1997), pp. 20–21.

6. Peter Humfrey and Richard MacKenney, "The Venetian Trade Guilds as Patrons of Art in the Renaissance," *Burlington Magazine*, May 1986, pp. 317–30.

7. Ibid., p. 317.

8. David Rosand, *Painting in Cinquecento Venice: Titian, Veronese, Tintoretto* (Yale University Press, 1982), pp. 10–11.

9. Ibid., p. 11.

12. WOMEN

1. Thucydides, *The Peloponnesian War*, 2.45.

2. Carlo Ridolfi, *Vite dei Tintoretto*, edition of 1648 (Filippi Editore, 1994), pp. 11–12. The painters were Marietta Tintoretto in her father's shop, Irene de' Signori di Spilimbergo in Titian's shop, Livinia Fontana, Chiara Varotari, and Giovanna Garzoni.

3. Margaret F. Rosenthal, *The Honest Courtesan: Veronica Franco, Citizen and Writer in Sixteenth-Century Venice* (University of Chicago Press, 1992), pp. 85, 89.

4. Guido Ruggiero, *The Boundaries of Eros: Sex, Crime and Sexuality in Renaissance Venice* (Oxford University Press, 1985), p. 153.

5. Ibid., p. 102, for Franco's meeting with Henry III, King of Poland.

6. Achille Olivieri, "Eroticism and Social Groups in Sixteenth-Century Venice: The Courtesan," in Philippe Ariès and André Béjin, *Western Sexuality* (Basil Blackwell, 1985), p. 97.

7. Bernard Aikema, *Renaissance Venice and the North* (Rizzoli, 2000), p. 236.

8. Jutta Gisela Sperling, *Convents and the Body Politic in Late Renaissance Venice* (University of Chicago Press, 1999), pp. 26–29.

9. Ibid., p. 30.

10. Ibid., pp. 11–12.

11. Ibid., pp. 208, 233, 237.

12. Ibid., pp. 226–27.

13. Ibid., p. 225.

14. Ibid., pp. 229–30.

15. Ibid., pp. 3–4.

16. Ruggiero, op. cit., pp. 77–78.

17. Ruggiero, op. cit., p. 78.

18. Ruggiero, op. cit., p. 113.

19. Peter Humfrey, *Lorenzo Lotto* (Yale University Press, 1997), p. 139.

20. Eve d'Ambra, "The Calculus of Venus: Nude Portraits of Roman Matrons," in Natalie Boymel Kampen, *Sexuality in Ancient Art: Near East, Egypt, Greece, and Italy* (Cambridge University Press, 1996), pp. 219–22.

21. Keith Christiansen, "Lorenzo Lotto and the Tradition of Epithalamic Paintings," *Apollo* 124 (1986), pp. 166–73.

22. Humfrey, op. cit., pp. 137–40.

23. Mauro Lucco, "Marsilio Cassotti and His Bride Faustina," in David Alan Brown et al., *Lorenzo Lotto: Rediscovered Master of the Renaissance* (Yale University Press, 1998), pp. 134–37.

24. The seventeenth-century view apparently reflected the fact that Giovanni Baglione painted a *Sacred and Profane Love* in 1603, in which the Sacred was clothed and the Profane was nude.

25. Maria Grazia Bernardini, "*L'Amor Sacro e Profano* nella storia della critica," in *Tiziano: Amor Sacro e Amor Profano* (Electa, 1995), p. 35.

26. Ibid., pp. 38, 44–45. Goffen still accepts the Wethey attribution of the stemma in the bowl: Rona Goffen, *Titian's Women* (Yale University Press, 1997), p. 290.

27. Mark Twain, *A Tramp Abroad* (Oxford University Press, 1996), p. 578.

28. Goffen, op. cit., p. 152.

29. Jean-Louis Flandrin, "Sex in Married Life in the Early Middle Ages: The Church's Teaching and Behavioural Reality," in Ariès and Béjin, op. cit., pp. 199–20.

30. Alison Luchs, *Tullio Lombardo and Ideal Portrait Sculpture in Renaissance Venice, 1490–1530* (Cambridge University Press, 1995), p. 60.

31. Sarah Wilk, *The Sculpture of Tullio Lombardo: Studies in Sources and Meaning* (Garland Publishing, 1978), pp. 61–67.

32. Luchs, op. cit., pp. 53, 148.

33. Letizia Panizza, introduction to Lucreza Marinella, *The Nobility and Excellence of Women, and the Defects and Vices of Men,* translated by Anne Dunhill (University of Chicago Press, 1990), p. 3.

34. Ibid., pp. 57, 60.

35. Ibid., p. 70.

36. Ibid., p. 95.

37. Peter Humfrey, "Portrait of a Lady as Lucretia," in Brown, op. cit., p. 185.

13. ARTISTS

1. Hans Tietze, "Master and Workshop in the Venetian Renaissance," *Parnassus*, December 1939, p. 35.

2. Ibid., p. 334, and Michel Hochmann, *Peintres et commandataires à Venise, 1540–1628* (Ecole Française de Rome, 1992), p. 79.

3. Carlo Ridolfi, *Vite dei Tintoretto* (Filippi Editore, 1994), pp. 111–13.

4. Tietze, op. cit., p. 32.

5. Hochmann, op. cit., p. 76.

6. Hochmann, op. cit., pp. 85–86.

7. Jennifer Fletcher, "Les Bellini," in Roberto Casanelli et al., *Ateliers de la Renaissance* (Desclée de Brouwer, 1998), pp. 134–36.

8. Ibid., p. 78.

9. Paul Hills, *Venetian Colour: Marble, Mosaic, Painting and Glass 1250–1550* (Yale University Press, 1999), p. 134.

10. Fletcher, op. cit., pp. 137–38.

11. Ridolfi, op. cit., p. 96.

12. Anthony Hecht, "Venetian Vespers," in *Collected Earlier Poems* (Alfred A. Knopf, 1990), p. 230.

13. Rodolfo Palluchini, *I Vivarini: Antonio, Bartolomeo, Alvise* (Neri Pozza Editore, n.d.), pp. 30, 103. Palluchini thinks Antonio might have had collaboration on the work by Francesco dei Franceschi.

14. Ibid., p. 116—date to the early 1470s.

15. Ibid., pp. 138–39. Also John Steer, *Alvise Vivarini: His Art and Influence* (Cambridge University Press, 1982), pp. 68–74, 158–62.

16. Maurice E. Cope, *The Venetian Chapel of the Sacrament in the Sixteenth Century* (Garland Publishing, 1979).

17. Manfredo Tafuri, *Venice and the Renaissance*, translated by Jessica Levine (MIT Press, 1989), pp. 85–88.

18. Tietze, op. cit., p. 34.

19. Fletcher, op. cit., p. 143.

20. M. Roy Fisher, *Titian's Assistants During the Later Years* (Garland Publishing, 1977), pp. 9–30.

21. Carlo Pedretti, "Giorgione e Leonardo," in Rodolfo Pallucchini, *Giorgione e l'umanismo veneziano* (Civiltà veneziana. Saggi 27, Olschki, 1981), vol. 2, pp. 485–504.

22. Ridolfi, op. cit., p. 8.

23. Ridolfi, op. cit., p. 95.

24. Eliska Fucikova, *Capolavori della pittura veneta dal Castello di Praga* (Electa, 1994).

25. Philip Rylands, *Palma Vecchio* (Cambridge University Press, 1992), pp. 114–15.

26. Jacob Burckhardt, *Die Kultur der Renaissance in Italien* (Verlag von Th. Knaur Nachf., 1927), p. 66.

14. OUTSIDERS

1. Thucydides, *The Peloponnesian War*, 2.39.

2. James Cleugh, *The Divine Aretino* (Stein and Day, 1966), p. 111.

3. Brünehilde Imhaus, *Le minoranze orientali a Venezia, 1300–1510* (Il Veltro Editrice, 1997), pp. 255–87.

4. Ibid., pp. 248–52.

5. Ibid., pp. 220–22.

6. Ennio Concina et al., *La Città degli Ebrei* (Albrizzi Editore, 1991), pp. 24–26.

7. Fritz Koreny, "Dürer e Venezia," in Bernard Aikema and Beverly Louis Brown, *Renaissance Venice and the North* (Rizzoli, 2000), pp. 306–9.

8. Philip L. Sohm, *The Scuola Grande di San Marco, 1437–1550: The Architecture of a Venetian Lay Confraternity* (Garland Publishing, 1982), p. 28. There was heated competition between the Scuola degli Schiavoni, the Scuola degli Armeni, and the Scuola degli Albanese.

9. Concina, op. cit., p. 34.

10. Concina, op. cit., pp. 34–40. Manfredo Tafuri, *Venice and the Renaissance*, translated by Jessica Levine (MIT Press, 1989), pp. 17–23.

11. Concina, op. cit., p. 36.

12. Imhaus, op. cit., p. 222.

13. Concina, op. cit., p. 27.

14. Concina, op. cit., pp. 22–23.

15. Brian Pullan, *The Jews of Europe and the Inquisition of Venice, 1550–1670* (Barnes and Noble Books, 1983), p. 147.

16. Ibid., p. 148.

17. Riccardo Calimani, *The Ghetto of Venice*, translated by Katherine Silberblatt Wofthal (M. Evans, 1987), p. 154.

18. For Nasi's life, see Cecil Roth, *The House of Nasi: The Duke of Naxos* (Jewish Publication Society of America, 1948).

19. Calimani, op. cit., pp. 107–15.

20. Pullan, op. cit., p. 156.

21. Marino Zorzi, "Bessarione e Venezia," in Gianfranco Fiaccadori, ed., *Bessarione e l'umanismo* (Vivarium, 1994), p. 209.

22. Pullan, op. cit., p. 159.

23. Concina, op. cit., p. 105.

15. CHRIST'S BLOOD

1. Maurice E. Cope, *The Venetian Chapel of the Sacrament in the Sixteenth Century* (Garland Publishing, 1979), p. 2.

2. Rodolfo Gallo, *Il tesoro di S. Marco e la sua storia* (Istituto per la collaborazione culturale, 1967), pp. 12, 20, 276, and Illustration 14.

3. Charles de Tolnay, "Il 'Paradiso' del Tintoretto," *Arte Veneta* 24 (1970), p. 104.

4. Virgil, *Aeneid* 2.255.

5. The Scripture scholar Joseph A. Fitzmyer doubts the authenticity of the passage, but stresses that the point is a "splashing to the ground": *The Gospel According to Luke*, (Doubleday, 1985), Vol. 2, p. 1,444. Tintoretto and his contemporaries, of course, accepted the verse as genuine.

6. Cope, op. cit., pp. 631–33.

7. Cope, op. cit., p. 368.

8. Paul Hills, "Piety and Patronage in Cinquecento Venice: Tintoretto and the Scuole del Sacramento," *Art and History* 6 (1983), p. 32.

9. Cope, op. cit., p. 271.

10. S. J. Freedberg, *Painting in Italy, 1500–1600* (Yale University Press, 1993), p. 530.

11. G. K. Chesterton, "The Ballad of the White Horse," in *Collected Poems* (Methuen, 1933), p. 276.

16. CHRIST'S CROSS

1. Giustiniani quoted in André Jean-Marc Loechel, "Le rappresentazioni della communità," in *Storia di Venezia*, vol. 4 (Istituto dell'Enciclopedia Italiana, 1996), p. 610.

2. Ibid., p. 608.

3. It is now a home for the elderly. Umberto Franzoi and Dina De Stefano, *Le chiese di Venezia* (Azienda Autonoma Soggiorno Turismo-Venezia, 1975), pp. 85–86.

4. Rodolfo Gallo, *Il tesoro di S. Marco e la sua storia* (Istituto per la collaborazione culturale, 1967), pp. 12, 276.

5. Lotte Labowky, "Per l'iconografia del cardinal Bessarione," in Gianfranco Fiaccadori, ed., *Bessarione e l'umanismo* (Vivarium, 1994), pp. 287–94. The Carità had another painting of Bessarion with the relic, which is now in Vienna. It, too, is based on Gentile Bellini's drawings. Gentile had recorded Bessarion's features because he was commissioned to include the cardinal in a painting for the Larger Council hall, one of those destroyed in the fire of 1477. For the lost painting, see Patricia Fortini Brown, *Venetian Narrative Painting in the Age of Carpaccio* (Yale University Press, 1988), pp. 272–29.

6. Fortini Brown, op. cit., p. 285.

7. Fortini Brown, op. cit., pp. 150–51. Bellini's account of the miracle shows contemporary members of

the *scuola* kneeling in reverent memory of the past event depicted. The fourth kneeling man from the left is a self-portrait of Gentile (it matches the portrait in Gentile's *Preaching of Saint Mark in Alexandria*, ibid., p. 207), and the worshiping women on the other side of the picture include Caterina Cornaro, the former Queen of Cyprus, and her attendant ladies.

8. John Ruskin, *Modern Painters*, vol. II, in *Works* (George Allen, 1903), vol. 7, p. 271.

9. David Rosand, *Painting in Cinquecento Venice: Titian, Veronese, Tintoretto* (Yale University Press, 1982), pp. 204–5.

10. S. J. Freedberg, *Painting in Italy, 1500–1600* (Penguin, 1993), p. 526.

11. Rosand, op. cit., pp. 202–3.

12. Ann Derbes, *Picturing the Passion in Late Medieval Italy* (Cambridge University Press, 1996), pp. 1,145–49.

13. Ignatius of Antioch, *Letter to the Ephesians* 9.1. See William R. Schoedel, *Ignatius of Antioch* (Fortress Press, 1985), p. 65.

14. Hippolytus, *Antichrist* 59.

15. Methodius, *Answer to Porphyrius Concerning the Cross* 1.7–10.

16. Schoedel, op. cit., pp. 66–67.

17. For *hypsoun* as "exalt," not merely "lift," see Raymond Brown, quoting Isaiah 53.13, *The Gospel According to John* (Doubleday, 1966), vol. 1, p. 146.

17. VENETIAN ANNUNCIATIONS

1. For Annunciation patterns, see David M. Robb, "The Iconography of the Annunciation in the Fourteenth and Fifteenth Centuries" (*Art Bulletin* 18, 1936), pp. 480–516; John R. Spencer, "Spatial Imagery of the Annunciation in Fifteenth Century Florence" (*Art Bulletin* 37, 1955), pp. 273–80; and Georges Didi-Huberman, *Fra Angelico: Dissemblance and Figurations*, translated by Jane Marie Todd (University of Chicago Press, 1995), pp. 105–235.

2. Penny Howell Jolly, *Made in God's Image: Eve and Adam in the Genesis Mosaics at San Marco, Venice* (University of California Press, 1997), pp. 60, 115.

3. The mosaic cycle, drawing on the apocryphal gospel of Saint James, set a precedent for treating Mary in very human terms. It even shows Joseph rebuking Mary when he discovers that she is pregnant and suspects her of infidelity (D 1.135). She holds her right hand out in protest, but touches her cheek with her left hand to show she is hurt by the accusation.

4. Erwin Panofsky, *Problems in Titian, Mostly Iconographic* (New York University Press, 1969), p. 17.

5. Giovanna Nepi Scire, in *Titian, Prince of Painters*, Catalogue of the 1990 Exhibit for Venice and Washington (Prestel, 1990), p. 320.

6. Ibid., p. 318.

7. Some examples are in Peter Humfrey, "The Prehistory of Titian's *Assunta*," in Joseph Manca, ed., *Titian 500* (National Gallery of Art, Washington, D.C., 1993), pp. 322–41.

8. Rona Goffen, *Piety and Patronage in Renaissance Venice: Bellini, Titian, and the Franciscans* (Yale University Press, 1986), pp. 73–106.

9. Of Mary of Egypt's spectacular sins and spectacular repentance, see Jacobus de Voragine, *The Golden Legend*, translated by William Granger Ryan (Princeton University Press, 1993), vol. 1, pp. 227–28.

10. The Anastasis is shown twice in the San Marco mosaics, once on the façade (left top lunette) and once in the first left vault on entry (D 2.192, 196).

18. THE VULNERABLE MARY

1. Rona Goffen points out that there is another version, by the Vivarini, in San Pantalon.

2. Sarah Wilk, *The Sculpture of Tullio Lombardo: Studies in Sources and Meaning* (Garland Publishing, 1978), pp. 94–98. For fourth-century examples not cited by Wilk, see Angela Donati, ed., *Pietro e Paolo: La storia, il culto, la memoria nei primi secoli* (Electa, 2000), pp. 50, 51, 132, 148–49, 155.

3. Ibid., p. 108.

4. Ibid., pp. 110–11.

5. For Lotto's training with the Vivarini, see Peter Humfrey in David Alan Brown et al., *Lorenzo Lotto: Rediscovered Master of the Renaissance* (Yale University Press, 1998), p. 5, but Anchise Tempestini puts him among the Bellini pupils (T 85).

6. Humfrey, op. cit., p. 191.

7. T. H. White, *The Book of Beasts: A Translation of a Bestiary of the Twelfth Century* (Jonathan Cape, 1954), pp. 90–99.

19. MARK: THE RELIC

1. Hippolyte Delehaye, S. J., "Loca Sanctorum," *Analecta Bollandiana* 48 (1930), p. 23.

2. Raymond Van Dam, "Relics," in George Bowersock et al., *Late Antiquity* (Harvard University Press, 1999), p. 667.

3. Yvette Duval, *Auprès des saints corps et âme: L'inhumation "ad sanctos" dans la chrétienté d'Orient et d'Occident du IIIe au VIIe siècle* (Etudes Augustiniennes, 1988), pp. 99–130.

4. André Grabar, *Martyrium: Recherches sur le culte des reliques et l'art chrétien antique* (Collège de France, 1946), vol. 1, pp. 32–37.

5. *The Martyrdom of Polycarp*, quoted in Eusebius, *Ecclesiastical History* 4.15.

6. Patrick J. Geary, *Furta Sacra: Thefts of Relics in the Central Middle Ages* (Princeton University Press, 1978).

7. Bernard Flusin, "Martyrs," in Bowersock, op. cit., p. 568.

8. Peter Brown, *The Cult of the Saints* (University of Chicago Press, 1981), pp. 88–89.

9. Peter Brown, *Society and the Holy in Late Antiquity* (University of California Press, 1982), p. 241.

10. Patrick J. Geary, op. cit., pp. 94–95.

11. This account of the picture is taken from Philip Rylands, *Palma Vecchio* (Cambridge University Press, 1988), pp. 241–45. The door area was filled in after the painting was returned from Paris, where Napoleon had taken it in 1797. Since the *scuola* was secularized by Napoleon, the painting went to the Accademia. There it hangs where there is no door to explain the lacuna in the painting.

12. Peter Humfrey, "Saint Nicholas in Glory," in David Alan Brown et al., *Lorenzo Lotto: Rediscovered Master of the Renaissance* (Yale University Press, 1998), p. 165.

13. Lucy's body was placed at first in the Benedictine monastery-church of San Giorgio Maggiore, where pilgrims went in large sea processions on the saint's December feast day. But in 1277, the jam of boats on a stormy day led to the drowning of some pilgrims. After that, the body was removed to the church

named for Lucy on the main island. When that church was secularized, the relic went to its present resting place, the Church of St. Jeremiah. Gino Damerini, *L'isola e il cenobio di San Giorgio Maggiore* (Fondazione Giorgio Cini, 1969), pp. 91–2.

20. MARK: THE LIFE

1. The cure of Anianus originally occurred in the Holy Land, and it was too important to be dropped— so it was transferred to Alexandria, and a demoniac's cure replaced it whenever the Holy Land sequence was included.

2. The episodes are out of their chronological order on the Pala d'Oro, the result of resetting as the Pala was progressively encrusted with precious stones and new details: W. F. Volbach, "Gli smalti della Pala d'Oro," in H. R. Hahnloser and R. Polacco, eds., *La Pala d'Oro* (Canal e Stamperia Editrice, 1994), p. 33. The Pala Feriale by Paolo Veneziano, which covered the Pala d'Oro except on feast days, has four episodes from the Vita (numbers 3, 14, 18, 19), though it contains one event from the Translatio and two from the Inventio, combining all three cycles in one narrative line.

3. The tomb was lacking the upper attic and circular pediment, added by Giovanni Girolamo Grapiglia when he cut down the tomb at the other end of the wall to subordinate them both to the new Mocenigo tomb over the entryway, making them all one huge monument. There may have been statues on the outer capitals of the original attic (McA 475).

4. This is one of the reliefs just inside the iconostasis (the screen with the row of statues along its top) before the high altar. The dragging of Mark is on the right side as one faces the altar.

21. WAR SAINTS: GEORGE AND THEODORE

1. There have been some modern doubts about Theodore's original patronage of the city, but the Venetians of the Renaissance believed that he had been their patron, and that is what matters here.

2. H. R. Hahnloser and R. Polacco, *La Pala d'Oro* (Canal e Stamperia Editrice, 1994), pp. 53–63.

3. Otto Demus, *The Church of San Marco in Venice* (Dumbarton Oaks, Harvard University Press, 1960), pp. 130–33.

4. For the relics in San Marco, see Rodolfo Gallo, *Il tesoro di S. Marco e la sua storia* (Istituto per la collaborazione culturale, 1967), p. 276 and Tables 21 and 22. For the arm from Fiore di Calabria, see Gino Damerini, *L'isola e il cenobio di San Giorgio Maggiore* (Fondazione Giorgio Cini, 1969), p. 94.

5. Rodolfo Pallucchini, *I teleri del Carpaccio in San Giorgio degli Schiavoni* (Rizzoli, 1961), pp. 72–73.

6. Jacobus de Voragine, *The Golden Legend*, translated by William Granger Ryan (Princeton University Press, 1993), vol. I, pp. 239–40.

7. Jill Dunkerton, Susan Foster, and Nicholas Penny, *Dürer to Veronese: Sixteenth-Century Painting in the National Gallery* (Yale University Press, 1999), p. 69.

8. Wolfgang Wolters, *La scultura veneziana gotica, 1300–1460* (Alfieri, 1976), vol. I, p. 136. Luisa Sartorio argues that the head of the statue comes from the first century B.C.E., confirmed from coins as that of the Emperor Mithridates VI wearing the oaken crown of Heracles, and that the torso comes from a century or so later. See Sartorio, "San Teodoro, statua composita," *Arte Veneta* 2, 1947, pp. I,132–34.

9. Manfredo Tafuri, *Venice and the Renaissance*, translated by Jessica Levine (MIT Press, 1989), pp. 18–19.

10. Lionello Puppi, "Il tempio e gli eroi," in Paolo Peruzza and Mario Piana, eds., *La grande vetrata di San Giovanni e Paolo* (Marsilio, 1982).

11. Serena Romano, "La vetrata: I maestri e gli artefici," in Peruzza and Piana, ibid., pp. 51–71.

22. PLAGUE SAINTS

1. Here I use the sixteenth-century Catholic translation into English (the Douay), since that was made from the Latin Vulgate, which the Venetians used. It was not (like the King James version) from the original Greek.

2. Job 16.17. All quotes from Job I give in the Douay version, for the reason given in the preceding note.

3. Jacobus de Voragine, *The Golden Legend*, translated by William Granger Ryan (Princeton University Press, 1993), vol. 1, p. 100.

4. Septicemic plague killed so fast that bubos did not have time to develop. Pneumonic plague affected the lungs, making the victims cough blood copiously.

5. Diane Cole Ahl, *Benozzo Gozzoli* (Yale University Press, 1996), pp. 141–42.

6. Antonio Niero, *San Rocco: Storia, legenda, culto* (ISG Vicenza, 1991), pp. 9, 13.

7. Ibid., pp. 23–24.

8. The painting is much restored, and the side panels are eighteenth-century additions by Sanato Piatti.

9. Bruno Bertoli, *Arte e teologia nel culto di San Rocco* (ISG Vicenza, 1996), pp. 24–27.

10. Gino Damerini, *L'isola e il cenobio di San Giorgio Maggiore* (Fondazione Giorgio Cini, 1969), pp. 94–95.

11. Louise Marshall, "Manipulating the Sacred: Image and Plague in Renaissance Italy," *Renaissance Quarterly*, 1993, pp. 506–18.

23. THE OTHER LION: JEROME'S

1. Sinding-Larsen says that "Tintoretto painted St. Mark in exactly the same manner in the *Virgin with Saints Mark and Luke* in Berlin" (S-L 239). It is true that Mark and Luke, paired evangelists, are shown in seminude hermit costume in Berlin, but Mark does not have the bald head and long beard of the Jerome in the Salotto Dorato.

2. Jerome is present in Palma's picture because the same doge, Girolamo Priuli, kneels to the right of the doorway this painting surrounds. To the left of the doorway is the doge's brother Lorenzo, who succeeded him. This doge is also accompanied by his namesake, Saint Lawrence.

3. Patricia Fortini Brown, *Venetian Narrative Painting in the Age of Carpaccio* (Yale University Press, 1988), pp. 49, 270–71.

4. Ibid., pp. 288–89.

5. Eugene F. Rice, Jr., *Saint Jerome in the Renaissance* (Johns Hopkins University Press, 1988), p. 39.

6. Ibid., p. 41.

7. Ibid., pp. 51–2.

8. Ibid., p. 108, for Van Eyck's use of Cardinal Niccolò Albergati as a model. Antonello's picture has had several suggested models, but "he clearly must have been an ecclesiastic of notable culture," according to Bernard Aikema—see Bernard Aikema and Beverly Louise Brown, eds., *Renaissance Venice and the North* (Rizzoli, 2000), p. 216. The powerful features of Botticelli's Augustine were taken from Giorgio Antonio Vespucci, the scholar and Medici favorite who tutored his nephew Amerigo, after whom

America is named: Nicoletta Baldini, in *Sandro Botticelli: Pittore della Divina Commedia* (Skira, 2000), vol. 1, pp. 110–11.

9. Guido Perocco, "La Scuola di S. Giorgio degli Schiavoni," *Atti del XVIII Congresso internazionale di Storia dell'arte*, pp. 221–224.

10. Patricia Fortini Brown, "Sant'Agostino nello studio di Carpaccio: Un ritratto nel ritratto?" in Gianfranco Fiaccadori et al., *Bessarione e l'umanesimo* (Vivarium, 1994), p. 315.

11. Augusto Gentili, "Carpaccio e Bessarione," in Fiaccadori, op. cit., p. 301.

12. Fabrizio Lollini, "L'iconografia di Bessarione: *Bessarione pictus*," in Fiaccadori, op. cit., pp. 275–83.

13. Fortini Brown, op. cit., p. 315. She thinks that another picture in the Scuola, the *Calling of Saint Matthew*, may be a tribute to a different member of the Valaresso family, Maffio Valaresso.

14. Marino Zorzi, "Bessarione e Venezia," in Fiaccadori, op. cit., pp. 216–22.

15. Michel Serres, *Esthétiques sur Carpaccio* (Hermann, 1975), p. 71.

16. Rodolfo Palucchini, *I teleri del Carpaccio in San Giorgio degli Schiavoni* (Rizzoli, 1977), pp. 92–94.

17. The best painting of this legend is Benozzo Gozzoli's fresco of 1465, at San Agostino in San Gimignano.

18. Another proof that Jerome is intended is the fact that Bellini was working to match the main altarpiece in the church, in which Sebastiano del Piombo placed another doctor of the church, Saint John Chrysostom, sitting in profile on a rock.

19. Since Jerome was, for a time, the secretary to a pope (Damasus I), it was assumed that, as a Curia official, he must have been a cardinal, though the office did not exist in his day.

24. FRANCISCAN LEARNING

1. Rona Goffen, *Piety and Patronage in Renaissance Venice* (Yale University Press, 1986), pp. 164–66.

2. John V. Fleming, *From Bonaventure to Bellini: An Essay in Franciscan Exegesis* (Princeton University Press, 1982).

3. Millard Meiss, *Giovanni Bellini's St. Francis in the Frick Collection* (Princeton University Press, 1964). Meiss hedges his stance, however, by adding, "This power [the light source] probably also is imprinting stigmata on the saint's body, *though we cannot be absolutely sure*" (p. 33, emphasis added).

4. Bernard Aikema and Beverly Louise Brown, eds., *Renaissance Venice and the North* (Rizzoli, 2000), pp. 210–11.

5. Ibid., p. 210.

6. G. K. Chesterton, "The Ballad of the White Horse," *Collected Poems* (Methuen, 1933), p. 257.

7. Thucydides, *The Peloponnesian War* 2.42.

8. G. K. Chesterton, *Saint Francis of Assisi* (Doubleday, 1957), p. 36.

9. Jerome, *Letters* 22.7: "Though my temples were wan with fasting, my mind boiled on within my icy limbs, and hot lust seethed in my half-dead flesh."

10. Fleming, op. cit., p. 38.

11. Ernst Axel Knauf, "Ishmaelites," in David Noel Freedman et al., *The Anchor Bible Dictionary* (Doubleday, 1992), vol. 3, pp. 515–20.

12. Fleming, op. cit., pp. 59–60.

13. Edward Muir, "Manifestazioni e cerimonie nella Venezia di Andrea Gritti," in Manfredo Tafuri, "*Renovatio Urbis*": *Venezia nell'età di Andrea Gritti, 1523–1538* (Collana di Architettura 25, Officina Edizioni, 1984), p. 59.

14. Manfredo Tafuri and Antonio Foscari, *L'armonia e i conflitti: La Chiesa di San Francesco della Vigna nella Venezia del'500* (Giuli Einaudi, 1983), p. 29.

15. Manfredo Tafuri, *Jacopo Sansovino e l'architettura del'500 a Venezia* (Marsilio, 1969), pp. 25–26.

16. Tafuri and Foscari, op. cit., pp. 21–23.

17. Rudolf Wittkower, *Architectural Principles in the Age of Humanism* (Norton, 1971), p. 102. Tafuri and Foscari, op. cit., pp. 48–49, 55–57.

18. The twenty-two letters of the Hebrew alphabet, with their variants according to their position in a word, come to twenty-seven, a sacred number in the Kabbalah. Cf. William Melczer, "Ermetismo e cabala cristiana nel pensiero di Francesco Zorzi," in Tafuri, *Renovatio*, op. cit., pp. 152–53.

19. The importance of Zorzi's *memoriale* to Titian's *Presentation* is stressed by Lionello Puppi, "Tiziano e l'architettura," in Rodolfo Palluchini, ed., *Tiziano e il manierismo europeo* (Olschki, 1978), pp. 217–22.

20. David Rosand, *Painting in Cinquecento Venice: Titian, Veronese, Tintoretto* (Yale University Press, 1982), p. 104.

21. Jacobus de Voragine, *The Golden Legend*, translated by William Granger Ryan (Princeton University Press, 1993), vol. 2, p. 152.

22. *Sebastiano Serlio on Architecture*, translated with commentary by Vaughan Hart and Peter Hicks (Yale University Press, 1996), p. 340. Doric columns should be used for martial saints (p. 291) and Ionic columns for scholarly male saints or matronly women saints (p. 320). For the praise of Titian in Serlio's treatise, see ibid., p. 99. The first part of Serlio's treatise was being printed in Venice during the 1530s, the period of Zorzi's church and Titian's painting, and those in his circle were familiar with the drawings that went into it.

23. Rosand, op. cit., pp. 126, 275.

24. John Onians, *The Bearers of Meaning* (Princeton University Press, 1988), p. 297.

25. Ibid., p. 294.

26. Tafuri, *Renovatio*, op. cit., pp. 233–35.

25. DOMINICAN LEARNING

1. Augusto Gentilli, "Fonti e problemi del simbolismo antiquario nella vetrata di San Zanipolo," in Paolo Peruzza and Mario Piana, eds., *La grande vetrata di San Zanipolo* (Marsilio, 1982), pp. 37–50.

2. Serena Romano, "La vetrata: I maestri e gli artefici," in ibid.

3. Though the book was published anonymously in 1499, by 1512 it was realized that the first letters of its chapters formed an acrostic: FRIAR FRANCESCO COLONNA WAS DEEP IN LOVE WITH POLIA (POLIAM FRATER FRANCISCUS COLUMNA PERAMAVIT). Some have tried to make Francesco Colonna a Roman layman (the Frater must then refer to some kind of unspecified lay brotherhood). But the evidence that this is the work of a Venetian (with a thread of Venetian dialect terms running through it), and that it was seen through the press by its author *in Venice*, is marshaled compellingly by Marco Ariani and Mino Gabriele, drawing on the work of Maria Teresa Casella, in the introduction to their edition of the *Hypnerotomachia Poliphili* (Adelphi Edizioni, 1998), pp. lxiv-xc. They note that another Dominican, Giordano Bruno, could write ardently about eros, in his *Dialoghi d'amore*.

4. For the progress of the book as "an education of the senses," see Ariani and Gabriele, op. cit., pp. l–lii

5. Thomas Aquinas, *Summa theologiae* I q 84 a 7 and I q 84 a 1.

6. Ibid., I q 14 a 2 and 3.

7. Ibid., II–II q 175 a 3.

8. Francesco Colonna, *Hypnerotomachia Poliphili*, edited by Marco Ariani and Mino Gabriele (Adelphi Edizioni, 1998), vol. 2 (text and introduction), p. 253.

9. For the importance of Apuleius to Colonna, see ibid., pp. xxxiv-xxxv.

10. Augustine, *Confessiones* 10.8–9.

11. Colonna, op. cit., pp. 72–73.

12. Colonna, op. cit., p. 354.

13. Colonna, op. cit., p. 209.

14. Colonna, op. cit., p. 254.

15. Colonna, op. cit., p. 172.

16. Colonna, op. cit., p. 249.

17. Colonna, op. cit., p. 478.

18. Umberto Eco, *The Aesthetics of Thomas Aquinas*, translated by Hugh Breslin (Harvard University Press, 1988), pp. 144–21.

19. Thomas Aquinas, *Summa Theologiae* I q 44 a 1 resp.

26. BOOK LEARNING

1. Martin Lowry, *The World of Aldus Manutius* (Cornell University Press, 1979), pp. 118–19.

2. Marco Ariani and Mino Gabriele, in the introduction to Francesco Colonna, *Hypnerotomachia Poliphili* (Adelphi Edizioni, 1998), vol. 1, pp. xcvii–cix.

3. The second volume of the Ariani-Gabriele edition is a reduced-size facsimile of the original text, giving a splendid feel for its appearance.

4. Giovanni Pozzi, "Il 'Polifilo' nella storia del libro illustrato veneziano," in Rodolfo Palucchini, ed., *Giorgione e l'umanismo veneziano* (Olschki, 1981), vol. 1, pp. 74–75.

5. Liane Lefaivre, *Leon Battista Alberti's Hypnerotomachia Poliphili* (MIT Presss, 1997), p. 9. Though Ariani and Gabriele make quick work of the claim that Alberti wrote the *Dream-Combat*, Lefaivre's book is full of useful information.

6. Ibid., p. 9.

7. Pozzi, op. cit., p. 92.

8. Lowry, op. cit., pp. 129–30.

9. Leonardas Vytautas Gerulaitis, *Printing and Publishing in Fifteenth-Century Venice* (American Library Association, 1976), pp. 11, 29–30.

10. Lowry, op. cit., p. 22.

11. Lowry, op. cit., p. 87.

12. Lowry, op. cit., p. 87.

13. Lowry, op. cit., p. 90.

14. Gerulaitis, op. cit., p. 89.

15. Lowry, op. cit., pp. 225–27.

16. Mario Carpi, "The Making of the Typographical Architect," in Vaughan Hart and Peter Hicks, eds., *Paper Palaces: The Rise of the Renaissance Architectural Treatise* (Yale University Press, 1998), pp. 158–69.

17. Ingrid D. Rowland, "Vitruvius in Print and in Vernacular Translation: Fra Giocondo, Bramante, Raphael and Cesare Cesariano," in ibid., p. 108.

18. Robert Tavernor, "Palladio's 'Corpus': *I quattro libri dell'architettura*," in ibid., p. 236.

19. Manuela Morresi, "Treatises and the Architecture of Venice in the Fifteenth and Sixteenth Centuries," in ibid., p. 274.

20. Vaughan Hart and Peter Hicks, "On Sebastiano Serlio: Decorum and the Art of Architectural Invention," in ibid., pp. 146–47.

21. Robert Tavernor, *Palladio and Palladianism* (Thames and Hudson, 1991), p. 113.

27. LEARNED ARCHITECTURE: CODUSSI

1. Loredana Olivato and Lionello Pupi, *Mauro Codussi* (Electa, 1977), pp. 52–58.

2. Ibid., p. 184.

3. Manfredo Tafuri, *Venice and the Renaissance*, translated by Jessica Levine (MIT Press, 1989), p. 6.

28. LEARNED ARCHITECTURE: SANSOVINO, PALLADIO

1. Deborah Howard, *Jacopo Sansovino: Architecture and Patronage in Renaissance Venice* (Yale University Press, 1987), p. 146.

2. Rudolf Wittkower, *Architectural Principles in the Age of Humanism* (Norton, 1971), pp. 332.

3. The medals can be seen on page 186 of Lionello Puppi, *Andrea Palladio: Opera completa* (Electa, 1973).

4. Wittkower, op. cit., pp. 89–97.

5. Wittkower, op. cit., p. 157.

6. Wittkower, op. cit., pp. 94–95.

7. James S. Ackerman, *Palladio* (Penguin, 1966), p. 146.

8. Ibid., pp. 146–48.

9. Puppi, op. cit., pp. 264–65.

29. LEARNED SCULPTURE

1. Debra Pincus, "Tullio Lombardo as a Restorer of Antiquities: An Aspect of Fifteenth Century Venetian Antiquarianism," *Arte veneta* 33 (1979), p. 29.

2. Debra Pincus, "An Antique Fragment as Workshop Model: Classicism in the Andrea Vendramin Tomb," *Burlington Magazine* 1981, p. 42.

3. Pincus, "Tullio Lombardo as a Restorer," pp. 35–39.

4. Ibid., p. 38.

5. Lorenzo Finocchi Gherhsi, *Alessandro Vittoria* (Forum, Udine, 1998), pp. 36–44.

30. LEARNED POLITICS

1. Gaetano Cozzi, *Il Doge Nicolò Contarini* (Istituto per la collaborazione culturale, 1958), pp. 14–27.

2. William J. Bouwsma, *Venice and the Defense of Republican Liberty* (University of California Press, 1968), p. 254.

3. Cozzi, op. cit., p. 37.

4. Cozzi, op. cit., p. 40.

5. Cozzi, op. cit., pp. 2–12.

6. Paul F. Grendler, *The Roman Inquisition and the Venetian Press, 1540–1605* (Princeton University Press, 1977), p. 214.

7. Ibid., pp. 115–26.

8. Ibid., pp. 140–45, 154–55. On the other hand, the republic did its own burning of some Jewish books.

9. Ibid., p. 212.

10. Ibid., p. 269.

11. Ibid., p. 278.

12. Paolo Sarpi, *Istoria dell'interdetto e altri scritti editi e inediti*, edited by Manlio Duilio Busnelli and Giovanni Gambarin (Giuseppe Laterza & Figli, 1940), vol. 6a, pp. 6–15.

13. Federico Chabod, *La politica di Paolo Sarpi* (Istituto per la collaborazione culturale, 1962), p. 74.

14. Ibid., p. 4.

15. Logan Pearsall Smith, *The Life and Letters of Sir Henry Wotton* (Clarendon Press, 1907), vol. 1, p. 344.

16. On the apparent contradiction, see Vittorio Frajese, *Sarpi scettico: Stato e chiesa a Venezia tra Cinque e Seicento* (Il Mulino, 1994), pp. 289–91.

17. Pearsall Smith, op. cit., p. 341.

18. Pearsall Smith, op. cit., p. 349.

19. Frajese, op. cit., pp. 198–208.

20. Pearsall Smith, op. cit., p. 347.

21. Ibid.

22. James Brodrick, S.J., *The Life and Work of Blessed Robert Francis Cardinal Bellarmine, S. J.* (Burns Oates and Washbourne, 1928), vol. 2, p. 132.

23. Sarpi, op. cit., 6a, p. 51.

24. Some complying Capuchins were brought in to replace their defiant brothers—see Ludwig von Pastor, *The History of the Popes*, translated by Dom Ernest Graf (Kegan Paul, Trench, Trubner, 1937), vol. 25, p. 1,141.

25. Pearsall Smith, op. cit., p. 350.

26. Ibid.

27. Pastor, op. cit., p. 153.

28. Cozzi, op. cit., p. 39, quoting Giuseppe Malatesta, "a fervent champion of the other side."

29. Fulgenzio Micanzio, *Vita del F. Paolo Sarpi*, p. 27. This is the basic biography, written after his death by Sarpi's fellow Servite and long-time ally. I cite it in the edition by Ivone Cacciavillani (Signum Verde, 1993), which has a useful introduction and chronology.

30. Cozzi, op. cit., pp. 53–54.

31. Pastor, op. cit., pp. 146, 153.

32. Sarpi, op. cit., 6b, p. 7.

33. Sarpi, op. cit., p. 14.

34. Sarpi, op. cit., p. 26.

35. Sarpi, op. cit., p. 30.

36. Sarpi, op. cit., p. 40.

37. Chabod, op. cit., pp. 60–61.

38. Sarpi, op. cit., pp. 48–49.

39. Sarpi, op. cit., p. 26.

40. Ibid.

41. Pearsall Smith, op. cit., pp. 86–88.

42. Pastor, op. cit., p. 155.

43. Pastor, op. cit., p. 174.

44. Chabod, op. cit., pp. 92–96.

45. Pastor, op. cit., p. 181.

31. LEARNED HISTORY

1. Federico Chabod, *La politica di Paolo Sarpi* (Istituto per la collaborazione culturale, 1962), pp. 112–13.

2. Manlio Duilio Busnelli, *Paolo Sarpi, lettere ai protestanti* (Giuseppe Laterza & Figli, 1940).

3. Chabod, op. cit., pp. 117–45.

4. Ibid., pp. 149–52.

5. Another body of Sarpi's writings, his private and aphoristic notes during the period of his greatest scientific activity, have prompted the view that he was a skeptic, a relativist, or an atheist. The range of views is suggested by authors who give Sarpi these identities:

   Lutheran: Manlio Duilio Busnelli, *Études sur Fra Paolo Sarpi* (Editions Slatkine, 1986), pp. 191–203.

   Calvinist: Ludwig von Pastor, *The History of the Popes*, translated by Dom Ernest Graf (Kegan Paul, Trench, Trubner, 1937), vol. 25, pp. 196–211.

   Primitive Christian: Corrado Vivanti, Introduction to Paolo Sarpi, *Istoria del concilio tirdentino* (Giuli Einaudi, 1974), vol. 1, pp. xxxviii–xlv.

   Relativist: Vittorio Frajese, *Sarpi scettico: Stato e chiesa a Venezia tra Cinque e Seicento* (Il Mulino, 1994), pp. 129–76.

   Atheist: David Wootton, *Paolo Sarpi: Between Renaissance and Enlightenment* (Cambridge University Press, 1983).

6. Fugenzio Micanzio, *Vita del Padre F. Paolo Sarpi*, edited by Ivone Cacciavillani (Signum Verde, 1993), pp. 31–32.

7. Vivanti, op. cit., vol. 1, p. cxxxiv.

8. James Boswell, *The Life of Dr. Samuel Johnson*, edited by George Birkbeck Hill (Oxford University Press, 1934), vol. 1, pp. 134–36.

9. Sarpi, op. cit., vol. 1, p. 10.

10. Ibid., p. 120.

11. Ibid. Sarpi's ironic use of "virtue" was drawn from his great model Tacitus—as when the Roman historian writes of a despotic regime, "High birth, wealth, appointive offices either declined or, if accepted, were dangerous—but virtue was the surest doom" (*Histories* 1.3). Some of the debates given deadpan renditions by Sarpi recall, also, things like the Tacitean debate the emperor Claudius stages to discuss the pros and cons of marrying one of two competing women (*Annals* 12.1–3).

12. Ibid., *Libro quinto*, p. 638.

13. Giovanni Getto, *Paolo Sarpi* (Olschki, 1967), pp. 261–64.

14. Ibid., 271–72, 334–35.

15. Sarpi, op. cit., *Libro primo*, pp. 5–6.

16. Getto, op. cit., p. 271, in the order "papi e principi e prelati."

17. The popes' struggle with the conciliar movement is masterfully recounted in Hubert Jedin, *A History of the Council of Trent*, translated by Ernest Graf (Thomas Nelson, 1949), vol. 1, pp. 5–138.

18. Ibid., vol. 2 (1957), pp. 29–48.

19. Sarpi, op. cit., *Libro secondo*, p. 377. Some think Sarpi joins the argument over free will by noting that the Zwinglian doctrine of predestination emphasizes God's providence, while the free will school prompts human presumption. But these are detached views on practical results, not an entry into the validity of the arguments themselves. He balances the issues by saying that the free will party "won when human reason was relied on, but clearly lost when it came to citing scripture" (*Libro secondo*, p. 354). This is more an attack on Sarpi's enemy, Jesuit scholasticism, than a denial of free will.

20. Ibid., *Libro secondo*, p. 267.

21. Ibid., *Libro settimo*, p. 1,005.

22. Ibid., *Libro secondo*, p. 438.

EPILOGUE: A FAREWELL TO EMPIRE

1. John Winthrop, "Christian Charity, A Model Hereof," in Edmund Morgan, ed., *Puritan Political Ideas, 1558–1794* (Bobbs-Merrill, 1965), p. 93.

2. Thomas Jefferson, First Inaugural Address, in Merrill D. Peterson, ed., *Writings* (Library of America, 1984), p. 493.

3. Abraham Lincoln, Speech on the Kansas-Nebraska Act, in Don E. Fehrenbacher, ed., *Speeches and Writings, 1832–1858* (Library of America, 1989), p. 340

4. Aristotle, *Politics*, Book 1, 1252a7.

5. David Hume, "Of Commerce," in Eugene F. Miller, ed., *Essays: Moral, Political, and Literary* (Liberty-Classics, 1985), p. 263.

6. Lisa Jardine, *Worldly Goods: A New History of the Renaissance* (Doubleday, 1996), p. 436.

7. Hume, op. cit., "Of Refinement in the Arts," p. 271.

8. Ibid., p. 270.

Some Leading Dates

491: Legendary foundation of Venice on March 25, the Marian feast of the Annunciation

828: Body of Mark brought to Venice

1204: Venice conquers Constantinople and seizes much of its empire

1297: Legislation (the Serrata) defines a closed patrician class

1378–1381: War of Chioggia with Genoa

c. 1415–1480: Antonio Vivarini's life span

c. 1430–1516: Giovanni Bellini's life span

1468: Mauro Codussi begins first Renaissance building in Venice (San Michele in Isola)

1473–1489: Caterina Cornaro reigns as queen of Cyprus

1469: John of Speyer given first license to print books in Venice

1481: Commission awarded for church to house miraculous painting of Mary (Antonio Lombardo's Santa Maria dei Miracoli)

1490: Aldo Manuzio establishes Aldine Press

c. 1490–1576: Titian's life span

1509–1516: In war with the League of Cambrai, Venice loses its terraferma empire, then regains it

1516: Jews sequestered in Ghetto Nuovo

c. 1519–1594: Tintoretto's life span

1523–1538: Doge Andrea Gritti launches renovation of city with the help of Francesco Zorzi, Jacopo Sansovino, and others

1570: Palladio publishes *Four Books of Architecture*

1571: Battle of Lepanto

1576: Doge Alvise Mocenigo pledges to build church (Il Redentore) as thank offering for deliverance from plague

1605–1606: Doge Leonardo Donà, assisted by Paolo Sarpi, defies papal Interdict

Acknowledgments

For valuable corrections and suggestions, I am deeply grateful to the Renaissance scholars who read and criticized the manuscript: Rona Goffen, Edward Muir, John O'Malley, S.J., and Anthony Hecht read parts and asked probing questions. I also thank the proprietor of the best bookstore in Venice (Libreria Sansovino), Cesare Zanini, who was always ready to hunt down a needed volume for me; the staff of the hotel Monaco and Grand Canal, for many years of wonderful service; and Carla. My editors, Alice Mayhew, and her associate Anja Schmidt, worked assiduously with the researcher on art reproductions, Natalie Goldstein. My agent, Andrew Wylie, and his assistant, Zoe Pagnamenta, were supportive, as ever.

Index

Page numbers in italics refer to illustrations.
Roman numbers in boldface refer to plates in the insert.

PHOTO CREDITS